The Sesquicentennial History of Illinois

Published for the

ILLINOIS SESQUICENTENNIAL COMMISSION

and the

ILLINOIS STATE HISTORICAL SOCIETY

The Frontier State, 1818–1848

STUMP SPEAKING

The Sesquicentennial History of Illinois, Volume Two

The Frontier State
1818–1848

THEODORE CALVIN PEASE

With a new Introduction by
Robert W. Johannsen

UNIVERSITY OF ILLINOIS PRESS
Urbana and Chicago

Publication of this work was supported in part by a grant
from the Illinois State Historical Society.

First published as Volume 2 of the Centennial History of Illinois
by the Illinois Centennial Commission, 1918.

Introduction by Robert W. Johannsen copyright © 1987 by the
Board of Trustees of the University of Illinois

This book is printed on acid-free paper.

Library of Congress Cataloging-in-Publication Data

Pease, Theodore Calvin, 1887–1948
  The Frontier State, 1818–1848.

  Reprint. Originally published: Springfield :
Illinois Centennial Commission, 1918. (The
Sesquicentennial history of Illinois ; v. 2)
  Bibliography: p.
  Includes index.
  1. Illinois—History—1778–1865. I. Title.
II. Series.
F545.P34 1987   977.3'03   86–19282
ISBN 0-252-01338-7 (alk. paper)

CONTENTS

ILLUSTRATIONS

INTRODUCTION

Robert W. Johannsen

More than four hundred people gathered in Springfield's Leland Hotel on December 3, 1917, to observe Illinois Day, the anniversary of the admission of the State of Illinois into the Union. The occasion had been observed annually for many years, but this one was no ordinary celebration. Three former governors (a fourth declined at the last moment) and a United States senator were present, and each spoke. Presiding was the incumbent, Governor Frank O. Lowden, who tersely reminded the audience of the day's importance: "We are just entering upon the one hundredth year of our existence as a State." Lowden, who bore the title of Centennial Governor, promised that the celebration of the state's one-hundredth anniversary would itself be "one of the epochal events in our one hundred years of history."

Illinoisans in late 1917, however, had more on their minds than the past one hundred years. Since April, the nation had been involved in a great war, the magnitude of which was unprecedented in the history of mankind. The shadow of that struggle hovered over the festivities and could not be ignored. Indeed, Governor Lowden found a singular relationship between the war and the state's centennial. There were some, he suggested, who believed that citizens of the state ought not to celebrate the anniversary because "of the great perils which environ us." On the contrary, Lowden declared, "a study of our past history would inspire us to be better men and women in this crucial present."

The governor returned to this theme throughout the period of centennial planning and celebration. Illinoisans, he stated in his centennial proclamation, would bear the burdens imposed by the war more lightly if they recalled the first hundred years of the state's achievements. "We have a hundred years of noble history as a back-ground," he wrote. "Whether we shall have another hundred years equally inspiring, depends upon the issue of this world-wide war." Others echoed Lowden's sentiments. Illinois had given the nation Abraham Lincoln during that earlier struggle to preserve free government; it was only appropriate that the state should celebrate its centennial at a time when Americans were once again fighting to preserve free government in the world.[1]

Planning for the state's centennial had begun early. In 1909, the state (and the nation) commemorated the one-hundredth anniversary of Abraham Lincoln's birth but, despite the urgings of many of its citizens, Illinois had not erected an enduring memorial to the Lincoln centennial. "We do not admit in its entirety the truthfulness of the trite expression that republics are ungrateful," wrote Jessie Palmer Weber, secretary of the State Historical Society, "but we must agree that republics and the states which make up republics, are forgetful." Ohio, the first of the Old Northwest states to complete its first century, had failed to observe its centennial in an adequate way; Indiana's efforts got under way too late to carry out all "the splendid plans" which were made by its citizens. For Illinoisans, the lesson was clear: start early and leave nothing undone "to insure a complete and well planned celebration" of the state's centennial in 1918.[2]

The effort was not without its problems. The Centennial Commission created in the spring of 1913 by the General Assembly was declared invalid two years later by the state Supreme Court. A new commission was organized in January 1916 but in the meantime valuable time had been lost. Among the first plans to be made was the preparation of an ambitious publication program, focusing initially on the history of the state. If nothing else, it was thought, the centennial should provide the state's citizens with the opportunity to reflect on their past. Illinois's history, one report urged, "is not very familiar to our citizens, but should become more and more so with the advance of education and with the aid of a complete historical story such as does not exist today." To the historical volumes would be added volumes on the natural history, agriculture, manufactures, transportation, social conditions, religion, education, and commerce of the state. To be known as the *Illinois Centennial Survey*, the series would consist of as many as sixteen volumes. "The preparation of some of the volumes of this series," the report conceded, "would be very difficult." The practical value of the series was stressed, especially if the volumes were prepared with "scientific thoroughness" by experts in the fields, for the information would prove highly useful "in the solution of

many present day problems which confront the people of the State."
Furthermore, it would disarm those critics who might otherwise complain that state money was being employed to publish books "of mere
academic value."[3]

To offer a proper contrast with the Illinois of 1918, an initial volume on the state's economic and social conditions in 1818 was
thought essential. If published before the centennial year, the report
argued, the book would arouse the public's interest and provide publicity for the celebration. A young research associate in history at the
University of Illinois, with degrees from Wisconsin and Harvard, Solon J. Buck, was immediately commissioned to write it and in 1917
his *Illinois in 1818* was published.[4]

By the spring of 1914, however, more realistic notions prevailed
and the publication plans were scaled down considerably. Five historical volumes only were to be published, covering the history of Illinois
from the late seventeenth century to the centennial year, a more modest and perhaps a more meaningful program. It was certainly more
manageable than the earlier proposal. To oversee the project, a publications committee was formed, chaired initially by Chicago physician
and president of the State Historical Society Otto L. Schmidt and
later, following Schmidt's selection to head the reorganized Centennial
Commission, by Evarts Boutell Greene, head of the University of Illinois history department. A prospectus for each of the five volumes
was issued on July 1, 1914. The *Centennial Memorial History* would
be the "greatest monument" that could be produced in honor of the
centennial; it would also fill the long-felt need for a complete history
of the state on a scale never before attempted by any other state.

The books were designed to serve both the scholar and the general
reader. "The narrative," according to the committee's early guidelines,
"should be so prepared as to be attractive to the intelligent general
reader, but there should be foot-notes and careful bibliographical apparatus for the use of scholars." Each of the five volumes was assigned
to a University of Illinois professor. Clarence W. Alvord, of the history
department, was selected as editor-in-chief of the series and author of
the first volume covering the years from 1673 to 1818. The second
and third volumes also were assigned to members of the history department: Theodore C. Pease, responsible for the state's frontier period, 1818–48, and Arthur C. Cole, the Civil War years. Economics
professor Ernest L. Bogart (with Pease as co-author) would do the

industrial state, 1870–1893, and John M. Mathews of the political science department was assigned the final volume, 1893–1918. The total cost of the series was set at $30,000, of which each author would receive $1,000.[5]

All five volumes, it was hoped, would appear during the centennial year but that hope dimmed as the project was beset with difficulties. The reorganization of the centennial committee, necessitated by the Supreme Court decision, delayed the work. New contracts with the authors had to be drawn up; funds to support the publication program were not appropriated by the legislature until 1916. America's entry into the war made unforeseen demands on the energies of the authors. Greene made a valiant effort to push the project ahead, repeatedly emphasizing the importance of publication in 1918. Failure to meet the deadline, he feared, would arouse criticism among those who already felt that the university "has kept the work too much in its own hands." At the same time, he was aware that no group of historians "could hope to complete in that time a 'definitive history.'" Obviously, compromises might have to be made. He urged each author "to consider carefully just what he can do within the limited time," to leave for future investigation topics that could not be treated quickly. While the work must be "absolutely scientific in its analysis of the facts and its interpretation of them," Greene advised, emphasis should also be placed on the picturesque and dramatic features of the state's history. He did not believe that such an emphasis would be incompatible "with strict adherence to truth." The implication was clear: painstaking (and time-consuming) research might have to be sacrificed in the interest of meeting the publication schedule.

Greene's fears were well-grounded. Although as late as April 1918 Alvord still predicted that all five volumes would appear in the centennial year, only one in fact did so. In December 1918, virtually coinciding with the one-hundredth anniversary of Illinois's statehood, Pease's *Frontier State, 1818–1848* was published by the Chicago publisher A. C. McClurg and Company. Disappointed that Alvord missed the deadline with his work on early Illinois, Greene consoled himself with the thought that it was Pease's book after all that provided the natural sequel to Solon Buck's already published *Illinois in 1818*.

Less than a month before the centennial anniversary, the great war, "this most frightful of all wars," came to an end. The conjunction seemed an omen for the state's future. Illinois's second century of statehood, it was confidently predicted, would see the "realization of a new democracy and a truer and broader citizenship."[6]

Theodore Calvin Pease was born in Cassopolis, Michigan, on November 25, 1887.[7] While he was a boy his family moved to Chicago and it was in the Illinois metropolis that Pease grew to maturity. He graduated from Lewis Institute in 1904, at the age of sixteen, and three years later received his bachelor's degree from the University of Chicago. His association with the University of Illinois began soon afterward, when he moved to Urbana with an appointment as a graduate assistant in the history department, a position that brought him his first acquaintance with Illinois history and his first experience with the state's source materials. In 1909, he assisted Clarence Alvord in preparing a report on the "Archives of the State of Illinois" for the public archives commission of the American Historical Association. Published in the association's annual report, it was deemed the most thorough examination ever made of the state's records.[8]

Pease's interests, however, lay in a different direction. He left both the University of Illinois and Illinois history behind when he enrolled in the graduate history seminar of Professor Andrew C. McLaughlin, the University of Chicago's distinguished constitutional historian, and embarked on the study of English and American constitutional history. Five years later, in 1914, he was awarded the Doctor of Philosophy degree. Research on his doctoral dissertation, a study of John Lilburne and the Levellers in seventeenth-century England, further sharpened Pease's skill in working with original documents, in this case the immense pamphlet collections in the British Museum and the Bodleian Library. Published in 1916 as *The Leveller Movement: A Study in the History and Political Theory of the English Great Civil War*, the work was awarded the American Historical Association's Herbert Baxter Adams Prize.

Frankly avowing a sympathy for the efforts of the Levellers to establish a "democratic government limited and bounded by law," Pease revealed an orientation that would color his view of early nineteenth-century American history. His study was an attempt "to show what is best in the men and their ideals" and to indicate "the contribution they made to the world's political ideas." He found the Levellers' vision particularly relevant to the American Revolution and to the development of American constitutional history. It was more, he wrote, than "an interesting coincidence." Furthermore he believed that the Levellers' program was in some ways better suited to the nineteenth, even the twentieth, centuries, than to the seventeenth, for it "demanded that the rank and file of a nation untrained in democracy abandon the guidance of its traditional ruling classes and attempt self-government." The constitutional and political doctrines espoused by the Levellers had all become "American doctrines." Pease's study prepared him well for his later work on America's Jacksonian period and indeed there are echoes of the Levellers in his *Frontier State*.[9]

Pease returned to the University of Illinois after receiving his doctorate, this time with an appointment to the faculty as associate in history. He plunged immediately into a whirlwind of scholarly activity that might have discouraged any ordinary historian. He resumed his examination of the state's archival records and in 1915 published an ambitious and comprehensive survey, *The County Archives of the State of Illinois*, a "pioneer of its kind" according to one reviewer. While he was preparing his book on the Levellers for publication, he also read and edited the chapters of Clarence Alvord's two-volume study, *The Mississippi Valley in British Politics*. And, from the moment of his appointment, he was at work on his volume in the *Centennial History*, searching out materials in libraries and depositories in the Midwest and in Washington, D.C. While doing his own research, Pease also located material and took notes for Alvord and Cole, whose volumes in the series would precede and follow his own. Initial plans (later abandoned) also called for Pease's collaboration with Bogart on the fourth volume, covering the latter decades of the nineteenth century, and he was alert to any material that would help them there.

Working in the collections of the Chicago Historical Society during most of 1915, Pease maintained a regular correspondence with Alvord, sending enthusiastic accounts of his discoveries and reporting on his progress. Alvord in the meantime was sending him chapters of his Mississippi Valley book (the completion of which necessarily preceded Alvord's work on the first volume of the *Centennial History*), which Pease read in his slack time. There were moments, however, when his attention was riveted to the problems of Illinois's early statehood years, to the exclusion of all else. "Unless you write me that there is need of haste," he informed Alvord upon receiving a package of manuscript, "I shall let it go two or three days. Just now I am in a death grapple with the problem of finance in 1818–24." When Pease was informed that Alvord wanted him to help Solon Buck with his research, he drew the line. Buck, whose study of Illinois in 1818 was nearing completion, "seems to expect to appropriate any material I may have down to 1820." Pease was not about to surrender any part of his domain. "I dont see that 1819 and 1820 come legitimately in the scope of his volume," he protested to Alvord, "and cant see that he needs to scoop quite so deeply into my work." Pease's resentment at Alvord's decision was hardly placated by the latter's reply. There was nothing for Pease to fear from Buck; "the field is plenty big enough, and if he does manage to appropriate one or two lightning bolts, there will be lots left in the sky for Jove to hurl." Alvord advised Pease to give Buck "all the help he needs, as his book is due right now." [10]

Pease also served occasionally as an informal liaison between Alvord and Otto Schmidt. The uncertain legal status of the commission raised questions about the funding of the state history and the possibility that the commission would be reorganized prompted Alvord to warn Pease to "go slow in running up bills." Pease met with Schmidt on several occasions and conveyed the latter's doubts that additional funds to support the *Centennial History* would be forthcoming. The attitude is, Pease wrote, that since the history is a "U of I affair," then "let the U of I look after it." The report had some effect for shortly afterward the university's dean of the Graduate College assigned $1,500 to the project and Greene contributed an additional $3,000 from history department funds. [11]

Finally, Pease was drawn into Alvord's own difficulties in maintaining his responsibilities as editor-in-chief of the *Centennial History*. Suffering from ill health and quick to take affront at decisions that seemed to threaten his freedom of action, Alvord threatened to resign from his position in late 1916. The crisis arose over pressures to hurry Buck's volume into print. Pease, writing from Chicago, urged Alvord to reconsider. Buck's 1818 volume, he reminded Alvord, "is only a secondary matter to the main history." By yielding to the pressure on this volume, Pease advised, Alvord would be able to "stand out with firmness" for his own way on the more important works. The situation was rendered more difficult when Alvord was admitted to an Indiana sanitarium to recover his health. In order to ease Alvord's burden, Greene proposed that Pease undertake the proofreading of Buck's book in addition to all his other tasks. A few days later, Greene himself assumed Alvord's editorial duties until the latter's health should improve. [12]

Through it all, Pease pushed his study toward completion. Two graduate students in history at the University of Illinois were appointed to assist him, one of them, Robert R. Russel, later becoming a distinguished historian of antebellum American politics in his own right. Furthermore, the services of a young archaeologist and ethnologist, Ralph Linton, were acquired to provide authoritative information on Illinois Indians, not only to Pease but to Alvord as well. "The study of Indian life is a separate science," Alvord wrote, requiring a special training that was "not part of the equipment of the average historian." Fresh out of undergraduate college but with some field experience already behind him, Linton not only made a careful study of Indian life from printed records but also conducted investigations of Indian mounds and other "relics" in the state. Alvord hoped that his appointment might lead to a permanent academic post at the University of Illinois. It did not but Linton did go on to develop a career as one of the nation's outstanding anthropologists.[13]

The *Centennial History* had been fraught with difficulties from the very start and its troubles were not over yet. A problem next appeared from a wholly unexpected direction when, in April 1917, the United States went to war. Suddenly the celebration of the state's first one hundred years no longer seemed to be the most important concern of Illinoisans and some even questioned its appropriateness at a time when the world was aflame with conflict. The uncertainties of life in wartime America and of the state's priorities in the coming months threatened to delay the completion of the history. On August 13, Pease sent Greene, by then serving as chairman of the publications committee, the news that he had been selected to enter reserve officers training camp at the end of the month for service overseas with the army. Not only would he be unable to complete his collaboration with Bogart on the fourth volume of the history, on which he had already collected notes, but there were now some doubts that he would be able to see his own study of the frontier state through to publication.[14]

When Pease entered the training camp, two chapters were yet to be written, one on the Black Hawk Indian War and one on social conditions in the state. The completed manuscript, except for these two sections, was submitted to Alvord before Pease reported for duty. Alvord turned the task of writing the missing chapters over to Agnes Wright, a recent graduate of the university and a member of what Alvord called "the office force." Notes for the Black Hawk chapter were provided by Pease but one wonders how much use Wright was able to make of them. Pease "had his own way" of taking notes, Alvord once wrote. No one "but he himself can read them and at times he finds himself unable to do so." It takes only a glance at Pease's notes to confirm Alvord's appraisal.

Pease's relationship with Alvord had not always been smooth and his sudden decision to enter military service did not improve matters between them. Complaining to Greene that Pease had left him "more work than he should have done," Alvord read the manuscript quickly and returned the chapters to the author for revision. His annoyance was evident. In the first place, Pease's handwriting was difficult to read. Returning one set of pages to the author, Alvord protested that "you have so burried [sic], or so hidden, your meaning under your fluid handwriting that no one so far has been successful in deciphering it." Then there was the matter of length. Pease had exceeded the word limit specified in the contract by 15,000 words. "How would you like the job of cutting it down?" Alvord asked, knowing full well that Pease was in no position to do so. The query elicited a prickly reply, for Alvord later apologized for having "worded my letter just as I did."

The question of length, however, remained bothersome. Alvord insisted that only Pease could shorten the manuscript, certainly it was impossible for him to do so, and he appealed to Greene to let the manuscript stand. Greene was cool to the suggestion. Not only would the added length increase the expense of publication but it might also discourage the general reader for, he pointed out, in a series of this kind "there is much to be said in keeping the volumes comparatively short." The possibility that Pease's brother, Albert A. Pease of Chicago, might be asked to cut the length was rejected by Alvord as posing a "serious detriment to the volume." Schmidt apparently agreed that the work could be published "as it stood." As it turned out, Pease's volume was the shortest of the five.[15]

Finally, questions were raised regarding Pease's objectivity. Frederic Siedenburg, a Jesuit priest, professor at Loyola University in Chicago, and member of the Centennial Commission, had already conveyed complaints from the American Irish Historical Society that Solon Buck's *Illinois in 1818* was anti-Irish and hence un-American, "a fraud upon the tax payers of Illinois." A committee had been established by the society to guard against a further "distortion of American history" and "misuse of public funds" in the remaining volumes of the *Centennial History*. America's entrance into the war aroused the sensitivity of minority groups and their emotions were at hair-trigger, ready to take affront at any supposed slight. Siedenburg endorsed the society's complaint, noting that Buck did not give adequate recognition to the work of the Roman Catholic Church, but he expressed his willingness to overlook "this bias" since he "did not think the book of much consequence." Pease's volume, however, promised to be "a work of merit"; hence any such bias in it, Siedenburg warned, would not be tolerated.

Siedenburg read Pease's first seven chapters and found much to complain about. While prominence had been given to the work of the Methodists, Baptists, and other denominations in frontier Illinois, there was "not a trace" devoted to Catholic activity. He protested against Pease's statement that Masonry provided an outlet to the spiritual aspirations of the settlers and objected to Pease's reference to the importance of private schools without specifying who conducted those schools. Siedenburg further believed that James Shields, Irish-born and a Roman Catholic, should receive greater recognition, if for no other reason than to demonstrate that "our historians are broad enough to record merit wherever they find it even when they see it in one who is not a descendant of the Pilgrim Fathers." Inasmuch as the *Centennial History* was a state production to be published at state expense, Siedenburg felt that "special pains" should be taken to give all elements of Illinois society their "just due."

The offending passages and omissions were addressed by Alvord, some of the changes being made in the proofs of the volume, and Pease's critics were apparently satisfied. A reviewer in the *Illinois Catholic Historical Review*, while still faulting Pease for not having given more space to Shields and for not extending his coverage to 1849 so that "the advanced state of Catholic temperance work" could have been discussed, found little to criticize in the book. Pease, in fact, was praised for his success in dealing with "the difficult and the more or less dangerous subject of nationalities" and for having written "rather meritoriously of the religious situation." [16]

Siedenburg's remonstrance touched a sensitive nerve among the centennial's planners. Several weeks later, after Pease's manuscript had been revised and sent to the printer, Alvord received a further complaint, this time from Otto Schmidt. Schmidt found a reference to "Canal Irish" in Pease's chapter on internal improvements, a term which Pease used to describe those Irish laborers engaged in construction of the Illinois and Michigan Canal, and immediately questioned its historical value. Alvord was clearly nettled by Schmidt's suggestion that the phrase be dropped and replied at length: "I have asked everybody connected with this office what is the objection to 'canal Irish' even putting it up to the only Irish lady in the department." None could understand why the term should be deemed objectionable. In order to "keep peace in the Illinois family," however, Alvord agreed to expunge the passage. With tongue in cheek, he suggested a substitute for "Canal Irish":

> Many Irish gentlemen, driven by the persecution of their native land by autocratic and perfidious Albion, and financially embarrassed by the depreciation in the value of their estates, had left their castles and all that they held most dear to seek for the liberty they loved in the wilderness of America. Many came to Chicago where they soon learned of the noble work being done on the Illinois-Michigan canal. Fired by an idealism not easily understood in our materialistic day and inspired by a love of their newly adopted flag—Old Glory, may it ever wave over bands of free men—they volunteered to aid in this noble work. Inspired by their enthusiasm for liberty and by a noble idealism they enlisted in the service that would cause the icy waters of the Great Lakes to mingle with the balmy waves of the Gulf of Mexico. Their enthusiasm did not fail them even when they were forced to wield in this struggle of freemen against the mighty forces of Nature those common implements of labor, the shovel and the pick axe—common implements did I say? No, noble implements, enobled by the perspiration that flowed from the consecrated muscles of the laborers.

The statement, Alvord conceded, was a bit more complicated than "Canal Irish" but he felt it should certainly satisfy the "amour propre of our Irish friends." Or perhaps, he added, something more simple like "Irish working on the canal" might suffice.[17]

Alvord's outburst was the last in what had been in some ways a long and frustrating experience. Pease completed the final revision of his manuscript during the brief period following his commissioning as a second lieutenant and before he was ordered to active duty. Because of his absence, the task of seeing the work through the press fell to others, notably his brother Albert, Agnes Wright, who supplied the two additional chapters and gave the manuscript its final scrutiny, and Alvord. Pease's last contribution was the preface, which he wrote "Somewhere in France."[18]

The publication of *The Frontier State, 1818–1848* in December 1918 not only coincided with the state's centennial but also forecast a series that, in the words of one historian, would serve as "a unique monument" to Illinois, placing in her debt "all students of history and all true admirers of genuine search for the truth."[19] Pease was lauded for the high standards of research and scholarship he established in the volume, standards against which the succeeding volumes in the *Centennial History* would be measured. Never before had a state history been attempted on so ambitious or so scholarly a scale.

The *Centennial History* would be the first Illinois state history to be published in over six decades. During the earliest years of statehood, Illinoisans had expressed a strong concern for the area's historical roots and background, for to discover the state's past was one way to lend legitimacy to the state's role in the progress of the nation itself. Americans in this romantic age were fascinated by the vestiges of the past and by the whole question of the origins of civilization, a fascination that was made doubly important (and difficult) by the fact of America's newness and its unique place in the world. They believed, moreover, that there was an inexorable link between past and present, that to know the past was to understand the present and to form a clearer vision of the future. In 1827, only nine years after admission to the Union, the state's first historical society was founded. The effort proved abortive but the interest that had spawned it remained high. Four state histories were published in the decade between 1844 and 1854. From that point until the end of the century and after, popular interest in Illinois history seemed to wane and no further efforts were made to create a state historical society or to write the state's history. The Chicago Historical Society, organized before the Civil War, assumed many of the functions of a state society; the Civil War itself diverted popular interest into other channels; and the creation of the Illinois State Historical Library by legislative enactment in 1889 provided the means for the collection and preservation of the state's historical materials normally exercised by a state society. It was not until 1899 that the present Illinois State Historical Society was established. The approach of the twin centennials—of Lincoln's birth in 1909 and of statehood nine years later—provided an immediate role for the new organization.[20]

Of the early state histories, the most influential was Thomas Ford's *History of Illinois, From Its Commencement as a State in 1818 to 1847*, published in 1854. Ford's book, called a "minor classic" by one scholar, covered virtually the same period treated by Pease and remained the only close study of early Illinois history until the publication of *The Frontier State* sixty-four years later.[21]

Ford, who served as governor of Illinois from 1842 to 1846, viewed the period almost solely in political terms, not surprising since, being himself an "insider," politics was what he knew best. More striking was the candor with which he described the state's political activity and the disdain, even scorn, in which he held politics and politicians. His book, he warned, was "about small events and little men." To Pease, Ford's account, written with a "pen dipped in the sharpest caustic," breathed "disillusioned cynicism." Nevertheless, Pease described the book sympathetically as "one of the clearest and most subtle analyses of American politics," an effort to explain to future generations "the seemingly inexplicable devotion of the people of the state to . . . partisan politics." It was, he noted, "one of the earliest books on the philosophy of American history," deserving a better fate than it had been accorded by historians. His admiration for Ford as a voice of responsibility and wisdom amidst the swirling passions of partisanship was unmistakable.[22]

That Pease shared some of Ford's cynicism is equally clear. The early years of the twentieth century, the period of the progressive movement, bred the same disillusion and disgust with politics that Ford reflected in the 1840s. It was not difficult for Pease to find in the early nineteenth century a reflection of his own twentieth-century attitudes. His judgments of men and motives in early Illinois were severe. Leaders lacked both courage and understanding in their efforts to resolve the state's problems; sobriety and responsibility among the state's voters were slow to develop. Politics was little more than a "maze of personal and factional rivalries" with the gratification of personal ambition as the primary goal. Political contests were decided by "trades and rumors of trades," logrolling, and (employing a popular phrase of the time) "bargain and corruption." Until, that is, the advent of "Jacksonism," with its new emphasis on measures as well as men and its closely fashioned ties with national politics.

In his discussion of party formation in Illinois, Pease anticipated the direction historical study would take for years to come. Some signposts had been erected already. As a field for investigation, the Jackson era was yet in its infancy. Historians had been more concerned with finding clues to the coming of the Civil War than in viewing the period for itself. An early exception was Columbia University political scientist John W. Burgess, whose book (published in 1897) gave the period one of its most persistent labels: *The Middle Period, 1817–1858*. The shadow of the Civil War, however, was not easily dispelled, not even for Burgess. The study of the Jackson era, usually defined as those years from the 1820s through the 1840s, did not come into its own until American historiography itself was revolutionized by Frederick Jackson Turner and his generation of young, dynamic historians. Imbued with the currents of progressivism in their own day, they turned the study of American history into a "pro-democratic" channel.[23] Pease, attaining intellectual maturity during these vibrant years, was caught up in the excitement of a movement that not only promised a new future to the American people but also a new meaning to the nation's past. *The Frontier State*, exhibiting the lineaments of progressive historiography, was as much a contribution to the Jackson era as it was to Illinois history.

Jacksonian democracy, Pease contended, rode into power in Illinois on a "rising tide of westernism." Like Turner, he found the springs of Jacksonism on the frontier; it was a western phenomenon, in tune with the interests of the settlers and espousing policies that looked particularly to the development of the West. There was no mistaking Pease's deep esteem for the Old Hero. In Jackson, he declared, "one catches an echo of the spirit of the American frontier"; his characteristics were frontier traits—directness, practicality, and impatience with abstraction and theory. Yet, Pease conceded, there was a complexity about Jacksonian democracy that defied simple explanation. Its central idea was so "intensely alive" that it was also "intensely variable." Jackson's cause was the cause of a new democracy that provided "the moving force in the war of the people against the moneyed interests." His party, which commanded the loyalties of most Illinoisans, was dedicated to "the rights of the many against the few" and to "the rights of man against the rights of property." No matter how inconsistent the party's actions, how knavish and sharp its politics, Pease insisted, "the ideal was always there." The chords of progressivism were unmistakable. Of Jackson, he concluded: "Beyond any other in American history his figure, aged, but not senile, vibrant, passionate, masterful, has the eternal vigor of the will of the people."[24]

To Pease, however, the promise of Jacksonian democracy was shortlived and the optimism with which he wrote of Jackson and his cause gave way to bitterness and dismay. "The democratic party in Illinois," he wrote, "had scarcely completed its physical growth before its de-

terioration began." The character of the party nationally had begun
to change as it became less western and more southern. The specter of
slavery loomed more ominously over national political life. The turning point, according to Pease, was the election of 1840, "one of the
strangest in American politics," when the Democracy was swept aside
by pageantry and sentimentalism. The party's stand for what Pease
believed to be a "sound financial policy" through Van Buren's bold
and statesmanlike subtreasury system was rejected in a campaign that
paid little attention to issues. Although Pease considered the subse-
quent death of William Henry Harrison and John Tyler's accession to
the presidency to be "one of the most ironical instances of retributive
justice in politics that history affords," the damage had been done.
Southern politicians took the party "out of pawn" and the "vigor of
its creed" departed. It was the last election, Pease lamented, "on which
the shadow of the aggression of slave power in the west did not fall
heavily." Yet Illinoisans continued to cling tenaciously to the Old
Hero's platform for years to come. "So strongly cemented was the
fabric of the democratic party, so great was the power of the democratic name that the destruction of the party there had to be the work
of years."[25]

In his estimation of Jackson's character and his place in American
history and of the frontier origins of Jacksonian democracy, Pease followed the path marked out by Frederick Jackson Turner. Although
Turner's work does not appear in Pease's bibliography, there is no
doubt that it helped shape his outlook, toward the role of the West in
national development as well as toward the nature of historical study
itself. Pease shared the "pro-democratic" stance of Turner and the
progressive historians. Elements of Turner's frontier thesis, first suggested in his famous 1893 essay and later incorporated in his study
Rise of the New West (1906), also found echo in Pease's account. For
example, Pease saw in Illinois the same development of civilization
from simple to more complex forms that Turner described. Pioneers
"passed over its territory in waves," first the hunters with their "half
savage life," then the more settled farmers, town builders, and professional men. Divergent cultural streams, one southern and one northern, intermingled on the Illinois prairie (Pease rejected the notion of
confrontation) to create a unique cultural zone that set this frontier
apart from areas to the east.

Like Turner, Pease viewed the civilizing process as organic. Evolutionary change was the "keynote" of frontier Illinois, he wrote, as

environmental influences helped mold the state's economic and social development and shape the ideas of those who settled the state. Easterners "ceased to be purely eastern" once they were touched by the "freedom of their new surroundings." In 1837, Pease suggested, Illinois's pioneer period ended with the adoption of the controversial, ill-considered internal improvement scheme. An "era of transition" followed during which Illinoisans groped for a solid foundation on which to rest their institutions, a maturing process in itself. The Illinois of 1837 and that of 1848 bore all the differences between "light-hearted reckless youth and sober responsible manhood." Politics reflected the growing complexity of life and Pease warned "the superficial historian" of the pitfalls inherent in the political story. Betraying the same vulnerability as the animal organism, the political organism, he asserted, moved quickly from maturity into morbidity, as the Jacksonian crusade lost its vigor and the ominous shadow of slavery began to lengthen.[26]

Although notions of liberty and equality were instilled in the state's early inhabitants, Pease found little to admire in the spirit of "wild freedom" that characterized the first stages of social evolution. "The virtues of man," he wrote, "living in the state of nature are alluring, but an analysis of the social life of the frontier discloses nothing of good that necessarily must be lost in a change to a higher civilization and much that might well be replaced by something better." He gave more credence than Turner to the importance of continuity and tradition, a point of view that undoubtedly drew its strength from his study of English constitutional history and from his mentor, Andrew C. McLaughlin. Pease shared McLaughlin's respect for the continuity of the Anglo-American legal tradition and McLaughlin's conviction that politics revolved about the effort to reconcile liberty and order. In Illinois law and constitutionalism, the mark of civilization, did not spring full-blown from primitive surroundings. Quoting a young English visitor to Illinois, Pease revealed his own attitude: "Tis the hand of man that makes the wilderness shine." The environmentalism of Turner was tempered by a realization that it was the continuities in history that ultimately counted. There was something analogous, as Pease pointed out, between the political struggles of Illinoisans in the early nineteenth century and those of the Levellers in seventeenth-century England. Yet like McLaughlin—and Turner—Pease clearly believed that (in McLaughlin's words) "democracy is a spirit and not merely a form of government" and that it was in the era of Andrew Jackson that this spirit most evidenced itself.[27]

Pease's study of frontier Illinois, indeed the *Centennial History* itself, exemplified the new professionalism that had taken control of historical study.[28] Beginning in the late nineteenth century, the traditional custodians of the past, those gifted upper-class "amateurs" whose broad narrative sweeps represented history written in its grandest manner gradually gave way before the onslaught of the graduate school. History fell into the hands of the professors, university-trained academics who democratized its study while they narrowed its scope. Their hold was strengthened by the growth of the American Historical Association (founded in 1887) and by the increased influence of its journal, the *American Historical Review.* By the early years of the twentieth century, the professionals were in command, penetrating even the ranks of the state historical societies. Two events in 1907, as John Higham has noted, brought "the formative era in the creation of the American historical profession" to a close. The first was the creation of the Mississippi Valley Historical Association by representatives of a number of midwestern historical societies and universities, for the purpose of promoting scholarly research and writing in western history. In the same year, the first monument to the new professionalism, the *American Nation* series, was completed—twenty-six volumes, twenty-four of which were written by authors trained in graduate schools. The series marked the "triumphant appropriation of the whole span of American history by professional historians" (and, incidentally, may have suggested a model for Illinois's *Centennial History*).

Plans for the *Centennial History* and the publication of Pease's volume must be viewed in the context of this new professionalism and of the close cooperation it spawned between the university and the historical society. Evarts Boutell Greene, the University of Illinois history professor whose involvement in the project has been discussed, was perhaps more instrumental than any other figure in the organization of the Illinois State Historical Society in 1899. Clarence Alvord was one of the founders of the Mississippi Valley Historical Association and later edited its journal, the *Mississippi Valley Historical Review.* At the association's first meeting, Alvord presented a paper, "The Study and Writing of History in the Mississippi Valley," in which he urged historians to dedicate their efforts to filling the need for scholarly monographs in western history. Alvord's operation at the University of Illinois, sometimes dubbed the "History Factory," represented the new professionalism at its height. A *New York Times* writer, visiting Alvord's offices in the summer of 1918, reacted with awe and wonder, noting that the popular image of the historian's workroom was completely dispelled. "You would probably feel that you had strayed by accident into, say, a big insurance office," he wrote. "There is such a lack of the dust and tome stuff." Instead the rooms were filled with filing cases, card indexes, typewriters, and dictaphones. Five or six typists were busy at their machines while others at desks were checking footnotes, collating manuscripts, and reading proof. Here the *Centennial History* was being produced, volumes in the *Illinois Historical Collections* (an ongoing project of the State Historical Society to collect and disseminate documents relating to Illinois history) were being prepared, and the *Mississippi Valley Historical Review* was being edited.[29]

Pease himself had been trained by one of the nation's eminent professional historians, who also had been both editor of the *American Historical Review* and president of the American Historical Association. During his brief academic career before entering military service in 1917, Pease had been active in the American Historical Association's public archives commission and had edited a volume in the *Illinois Historical Collections*.

The milieu in which the *Centennial History* was launched with the publication of *The Frontier State* is only partially described by the professionalization of historical study. Hand in hand with the new professionalism went a changing view of history's nature and function. Historians spoke of history as a science and urged students and colleagues to turn to "scientific history," a loose and ill-defined concept that seemed to include not only a more critical approach to sources but also a spirit of scientific inquiry—a detached, dispassionate, and objective pursuit of truth, wherever it might lead. Whatever it meant, the scientific spirit became a hallmark of professionalism, and if the substance was not always apparent, the words were there. "This is the day of the professional, or rather of the professorial historian," wrote Alvord in *The Nation*. "This change is in harmony with the rapid development of the scientific spirit in America. The historical science is a difficult one to acquire, and hence there is need of training and apprenticeship, which can be most easily acquired in the graduate school."[30] Early in the twentieth century, the scientific spirit encountered the challenge of progressivism; historians became more concerned with the economic and social problems of their day and with history's potential for resolving them. The result was an approach to the past that came to be known as the "new history."

With the new history, the study of the past regained its purpose. In the words of James Harvey Robinson, the movement's most effective spokesman, history "is to help us to understand ourselves and our fellows and the problems and prospects of mankind." No longer conceived in narrow political terms, history reached out to embrace "the multitudinous forces" that shaped man's actions. "In its amplest meaning," Robinson insisted, "history includes every trace and vestige of everything that man has done or thought since first he appeared on the earth." The common man moved once again to center stage.[31]

Pease reflected the new history in ways that have already been suggested: his broad view of the past encompassing economic and social as well as political forces (although politics admittedly received the greatest attention), the stress on evolutionary development, the balance of environmental and inherited influences, the feel for the common folk, and the measurement of progress in terms of expanding democracy. Implicit throughout is the assumption that there are lessons to be learned from history and that an understanding of Illinois's early statehood years will enable its people to meet the challenges of the future. But the new history involved more than the substance of historical study; it called for new, more rigorous (or "scientific") modes of research as well. If the historian was to widen his "vision of the past" and to pursue its truth wherever it might be found, he must expand and enlarge his investigation, principally through an exhaustive study of primary sources.

Pease had been trained in the methodology of the new history and had learned the value of those sources that emanated from the common people. He had been among the first to examine the vast pamphlet collections of seventeenth-century England and his early recognition of the importance of manuscript collections, as well as the more formal archival materials, resulted in long hours spent sifting and sorting documents for the light they might shed on Illinois's early experience. His *Frontier State* marked the first time that the state's newspaper sources had been exploited fully and effectively. Indeed, one less than enthusiastic reviewer found in Pease's use of newspapers a "novel method of history writing." Newspapers, even (or especially) those "low grade" sheets of which the reviewer complained, provided a touchstone for an understanding of the "aspirations and life of the people." Pease was aware of the novelty, as witness the apologia for his use of newspapers which he inserted in his bibliography: "Newspapers form a source of inestimable value in writing Illinois history of this period. Indeed, for any approximately full or continuous record, it is only through them that the pioneer state may be pieced together; economically, socially, and in especial politically, they preserve for the critical student, a reflection of early Illinois." Pease's efforts were not unappreciated. His almost exclusive reliance on primary sources won praise from the more eclectic reviewers. "One who has not tried," wrote Indiana historian Logan Esarey, "can never realize how difficult it is to wring a connected consequential story out of such materials." Pease's skillful use of sources set him apart from the "commercial or hack historian" as the artist is set apart from the photographer.[32]

Although *The Frontier State* is clearly a product of the early twentieth century, it also possesses enduring qualities. Perhaps it is because the point of view from which it was written dominated American historiography for decades following its publication and even now continues to influence historical study. Historians were slow to follow up the promising start made by Jacksonian scholars early in the century. It was not until the immediate post–World War II years that the Jackson period was "re-discovered," and then the impetus was provided by a single book. Arthur Meier Schlesinger, Jr.'s prize-winning *The Age of Jackson* (1945), a study not unlike those called for by the practitioners of the new history, turned Jacksonian research into new and fruitful channels. While retaining the pro-democratic orientation of earlier scholars, Schlesinger found the roots of Jacksonism, not on the frontier, but in the urban industrialized East. Since 1945, the popularity of the Jackson era as a subject for investigation has burgeoned. New methodological techniques and the application of new technologies to historical study, along with a more intensive scrutiny of a wide variety of sources, have brought a greater understanding of early nineteenth-century American history than ever existed before. Pease's story has weathered the onslaught of new information, its basic premises and structure unchanged. Indeed, Jacksonian historiography may be said to have come full circle since Pease published his study of frontier Illinois, for the leading interpreters of the Jackson period today, according to one historian, may aptly be characterized as "neo-Progressives."[33]

Pease's account then has stood the test of time. State history at its best, the book still enlightens students of the early nineteenth century, not only about Illinois's experience during those dynamic years but about that of America as well. *The Frontier State* is the story of America's, as it is of Illinois's, coming of age.[34]

NOTES

1. *The Centennial of the State of Illinois: Report of the Centennial Commission*, compiled by Jessie Palmer Weber (Springfield, 1920), 52–54; *Centennial Bulletin*, no. 2 (Nov. 1917), front cover; no. 5 (Feb. 1918), 2.

2. *Centennial of the State of Illinois*, 15; *Report of the Illinois Centennial Commission to the Forty-Ninth General Assembly* (Springfield, 1915), 7.

3. *Report of the Committee for Publications of the Illinois Centennial Commission, November 19, 1913* (Springfield, 1913), 3–9. In support of this publication program, the Illinois Historical Survey, created at the University of Illinois in 1910, was charged with the task of collecting materials and encouraging research in the state's history, a function it has continued to serve down to the present day. Clarence W. Alvord became the survey's first director.

4. Before his book was published, Buck left Illinois to assume the position of superintendent of the Minnesota Historical Society. *Illinois in 1818* was reprinted in 1967 by the University of Illinois Press with an introduction by Allan Nevins.

5. *Report of the Committee for Publications of the Illinois Centennial Commission, November 19, 1913*, 4; *Centennial Bulletin* no. 6 (Apr. 1918), 3; *Centennial of the State of Illinois*, 33; Evarts Boutell Greene to Otto L. Schmidt, Apr. 1, 1916, Illinois Centennial Commission Papers, Illinois Historical Survey, University of Illinois, Urbana. The authorship of the last two volumes was subsequently changed; Bogart and Charles Manfred Thompson, also an economics professor, collaborated on the fourth volume (with a chapter by Chicago novelist H. B. Fuller) and the fifth volume was written by Bogart and Mathews (with chapters by Cole and Fuller). For the complete story of the *Centennial History*, I am indebted to John Hoffmann's fine paper, "A History of *The Centennial History of Illinois*, 1907–1920," prepared for the Third Annual Illinois History Symposium, Dec. 3, 1982, and published by the Illinois State Historical Society in *Selected Papers in Illinois History 1982*.

6. Greene to Schmidt, Jan. 8, Mar. 10, Apr. 27, 1916; Greene to Alvord, May 9, 1916, June 15, Mar. 12, 1917, Illinois Centennial Commission Papers; *Journal of the Illinois State Historical Society*, 11 (Jan. 1919), 596. The third (Cole) volume was published in 1919; the first (Alvord), fourth (Bogart and Thompson), and fifth (Bogart and Mathews) in 1920.

7. Information in this and following paragraphs has been drawn from J. G. Randall's informative article, "Theodore Calvin Pease," *Journal of the Illinois State Historical Society*, 41 (Dec. 1948), 353–66.

8. Clarence Walworth Alvord and Theodore Calvin Pease, "Archives of the State of Illinois," *Annual Report of the American Historical Association, 1909* (Washington, 1911), 383–463.

9. Theodore Calvin Pease, *The Leveller Movement: A Study in the History and Political Theory of the English Great Civil War* (Washington, 1916), 1, 6, 2, 360, 363 (in order of quotation).

10. *Minnesota History Bulletin*, 1 (Nov. 1915), 220; Pease to Alvord, Apr. 9, Oct. 18, 1915; Alvord to Pease, Oct. 20, 1915, Illinois Centennial Commission Papers.

11. Alvord to Pease, June 25, 1915; Pease to Alvord, July 29, Sept. 8, Oct. 25, 1915, Illinois Centennial Commission Papers.

12. Pease to Alvord, Nov. 25, 1916; Alvord to Schmidt, Dec. 6, 1916; Greene to Alvord, Nov. 24; and Memorandum of Conference with Professor C. W. Alvord, Dec. 9, 1916, Illinois Centennial Commission Papers.

13. Alvord to the Illinois Centennial Commission, Feb. 24, 1916; Ralph Linton to Alvord, May 28; Alvord to Linton, June 8, 1915, Illinois Centennial Commission Papers.

14. Pease to Greene, Aug. 13, 1917, Illinois Centennial Commission Papers.

15. Theodore Calvin Pease, *The Frontier State, 1818–1848*, vol. 2 of *The Centennial History of Illinois* (Chicago, 1918), preface; Alvord to Greene, Aug. 22, 1917; Alvord to Schmidt, Jan. 4, 1918; Pease to Paul M. Angle, Jan. 11, 1934; Alvord to Greene, Sept. 26; Alvord to Pease, Sept. 20, 29; Greene to Alvord, Sept. 19, 1917, Illinois Centennial Commission Papers.

16. Frederic Siedenburg to Alvord, Dec. 13, 1917, Illinois Centennial Commission Papers; Joseph J. Thompson, in *Illinois Catholic Historical Review*, 1 (Apr. 1919), 516–18. In response to objections from the Reorganized Church of Jesus Christ of Latter-Day Saints, Pease's chapter on the Mormon War was also "toned down." For the full story of these attacks on the objectivity of the *Centennial History*, see Hoffman, "History of *The Centennial History of Illinois*," 29–40.

17. Schmidt to Alvord, Mar. 3; Alvord to Schmidt, Mar. 5, 1918, Illinois Centennial Commission Papers.

18. Pease, *Frontier State, 1818–1848*, preface.

19. Lester Burrell Shippee, in *Minnesota History Bulletin*, 4 (Feb.-May 1921), 49.

20. For accounts of the early interest in Illinois history and the eventual organization of the Illinois State Historical Society, see Robert W. Johannsen, "History on the Illinois Frontier: Early Efforts to Preserve the State's Past," *Journal of the Illinois State Historical Society*, 68 (Apr. 1975), 121–42; and

Roger D. Bridges, "The Origins and Early Years of the Illinois State Historical Society," ibid., 98–120.

21. [Mark E. Neely, Jr.,] "A 'Great Fraud'? Politics in Thomas Ford's *History of Illinois*," *Lincoln Lore*, no. 1687 (Sept. 1978), 1. With the publication of the *Centennial History*, the need for a single-volume state history obviously still remained. The need was filled by Pease himself in 1925, when his *Story of Illinois* was published. Based on the five volumes of the *Centennial History*, the book became the standard history for many years.

22. Thomas Ford, *A History of Illinois, From Its Commencement as a State in 1818 to 1847* (Chicago, 1854), xiv; Pease, *Frontier State*, 316, 314.

23. For the shifts and changes in Jacksonian historiography, see Charles Grier Sellers, Jr., "Andrew Jackson and the Historians," *Mississippi Valley Historical Review*, 44 (Mar. 1958), 615–34.

24. Pease, *Frontier State*, 114–15, 188, 262–63.

25. Ibid., 265, 271, 339.

26. Ibid., 1, 410, 189, 326, 136, 339 (in order of citation).

27. Ibid., 1, 6–7, 17, 31–32; Andrew C. McLaughlin, "American History and American Democracy," *American Historical Review*, 20 (Jan. 1915), 256 and passim.

28. For a discussion of the centennial history from the perspective of early twentieth-century American historiography see Clarence W. Alvord, "The Centennial History of Illinois," *Transactions of the Illinois State Historical Society, 1918* (Springfield, 1919), 74–82.

29. John Higham, *History: The Development of Historical Studies in the United States* (Englewood Cliffs, N.J., 1965), 6–25 (quotations, 19, 20); Bridges, "Origins and Early Years of the Illinois State Historical Society," 105; Clarence W. Alvord, "The Study and Writing of History in the Mississippi Valley," Mississippi Valley Historical Association, *Proceedings for the Year 1907–08* (Cedar Rapids, 1909), 98–110; *New York Times*, July 14, 1918, 6:3 ("Up-to-Date Methods of Illinois Centennial Historian").

30. Clarence W. Alvord, "The New History," *The Nation*, 94 (May 9, 1912), 457.

31. James Harvey Robinson, *The New History: Essays Illustrating the Modern Historical Outlook* (1912; rpt. New York, 1965), 17, 1 (in order of quotation); Higham, *History*, 110–16.

32. Alvord, "New History," 458–59; *Illinois Catholic Historical Review*, 1 (Apr. 1919), 516 (Joseph J. Thompson); Pease, *Frontier State*, 443; *Mississippi Valley Historical Review*, 6 (June 1919), 133.

33. Frank Otto Gatell, "The Jacksonian Era, 1824–1848," in William H. Cartwright and Richard L. Watson, Jr., eds., *The Reinterpretation of American History and Culture* (Washington, 1973), 320.

34. Following two years of military service, Pease returned to the University of Illinois, where he remained a member of the history faculty until his death

in 1948 at the age of sixty. He attained the rank of full professor in 1926 and served as head of the department during the last six years of his life. His contributions to the historical profession were manifold, his bibliography was extensive, and his service to his university, as both teacher and administrator, was tireless.

THE CENTENNIAL HISTORY OF ILLINOIS
VOLUME TWO

THE FRONTIER STATE

1818-1848

BY

THEODORE CALVIN PEASE

UNIVERSITY OF ILLINOIS

PUBLISHED BY THE

ILLINOIS CENTENNIAL COMMISSION

SPRINGFIELD, 1918

PREFACE

THE time available for the writing of this volume was necessarily shortened by the entrance of the United States into the European war and my consequent decision to apply for admittance to a Reserve Officers' Training Camp. The final revision was done during the short interval between the time when I was awarded my commission and the time of my reporting for duty. Much of the work of revision, therefore, that I should under normal conditions have done, I have of necessity intrusted to others. When I entered the training camp two chapters (8 and 21) were unwritten. Miss Agnes Wright, my assistant, has supplied these and, in addition, has given valuable assistance during the preparation of the manuscript of the entire volume. My brother, Albert A. Pease, has carefully read the volume in manuscript and has suggested many improvements in the text. The editor-in-chief of the series, Clarence W. Alvord, has very kindly added to the customary duties of an editor a care for details which of right falls to the author. I congratulate myself that in the emergency I have been able to draw on my friends for competent assistance ungrudgingly given.

It is a pleasant duty to acknowledge my indebtedness to individuals not connected with the work of the Centennial Commission. I am under obligation to Mr. Milo M. Quaife for several important suggestions and for permission to reproduce the copy of the Peck-Messenger map in the Wisconsin History Society's library. Mrs. J. B. Dyche has assisted me with material of various sorts. The Chicago Historical Society through its librarian, Miss Caroline M. McIlvaine, has accorded me every imaginable assistance and privilege in connection with the prosecution of the work in Chicago.

THE FRONTIER STATE

Among those immediately connected with the enterprise I must particularly mention Dr. Otto L. Schmidt and Mr. Evarts B. Greene of the Centennial Commission, who officially and unofficially have afforded me every possible assistance. A third member of the Commission, Mrs. Jessie Palmer Weber, in her capacity of librarian of the State Historical Library, has given me the privilege of working there during the collection of material at Springfield and has assumed responsibility for the correctness of many quoted passages. My special obligations to the editor-in-chief I have already mentioned. At every stage he has done everything in his power to facilitate the work.

THEODORE CALVIN PEASE.

Somewhere in France.

I. THE LAND AND THE PEOPLE

THE task of reconstructing for the student of history the politics, manners, and customs of a frontier community such as the Illinois of the first decade of statehood is not an easy one. The newspapers of that day only dimly reflect the life about them and contain no information whatever about the phases of it which their readers took for granted. The contemporary traveler too often saw only a small part, and that inaccurately, detached from its surroundings save in so far as the inhabitants condescended to explain them to him, while too often his prepossessions in favor of the land of political liberty or his disgust at the impossibility of continuing his accustomed habits of life lent a roseate or a dingy hue to his picture. The reminiscences of the pioneer, set down long after the occurrence of the events he tried to describe, are generally open to the suspicion that they have been unconsciously foreshortened so that the descriptions of the rapidly changing life and conditions of the frontier are focused at but one point and that perhaps not the most important. Under such limitations of information the picture of Illinois a hundred years ago, if it is to be accurate, must be somewhat indistinct.

Change and evolution sound the keynote of frontier Illinois. For the first thirty years of statehood its politicians sprang up, flourished, changed sides, and left the state to seek new careers with a rapidity that is the despair of the chronicler. Pioneers passed over its territory in waves with varying manners, ideals, and habits of life. Civilization first of simple, then of more complex, gradations sprang up with amazing rapidity behind and among the frontiersmen. The half savage frontiersman and the college-bred lawyer, the woman of the backwoods and the fine lady rubbed elbows in the little village where the frame house was rapidly replacing the log cabin. Into communities without religion came numerous denominations striving to supply the lack of spiritual life. Churches were organized, were torn by quarrels and secessions, and yet reached out for better education. Above all, this community ready and eager to go up and possess the land continually had to fight politically in the hope of obtaining from its landlord, the federal government, better and better terms for the acquisition of its land.

In the beginning was the land; the vast stretch of diversified hill and plain, forest and prairie, scrub oak, barren, and swamp stretched before the people. Shutting off the greater part of it from them were the intangible but nevertheless annoying restrictions of the United States government, and the more concrete barriers of Indian tribes, jealous of the presence of the white settlers among them, and of the wilderness itself, untraversed by roads and locking from the settler with its standing timber and tough sod the cornfields of the future. The story of the acquisition of this domain, of how the little community of frontiersmen waxed to conquer its lands to cultivation, of how successfully or unsuccessfully they sought to drive through it lines of transport which might connect them commercially with the outside world, and of how they wrestled politically with their brethren of the eastern states for a freer hand at its legal conquest is the material side of the history of provincial Illinois.

On the day when Illinois was both territory and state its population of some 35,000 lay in two columns on opposite sides of the state, resting on the connection with the outside world furnished by the Mississippi, the Ohio, and the Wabash rivers respectively. The population clustered in the rich river bottom, gift of the Mississippi, where Illinois history began, and in the neighborhood of the United States saline in Gallatin county. It tended always to make settlements on water courses for the sake of securing timber, water, and easy communication. Away from the rivers lay an unpopulated region in the interior of southern Illinois, where the traveler to St. Louis or Kaskaskia who preferred to cut across by road from Vincennes or Shaw-neetown rather than pole up the Mississippi, could still stage tales of robbers, murders, and hairbreadth escapes. On the east population had crept north, clinging closely to the Wabash, as far as the present Edgar county. On the west settlements had reached the southern part of Calhoun county and were pushing up the creeks into Greene and Macoupin; they had also followed the Kaskaskia and its south-flowing tributaries, so that settlements lay in Bond, Clinton, and Washington counties. Elsewhere there was wilderness.

To the north of the area of settlement lay another world distinct and independent from that to the south. The Kickapoo Indians still inhabited central Illinois, and the Sauk and Foxes, chastised in the War of 1812, but still morose, occupied a little of the territory northwest of the Illinois river — the Military Bounty Tract — though this had for some time been surveyed and allotted in military bounties to soldiers of the War of 1812. The main strength of the Sauk and Foxes in Illinois, however, lay in the territory near the junction of the Rock and the Mississippi, where Fort Armstrong on Rock Island had lately risen to overawe them. In the territory east of them lay villages of Winnebago and Potawatomi. Among them in northern Illinois and on the Illinois and the Wabash rivers wandered the fur traders of the American Fur Company; these came south down the lake in their Mackinaw boats each fall, dragged their boats over the Chicago portage to the Des Plaines river, went into winter trading posts along the Illinois from which trading expeditions were sent out during the winter, and carried their harvest of furs to Mackinac in the spring. Besides Fort Armstrong there lay in this district Fort Edwards on the Mississippi, Fort Clark at the present site of Peoria, and Fort Dearborn; though as Indian dangers waned and Indian cessions were consummated, the forts were successively abandoned.

The terms upon which the United States government disposed of its domain in Illinois materially affected settlement in the state. From an early period in the history of the United

States land policy the method of regular surveys had obtained. The face of the country was surveyed into rectangular townships approximately six miles square. These were defined by their number north or south of a line called the base line and in ranges east and west of a principal meridian. Each township was divided into thirty-six sections, each containing 640 acres and capable of division into quarters and similar subdivisions.

In the method of disposing of these the federal government had grown more and more liberal as the years passed. Starting from the concept that the lands were a fund for the payment of the national debt, it had gradually offered better and better terms to the small purchaser. In 1818 the system of sale was as follows: Lands put on sale for the first time were set up at auction at the land office in the district containing them. In Illinois in 1818 there were but three offices — Kaskaskia, Edwardsville, and Shawneetown — soon to be increased considerably in number. If not bid in at auction for two dollars an acre or more, lands might be bought at any time thereafter at private sale, the terms being two dollars an acre, payable in four annual installments. In 1820, however, in spite of strenuous opposition from the western representatives, the credit system was abolished, and the land after having been put up at auction sold at one dollar and twenty-five cents cash per acre.

The first result of the measure was to cut down sharply purchases from the government. Great amounts of land in southern Illinois had already passed out of the hands of the government, partly as gifts to the old French inhabitants and partly by speculative entries under the credit system. Numbers of speculators as well as settlers had been lured by the low initial payment into contracting for more land than they could pay for; and it took act after act permitting the application of a first installment on a large piece of land to apply as payment in full on a smaller before they were extricated from their difficulty. Meanwhile sales of the great body of land that remained were slow. In 1822 sales were as low as 27,000 odd acres; in 1826 they were some 80,000, the next year they fell off to

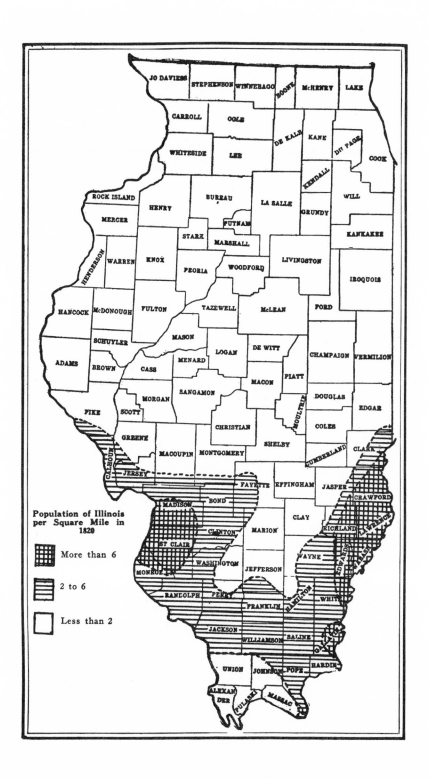

Population of Illinois
per Square Mile in
1820

More than 6

2 to 6

Less than 2

50,000, and not till 1829 did they pass the hundred thousand mark. From 1820 to 1828 the equivalent of twenty townships was sold. Of this the greater part lay in the Springfield land office district, sales in the Edwardsville and Palestine districts coming next in amount. In the Kaskaskia, Vandalia, and Shawneetown districts, which served southern Illinois, the sales were insignificant; in 1821 the three offices sold some 14,000 acres, but in 1822 they sold 5,916; in 1823, 2,636; in 1824, 4,160; in 1825, 2,963; in 1826, 5,459; in 1827, 7,339; and in 1828, 11,518. The significance of this situation is that the course of settlement by men with money had shifted from the south and had passed on to the Sangamon country and northern Illinois. In the south settlers were squatting on the public land. In 1828 W. L. D. Ewing estimated that in the counties of Clay, Marion, Shelby, Tazewell, and Fayette there were 1,230 voters of whom 217 were freeholders.[1] The large sales under the credit system with the great numbers of Military Bounty tracts thrown on the market had created such a glut that men with cash to pay for land would buy only the land of their choice. Otherwise the newcomers to the state held their land by squatters' right, and by the force of public opinion they were able to maintain themselves against those who would buy the improvements over their heads. The west was ripe for agitation for new legislation in favor of the squatters — legislation which directly or indirectly would be opposed by men with heavy landholdings.

In the Illinois of 1818 the French *habitants* still mustered strong in numbers in the villages of the American Bottom, though with a few exceptions, such as the Menards, the well-to-do and better educated of their race were to be found across the Mississippi. Their economic and social life has been the subject of the preceding volume of this series and furthermore requires no special attention here, since the influence of the French upon the development of Illinois in the nineteenth century was negligible.

[1] *American State Papers, Public Lands*, 5:554-556.

It is not easy to describe, or even to divide into classes, the newcomers who were sweeping over the land of Illinois. On the outskirts of settlement was a fringe of hunters leading a half savage life in the forests, supporting their families by the products of the hunt and by the produce of a few acres of corn-land planted among the girdled forest trees. Their life was a series of retreats before the advance of civilization, and they were ever ready to sell their improvements to a newcomer and to push out one stage further into the wilderness.[2]

It is possible to differentiate this first class from later comers only in degree, since the men of the whole frontier were more or less migrating. The men who succeeded the hunters came also from the south for the most part, yet they were in various degrees more civilized in their habits, laid less emphasis on hunting and more on building, making improvements, and clearing land for the cornfields. They very often possessed hogs and cattle which furnished to the little towns a continually increasing amount of raw products to be traded for store goods and to be freighted in flatboats or keel-boats down the Ohio and Mississippi as articles of commerce. This produce of the farm was not only corn, ginseng, beeswax, salted pork, tallow, hides, and beef, the last named sometimes bought by the store-keepers on the hoof and slaughtered for market, but also various rough wool and flax fabrics. Important in the frontier market were such items as deer skins and venison hams, distinctly the products of the rifle rather than of the hoe.[3]

The habit of some writers to classify these southern men as hunter pioneers and to contrast them with the New England and northern farmers who settled the prairies of the north is misleading unless the contrast is carefully limited and defined. The settlers of the south hunted, as did white men everywhere in the wilderness where there were no game laws. They enlarged their cornlands by clearing the forest instead of cultivating the prairies because, in the decade in which they settled

2 Fordham, *Personal Narrative*, 125-126; Flower, *History of the English Settlement*, 129.
3 Fordham, *Personal Narrative*, 181; Birkbeck, *Notes on a Journey*, 155.

the state, farmers preferred such lands, chiefly because the forested lands offered greater accessibility to wood and water, partly because they lacked the capital necessary for breaking up and fencing the prairie, and partly because the scarcity of markets offered no temptation to raise grain that could not be sold. Without a heavy ox team breaking the prairie was almost impossible, and without improved transportation produce could not be carried to market.

There has grown up a traditional interpretation of events sanctioned now by age, that would explain the stoppage of the northern thrust of the southern pioneers by the downpouring of immigrants from the northeast into the valleys of the upper Illinois river. There is little in the sources of information that gives warrant for interpreting the encounter as a meeting of opposing forces. It is true that the immigration of the northerners followed closely on the heels of the backwoods hunters, but this relation in the time of the two movements has only apparently justified the interpretation, for to all appearances the two peoples settled down side by side in peace and concord throughout the state, the southern element naturally enough preponderating in the southern counties and the "Yankee" element in the northern.

Besides this class of so-called hunter pioneers the community had a set of young men of education, of legal training, and of good address, who aspired to the leadership of the community. Frequently they had a few hundreds or thousands to invest in land speculations. Some of them married into the well-to-do French families. They were men of more finished manner than the average pioneer, and their wives and daughters speedily gave the community a touch of sophistication. Doubtless it was for this class the stores advertised the finer goods such as silks, crêpes, and other fabrics of similar character, and kept the choicer wines, liquors, and groceries.[4]

The conditions in the towns are more or less truthfully

[4] In this chapter I have made much use of an unpublished monograph by my assistant Miss Agnes Wright on the subject of social conditions in early Illinois.

mirrored in the contemporary newspapers. In the towns, when the state was young, the rising brick and frame houses contrasted sharply with the log cabins of the territorial days; yet the stage of civilization must not be overestimated, for even in 1821 Shawneetown had no courthouse, jail, church, or school. The towns were disorderly places at best, a Shawneetown Sunday being a byword. Frequently they were rendered unhealthy by pools of stagnant water and by the lack of all sanitation. In 1822 the trustees of Shawneetown had to pass an ordinance providing for the removal of dead animals and for the laying of sidewalks. Town government in so far as it was distinct from other local government was rudimentary. Towns were incorporated by individual acts which gave the trustees power to legislate for the order of the town and to levy taxes on town lots.[5]

The towns of the early days could boast of only the most rudimentary manufactures. The newspapers contain numerous advertisements of grist mills, steam distilleries, log stills, sawmills, etc. In 1817 Jesse B. Thomas set up a carding machine in Cahokia, which was managed by Adam W. Snyder. Promoters of towns were continually offering special inducements to mechanics and skilled workmen to settle within their communities in order that the simplest needs of the inhabitants might be supplied, and the advertisements in the newspapers show the presence of coopers, tanners, clock and watchmakers, hatters, and milliners. There is some evidence, however, that the economic position of such artisans was not altogether prosperous; at least the *Illinois Gazette* in 1820 complained that high rents had driven the mechanics from Shawneetown.[6]

The most important function which the towns performed was that of furnishing a buying and shipping point for country

[5] *Illinois Gazette*, May 19, December 8, 1821, May 25, November 30, 1822; Tillson, *Reminiscences*, 35 ff.; *Laws of 1819*, p. 249, 259; *Laws of 1821*, p. 160, 176.
[6] *Illinois Gazette*, March 30, July 1, 8, 1820, April 10, 1824; *Edwardsville Spectator*, May 23, 1820, May 4, 1822; *Illinois Intelligencer*, February 17, December 15, 1819, September 9, 1820; Snyder, *Adam W. Snyder*, 28. A manufacturing company in Bond county was incorporated. There was also a general incorporation law. *Laws of 1825*, p. 113.

produce and a distributing point for store goods. Stores were ordinarily kept by men of considerable means. They advertised in the local papers alluring lists of goods "just in" and offered to dispose of them "cheaply for cash, for produce, or on terms." Shawneetown, Edwardsville, and Carmi apparently did a wholesale trade as well. Moreover, some storekeepers at Edwardsville and one at Shawneetown regularly advertised semiweekly auctions of goods. Occasionally merchants employed peddlers to go through the country to sell their merchandise. The *Illinois Gazette* contains an indignant advertisement for a runaway peddler "from Connecticut, and is no doubt a perfect chip of the old block!" One notices frequent insistent advertisements calling on delinquent debtors to settle.[7]

In the Illinois of 1818 Shawneetown seemed to hold a favorable position as the gateway, a fact which had been recognized by the United States government by the designation of the town as a port of entry. It was the natural Illinois *entrepôt* for the eastern part of the state and for the country up the tributaries of the Wabash. One rival to its trade near at hand, however, was the New Harmony settlement of Frederick Rapp, which in 1823 maintained a store in Shawneetown for the sale of its goods, woolen cloths, cottons, hats, shoes, stockings, leather, flour, wine, whisky, brandy, beer, etc., as well as a line of eastern goods from Philadelphia. Rapp's failure to buy as well as sell made him unpopular, however, with the resident merchants.[8]

On the west side of the state St. Louis had the position of dominance. It held western Illinois subject to it commercially, despite the attempts at Alton and at Cairo to build up rivals on Illinois soil. Its merchants advertised in western Illinois papers, and they were even able to regulate the discount at which Illinois bank notes should pass; indeed, they exercised some influence on the politics of the state.

[7] Frequently merchants bought and sold goods on commission, see *Illinois Gazette*, September 9, 1820. See also *ibid.*, October 9, December 4, 1819.
[8] *Ibid.*, November 8, 1823.

In the Illinois of 1818–1828 transportation was a serious problem, and the means available for it necessarily influenced the state's contact commercially and intellectually with the outside world. Transportation overland was an extremely difficult matter. The so-called roads of southern Illinois were of but little account and transportation facilities were meager. Not till 1819 was a stage line from Kaskaskia to St. Louis in operation. In the summer of that year a second line from Shawneetown to St. Louis was projected. In 1822 a stage wagon was advertised to run from Springfield to St. Louis once in two weeks, taking two days for the trip.[9]

The state's main reliance had to be on river transportation. At the time of the admission of Illinois to the union the steamboat was just replacing the flatboat and keel-boat. The keel-boat or flatboat was often of considerable size, nineteen and even twenty-seven tons. The farmer who chose to eschew steamer transportation to his market either himself navigated a flatboat or keel-boat with his produce [10] or intrusted it to the tender mercies of the river boatmen, hard drinking, desperate men who terrorized the villages along the river, governing themselves by a rough and ready code of their own in which stealing under certain circumstances was permissible and murder an ordinary matter. Year by year their importance was destined to wane as law and order grew stronger in the river towns and the steamboats multiplied in number. Sweeping down the river to the tune of such doggerel boat songs as "Hard upon the beach oar! She moves too slow; All the way to Shawneetown, Long time ago," they lent to the frontier a touch of the picturesque and romantic peculiarly grateful to the literature of the next generation.

The river steamer, which was ultimately to displace these men's monopoly, had its difficulties with the Ohio river. February 10, 1820, the *Illinois Gazette* noted the passage up the river to Louisville of six or seven steamboats, delayed since

[9] *Illinois Intelligencer*, January 20, 1819, July 5, 1823; *Edwardsville Spectator*, August 7, 1819, April 27, 1822.
[10] *Illinois Gazette*, December 15, 1822; *Illinois Intelligencer*, May 31, 1820.

June by low water. The previous spring, on the other hand, high water had cut Shawneetown off from the outside world.[11] During the twenties the navigation of the Ohio and Mississippi were improved by the federal government to the extent of the removal of obstructions, the channeling of sand bars, and the grubbing out of " snags " and " sawyers."

Even with improvement in the navigation of the Mississippi river the problem of transportation was still a serious one. The inevitable tendency of trade in the west until the coming of the railroad was toward water routes. Down every Illinois creek or river, produce naturally poured to the Ohio and Mississippi, thence to pile up on the wharves of New Orleans. Manufactured goods had to come from the east whether they were shipped by sea from Philadelphia and Baltimore to New Orleans and thence brought up the Mississippi, or whether they followed the stream down from Pittsburg. The balancing of credits was an exchange problem that the age was not able to solve; and with her credits receivable at New Orleans and her debits due in the east, Illinois was facing an impossible situation that drained her scanty currency in remittances and lent a specious excuse for the founding of unstable banks.[12].

Some, foreseeing that Illinois could never prosper without new outlets for its commerce, turned to the hope of internal improvements. In 1824 George E. McDuffie pronounced in congress that if the west's relations were to continue solely with New Orleans, the union could not last fifty years. It was said that the produce of the west was floated down the Mississippi at high water to pile up at New Orleans in the unhealthy season; that Illinois beef and pork which was not put up with imported salt spoiled in the New Orleans market; that in the last five years one-sixth of the flour unloaded there had spoiled; and that even then the trade route to Europe was too long. Thomas Hart Benton, in debate on " Foot's Resolution," laid down a counter-proposition that internal improvements over

[11] *Illinois Gazette*, March 27, April 3, 1819.
[12] In 1821 a firm tried to devise an exchange of produce for goods at New Orleans. *Ibid.*, December 15, 1821; *Edwardsville Spectator*, June 18, 1820.

the mountains were useless to the west, and that she must still find her market at New Orleans; but every year was to add fresh demonstration that Benton's proposition was fallacious. The Illinois-Michigan canal whereby the Illinois river might be made tributary to a transportation system which would lead over the Great Lakes to the Erie canal and the east was the measure which to Daniel Pope Cook and to an increasing number of Illinoisans appeared the best remedy.[13]

The history of the development of Illinois between 1818 and 1822 would be incomplete without mention of a concerted scheme of colonization that, running in channels completely different from those which carried the ordinary course of settlement, was to influence the development of the state out of all proportion to the numbers engaged in it. This enterprise was the settlement of English Prairie in Edwards county by Morris Birkbeck and the Flowers. At its inception the motive force in the movement was the discontent with economic and political conditions in England that affected men of the comparatively affluent classes. For example, Morris Birkbeck by his industry and ability had raised himself to the position of a tenant farmer, farming on long lease a holding of 1,500 acres in the hamlet of Wanborough; yet he was not a freeholder and therefore not entitled to the vote; he chafed at the social and political inferiority which thus marked him, as well as at the heavy taxes and tithes levied on him by the parliament in which he had no voice and by the church in which he was not a communicant.[14] He aspired, to use his own words, to leave his children citizens of "a flourishing, public-spirited, energetic community, where the insolence of wealth, and the servility of pauperism, between which, in England, there is scarcely an interval remaining, are alike unknown."[15] The United States seemed to him the realization of his political ideals; and except for his detestation of slavery he looked on its institutions and the assumed political and social virtues of its republic and citizens through glasses

[13] *Illinois Intelligencer*, February 8, 1823.
[14] Birkbeck, *Notes on a Journey*, 8-9; Birkbeck, *Letters from Illinois*, 28.
[15] Birkbeck, *Notes on a Journey*, 10.

of rose tint. No less attractive perhaps was the opportunity it afforded him of becoming a freeholder at a rate comparable to English rental values. George Flower, son of Birkbeck's friend, Richard Flower, who had been sent to the United States in search of land, had conceived a romantic affection for the prairies of which he had read in Imlay's *Topographical Description of the Western Territory of North America.* When at last he and Birkbeck crossed the Wabash into Illinois and attained the Boltonhouse prairie, depressed as they had been by the mighty forests through which they had journeyed, the broad expanse of meadow stretching for miles embayed in the surrounding timber seemed to them the manor park that they coveted, and they hastened to acquire as much of it as their funds would permit.[16]

In presenting their design of a colony to the English public by the publication of Birkbeck's letters, the promoters strove to induce men of their own social status — tenant farmers possessed of capital and desirous of becoming landholders — to take up land from them or in their vicinity. As a complement this necessarily required the establishment of a class comparable to English agricultural laborers or cottagers; and in fact the enemies of the enterprise later insinuated that while holding great tracts for wealthy emigrants who never came, the promoters refused to sell smaller tracts to poorer men. The accusation was made that they had founded a rich man's settlement. The first settlers to come, however, were mechanics and laborers, who had not been concerned in the original enterprise but who were attracted by Birkbeck's books.[17]

Birkbeck, who remained on the ground over winter with the uncertain labor obtainable from the backwoodsmen — half hunters, half farmers — who surrounded him, was not able to

---

[16] Birkbeck, *Notes on a Journey,* 16 ff., 37, 57, 58, 98, 107, 113; Birkbeck, *Letters from Illinois,* 28-29, 41; Flower, *History of the English Settlement,* 64; Flower, *Letters from Lexington and the Illinois,* 102-103; Faux, *Memorable Days in America,* 254-255.
[17] Birkbeck, *Notes on a Journey,* 132-133, 141-163; Birkbeck, *Letters from Illinois,* 10, 18-19, 75; Faux, *Memorable Days in America,* 235, 238-239, 244; Flower, *History of the English Settlement,* 96.

get accommodations completed for newcomers. Food for the first year had largely to be procured from the nearby Rapp community at New Harmony in Indiana. The newcomers and such wealthier immigrants as followed fared well or ill, according to their ability to work for themselves and to make the best of backwoods conditions. Men without large capital or enterprise missed the agricultural laboring class of England and the presence of women servants, and they were described by persons not well disposed to the enterprise as for the time reduced to squalid wretchedness. Attacks inspired by the "borough managers," so the leaders believed, and by men interested in eastern lands who enlisted in their behalf the sharp pen of Cobbett—sometimes known as Porcupine Cobbett—spread the tales of the wretchedness and woe existing at English Prairie. They made the most of expressions of pleasure by Birkbeck at the absence of all religious observance on the frontier and used them to brand the enterprise as irreligious; this accusation was met by the building of churches, in one of which Unitarian and in the other Episcopal services were installed by Flower and Birkbeck, respectively.[18]

To add to the difficulties of the settlement a feud broke out between Birkbeck and George and Richard Flower. The causes of it undoubtedly were connected with the marriage, during the exploratory trip, of George Flower to Miss Andrews;[19] but whether Birkbeck's anger was the jealousy of a rejected suitor or the just resentment of a man who had unconsciously been made a party to an impropriety in offense of good taste, if not of good morals, it is not necessary to decide. On George Flower's return Birkbeck refused to have any dealings with him, and he was left to establish a home for his father's family as best he might. The settlement clustered in two groups, one centering in Wanborough, the town founded

[18] See the descriptions of the various families in Faux, *Memorable Days in America*, 252-273. Fordham, *Personal Narrative*, 216, 227 ff.; Birkbeck, *Letters from Illinois*, 23 ff.; Flower, *Letters from Illinois*, 124, 129, 131-132, 144-145.
[19] Faux, *Memorable Days in America*, 271 ff. Contrast this gossip with the discreet silence of Woods, *Two Years' Residence*, 348-349.

by Birkbeck in August, 1818, the other in Albion, the town some two miles to the east laid out by George Flower with Elias Pym Fordham and others two months later. In the course of two or three years the men who were determined on success had made headway. By 1819 there were 400 English and 700 Americans in the settlement. They had established comfortable homes and large farm structures, had discovered the futility, in default of labor, of extensive grain farming, were turning their attention to the raising of cattle, sheep, and hogs, and were making progress. Practical farmers with money and industry were doing well, and good laborers imported by the leaders were acquiring lands of their own.[20] The leaders had perhaps totally abandoned their desire of a cluster of manors in southeastern Illinois, as they discovered that the English agricultural laborers they imported also caught the land fever. Men of narrower views believed they saw in the lack of labor a justification of negro slavery and a necessity for it. Men like Birkbeck were able to accept the facts as they were and at the same time to foresee an Illinois of free farmers, neither masters nor servants.

The enterprise had done much for Illinois. It had brought the prairie into notice if not into vogue. Against the agriculture necessarily practiced by the farmer of small means — a corn-patch among trees girdled by the ax, growing larger year by year — it had set the utility of prairie land either for grazing or for grain when broken as it could be by men able to afford a six-ox team. Through the numerous books of Birkbeck, the Flowers, and others, it had brought Illinois into notice not only in England but in the eastern United States and in continental Europe as well. More important still, it had in Morris Birkbeck brought to the state a leader whose services in the struggle with slavery were past all estimate.

Almost equally important was Birkbeck's influence in the advancement of scientific agriculture. The call for the forma-

[20] Flower, *History of the English Settlement*, 130; Flower, *Letters from Lexington and the Illinois*, 104, 137-142; Woods, *Two Years' Residence*, 258-259, 339.

tion of an agricultural society appeared October 8, 1819, in
the *Edwardsville Spectator*. It was signed "A Farmer of
Madison" and hence may very possibly have originated with
Edward Coles. At the meeting for organization held on November 10, the society elected Birkbeck president and Coles
first vice president, and it speedily drew the support of the
prominent men of the state. It offered premiums not only for
wheat, corn, hay, and fine livestock, but also for hemp, flax, cotton, homespun cloth — the premium for this last was in 1823
awarded to Governor Bond — tobacco, castor oil, wool, malt
liquor, salt, and cheese. Agricultural societies, with some
emphasis on the policy of non-importation due to the hardness
of the times, were founded in Madison and Bond counties; and
these were affiliated with the state society. In 1825, however,
the society disbanded, turning over its funds to Sunday
schools.[21]

The most interesting work of this society was the series of
proposals for better agriculture that emanated from its members. Birkbeck's suggestions are of most interest. He repeatedly urged on the society the importance of turning a large
share of attention to grazing and dairying, insisting on the
need of growing finer grasses before fine wool could be hoped
for, and insisting on the need of stringent measures against
wolves, as a prerequisite to successful sheep raising.[22] In 1820
he voiced a prophetic warning against the danger of skinning
the soil, a practice already too prevalent in the older states.
He suggested various devices for successful prairie farming,
recommending also in an article in the *Illinois Gazette* the use
of ditches for prairie fencing. Coles came forward with a
method which he thought would reduce the expense of breaking
prairies, a second surface plowing followed by harrowing.[23]

[21] *Illinois Intelligencer,* January 19, 1822, December 13, 1823, January 25,
1826; *Illinois Gazette,* March 1, 1823.
[22] In 1823 the legislature offered a premium of $200 for the greatest number
of wolves above sixty killed in the state, and a premium of $40 for the greatest
number killed above ten in each county. In 1825 they substituted a general
bounty of one dollar per head. See also *Illinois Intelligencer,* May 13, 1820.
[23] *Illinois Gazette,* May 5, 1821, January 5, 1822.

One point of especial interest treated by the society was the need of improving the health of the country by draining standing and stagnant waters. These conditions were often perpetuated in the small running streams of Illinois by mill dams designed to afford pressure for water mills. In 1821 the Agricultural Society announced a premium for an essay on the subject which detailed the foregoing objections to water power and proposed animal power in its place.

If it is difficult to describe frontier Illinois in its physical aspects since it is impossible to describe it in its mental and spiritual; the evidence is even more fragmentary and more subject to bias in the observers. Again, it is to be regretted that the newspapers which might seemingly furnish unconscious evidence on this subject do not reflect the mental attitude of great parts of the population, since their circulation was very limited. One wonders often how far the traditional shibboleths of frontier Illinois are humorous exaggerations; for instance, how far was the oft-cited prejudice against Yankees based on a piece of popular humor comparable to the mother-in-law joke?

Some general characteristics can be positively described. English observers, friendly or hostile, commented on the open and unabashed manner of the people. In the Illinois frontiersman there was none of the self-conscious awkward rusticity of the English peasant. The instillation of the doctrine of liberty and equality undoubtedly had so far borne fruit as to make the conviction of his own dignity apparent in the conversation of every man. The interpretation put upon this attitude and the form it took naturally varied with the attitude of the observer. If he expected his money to buy him obsequiousness he was disappointed and had to complain often of a positive bad faith and trickiness which at times may well have been a desperate attempt on the part of the native to vindicate an affront to his dignity. If the traveler met all men with an open friendliness, he generally encountered in return a real kindliness and courtesy. If the frontiersman was appealed to as a man for help and sympathy he usually responded in liberal measure. If he was hired as a servant, little good could be expected from him.[24]

Probably the jarring with backwoodsmen and accusations of bad faith and trickiness in bargains made against them frequently arose from the fact that on the frontier specific performance of contract had hardly come to be regarded as the touchstone of honesty. In a wild country where natural elements continually intervene to prevent the performance of a set duty at the proper time, it is an easy and natural step to regard personal convenience or even personal whims as worthy to be taken into account. In Illinois men from older settled communities might fume in vain, if they had not tact to wheedle a performance of contract out of the party bound.

Probably this furnishes a clue to the reason for the dislike of the Yankee so far as it was not a half humorous attitude. Even in a moderately well-to-do settlement of southern men, the Yankee's insistence on writings, mortgages, bonds, and the like, and his superstitious observance of days and times contributed to render him unpopular as being unneighborly. To ask a man on the frontier to hire out his oxen rather than to lend them was thought to imply a belief that he would " act like a Yankee." Furthermore, the frontiersman divined the prim New Englander's suppressed feeling of criticism for all the shiftless, easy-going habits of frontier life. Taking thought for the morrow and multiplying mechanical devices to meet it were considered especially "Yankee;" and Mrs. John Tillson found her clothespins looked upon as the latest Yankee notion. In spite of the prejudice against Yankees, they were repeatedly, as in Tillson's case, placed in situations of importance, often probably because their education and disciplined attention to business rendered them indispensable for many duties.[25]

How far social distinctions divided the frontier state into

---

[24] Fearon, *Sketches of America*, 398, 437 *passim;* Birkbeck, *Notes on a Journey*, 107; Fordham, *Personal Narrative*, 196.

[25] Woods, *Two Years' Residence*, 261, 317; Buck, " The New England Element in Illinois Politics before 1833," Mississippi Valley Historical Association, *Proceedings*, 6:49-61.

classes, it is difficult to say. Most observers remarked that, the backwoods pioneer being omitted, the various classes did not vary nearly so much in intellectual grasp as in England. "In this remote part of America, judges, generals of militia, colonels, captains, and esquires, are not generally men of property or education; and it is usual to see them employed in any common kind of labour. Yet I have seen men among them that possess very good abilities; far from ignorant, and much better informed than could be expected from their appearance."[26] So far as wealth and its means of display were concerned, however, the basis for social distinction existed. When Shawneetown was a village of one brick and several frame houses amid a cluster of log cabins, it boasted one jewelry store which at least advertised a surprisingly wide selection. Advertisements of silks, satins, broadcloths, muslins, cambrics, and silk gloves, among plaids and cheap stuffs and offerings of fine groceries and Madeira wine as well as of whisky by the barrel prove the existence of such distinctions. To take action against the importation of such luxuries, societies were formed between the years 1819 and 1821. The political aspirations of the well-to-do men doubtless induced them, especially at elections, to keep such distinctions in the background. Nevertheless the society of afternoon teas and great dinners must have lived side by side with the simple society whose social events were the dance after the corn husking or barn raising and the gathering at the county seat on court day or at the camp meeting, the last two probably partaken of by rich as well as by poor. Woods mentions husking, raising, reaping, rolling, picking, sewing, and quilting frolics; and they were much more common than their mention in the contemporary literature of the frontier might lead one to suppose.[27]

Patriotism of a higher or lower type flourished in pioneer Illinois. In the frontiersman, according to Fordham, it might be described best as a belief that Americans, especially the

[26] Woods, *Two Years' Residence*, 346.
[27] Fordham. *Personal Narrative*, 219; Woods, *Two Years' Residence*, 300.

people of his own state, were the best soldiers in the world. In the class reached by the newspaper, it took a finer form. At the Fourth of July dinners so often noted in the papers "The memory of Washington" usually was drunk in silence, and there was almost always a toast to the heroes of the Revolution, both toasts indicating a pride in what rapidly was coming to be hallowed by distance as a great and glorious past. The valor of the frontiersman and of the jack tar in the War of 1812 offered a new stimulus to national pride. Further, as the newspaper reported for its readers, the monarchical weaknesses of the old world, the contemptible foibles of the libertine George IV and his immodest queen, the stirrings of revolution and liberty in Europe and South America under the influence and example of republican America made the nation seem destined to an even nobler and more significant future as the standard bearer of republican principles. Adherence to these principles as yet seemed a bond of political unity beside which considerations of dynastic allegiance or racial ties seemed frivolous. In 1820 men were well content to ask no other unity for the American nation. The doubts and fears that beset the whigs in later days as to the influence of the foreigner and the rabble on the future of the republic were thus far characteristic only of the despised federalist minority.

The part which the newspaper played in the community is an interesting one. The present day definition of news was unknown to editors who thought it their duty to keep from their readers anything that might be considered contrary to good manners and morals; an editor might even rebuke as mere idle curiosity the desire for the details of murders and steamboat explosions. The paper's main function was to furnish a medium of polite communications from the editor to his patrons. Usually he regaled them with foreign news, accounts of the proceedings of congress, and the state general assembly, with occasional speeches made in congress, political articles, and forecasts, accounts of improvements in agriculture or manufactures, and moral anecdotes in the manner of Franklin, interspersed with jokes about the sea serpent — matter nearly all obtained by clipping from papers nearer the center of the great world or of the United States. In times of election, however, politics displaced all else.

The scissors usually supplied the literature, which was sentimental in imitation of Goldsmith, humorous after the manner of Sterne, or romantic in the fashion of the author of Waverley — in any case distinctly exotic in character. This was supplemented by local contributions, political, controversial, and humorous, though the point of many a satire, doubtless keen enough in its hour, has long since rusted away completely. On the whole the newspaper was much less a suggestive index to the intellectual habits and tastes of the country than it was ten years later.

The economic status of the newspaper was usually based on the possession of state or national printing contracts or on the desire for them. The printing week by week in their columns of national laws and treaties or the issuing of laws and journals of the state general assembly made the newspaper business profitable. Editors were, in many cases, itinerant — editors partly by grace of their editorial capacity, partly by their knowledge of printing. Such men were free lances willing to enter the pay of any aspiring politician who was ready to provide a press and type, usually veterans of former wars, to loan a few hundred dollars, and to drum up a small subscription list. Without the bounty of public printing, newspapers could not live save by subsidy. Four hundred was a very good list of subscribers; and subscriptions often ran unpaid for years despite the pleadings, threats, and blacklisting resorted to by the editor. There are traces of other intellectual influences. Lists of books advertised for sale are short but contain the titles of some good books; and no doubt the few persons with genuine tastes for good reading could satisfy them as well as if they lived in the east. There were literary and debating societies in Fayette and in two neighboring counties. There was even a Handel-Haydn society. That an outlet to spiritual aspirations was doubtless offered by Masonry is indicated by the St. John's Day orations published from time to time, though apparently Masonry met disapproval from a section of the clergy.[28]

Such systematic education as the state afforded was supplied by private schools and for a price, for the state during the first decade made scarcely any use of its endowment from the federal government. Some of the schools were of about the grade of grammar schools; and girls' schools where needlework, painting, and similar subjects were taught for an extra charge were not uncommon. Frequently board was offered also. Charges for tuition varied from three dollars and fifty cents to seven dollars a quarter, according to subjects taught, needlework in girls' schools usually being an extra.

There were not wanting, however, more ambitious establishments. One at Salu was kept by a New England schoolma'am. The Reverend Mr. Desmoulin had a school in Kaskaskia in which he taught Latin and French. At Ebenezer they advertised for a preceptor who was qualified to teach Greek, Latin, and the higher mathematics. At Galena in 1829 a school (Aratus Kent's) purported to teach Latin and Greek. One public school at Alton was free to the children of parents residing in the corporation, for Alton had been incorporated with an endowment of one hundred lots for religious and educational purposes.[29]

The foundations of collegiate education were laid before the end of the period. In 1827 the indefatigable John Mason Peck opened a seminary at Rock Spring as a theological training school, equipping it with the books and other property that he had collected in the east. It was intended primarily for the education of ministers, but in addition it offered courses in literature and the sciences. At a meeting at Rock Spring, January 1, 1827, Peck was appointed superintendent and agent to obtain funds. It was decided that a farm for student labor be operated and that subscriptions be solicited for buildings

[28] *Illinois Gazette*, January 1, December 2, 1820; *Illinois Intelligencer*, May 15, 1821; *Edwardsville Spectator*, July 3, 1821.
[29] *Illinois Intelligencer*, April 7, 1819.

payable in provisions, cattle, labor, books, or building materials. Contribution entitled a subscriber to send his children or wards without charge for rent or for the use of the library. The school was to have a theological professor and one for mathematics, natural philosophy, and languages.[30]

Religion came to be the most universally pervasive intellectual force of the frontier. As might be expected, on the frontier the first tendency was toward a disregard of religious observances. The emigrant from the older settled regions left behind him the machinery and the establishment of sectarian religion. Until that machinery could be set up again on the frontier he lived without formal worship and often for the time at least the sense of the need of it passed out of his life. In cases where observance had been due to social convention there was no doubt a welcome feeling of freedom and restraint.

Normally the frontiersman was unreligious. Birkbeck noted with relish the absence of ceremony at baptism or funeral and the tolerance of all backwoods preachers alike, whether they raved or reasoned. Sunday was a day for riot and disorder. Other observers looked with horror on such a state of things, did their best to set up at least stated regular worship, and noted an improvement in morals as a result.[31] Yet for years the riot and license of a Shawneetown Sabbath was a shocking thing to a prim New England bride. Further, if one may believe the early preachers of both Baptists and Methodists, deistic and atheistic belief flourished on the frontier among even the better classes. Evidence is not lacking to corroborate the frequency of this attitude of mind, which accentuated the sharp line drawn among men between the religious and the irreligious, the good and the wicked. The latter term connoted those who did not fall in with the beliefs and practices of the denominationally pious. The idea of the sheep and goats divided by observances and beliefs, possibly

[30] *Edwardsville Spectator*, February 19, 1820; *Illinois Intelligencer*, March 24, 1824; Babcock, *Memoir of John Mason Peck*, 225-228.
[31] Birkbeck, *Letters from Illinois*, 24-25; Flower, *Letters from Illinois*, 124-125.

also by such habits as profane swearing and drinking, persists in the pioneer narratives. "A man of good character," wrote Fordham, "is an acquisition; not that there is a small proportion of such men, but because the bad are as undisguisedly bad, as their opposites are professedly good. This is not the land of Hypocrisy. It would not here have its reward. Religion is not the road to wordly respectability, nor a possession of it the cloak of immorality." [32]

Into this western wilderness containing many who had grown accustomed to the lack of religious food, many who openly professed diabolism, and many who yearned for religious observances, the organizations of the Protestant denominations threw themselves.

At every point the Methodist order was best equipped for waging a systematic and thorough campaign against the indifferent and hostile. Its organization was ideal for such a purpose. In effect, under the executive leadership of the bishops of the church, elected by delegates from local conferences to the general conference, but holding for life, it was a self-perpetuating aristocracy of the traveling elders organized in their various conferences; while in its quarterly meetings, love feasts, class meetings, and the like, it gave opportunity for lesser officers, local preachers, and class leaders, and even the rank and file to bear their share in their local government under the guidance of the traveling eldership. For a man to be "settled" was to lose his place in the government; he could hold his position in this aristocracy with its ridiculously meager stipend only by continuing itinerant until under burdens that equalled St. Paul's his strength gave out.

The whole organization was an elastic one, capable of adaptation to the changing march of the frontier and yet always ready to respond to the touch of the executive officers. The best men, transferred from circuit to circuit year by year, could be thrown at one community after another until vast numbers of people at some time had come under the influence of their

[32] Fordham, *Personal Narrative*, 128.

preaching. The faith and theology of the Methodist rejected the stern predestinarian doctrine of Calvin and proclaimed a divine grace freely offered. They looked toward the sudden working of the grace of God in the hearts of great audiences gathered to hear impassioned preaching. The great Methodist preachers of the backwoods were men with a tremendous gift of eloquence which could sway congregations back and forth like fields of waving grain while sinners by the hundreds " fell slain," as the preachers said, and were led to the mourners' bench to be exhorted and prayed with till the divine ecstasy took the form of rapture and peace. This power the ministers commonly used and struggled for, and they were depressed when they could not exercise it. Its importance in the development of the church was tremendous. Once the preaching of Peter Cartwright or James Axley had wrought this experience in a man the local organization of exhorters, preachers, and class leaders was at hand to lead and instruct him.

The men who were the most successful in the struggle for the conquest of the frontier to Christ were a distinct type, unlearned, well-nigh unschooled, only a stage or two above illiteracy. They had a strong contempt for college-bred ministers as unfit to follow in their footsteps, unable with their written sermons to get the effects that the native eloquence of the pioneer attained. Men who had spent four years in rubbing their backs against the walls of a college[33] were not the men to ride wretched roads week in and week out, swim their horses over creeks, and by address, by stratagem, or by force of superior muscle defeat the efforts of the rowdies to break up camp meetings. The pioneer preached a christianity emotional rather than intellectual. His exegesis was often astonishing. In the sermon attributed to Axley preached from the text " Alexander the Coppersmith did me much evil," Alexander figures as a reformed still-maker who turned class leader, but who under the influence of a heavy peach crop, backslid, and made stills for the brethren to the destruction of sobriety in

[33] Sturtevant, *Autobiography*, 162.

the neighborhood. Yet the pioneer preachers worked a revolution in the moral life of the communities they served. Methodists for many years were known by a plainness of dress. Wherever they were, Axley and Cartwright on all occasions struck straight from the shoulder at the vice of liquor drinking and the sin of slaveholding.

The Baptist polity, on the other hand, represented the natural centrifugal tendency of the frontier. The wilderness congregations united by loose associational ties tended to split or to divide. The application of the faulty logic of untrained minds to the interpretation of the doubtful things of scripture was continually resulting in the production of strange and weird doctrines; and since there was lacking the organization by which the Methodist church secured uniformity, the Baptists were in their remote congregations likely to become far separated from each other in matters of belief and practice.

Among the various denominations in Illinois — Baptist, Methodist, and Presbyterian — differences of opinion arose in general upon the various doctrines of predestination and of baptism. These, however, were only the starting points for subdivision. Thus the Cumberland Presbyterians in their practice came somewhat near to Methodism, while they were scarcely Calvinistic in their beliefs. The Campbellites, on the other hand, were non-Calvinistic Baptists.

When Illinois became a state, Methodism had long been established in it. At that time the district of Illinois was united with the Missouri conference, and there were a presiding elder and seven circuit preachers. The church had a membership of 1,435 whites and 17 blacks. In 1824 a separate Illinois conference including a part of Indiana was formed. Illinois itself had a presiding elder and nine circuits with eleven preachers. At that time the membership had increased to 3,705 whites and 27 colored. Jesse Walker, the indefatigable preacher who had first worked in Illinois in 1806, was assigned as missionary in the settlements between the Illinois and Mississippi rivers and Fort Clark. There he formed the first class at Peoria. In

1825 he was assigned as missionary to the Potawatomi located on the Fox river above the Illinois. The expense of the enterprise was $1,000 a year. In 1829, however, when their lands were sold, the mission among the Potawatomi was abandoned, and missions at Galena and Fox River were opened.[34]

The only other denomination of comparable strength in the state was the Baptist. In 1825 the Baptists were estimated to have fifty-eight preachers and exhorters, and the Emancipating Brethren and the Christian Body had thirteen each.[35] In the midst of the individualism characteristic of the denomination there stands out the figure of one man, John Mason Peck. Peck was born in 1789 in the Congregational atmosphere of Connecticut. The birth of his first child in 1810 first discovered to Peck his disbelief in efficacy of pedobaptism. Becoming at length a Baptist by conviction, he began to preach a little and in 1813 was ordained. In 1816, to prepare himself for a missionary career, he studied in Philadelphia, gaining some knowledge of Hebrew and a greater mastery of Latin and Greek, as well as some acquaintance with medicine. In 1817 he was dispatched by the Baptist Board of Foreign Missions as missionary to the west, where he settled himself for the time at St. Louis. His duties soon carried him to the Illinois side of the river. In 1820 the board abandoned the St. Louis mission. In 1822 the Massachusetts Missionary Society appointed Peck a missionary; and in April of that year he removed to Illinois, still keeping an eye to the maintenance of his hard-won foothold in St. Louis.

Peck's activity was tireless. From the time of his coming to the west he rode circuit as assiduously as a traveling Methodist elder, braving the dangers and hardships of the wilderness. With indefatigable Yankee energy he was ever founding, establishing, and sustaining Sunday schools, Bible societies, missionary societies, and their auxiliaries, laboring for better schools, striving with the perversions and oddities of doctrine

[34] Leaton, *Methodism in Illinois*, 48, 151-152, 213.
[35] *Edwardsville Spectator*, October 22, 1825.

that had grown up in the wilderness.   He was not successful in
avoiding the excitement of enmity among the Baptists, partly
as the result of the jealousy of local illiterate preachers who
feared that the better educated missionary preacher might
lessen their prestige among the people, partly from a distrust
that the mission system was an approximation to Methodism
and that the organization of general societies was an encroach-
ment on the autonomy of the individual church governments.
Peck soon had a growing opposition to contend with in Illinois.
His opponents in clumsy satires made light of educated ministers.   They opposed all concerted denominational methods,
such as the establishment of Bible societies, missionary societies,
and Sunday schools.   This opposition they justified partly, one
would judge, on predestinarian grounds, considering that such
aids to salvation were flying in the face of divine election.   A
further development of this opposition was the "two seed"
doctrine of Daniel Parker, at one time Illinois senator, which
predicated the fact that the seed of the woman and the seed of
the serpent were fixed to all eternity, declining any attempts of
the missionary methods to change the one to the other.[36]

Sometimes the opposition took unusual or interesting forms.
In Sangamon county in 1823 an association debarred from
membership any Baptist holding membership in a missionary
society.   In the legislature in 1828 Cartwright and James
Lemen sponsored a bill for the prevention of vice and immorality, and a member proceeded to amend the clause
prohibiting the disturbing of congregations in this fashion:
"that if any person on the Sabbath or first day of the week,
should attempt to disturb the peace or good order of any congregation or body of people gathered together for the purpose
of worshiping Almighty God, by offering to sell pamphlets or
books of any description whatever; or by begging money, or

36 Babcock, *Memoir of John Mason Peck*, 12-14, 30, 106-110, 172. See *Illinois Intelligencer*, December 7, 1822, for a letter by Parker, declaring a Baptist
paper was full of philosophy and enticing words of men's wisdom. Training
preachers he pronounced a mark of the beast. His declaration that not one association in five in the west corresponded with the Board of Missions is interesting.

any other thing for the support of Missionary Societies, Bible Societies, or Sunday Schools, shall be fined any sum not more than $15, nor less than $5." [37]   Strangely enough twelve votes were mustered in the house of representatives for this amendment.   Occasionally a charge of attempts to unite church and state was used against some particular candidate.   It was undoubtedly true that appeals were occasionally made to religious people to vote against " an enemy to religion."   John Russell was several times attacked on charges that he wished to set up Presbyterianism as the state religion and the same charge was frequently brought against S. H. Thompson with reference to his Methodist connections.   The supporters of a convention in 1824 attempted to argue that the Methodists were trying to run the state. [38]

Other denominations in Illinois were of minor importance. In 1825 it was said that there were fourteen Cumberland Presbyterian ministers and two Presbyterian, with one each for the Covenanters, Dunkards, and Independents.   In Bond county in 1824 it was said that the Methodists, Presbyterians, and Cumberland Presbyterians would frequently unite in services. [39]   There was enough Universalism to cause much annoyance to the orthodox ministers.   Catholic activity, at first confined to a few French parishes and missions in the southern part of the state, was, in the late twenties and early thirties, beginning to follow the thickening population into central and northern Illinois.

As a corollary to the efforts of distinctly denominational religion on the frontier must be noted the activities resulting in the spread of Sunday schools and Bible societies.   It is said that the first Sunday school in Illinois was established at Alton in May of 1819.   In 1821 a female society at Edwardsville had been in operation over a year.   In 1822 the ladies and gentlemen of Vandalia were asked to meet to form a Sunday school.   In 1824 societies to promote the formation of Sunday

[37] *House Journal*, 1828-1829, 1 session, 78.
[38] *Illinois Intelligencer*, July 27, 1822, December 9, 1825.
[39] *Ibid.*, November 12, 1824.

schools were established in Greene, Madison, Sangamon, Morgan, and St. Clair counties, as well as in a few others. The total number of schools was thirty-five with 1,047 scholars, who had recited according to report, 82,441 verses, the Bible verses memorized being the important quantitative unit of measure. The purpose of the schools was to furnish a little education in communities that could not sustain ordinary schools, to teach reading, instill moral habits, induce a due observance of the Sabbath, but chiefly to commit scripture to memory. In 1826 a general Sunday School Union for Illinois and Missouri was formed, which in its second annual report, claimed 77 schools, 340 teachers and superintendents, and 2,546 scholars in Illinois. It planned to establish depositories of books at Kaskaskia, Shawneetown, Vandalia, and Springfield. Its appeal was to all denominations. Apparently both the county and the state societies were founded under Peck's leadership in the hope of checking the anti-mission movement. In December of 1823, perhaps under his guidance also, Bible societies were formed in Greene and Madison counties; in 1824 one was also formed in Bond county. In 1825 there were said to be twenty-two auxiliaries and branch Bible societies in the state.[40] These societies appear to have encountered opposition from the same source as that to missions, even in such an important task as the distribution of Bibles. In 1826 it was estimated that in Madison county there were 720 families in which were 3,237 persons able to read and 27 families in which no one could read. There were 79 families in which some person could read and which had no Bibles. In 1828 a state Bible society, on the call of the Bond county society, was formed at Shoal Creek.

With a purpose closely akin to these the American Tract Society depository was founded in Greenville in 1824 and 1825 with William M. Stewart as agent; Bond county, it may be noted, seemed to take a prominent part in many enterprises of the sort. In November of 1824 a temperance society was

---

[40] *Edwardsville Spectator,* October 22, 1825; Babcock, *Memoir of John Mason Peck,* 185, 192; *Illinois Intelligencer,* August 28, 1821.

formed there which a year later served as the nucleus of a state society; the members pledged themselves to abstain from offering liquor at house raisings, a habit apparently already frowned upon in the county. They attacked the use of liquor upon the ground, familiar enough nowadays, that it was the fruitful source of idleness, profanity, and crime, depicting drunkenness as a vice that produced tenfold more misery than stealing or dueling, caused 10,000 deaths a year in the United States, and wasted $12,000,000 directly for spirits and $60,000,000 indirectly through its use. The society, however, did not insist upon prohibition but rather upon the barring from public office all those addicted to strong drink.[41]

Crude and artificial as often were the forces promoting a higher culture on the frontier, one feels as he takes his leave of the period no reason to regret their work. The virtues of man living in the state of nature are alluring, but an analysis of the social life of the frontier discloses nothing of good that necessarily must be lost in a change to a higher civilization and much that might well be replaced by something better. The neighborliness that found expression in the barn raising does not seem so great when compared with the every day acts of kindness that flourish in a rural community today, when the comparative value of time and labor in the one and the other case is considered. Side by side with the honesty and open-hearted hospitality existed the villainy of the scoundrel who had fled to the backwoods to evade the law. The summary punishment inflicted on the outlaw by the backwoodsman was well replaced by the due forms of law. The squalid surroundings of the backwoods cabin happily disappeared before the trim farmhouse. And even the emotionalism or dogmatism of the early preacher compared favorably with the intellectual darkness of the years before Peck and Cartwright, or the intellectual self-complacency of the shallow freethinker. A young Englishman at first fired with enthusiasm for the free life of the frontier finally came to see in the freedom little but lawless-

[41] *Illinois Intelligencer,* November 13, 1824, April 21, 1827.

ness. On the page after that on which he records the killing
of six Indians, men and women, on English Prairie in the spring
of 1817, he wrote "Instead of being more virtuous, as he is
less refined, I am inclined to think that man's virtues are like
the fruits of the earth, only excellent when subjected to culture.
The force of this simile you will never feel, until you ride in
these woods over wild strawberries, which die your horse's
fetlocks like blood yet are insipid in flavour; till you have seen
waggon loads of grapes, choked by the bramble and the
poisonous vine; till you find peaches, tasteless as a turnip, and
roses throwing their leaves of every shade upon the winds,
with scarcely a scent upon them.   Tis the hand of man that
makes the wilderness shine.   His footsteps must be found in
the scene that is supremely & lastingly beautiful." [42]

[42] Fordham, *Personal Narrative,* 225.

II. THE NEW STATE GOVERNMENT,
1818 – 1828

THE constitution of 1818 and the laws under which the people of the state lived for the first ten years of its existence afford an interesting elaboration and commentary on certain phases of the general life of the people already described. Such material, of course, has to be used cautiously; the passage of a law by no means implies that the condition toward which it is apparently directed prevailed to any considerable extent. Without some such study, however, the picture of early Illinois would be incomplete. Reserving the financial legislation to a later chapter, the important elements in Illinois' early legal history will be next considered.

The government of Illinois in its constitution and in its tendency for the first fifteen or twenty years after 1818 was a government by the legislature. The observer is impressed not only by the extent of the power exercised by the general assembly in comparison with that exercised by the judiciary and the executive, but by its assumption of the choice of local officers which are now by almost universal practice chosen by individual communities.

The legislature by the terms of the constitution was to meet biennially; there were to be between one-third and one-half as many senators as representatives. In practice the first and second general assemblies consisted of fourteen senators and twenty-nine representatives; there was a slight increase thereafter until 1831.[1] The representatives were elected annually for each assembly and the senators for terms of four years, half of the senate retiring every two years. In addition to its

---

[1] Up to that time the senate regularly had eighteen members excepting the fourth with nineteen. The house was composed of thirty-six increasing to thirty-seven in the third and forty in the fourth.

powers of legislation the assembly enjoyed the usual powers in impeachment, counted the votes in gubernatorial elections, elected members of the supreme court, appointed the auditor, attorney-general, state treasurer, state printer, and other necessary state officers. By a two-thirds vote it could submit to the voters the question of calling a convention to amend the constitution. The senate could pass on the governor's nominee for secretary of state and had a similar voice in the selection of other officers created by the constitution without a specific provision for their election.

On the legislative department the constitution grafted a very curious body, almost indeed a third house — the council of revision. The origin of this institution was generally traced to a similar one in New York, and when it became unpopular Elias Kent Kane was usually charged by his enemies with responsibility for it. The council was composed of the governor and the justices of the supreme court; its duty was to examine all laws passed by the house and senate and to return such as it disapproved, which last could be passed over its veto by a majority of the members in each house. In practice the institution prevented some useless legislation by calling to the attention of the legislature technical defects in laws passed; but the council's vetoes of laws on grounds of public policy or of unconstitutionality were apt to be futile or merely irritating, because legislators in early Illinois were rarely absent during the session and the majority of members elected in each house required to pass a bill over the veto of the council was usually only one or two greater than the vote by which it originally passed. Furthermore, the supreme court in deciding cases involving the constitutionality of state laws was continually embarrassed by the fact that the justices in the council of revision had already passed on them. This function of the justices undoubtedly heightened the political character, already too apparent, of the early Illinois judiciary.

The powers of the executive of the state were defined by the constitution within narrow limits. The governor could pardon and reprieve and could nominate to the senate for appointment all officers whose choice was not otherwise prescribed by the constitution or whose functions were not exclusively local. He was commander-in-chief of the army and navy of the state and of the militia. In case of his impeachment, resignation, or absence from the state he was to be succeeded by the lieutenant governor, who normally presided over the senate. The veto power, however, which has come to be an important function of the governorship, he could exercise only by his single vote in the council of revision.

The judiciary was only sketched in by the constitution. Inferior courts could be established and their judges appointed by the legislature and removed by it on the formal application of two-thirds of each house. The supreme court till 1824 was to consist of four justices chosen by joint ballot of the assembly, and charged with both circuit and supreme court duties. At the end of that period the legislature might remodel the supreme and circuit courts and elect judges who were to hold office during good behavior. As might have been foreseen this gave a political cast to the first supreme bench; and it is not surprising that in 1822 two justices should have been openly candidates for governor and a third a potential candidate for either the governorship or the senate.

The court as first constituted consisted of Joseph Phillips, Thomas C. Browne, William P. Foster, and John Reynolds. Of these men Foster never acted and was succeeded by William Wilson; Phillips resigned in 1822 and was replaced by Thomas Reynolds. In 1825 the legislature reconstituted the court with a chief justice, three associate justices, and five circuit judges. The justices elected under this law, however — Samuel D. Lockwood, Theophilus W. Smith, Thomas C. Browne, and William Wilson — by an act of 1827, were compelled to return to circuit duties; and the circuit judges were legislated out of office.[2]

[2] In this and in following chapters when the date of a law is given in the text, no further reference is made.

The displaced circuit judges drew up a communication to the senate protesting against the act as calculated to displace the balance of the three divisions of government and leave the tenure of the judiciary at the whim of the legislature. This was the main argument advanced by their supporters; while those who favored the abolition of their offices urged economy and the advantage of keeping the supreme justices fresh in the law by service in the circuits, instead of leaving them to be in session twenty-eight days in a year and a half to decide sixty-three cases. They discounted the argument that the benefit of appeal would be destroyed by referring to the supposedly similar experience of Great Britain, the United States and New York state. On one ground or another probably the majority of the people were in favor of the repeal.[3]

Local government in Illinois for its first decade was as rudimentary as the state government. The constitution had little to say on the subject. It provided that three county commissioners be elected in each county to transact all county business but left their duties and term of service to be regulated by law. The first general assembly expanded the constitutional provision regarding county commissioners by defining their duties as follows: "That said court in each county, shall have jurisdiction in all matters and things concerning the county revenue, and regulating and imposing the county tax, and shall have power to grant license for ferries and for taverns, and all other licenses and things that may bring in a county revenue; and shall have jurisdiction in all cases of public roads, canals, turnpike roads, and toll bridges, where the law does not prohibit the said jurisdiction of said courts; and shall have power and jurisdiction to issue all kinds of writs, warrants, process, and proceedings, by the clerk throughout the state, to the necessary execution of the power and jurisdiction with which this court is or may be vested by law." The court, it was expressly stated, had no legal jurisdiction in the ordinary sense, "but

---

[3] *Illinois Intelligencer*, January 6, 27, 1827; *Edwardsville Spectator*, February 25, September 29, 1826; *Illinois Gazette*, October 14, December 2, 16, 1826.

said court shall have jurisdiction in all cases where the matter or thing brought before the said court, relates to the public concerns of the county, collectively, and all county business." The function of the court was clearly designed to be administrative.[4] This act, however, did not specify the term of office of the members and indeed none did until 1829.

Of other county offices the sheriffs and coroners were by constitutional provision to be elected biennially. Notaries public, public administrators, and recorders were appointed by the governor and senate, surveyors by nomination of the house of representatives to the senate. The first general assembly assigned probate functions to the county commissioners; the third to a probate judge who was to hold office till the end of the next general assembly. In 1825 the assembly installed new probate judges elected by the legislature on joint ballot. The county commissioners and the circuit judge both appointed their own clerks. In most cases the returns from fees were small and the county offices themselves were held as minor prizes and rewards in the political game. Very often, especially in the case of a new county, several of these offices were held by the same man. "The offices in a new county" was a not uncommon political proffer or request. In such cases through long tenure county clerkships sometimes became almost private political freeholds especially in view of the fact that the law recognized little or no responsibility on the part of the county to provide clerks with offices or equipment. It will be seen that the legislature allowed to the people of the counties a voice in the selection of few of their officers.[5]

As defined by the constitution and the earlier statutes there was nothing unusual in the duties of the Illinois justices of the peace. By the act of 1819 they were to be elected by the senate on the nomination of the house of representatives; constables were to be appointed annually by the county commissioners'

---

[4] *Laws of 1819*, p. 175.
[5] *Laws of 1819*, p. 18, 31; *Laws of 1821*, p. 62; *Laws of 1823*, p. 87,132; *Laws of 1825*, p. 70; Washburne, *Edwards Papers*, 397-398; Reynolds to Grant, 1830, in Eddy manuscripts.

courts. In 1827, however, the law was changed to provide for their election by districts. The jurisdiction of the justice as first defined extended to civil matters not exceeding one hundred dollars, with appeal in all cases in which over four dollars was at stake. The act of 1819 gave him general powers in criminal cases to commit for all offenses and to free on recognizance in minor cases. He was also given a rather vague jurisdiction in criminal matters, which later acts rendered more specific. He could commit vagrants and could discharge apprentices from their masters, subject to appeal, or could correct them for misbehavior.[6]

One minor function of local government may here be discussed. Poor relief was provided for by a statute of 1819 which called for the annual appointment of overseers of the poor in each township by the county commissioners. They were directed to farm out the poor and to apprentice poor children, and they might in behalf of the poor administer bequests not aggregating in yearly value $1,200. There were added elaborate provisions as to how a person might obtain a settlement in the district and penalties for being without one, which sound strangely on the frontier. Indeed the whole matter was one of form only and Governor Coles, in answering a query from New York regarding the Illinois poor system, was happy to be able to remark that in no county had the poor been sufficient in numbers to exercise the statutes.[7]

The constitution had left the appointment or election of many officers now chosen by popular vote in the hands of the governor and the general assembly. For the limited number left to the popular choice any male white inhabitant above the age of twenty-one residing in the state six months was entitled to vote. For members of the general assembly the constitution prescribed the payment of a state or county tax and United States citizenship and for the governor United States citizenship for thirty years. The specific laws relating to elections

⁶ *Laws of 1819*, p. 5, 88, 162, 186-195.
⁷ *Ibid.*, p. 127-139; *Laws of 1827*, p. 309-310; Greene and Alvord, *Governors' Letter-Books, 1818-1834*, p. 51.

were altered rapidly by the various general assemblies. The successive laws provided for the division of the counties into election districts with judges chosen by the county commissioners' court. In 1819 and 1823, provision was made for vote by ballot, in 1821 and 1829, by viva voce. All the acts after 1823 allowed the voter to cast his vote at any polling place in the district in which an office for which he had the franchise was to be filled.

The question between viva voce and ballot voting gave rise to some interesting political discussion. In 1819 there seemed to be a tendency to defend viva voce voting as a necessary complement to the hustings, where the candidate appeared, to be interrogated or pledged by the voter if he wished. Vote by ballot, on the other hand, was held to imply some form of previous nomination; and a nomination by clique or meeting enabled a man to stand aloof and unpledged and be elected by his friends.[8] Whatever force this theory may have possessed disappeared with the multiplication of polling places. One has more sympathy with the attacks made in 1821 on viva voce voting as a relic of British tyranny which admitted of overawing voters. The general assembly was attacked for ordaining viva voce vote in popular elections and for conducting its own by ballot; and as a result of this criticism the assembly in 1829 provided by law that its own elections should be viva voce.[9]

At first the quinquennial state census was apparently designed as an aid to apportionment. The laws of 1819 prescribed only returns of heads of families, free white males of twenty-one years, other free whites, free people of color and slaves. The laws of 1829, however, contained additional provisions for returning the number of persons of both sexes and colors in ten-year age periods, the number of males eighteen to forty-five subject to militia duty, and the number of factories, machines, distilleries, etc.

In the legislation of Illinois during the period of its first

[8] *Illinois Intelligencer,* March 17, June 9, 1819.
[9] *Ibid.,* January 16, July 31, 1821; *Senate Journal,* 1821, 1 session, 68.

constitution the militia occupies a much more prominent place than a legislature of this day would assign it. Indications are not wanting that its importance was much less than the bulk of legislation would imply. The constitution defined the militia as all free white males from eighteen to forty-five except those exempted; it provided for the exemption of conscientious objectors, it prescribed the election of company and regimental officers by the whole of their respective commands, and election of general officers by the officers of the commands in question. The legislature provided for conscientious objectors by allowing them to obtain release from drill, not from active service, by payments for flags and martial musical instruments or for the poor of the county, or by additional road service.

The militia was organized on a territorial basis; its unit was the company whose captain was to enroll in a specific district all those liable for duty; the regiment represented a county, and the brigades and divisions, groups of counties. The men were brought together in company, battalion, or regiment for drill several days in each year. The officers formed regimental courts-martial which assessed petty fines for nonattendance at musters or for improper equipment.[10]

In spite of elaborate militia statutes, notices in newspapers of militia elections, and even store advertisements of martial trappings, one doubts if the militia service was a very important one in men's minds, or even if the musters gained in the social life of communities such a place as that held by the circuit court days. Coles in reporting to the war department in 1826 expressed the belief that a volunteer corps would be far more valuable. He thought that the musters were productive of little military knowledge and that their effect on society was bad. He believed one muster a year for companies and regiments would be enough, though he thought the officers would need additional training in "the duties of the field and camp." "The Militia," he said, "as now organized is a mere school of

10 *Laws of 1819*, p. 13-14, 270-296; *Laws of 1821*, p. 13, 106-112; *Laws of 1823*, p. 40; *Laws of 1827*, p. 296; *Laws of 1829*, p. 107-108.

titles where honors are conferred more from a momentary impulse of personal kindness than from a sense of the qualifications of the individuals."[11] This criticism was amply justified in the course of time, for when in 1861 the call came for six regiments of militia, there were "no available, efficient, armed and organized militia companies in the State, and it is doubted whether there were thirty companies with any regular organization."[12]

The problem of transportation in pioneer Illinois was a most important one. By general acts, by special licenses to individuals and corporations, by state aid, successive legislatures labored at the problem, and none too successfully. The general acts left the handling of this problem in its primary sense of good local roads under the charge of the county commissioners' courts. In local districts in their counties these courts were required annually to appoint supervisors of highways who were empowered to call on the people of their districts for specific amounts of labor or for money commutation in lieu of them which might be expended for hiring extra labor and teams and buying scrapers or materials. These acts generally laid the burden of labor on the highways on all males of from eighteen to fifty years, but the act of 1825 allowed in addition a levy of one-half per cent on all taxable property to be collected in labor or money. The provision was repealed in 1827. In this provision lay a direct issue as to whether good roads were to be considered so universal a benefit that the poll tax principle was properly applicable, or whether the benefit to property was sufficiently great to warrant its taxation. The debate assumed a class character; and while in Illinois legislation the poll tax principle prevailed, it may be questioned if it was a triumph of justice.[13]

In dealing with tne problem of long distance transportation the legislature was inclined to rely on private enterprise. In

---

[11] Greene and Alvord, *Governors' Letter-Books, 1818-1834*, p. 110.
[12] *Reports General Assembly*, 1863, 1:467.
[13] *Laws of 1825*, p. 130, 135; *Laws of 1827*, p. 340, 346; *Edwardsville Spectator*, May 9, 1820, January 15, 1826.

1819 it allowed county commissioners' courts to authorize the establishment of ferries and to fix rates for fares, which rates the owners apparently sometimes tried to alter at pleasure. It further authorized by similar means the construction of toll bridges and turnpikes. In addition the legislature was free with special acts allowing individuals to erect toll bridges or build turnpike roads, sometimes with a provision allowing county purchase after a term of years. Sometimes a lottery was authorized for some such purpose as improving the Grand Rapids of the Wabash or draining the American Bottom. In 1825 the county commissioners of Sangamon county were allowed to receive subscriptions and to levy a tax for the improvement of the Sangamon river.

Sometimes the state legislature made grants in aid. Thus in 1823 it provided for the laying out of a series of roads radiating from Vandalia and appropriated $8,000 to build them in Fayette county. Frequently it passed acts appointing commissioners to lay out specified roads. "Vast sums from the public Treasury," protested the council of revision in 1827, "have been thrown away on commissioners to view and mark out roads, which have never been and never will be opened." [14]

In 1827 and 1829 the legislature set about appropriating the proceeds from the sale of the surplus saline land which had been authorized by congress. The act of 1827 provided for its use in improving Saline creek, for a local road, and for a canal on the Little Wabash, allotting the proceeds from the Vermilion saline to the improvement of the Great Wabash. In 1829 it distributed all the proceeds above $10,000 to various counties for miscellaneous public works. This was apparently the triumph of a scheme of legislative logrolling in which amendments and additions without number were proposed for the benefit of various localities and vain appeals made for economy or for reimbursing the school fund instead. Two broad projects of internal improvement by federal activity or federal aid — the Cumberland road and the Illinois and Michigan

[14] *Senate Journal*, 1826-1827, 1 session, 126.

canal — though projected in this period, were not undertaken till later and may most appropriately be considered elsewhere.

From the first session of the general assembly the question of the establishment of an adequate code of statute law came up repeatedly. The first legislature was criticized sharply for repealing the territorial code and for the alleged discrepancies and omissions in the laws with which they sought to replace it. In the session of 1823 a joint committee of the general assembly decided against revision of the laws until a permanent judiciary could be established, possibly intending to postpone consideration till the question of a revised constitution was settled also. That question settled, the legislature of 1825 required the justices of the supreme court to digest the statutes and report discrepancies to the general assembly for adjustment. They were also directed to consider the expediency of printing with the statutes the English statutes in force in the state, a reminiscence of the act of the first general assembly which had made the rule of decision, subject to legislative alteration, the common law of England and all statutes with certain exceptions made in aid of it before 1606.[15]

In reporting to the general assembly of 1827 the justices excused themselves for not undertaking the prescribed research in early English laws on the plea that many of the statutes were barbarous, long since obsolete and at variance with free institutions, as well as by the fact that there was no set of the *Acts of Parliament* in the state. They had further decided it would be inexpedient to prepare a digest since a permanent statutory code was designed. Meanwhile they wished to examine the new Louisiana code and, if they might take the time necessary, the new New York code. Their uncertainty as to the sense of the legislature on the revenue and execution laws, they concluded, prevented them from having the work completed. The legislature appointed a joint committee of fourteen which set to work on the judges' recommendation. Their work, though

[15] *Illinois Intelligencer*, May 25, 1819; *Edwardsville Spectator*, December 27, 1819; *Senate Journal*, 1822-1823, 1 session, 77; *Laws of 1819*, p. 3.

partly enacted into law in the form of statutes, was not finished until the session of 1829.

The early criminal codes of Illinois were influenced in their tenor by the impossibility of providing for punishment by imprisonment. In spite of repeated statutes requiring county commissioners to provide strong jails, there were probably even as late as 1829 many counties without them. A state penitentiary did not exist, and the expense of keeping malefactors to serve out prison terms was a burden which counties were unwilling to assume. Accordingly, when fines could not be collected, the most feasible method of punishment for the more serious offenses appeared to be whipping. In spite of such traces of savagery as the fact that an act providing for punishment by extreme mutilation was lost in the Illinois house in 1823 by a vote of but fourteen to eighteen, it is probable that tenderhearted juries often neglected to apply the punishment of whipping. None the less, the early codes have on their face savage penalties in which the whipping post and even the brand play a part.[16]

By the criminal act of 1819 only four offenses were punishable by death. From this list the code of 1827 subtracted assault and arson, unless a life were lost in the fire, while adding two corollary offenses. As to punishments by whipping, the code of 1827, while applying it to nine offenses including crimes of violence, forgery, counterfeiting, and altering marks and brands, cut down the number of lashes; in certain cases the code of 1819 prescribed five hundred lashes, but the later code in no case exceeded a hundred. The large number of additional offenses created by the act of 1827 were punished by fine or by civil disability.

Some of the offenses specified in the early act are interesting commentaries on the economic conditions of the day. In the act of 1819 were penalties for hog stealing, altering marks — punished by a fine of fifty to one hundred dollars and from twenty-five to thirty-nine lashes — and for defacing brands —

16 *House Journal*, 1826, 2 session, 58; *ibid.*, 1828-1829, 1 session, 7.

punished by a fine of five dollars plus the value of the animal and forty lashes if a first offense and by branding for a second. Persons killing cattle or hogs in a wood were required to show the head, ears, and hide to the next magistrate under penalty of ten dollars. Every person owning livestock was required to record his brand or earmark with the county commissioners' clerk, and a person buying neat cattle must within eight months brand them with his own brand before two credible witnesses. Any man bringing earless hogs to a house was to be judged a hog stealer. The act is strangely reminiscent of the custom of the Anglo-Saxon frontier a thousand years earlier.

Certain interesting aspects of social life are touched in the various Illinois codes. In 1819 and 1827 acts were passed against dueling, the first of them limiting the death penalty to the principal, and the second making any participation in a fatal duel murder. Both acts punished anyone concerned in the formalities of a duel with civil disability. There was repeated legislation from 1819 against gambling. In 1825 the purchase or importation of packs of cards or other gambling devices was punished by a fine. In 1827 a curious provision was enacted making payments of gambling debts recoverable at law at treble value by the loser or, if he did not act, by any other person. There was a severe penalty prescribed against tavern keepers who tolerated gambling or who kept open on Sunday. The term tavern was given a definition by an act of 1823 which had forbidden county commissioners to grant "grocery" licenses unless the applicant gave security to provide lodging for four persons besides his family. The code of 1827 continued the penalty against tavern keepers who tolerated gambling; further it provided a fine for tavern keepers who sold liquor without a license or sold it to a slave without his master's consent. There was a general penalty for keeping a tippling house open on Sunday or for keeping a gambling or disorderly house.

Most curious of all, both for the spirit that prompted them and for the spirit which they were intended to combat, were the Sunday laws. The act of 1819 assessed a fine of two dollars on persons fighting, working, shooting, or hunting on Sunday. Further it assessed swearing of oaths at from fifty cents to two dollars. Persons swearing or behaving in a disorderly manner before a court or a congregation were fined from three to fifty dollars. No provisions on the subject appear in the code of 1827, but in 1829 an act provided that any person disturbing Sunday by work be fined not to exceed five dollars, and anyone disturbing a congregation be fined not to exceed fifty dollars.

Acts of 1819, 1825, and 1827 provided for divorces to be granted by circuit courts. The act of 1825 allowed divorce from bed and board for cruelty or for habitual intoxication. Otherwise only impotence, adultery, and the existence of a previous spouse were recognized as valid reasons. In spite of these provisions, the legislature was repeatedly appealed to for special divorces and was usually in the throes of contest over the principle of granting them. A limited right of imprisonment for debt was granted by the act of 1823, but it applied only in case of an affidavit that the debtor was on the point of absconding and lasted only till security was given or an oath of insolvency taken.

It is comparatively difficult to determine the character and the amount of crime that flourished in the Illinois of the first decade of statehood. In default of searching court records one is thrown back on the newspaper accounts, which of course are far from complete and indeed difficult to estimate. Crimes of violence exclusive of those resulting from mere affrays like that one at Vandalia when James Kelley, cashier of the state bank, was killed in the act of cowhiding his assassin, found their most fruitful source in the gangs of desperadoes, half counterfeiters and horse thieves, half robbers and murderers, such as the one which infested southeastern Illinois in the early years of statehood. These gangs, having their rendezvous at taverns where they trapped unwary travelers well supplied with money, often mustered sufficient strength to make open war on the posses sent out against them. Occasionally the inhabitants in desperation enforced a lynch law of their own, as for instance when in Hamilton county in 1823 two persons were acquitted of the death of a bad character whose house they had gone to search.[17]

Among lesser crimes counterfeiting and horse stealing throve exceedingly. The temptation to the former was irresistible when the large number of banks of issue and the comparative ignorance of the people is considered, and the plates once made the business could be conducted as well in the seclusion of the woods as in cities. Horse stealing was so prevalent in Madison county in the first years of statehood that Mrs. Ninian Edwards was compelled to lead the family horses through the house into the yard every night.

From the beginning Illinois had a savage black code. By act of the first legislature all Negroes and mulattoes settling in the state must produce a certificate of freedom to be recorded by the clerk of the circuit court. Any person bringing in Negroes to be emancipated must give bond of one thousand dollars for each. All resident blacks must enter their names and evidence of their freedom with the circuit clerk, and no one was to hire them unless they produced the clerk's certificate to their freedom. Harboring runaway slaves, like receiving stolen goods, was felony. Blacks without certificates were to be advertised in the papers and hired out for a year. If no owner appeared within that time the black was given a certificate of freedom. No Negro might be a witness, except against a Negro, a mulatto, or an Indian. The code of 1827 stated that justices of the peace had jurisdiction over free Negroes, indentured servants, or slaves in cases of larceny and with the verdict of a jury might condemn them to stripes. The act of 1819 had also left to justices power of inflicting similar punishment on insubordinate servants. The law of 1829 provided that no black or mulatto, not a citizen of one of the United States, was to enter the state unless he gave bond of a thousand dollars and exhibited a cer-

[17] *Illinois Gazette*, July 19, 1823.

tificate of freedom. This law was ushered in by a report by Joseph Kitchell which pronounced the presence of negroes with masters a moral and political evil and their presence without them a greater one, especially as they could never be citizens. This measure passed the house by a vote of twenty-five to eleven and probably represents the sentiment of the day.

The clause of the act of 1819 which penalized the bringing in of servants without giving bond caught at least one illustrious victim in Edward Coles, who had brought in his slaves a month after the passage of the act but five months before it was published and had, through ignorance, neglected to comply with its provisions. He was sued on behalf of Madison county late in 1823 or early in 1824, and a verdict for $2,000 was given against him. The next legislature passed an act releasing all penalties, judgments, or verdicts under the provision of the law of 1819, as Coles' enemies alleged at his special instance. Samuel McRoberts, however, who was now the presiding judge, overruled a plea to set aside the judgment and verdict, arguing that the legislature could not legally revoke the penalty. His decision was reversed by the supreme court in 1826. Meanwhile it gave rise to a long newspaper controversy between Coles and McRoberts.[18]

With the presence of free blacks in the state the kidnapping of them into slavery in the south was all too common, especially in the decades 1820–1840. For instance in 1823 certain freedmen from Vincennes were kidnapped and carried off through Shawneetown in spite of the fact that a son of William Henry Harrison endeavored to raise a pursuit.[19] There were repeated laws on kidnapping. The act of 1819 penalized it by a fine of one thousand dollars. The act of 1825 made it a felony punishable by twenty-five to one hundred stripes, by two to four hours in the pillory, and by a fine of one thousand dollars. It was much more closely drawn than its predecessor and included the case of kidnapping from one county of the state to

18 *Edwardsville Spectator*, April 12, 26, 1825.
19 *Illinois Gazette*, August 2, 1823.

another and prohibited the selling of indentured servants out of the state. The code of 1827 had somewhat similar provisions. The act of 1829 prohibited marriage between the races under penalty of stripes, fine, and imprisonment. Jacob Ogle in 1823 was not permitted by the legislature to introduce a petition from persons of color begging for the suffrage. When Flower sent some freed Negroes from Illinois to Haiti, they were stopped in Shawneetown under suspicion of being fugitive slaves. It was intimated that the men in charge of them might design to sell them at New Orleans. The prevailing attitude toward the Negro or his friends was distinctly one of distrust and dislike.[20]

There were Negroes other than freedmen in Illinois not only the slaves of the old French inhabitants supposedly guaranteed them by the Virginia act of cession but numerous indentured servants as well, held on long terms that made them slaves in all but name. Exactly what the economic status of these indentured servants was is hard to say. The indenture records kept in various counties, however, afford some light on the problem. Sometimes a cash consideration as high as $500 is named, but probably in such cases the sum was paid to the former owner of the slave in or out of Illinois. Oftener the consideration was a suit of clothes, a blanket, or something of the sort. The term of service varied widely, but the normal period usually was one that terminated at the slave's sixtieth year. Sometimes whole families down to the babe at the breast were indentured, but more frequently the indentures represent the acquisition of an adult slave. Except near the saline at least as many women as men were indentured. Undoubtedly this points to the presence of southern women unable to handle alone the task of housewifery or to procure white help. The need of servants in his own home doubtless caused many a young man, who was making his way to prosperity without being able to give his wife the benefits of it, to favor slavery.

The indenturing of new servants ceased of course with

[20] *House Journal*, 1822-1823, 1 session, 36; *Illinois Gazette*, April 3, 1829.

the new state constitution. A rush to indenture servants is especially noticeable in White and Gallatin counties at the time when the first draft of the new constitution would have reached them, about August 25, 1818. After the admission of the state there was open trading in French slaves and in indentures with varying terms to run. Slavery was not to be pronounced legally at an end in Illinois for a quarter of a century thereafter.

Upon the first legislature the duty of providing a new capital had been laid, not by popular demand, but by the influence of speculators in the constitutional convention. Kaskaskia, for a hundred and fifty years the seat of empire in the central west, was still by post road, by water, and by commercial connection, the most important city of the state; a change from this logical capital was premature and unnecessary. But in a day when the projection of a new town was the favorite get-rich-quick scheme, speculators were not likely to let slip so fat an opportunity as the promotion of a new capital. The question was brought before the convention by the introduction of three written proposals from proprietors of sites on the Kaskaskia river north of the government surveys, offering to donate land to the state for a capital site. At once the convention took issue. A bitter wrangle ensued with the outcome a draw, for the resolution finally adopted, though it made a change necessary, was designed to remove the transaction from the field of private speculation. As incorporated in the constitution, it provided that the first legislature should petition congress for four sections of land for a capital site " on the Kaskaskia river, and as near as may be, east of the third principal meridian;" if the petition was granted commissioners were to be appointed to select and lay out a town site to be the seat of government for twenty years. In case the petition was refused, the general assembly was to fix the capital where it thought best. By requiring that the site be located east of the third meridian where no individuals had land claims, it was thought that the state, and not private enterprise, would profit from the sale of lots. The gains from this source were practically the only advantage reasonably to be expected from the change, and to many minds they seemed trifling indeed as compared to the sacrifices entailed.

In spite of some such protests, the legislature, when it convened, proceeded as directed by the constitution. Its petition was granted by congress and five commissioners selected as the new site for the capital Reeve's Bluff, a beautiful spot in the midst of an unsettled wilderness eighty miles to the northeast of Kaskaskia.

The legislative ruling that only one hundred and fifty lots of the new site were to be put on sale caused such absurdly high prices to be bid for them that on paper the state realized over $35,000. Only a small portion of this sum was paid in cash, however, and it became impossible to exact full payment when in a short time the dream of a swift-growing city was seen to be chimerical. This uninhabited spot was christened Vandalia;[21] having thus been chosen as the repository of the state archives, these were bundled into a small wagon and carried through the forest to the temporary building erected for them.

[21] The name was probably taken from the name of the proposed colony of Vandalia that was an issue in British politics and later American during the last quarter of the eighteenth century.

III. TEN YEARS OF STATE FINANCE

THE public finance of early Illinois introduces the student to a strange world, in which currency normally circulates at a score of different discounts from par, in which banks are organized to loan money on the state's credit to hard-pressed citizens, and in which the state derives but a small portion of its little revenue from the taxation of its own citizens. Illinois state finances, while not expressed in sufficiently great sums to be impressive, are sufficiently bizarre to be interesting.

As an introduction to the public finance of the state it will be necessary first to consider the currency and private finance. The currency in circulation in Illinois for the first years of its majority was emphatically of an *opéra bouffe* character. Not merely did the notes composing it pass at a discount; they passed at forty different discounts, varying with the reputation of the banks from which they issued or purported to issue. Some were issued by solvent banks, some by specie paying banks, some were issued by banks that had failed, some were counterfeit notes of existing banks and others of purely fictitious ones. Of the notes in circulation, a few were issued by New England banks, a few came from western New York, more came from Pennsylvania and the District of Columbia, still more from the banks of Ohio and of the south, in particular Tennessee and Kentucky. Local notes composed but a small fraction of the total, and notes of the Bank of the United States were very rare.

In great measure the uncertainty of the note issues in circulation was due to the course of western trade. Illinois was poor; her agricultural products were her main source of wealth; and these, poured down the Mississippi in such quantities as to glut the markets of New Orleans, afforded meager returns. Furthermore, New Orleans was not able to act as the source of supply for the needs of the state; and the manufactured luxuries and necessaries that Illinois drew from older communities came from the northeast, notably from Philadelphia and Pittsburg. Means of making payments in the eastern cities were scanty in the extreme. The good eastern money brought in by immigrants found its way to the land offices and from them it was drawn into the government treasury to be spent in the east. The west was accordingly compelled to drain out the dregs of its good money to pay its eastern debts. The one means of relief would have been a commercial or exchange organization capable of setting off credits at New Orleans against debits in the east, but no such organization existed. The Bank of the United States had hoped to establish a uniform currency by making notes issued at one branch redeemable at all others; but the western branches had issued such floods of notes to be applied in local improvements or land speculation that the United States Bank was threatened by the drain of its specie in the east. The fact that it was compelled to receive for the government the notes of any bank at all prevented it from circulating its own notes locally in the west and providing a different system of exchange; and it refrained for some years from any issue of notes whatever in the west.

Under these circumstances the question whether or not the government land offices would accept the uncertain currency of the west was vital to the people of the state. William H. Crawford, secretary of the treasury, undertook the task of devising a means whereby the government might accept the better notes current in the west and convert them into eastern funds. The Bank of the United States had at first agreed in localities where it had no branches to designate local banks to receive the public money from land offices. It soon discovered that in spite of the treasury limitations as to notes which were land office money, it was becoming responsible for vast sums of paper it could not convert into current funds without delay and loss by exchange. In June, 1818, therefore, it announced that it would henceforth be responsible only for the transmission of legal currency of the United States or of funds convertible into it. Crawford then undertook to use state banks in the west as deposit agencies, requiring them to transmit the government funds in their possession by degrees to the United States Bank; and in 1819 he granted them fixed government deposit balances. At the same time he required them to be responsible for the transmission without depreciation of bank notes deposited by land offices, but allowed them to discontinue receiving notes of any particular bank on due notice to the receiver of the depositing land office.[1] In 1820 he entered into arrangements by which the depository banks were to receive and remit at par notes of certain eastern banks and of specie paying banks in their own community. This was a distinctly able measure toward building up sound local currencies.

Undoubtedly this policy saved the west from much hardship. Had it not been entered into, the government could have received only specie, United States Bank notes, and good eastern notes, all of which were rare in the west. Undoubtedly as Crawford's enemy, Ninian Edwards, later charged some government money was lost in transactions with fraudulently conducted banks; possibly also Crawford used the measure to favor his political friends; but when all has been said the policy was essentially statesmanlike in character and was executed, if one can judge from the *State Papers*, with much skill.

The Bank of Missouri served the longest as a depository bank for Illinois. Crawford had designated it first as the depository for the Illinois receivers. In 1819 he allowed it a fixed government deposit of $175,000. At one time it held as much as $600,000 of government funds awaiting transmission, much of it in such notes as the United States Bank would not accept, and much of it of uncertain value from any standpoint. Yet only $152,000 was caught in the bank when it finally suspended; and part of that may have been in uncurrent notes received before the bank had a right of veto on the paper it

[1] *American State Papers, Finance*, 3:725, 741, 747-750, 4:583, 587, 844, 853.

received.[2]   It suffered heavy drains of specie to pay accounts for which exchange could not be procured — $90,000 in a year; in June, 1821, it appealed to Crawford for an additional deposit of $50,000 and in August suspended.   It had loaned nearly the full amount of its paid-in capital, $210,000, over half the sum going to the directors, who had in addition borrowed $80,000 on mortgage, $60,000 on personal security, and $37,000 as indorsers.   The reason for its downfall is obvious, but considering conditions in the west it had served with fair efficiency as the government's fiscal agent.

Needless to say, there was from the beginning jealousy in Illinois at the preference accorded to the bank across the river in receiving deposits from United States land offices.   At the time of admission Illinois had two banks in operation, the Bank of Edwardsville and the Bank of Illinois at Shawneetown; the banks of Cairo and Kaskaskia, though chartered, were not in operation.   The Bank of Illinois numbered among its officers many of the most substantial men of Shawneetown — John Marshall, Leonard White, Samuel and John Caldwell, John McLean, Michael Jones.   Through the earlier part of its career it was distinctly well managed.   The Bank of Edwardsville, though displaying on its list of sponsors the great name of Ninian Edwards, had men in its directorate whose financial stability was seriously questioned.   The bank was backed by Richard M. and James Johnson and General Duval Payne of Kentucky.   In 1819, $214,250 of its stock was held in Kentucky, $18,000 in St. Louis, and $66,750 in Illinois.   Only a tenth of this was paid in.   Both the Bank of Illinois and the Bank of Edwardsville were made government depositories late in 1818.[3]

The career of the Bank of Edwardsville as a government agent was short and troublous.   Its ownership apparently involved it in a series of associations with several other banking enterprises of uncertain character and in resulting rivalries

[2] *American State Papers, Finance,* 3:753, 758.
[3] *House Journal,* 1819, 2 session, 107; *American State Papers, Finance,* 3:741.

with other banks. It was connected with the Bank of St. Louis, a rival to the Bank of Missouri, which finally failed. Crawford was continually assailed by recriminations from the two rival banks, the Edwardsville institution accusing the Bank of Missouri of robbing it of specie through presenting its notes received in land office deposits. The Bank of Edwardsville was never allowed to decide what notes it should accept. It was in continual difficulty with the government over failures to make remittances, for which it excused itself by the plea that eastern funds could not be procured in the state and that it was impossible to ship specie. Benjamin Stephenson, the president, in his capacity as receiver of the land office, failed to make deposits regularly. Ninian Edwards cautiously disclaimed responsibility for the institution in 1819, and in 1821 it failed, carrying a heavy government deposit with it.

The Bank of Illinois had a better record than its rival in its career as a government agent. It made its remittances with comparative regularity and in good funds. Its notes passed at par in Illinois in 1822. In 1824 it declared a seven per cent dividend. Its sound condition undoubtedly was due to the fact that late in 1819 it voted for the future to discount bills of lading only; thus it practically confined its discount business to the equivalent of good commercial paper, representing bona fide transactions. Eventually it abandoned business, only to resume it ten years later at the time of the internal improvement excitement.[4]

The first general assembly under the provision of the state constitution attempted to contribute to the financial world of Illinois a state bank with a capital of $4,000,000 half subscribed by the state and half by private persons. Of the capital only one-fifth was to be paid in during the first six months. The bank's notes were to be receivable for state dues at par so long as they were payable on demand and were to draw twelve per cent interest a year when they were not so payable. The

[4] *American State Papers, Finance*, 4:956; *Illinois Intelligencer*, June 15, 1822, July 17, 1824; *Illinois Gazette*, December 11, 1819.

enterprise from the first encountered the bitter hostility of the *Illinois Emigrant* which claimed that it was the work of a Kaskaskia clique. The *Intelligencer* retorted that the *Emigrant's* hostility was due to the solicitude of the Shawneetown newspaper for the welfare of the Bank of Illinois. The debate, however, was futile as the bank never went into operation.[5]

Undeterred by the fiasco the second general assembly of 1820–1821 proceeded with a scheme for another bank. It was to be administered by a head office and four branches, each with a local directorate. Its capital was to be $500,000, and it might issue $300,000 in notes bearing two per cent interest which were to be loaned among the counties, each citizen being entitled to a total discount not in excess of $1,000. Loans in excess of $100 were to be secured on real estate. The faith of the general assembly was pledged to the redemption of these precious notes in ten years, one-tenth of them each year. Against money received from the United States government by the state treasurer which was to be deposited in the bank, demand notes to the amount of twice the sums deposited were to be issued and loaned in sums not exceeding $300 at six per cent. A replevin law, applicable for three years to all executions in satisfaction of which state notes were not accepted, indicates the purpose of the whole act. Times were hard and money scarce, and a benevolent state accordingly issued money in plenty to loan its citizens and protected their debts in case these could not be satisfied in it.

Men were not wanting in the legislature to point out the obvious arguments against the plan. Wickliffe Kitchell and three others protested in the house, holding that the operations of the bank would be a palpable evasion of the constitutional provision against state emissions of bills of credit. Further they held that the bank would encourage speculators and make bankruptcy easy. Joseph Kitchell in the senate had previously offered a resolution denouncing the establishment of a bank

[5] *Illinois Intelligencer*, March 17, April 21, May 19, 1819; *Illinois Emigrant*, April 17, June 5, 12, 1819.

without specie capital with which to redeem its paper on demand. The council of revision objected to the bill on the "bills of credit" ground and provoked only an overruling which was preceded by a peevish report adducing among other arguments for the bill that as the notes would not be accepted outside the state they would remain at home for the use of the citizens of Illinois! In spite of the opposition of McLean, the speaker of the house, the bill became a law.[6]

The measure once passed, the *Illinois Gazette,* while deploring it, was inclined to make the best of it and even attacked the Shawneetown merchants for receiving state bank paper only at a fifty per cent discount. The *Edwardsville Spectator* approved the measure from the first. Some of the bank's opponents, such as Joseph Kitchell, were apparently conciliated by offices in the bank. The notes were speedily disposed of at a fifty per cent discount. A further issue of notes proposed in January of 1823 was fortunately voted down.[7]

The state bank indeed is not to be judged and condemned by the ordinary principles of banking, for this most extraordinary bank was, if its officials may be believed, almost philanthropic in purpose. "When it is recollected," said a document of 1827, "that the establishment of the State Bank was a MEASURE of RELIEF — that its object was not to loan money on usury to the wealthy, for the purpose of gain, but to lighten the burthens of our indigent and embarrassed citizens — and that, therefore, if any preference was to be shewn among applicants for loans, it was to be exercised in favor of those who were encumbered by debt — the only real matter of surprise is that loans made under provisions so liberal, would have been reduced with so much promptitude, and so little loss."[8] On reading this statement the professed economist will cheerfully resign the subject, although colorably pertaining to him, to the historian.

[6] *House Journal,* 1820-1821, 1 session, 145-227.
[7] *Illinois Gazette,* July 8, 1821.
[8] Replication of William Kinney, Abraham Prickett, and Joseph A. Beaird to Edwards' charges, *Illinois Intelligencer,* February 3, 1827.

The capital was divided, \$83,516.86¾ to the Edwardsville branch, \$48,834 to Brownsville, \$84,685 to Shawneetown, \$47,265.02 to Palmyra, and \$35,699.11¼ to the head office at Vandalia. The capital of the Edwardsville and Shawneetown branches was practically loaned out a few months after the banks went into operation. The *Illinois Gazette* sarcastically suggested that the only way one could obtain a loan from the bank was by being indebted to a director. This suggestion may explain the attitude of a storekeeper like William Kinney connected with the Edwardsville branch who accepted the notes in satisfaction of specie claims of \$20,000. The reader may wonder whether the claims were good or bad. There is not very much doubt that the Edwardsville branch loaned some money for political reasons, some for the establishment of a proslavery press. Loans were frequently made on real estate of value insufficient to cover them. To add to the *opéra bouffe* character of the situation the justices of the supreme court declared that in their opinion the act establishing the bank was unconstitutional and their opinion made the directors chary of legal proceedings to enforce collections from debtors.[9]

The situation was brought to the attention of the legislature in 1823 by the auditor, who in his report pointed out that the notes were circulating at fifty per cent discount, thereby taxing unduly state officers who were paid in them at par, and giving an advantage to nonresidents who paid their taxes at par in the depreciated paper. He offered the wise suggestion that while the measure was one of relief and had been salutary, the time had now come to press the liquidation of the bank as the law prescribed. A legislative committee suggested a repeal of the replevin provision in the law, and the legislature voted an increase of fifty per cent in the salaries of state officers; but the main difficulty in the application of any adequate reform measure was found to be the lack of reports from which the conditions of the branches could be learned.[10]

[9] *Illinois Intelligencer*, December 23, 1826, February 3, 1827; *Edwardsville Spectator*, December 11, 1821; *Illinois Gazette*, July 28, 1821.
[10] *Illinois Intelligencer*, January 11, 1823; *Laws of 1823*, p. 131, 181.

The legislature of 1825, after an investigation, found the condition of the bank hopeless. Except at Edwardsville and Palmyra the expenses of the institution had exceeded its profits from discounting. The books of the Shawneetown branch were in hopeless disorder and those at Brownsville little better. Legislation was needed to force the Shawneetown branch to turn over to the head office the funds necessary to advance the work of liquidation. The assembly reënforced the legal provision requiring the cashiers to retire annually ten per cent of the notes and provided that cancelled notes be burned or, if reissued, be stamped so as not to draw interest. It put an end to the business of the branches except as collecting agencies. By one act, however, it fatally involved the state finances with those of the bank since it provided that auditor's warrants for appropriations made in terms of "state paper" should issue at its current value to be determined by state officers; the law recognized the current value as thirty-three and one-third cents on the dollar. Probably this was due to a desire to issue in auditor's warrants a currency in which debtors could pay their debts; but the effect on state finances was disastrous.[11]

The auditor's report for 1826–1827 summarized the result of this policy. The value of state paper rose to seventy cents on the dollar, approximately one-half the warrants being issued at or above fifty. About one-third of the state paper had been retired and destroyed. The house in 1825–1826 was inclined to oppose further relief and passed a measure that warrants be issued at specie value and be payable in state paper at fifty per cent discount; but the friends of relief were strong in the senate and secured the retention of the old system. Edwards in his campaign for the governorship in that year criticized acutely the fatuous policy of the legislature. He pointed out that in the first place the issue of auditor's warrants was made necessary by the fact that nonresidents were required to pay taxes only biennially. The debased warrants could then be used by nonresidents to pay their taxes at their face value and

11 *Laws of 1825*, p. 16, 82, 182; *Illinois Intelligencer*, August 3, 1826.

must themselves ultimately be paid at par.   If yearly settlements of taxes were required, he declared, the notes would rise in value because of the need of a medium in which to pay.[12]

As governor, Edwards hampered himself by his own actions from carrying through a wiser policy.   The legislature enacted a law for a gradual scaling up of the rate of discount at which warrants were to issue which would carry them to par by November 29, 1830.   But Edwards frittered away his influence by violent attacks on his political enemies which brought him no advantage.   He attacked James M. Duncan, cashier at the head office of the state bank, for failures in duty which certainly did not amount to malfeasances and of which a legislative committee acquitted him.   He attacked T. W. Smith, Kinney, and the other directors and cashiers of the Edwardsville bank.   There can be little doubt that they were guilty at least of improper conduct but the legislature in Smith's case took refuge behind the fact that his charges against the bank for services were a proper matter for judicial determination; and the men accused were cleared.[13]

The intent and purpose of the act in the first instance had been that the bank should by gradually retiring its notes automatically liquidate as its loans were paid.   A series of acts reduced the organization of the bank to a collecting agency. Thus in 1829 the position of cashier of the head office was abolished, the auditor and treasurer performing his duties. The collections came slowly.   There was the troublesome question of constitutionality already adverted to; and further there can be little doubt that the directors and presidents used to the fullest extent the borrowing privilege which the original law granted them.   In 1827 a statement of the Brownsville branch showed that William M. Alexander had borrowed $1,900.83; Abner Field, $1,700; William McFatridge, $750; Joseph Duncan, $2,000, and Edward Cowles, a well-known merchant of Kaskaskia, $1,750.   Of these, Cowles had paid in full,

[12] *Illinois Intelligencer,* August 3, 1826.
[13] *Laws of 1827,* p. 81; *Illinois Intelligencer,* January 20, February 3, 10, 17, 1827.

Field had paid $922, and Duncan $275. The statement speaks for itself. With such influential debtors the cry for leniency in dealing with bank debtors was soon raised. In his farewell message Governor Coles had deprecated the extension of inducements to debtors to pay up. Meanwhile he urged as the true remedy as simple an administration of bank affairs as possible. A contrary point of view was set forth in a house resolution offered by John Reynolds, January 19, which urged that inducements to secure immediate payments would save the expense of administration. An act was passed allowing debtors on paying up past due installments to renew their notes. Two years later they were allowed to pay up in three annual installments with interest. The bank lingered as a problem after the passage of the first decade of state history.[14]

Some of the complications in the revenue of Illinois introduced by the currency and the banks have been already hinted at. A clearer understanding of the problem may be obtained by an analysis of the source from which the state's revenue was derived. In 1821–1822 it received but $7,121.09 from resident taxpayers and $38,437.75 from nonresidents owning land in the state; in its capacity as landed proprietor the state received $10,563.09 from the rental of the salines and in its capacity of land speculator, $5,659.86 from the sale of Vandalia lots.

The importance in the state finances of the method of taxing nonresidents is self-evident. The enabling act had prohibited the state from taxing nonresidents at a higher rate than residents, from taxing land within five years from the time of patenting, or taxing the bounty lands remaining with the patentees for three years after the date of the patent. The state's dealings with nonresident landholders under these provisions are interesting. The first revenue act of 1819, while prescribing a triple tax on landholders who did not schedule their lands and bank stock before a certain day, left nonresidents too short a time to comply and caused them to believe the state was

14 Greene and Alvord, *Governors' Letter-Books, 1818-1834*, p. 132.

swindling them out of their lands.   The second general assembly allowed those subject to triple tax till January 1, 1822, to redeem for a single tax plus interest and provided for the advertising in the eastern cities of lands on which taxes were unpaid. The auditor even under the circumstances thought it unwise actually to force a sale and contented himself with an advertisement as a threat to secure payment of delinquent taxes.   The act of 1825 gave nonresidents till January 1, 1826, to redeem for a single tax and interest all lands stricken off to the state under the act of 1819 and 1823; it further allowed a period of two years in the future during which land could be redeemed for one hundred per cent penalty.   The legislature of 1826 provided that sales for taxes of lands owned by nonresidents thenceforth be held once a year instead of biennially.   A further provision designed to prevent nonresidents from taking advantage of their virtual monopoly of state paper by allowing residents only to pay in specie and at the prevailing premium was dropped at the suggestion of the council of revision.[15]

The nonresidents, however, were not without their revenge for the treatment which the laws clumsily accorded them.   Time and again, as nearly as one can judge, they forced the state to terms by refusing to pay the excessive penalties laid for failure to pay taxes.   It was believed also that the nonresident taxpayers in the east had bought up the notes of the state banks at a discount to use them at par in paying their taxes.   Thus they deprived the people of the use of the notes as a medium of exchange and taxed them the amount of the depreciation. Edwards claimed for himself at least part of the credit for the attempt to obviate this situation by forcing annual sales of nonresidents' lands.[16]

Administratively the state's first revenue law was as bad as it well could be and it was only gradually that the defects in it were remedied.   It was questionable if, in dividing lands into three classes and setting an arbitrary value on each, the law of

[15] *Laws of 1825*, p. 106.
[16] About 6,000 tracts were sold in 1827, most of them for the whole tract. Few were stricken off to the state. *Illinois Intelligencer*, January 27, 1827.

1819 did not violate the constitutional provision that all property be taxed according to value. Taxation was made on the basis of lists turned in by the taxpayers, resident and nonresident. Furthermore, while the auditor was authorized to obtain from land offices abstracts of lands entered, it must have been impossible for county assessors to know surely whether land was listed or entered; and the auditor had no check as to the amount of tax he was entitled to receive from the sheriff. The auditor gave as a reason for not selling lands for taxes in 1822 that the validity of both the tax law and the law allowing state sales for nonpayment of taxes was seriously questioned. The auditor's report of that year is important because of its suggestion that local taxation records be based on lists sent to the counties by the auditor showing lands entered in the county according to the United States land office records. A further suggestion that the auditor be allowed to fix the necessary tax rate was premature.

The most important part of the local machinery of taxation perhaps is the dividing by whatever method of state from county revenues. The act of 1819 retained for the state the tax on bank stock, on nonresidents' land, and two-thirds the tax on residents' land, giving the county the tax of one-half per cent on slaves and servants and permitting it to levy an additional tax of one-half per cent on personal property. The act of 1821, when the state revenue seemed likely to be superabundant, assigned the county two-thirds of the residents' land tax. In 1827 in answer to an urgent need of more county revenue the county was allowed all the land tax paid by its residents. The counties in the Military Tract were dealt with in a somewhat different fashion. A subsidy of $750 was granted to Pike county in 1821. In 1823 this grant was continued and Fulton county received $450. In 1827 this was altered to a gift of $275 to each Military Tract county, in return for which the state took all the land tax.[17]

[17] The grand jury of Madison county represented the county revenue as inadequate. *Edwardsville Spectator*, September 27, 1823.

By virtue of the enabling act the state came into possession of the salines including the reservations made to supply firewood for salt boiling. The state thus had the regulation of a large landed estate that normally would have furnished no inconsiderable portion of the revenue. In 1823 Thomas Mather estimated the income from the saline as one-seventh of the state revenue. The state, however, was to learn by experience the difficulty of making this estate productive.[18]

The difficulty was the securing of punctual payments of rent from the persons to whom the saline was leased. At the state's admission the saline, of course, was in the hands of private lessees holding under leases from the United States government. They asked for a renewal of their leases and offered $8,000 a year if they were permitted to sell salt at $1.25 a bushel and $10,000 if they could sell at $1.50. The legislature at its first session rejected both propositions. At the second session the legislature leased the saline to the former lessees, probably on the basis of salt at seventy-five cents a bushel and a rent payable in salt. In the carrying out of the leases there was continual difficulty. The lessees refused to pay over to the state the salt due on the unexpired portion of the 1818 rent; and by March, 1820, some were still delinquent.[19]

The assembly of 1821 created the office of superintendent of the saline and charged it with the duty of taking possession of establishments which had forfeited their leases. In practice, however, it proved difficult to make the agent answerable to the auditor; and in 1823 the assembly had to pass an act requiring reports of leases not yet entered to the auditor and accounts regularly kept with him.

As a matter of practice the state found it impossible to collect from the lessees of the saline the rents which they had agreed to pay; and the legislature of 1823 began the practice of condoning the nonpayment of them by releasing the securities of one of the lessees from liability for a balance of $1,511.11

[18] *House Journal*, 1822-1823, 1 session, 157.
[19] Greene and Alvord, *Governors' Letter-Books, 1818-1834*, p. 16, 19, 23, 26, 27.

due the state. In great measure the loss was probably due to the fact that the salt spring gave too weak a solution to furnish a commercial product that could compete in price with Kanawha salt. Much of the legislation of relief was directed to the purpose of encouraging the lessees to search for springs of a greater strength. Thus in 1823 it offered to those lessees who had paid up their rent an extension of their leases for ten years in case they found salt water stronger by a third than that previously used. In 1825 certain of the Shawneetown lessees were excused from paying the state arrears of rent in case they expended them in searching for stronger salt water. In 1822 the *Illinois Gazette* had announced that the discovery of a new salt spring had cut the price of salt to fifty cents a bushel.[20] Governor Coles, who during his term had taken much interest in the problem of the saline and had inquired particularly into the practice of older states in managing theirs, in his farewell message advocated that a tax per manufactured bushel be substituted for the fixed rents, which indeed had been calculated upon the basis of a much higher price for salt than could be obtained in the face of the competition from Kanawha and imported salt. The inferior quality of the salt rendered it unfit for salting provisions for the southern market, which was the most important commercial use for it. The legislature in 1827 passed an act leasing the saline until 1836 to two lessees at a price proportioned to the strength of the water they should find. The surplus land attached to the saline and to the Vermilion saline was sold under the authority of successive acts of the federal government.

The state of Illinois started on its career with an endowment for schools from which much more might have been expected than actually was obtained. The state received section sixteen in each township for the benefit of its schools, two townships of thirty-six sections each for a seminary, and three per cent on net proceeds from the sale of lands in the state. Of this amount one-sixth was for a college or university.

[20] *Illinois Gazette*, February 11, 1822.

Legislation on the subject of the school land was at first limited to a provision authorizing local renting of it for the benefit of schools and preventing waste on it.[21]   The school act of 1825 was more general in scope and was really an able attempt to establish at any cost a good system of primary education at public expense.   The act made provision for the creation by local initiative of school districts containing not less than fifteen families which might levy taxes on themselves for the support of schools, provided they did not exceed one-half per cent or ten dollars a person.   It provided also in the interest of the district schools for the regulation of the share of school land pertaining to each district and for state aid to the amount of the state's school fund and of a fiftieth of its revenue in addition.   The law, which was defended because it taxed rich and poor alike for schools, was attacked as a "Yankee device" and was repealed by the next general assembly, which left the payment of the tax purely optional with the payer; it retained, however, the provision for the apportionment of the section sixteen lands among the school districts interested in them.   In 1829 an act, passed subject to the assent of congress, allowed the sale of school lands at a minimum of a dollar and twenty-five cents an acre and the investment of the proceeds in mortgages.   The same legislature passed an act for the sale of the seminary lands.

Meanwhile there had already begun the process by which the school fund of the state arising from the three per cent of the sales of public lands was diverted to other uses.   The act of 1821 had required the treasurer to pay into the state bank the payments made by the federal government for the fund. These payments as being made in good funds were made the basis for the issue of bank notes to double their amount payable on demand in specie.   The legislature of 1825 in spite of its excellent school law was guilty of directing the use of the school fund to redeem state bank notes, auditor's receipts payable in legal United States currency being placed in the fund.   In 1829

[21] *Laws of 1819*, p. 107, 260; *Laws of 1821*, p. 60.

the fund was invaded not for an emergency but to supply the ordinary expenses of the government. The governor was authorized to borrow all the specie in it and in the seminary fund at six per cent interest and to use it in paying warrants drawn at their specie value. The fact that this was the device used to get the state warrants back on a specie basis cannot excuse the act.

Considered as a whole, the administration of the state's finances during the first decade of statehood cannot be commended. The state in 1818 had found it necessary to authorize a loan of $25,000 to pay the territorial debt and to meet the expenses of the first year of statehood. In 1820 Bond had been able to report that the territorial debt had been extinguished and that the treasury was in a flourishing condition. In 1823 the auditor's report showed receipts of $79,946.83 against warrants of $46,285.72 leaving a net balance of about $33,661.11. The items comprised are of interest. The general assembly cost $14,966.18, the judiciary, $7,932.33. Salaries of state officials amounted to $8,470.74 and the printing of the laws and journals cost $2,976.22. The device introduced by the legislature of 1825 of issuing warrants at three for one soon changed the aspect of the finances of the state. The auditor's report for 1826 showed a total fund of $132,000 to meet warrants amounting to $154,000; but as $29,000 of these were in the school fund, representing sums extracted from it for state expenses, the state was practically solvent. It had due from nonresidents $26,000 in taxes and from the saline lessees $24,000, which on account of the exemption from rent of the lessees in return for boring for salt water could not be collected.[22]

In short, the history of the first ten years of Illinois finance, public and private, is the story of the struggle of men with conditions which they did not understand and which they had not the courage to meet, even according to the intellectual light that they possessed. In the beginning they had sought to establish

[22] *Senate Journal,* 1818, 1 session, 7.

banks, public and private, in order to remedy by abundant issues of notes the dearth of money in the country or to relieve the financial distress of hard-pressed individuals. In the case of one bank, good management made it efficient and safe; in the case of the other bad management led to complete failure. The state bank, begun as a measure of relief, threw the expense of the relief that it afforded to individuals upon the people of the state at large. Because the legislatures did not have the courage to pay for liquidating it, they diverted to this end the trust fund of the schools and borrowed of the future by warrants issued at triple the value of the service for which they paid. In part the obliquity exhibited in Illinois finance may be attributed to the fact that so little of the state's revenue was actually drawn from its citizens. The state wisely parted with its potential revenue as owner of the saline in order to reduce if possible the price of salt; but it relied for years on possible speculative returns from Vandalia lots and developed its system of taxation with an eye to the fact that much of it was paid by nonresidents. Among the evils of absentee landlordism in Illinois was the fact that the state was slow to attain the sense of sobriety and responsibility arising in a state of things in which the voter realizes that his demands on his government in the way of service must be reimbursed by him in his capacity of taxpayer.

IV. THE CONVENTION STRUGGLE

THE union into which Illinois entered on the third of December, 1818, was a union already at the verge of sectional strife on the issue of slavery. The session of congress in which the first Illinois representatives took their seats saw the beginning of the struggle as to whether Missouri was to be slave or free; and the last aftermath of that struggle was not gleaned till in the summer of 1824 the people of Illinois finally registered their resolution that their constitution should not be altered to admit slavery. For the first six years of Illinois' existence as a state, the question of slavery hung like a threatening storm over her politics.

Distrust of the effectiveness of the more or less ambiguous antislavery clause in her constitution led the opponents of slavery in congress to cloud the title of Illinois to statehood. John McLean, the first representative from Illinois, appeared in the house Tuesday, November 19, after the session had begun. The house decided, however, that he should not be admitted till it was satisfied that the constitution of Illinois corresponded to the enabling act. When the resolution for admission came up for third reading four days later, opposition, hitherto in the interest of orderly procedure, was now directed against the constitutional provisions allowing indentured service and limited slavery. James Tallmadge of New York, later famous for his part in the Missouri struggle, declared that in these provisions the Illinois constitution contravened the Ordinance of 1787. Richard C. Anderson of Kentucky replied that the ordinance was not a compact either with Virginia or with the people of the territory, and that Virginia by her deed of cession had protected the right of the French inhabitants to their slaves. William Henry Harrison of Ohio defiantly assured Tallmadge that the people of Ohio would never come to congress or to New York for permission in case they desired to repeal their constitutional prohibition of slavery. Finally, only thirty-four representatives in a house of one hundred and fifty-one followed Tallmadge in voting against the admission of the new state; and Illinois took its place in the union.

The validity of the northwest ordinance again came into discussion during the Missouri debate which followed hard on that over the admission of Illinois. If the slavery restriction in that ordinance were a valid limitation on the states that had grown up under it, these latter could hardly be considered on an equality in all respects with the older states, which could lawfully admit or exclude slavery. The supporters of the slavery restriction pointed to the ordinance as a proof that the new states need not necessarily be on a complete equality with the old; the supporters of the Missouri constitution naturally argued that in view of the federal constitution's guarantee of equality, the ordinance could not prohibit slavery to the states that had been under it. The representatives from the northwest, among them Daniel Pope Cook of Illinois who had succeeded McLean, generally maintained the validity and the sacredness of the ordinance. "This ordinance," said Benjamin Ruggles of Ohio, "has been to the people of the Northwestern territory a rule of action—a guide to direct their course—'a cloud by day, and a pillar of fire by night.'"[1] On the other hand representatives from the south argued that in spite of the ordinance the people of Ohio, Indiana, and Illinois might alter their governments as they saw fit. John S. Barbour of Virginia was inclined to argue that the Virginia cession required that the new states must be as sovereign as the old. In view of such doctrine the slavery leaders in Illinois may well have wondered if the decision of 1818 need be regarded as final.

The votes of the Illinois delegation in congress were not

[1] *Annals of Congress,* 16 congress, 1 session, 281; see also *ibid.,* 15 congress, 2 session, 1170 ff., 1411 ff.

calculated to inspire in the foes of slavery a conviction that the new state would make an unflinching resistance to the introduction of that institution. The two Illinois senators, Ninian Edwards and Jesse B. Thomas, consistently supported the cause of Missouri. Their votes in no instance would have altered the result; but McLean, voting in the house on one crucial roll call with the majority of one, may possibly have turned the tide.[2] Daniel Pope Cook, who replaced McLean in the session of 1819–1820, voted against the Missouri Compromise; but he was not above countenancing the use of the popularity Edwards had gained in Missouri to endeavor to secure the election of his brother John Cook as senator from that state.

It was on the Missouri question, however, that Cook beat McLean in the Illinois congressional election of 1819. McLean defended his vote on the ground that the attempted dictation to Missouri of an antislavery proviso was a violation of state sovereignty. He attempted to evade Cook's assaults by accusing the latter of being really proslavery and of concealing his belief as a matter of policy. Cook's friends insisted that he had always been the unflinching foe of slavery. They accused McLean of having made in the former canvass antislavery pledges which he had violated. Worse still they alleged he was the tool of John Scott, the Missouri territorial delegate; Missouri when admitted a slave state as McLean wished would give the slave states control of the senate. "McLean," said one writer, "will vote us under the feet of slaves."[3] Cook's supporters in their publications usually assumed that the people of Illinois were generally opposed to slavery — three-fourths of them according to one writer — and that her representatives had misrepresented and disgraced her.

The congressional election of 1820 indicated in its course the possible relation between the triumph of slavery in Missouri and its adoption in Illinois. Early in July the *Edwardsville*

[2] *Annals of Congress*, 15 congress, 2 session, 1273.
[3] *Edwardsville Spectator*, June 19, 1819; *Illinois Intelligencer*, June 30, July 14, 1819.

Spectator, edited in Edwards' interest by Hooper Warren, charged Kane who was Cook's opponent with a share in a deliberate plot to amend the constitution to introduce slavery. Kane was to be put forward for congress to test the strength of the party; control of the *Illinois Gazette* and of the *Illinois Intelligencer* was to be secured; and a third proslavery press was to be established at Edwardsville. Cook's friends took up the cry, recalling that in the midst of the Missouri debate Missouri slaveholders had talked of setting up at Edwardsville a press to advocate the extension of slavery in Illinois in order to keep the people of Illinois busy at home. Denials appeared speedily from Kane and from the various persons accused in the plot. Kane insisted that Edwards was responsible for the attack on him and that it was made to aid Cook's cause. With some pertinence he adverted to Edwards' twenty-two slaves and to the fact that Edwards had voted on the same side with McLean, who had been defeated the year before. Edwards retorted with a denial.[4] If the plot actually existed, however, the defeat of Kane in the election shortly afterward checked it for the time being.

That same year saw an open proposal for amending the constitution to admit slavery, which emanated from a new quarter and from a man who strangely enough has frequently been set down as an anti-convention man, Henry Eddy. In offering himself as a candidate for the legislature in 1820, he addressed the voters of Gallatin county as follows: "With regard to the Saline, then, I am clear for extending to it, for another term of years, the privilege which it now enjoys of hiring and indenturing servants for the purpose of working the same. And being of this opinion, I am, of course, in favour of a convention, for that object can only be effected through the means of another convention, our present constitution having limited the time during which that privilege may be

<hr />

[4] *Edwardsville Spectator,* July 4, 11, 25, August 1, 1820; *Illinois Gazette,* August 5, 1820. Much of the material for the remainder of the chapter is found in contemporary numbers of the *Illinois Intelligencer* and *Edwardsville Spectator.*

claimed to the year 1825."[5]   He alleged as reasons for speedy action the fact that the salines in the neighborhood kept money in circulation and business good, and the time when western Illinois was still dependent on Illinois salt was, he thought, the favorable moment to strike.   The economic interest of eastern Illinois in the call of a convention is obvious.   Eddy was elected and duly introduced into the Illinois general assembly resolutions corresponding to his proposal.

Widespread financial distress in Illinois in the years immediately following 1820 insured a favorable hearing to advocates of a fundamental change in the economic order.   The act of 1820 abolishing credit sales and lowering the price of public lands to a dollar and a quarter necessarily caused financial embarrassment and reduced the value of lands in private hands.[6]   It was a period of hard times which in 1821 prompted the establishment of a state bank distinctly as an institution to afford relief.   It was not surprising that many should have listened to the assertions of the slavery party that the admission of the institution would bring in planters with ready money who would spend it freely and who would especially use it in buying up at good prices the farms of those anxious to leave the state. Many a man naturally opposed to slavery may well have wished for the institution that he might sell his property and flee from the wrath to come.

The canvass for governor in 1822 turned frankly on the question of slavery.   Joseph B. Phillips, who announced his candidacy February 20, 1821, was soon accused by letters in the *Spectator* of designing to introduce limited slavery and thus pave the way for a complete extension of the institution to the state.   At first Phillips' friends denied the charge; but July 3 the *Intelligencer* published a letter which admitted Phillips' proslavery leanings, assured the proslavery forces in the state that they had a majority, and called on them to rally for the

[5] *Illinois Gazette,* July 8, 1820.
[6] *Ibid.,* July 31, 1824.

cause and no longer to be withheld by mere sentiment from pursuing the true interests of the state.[7]

Curiously enough such announcements did not seem to cause excitement. The *Intelligencer* began publishing a series of scriptural parodies which touched on Phillips' alleged conversion from slavery advocacy on a former occasion for the sake of a seat in the supreme court. The *Spectator* contented itself with pronouncing the scheme chimerical and with warning the voters to beware of the many wealthy men who wished to own slaves and to use care in selecting their representatives. Instead of pressing the proslavery charge against Phillips it printed letters depicting the evil results of the activity of judges in politics and accusing Phillips of blasphemy, irreligion, and gambling.[8]

Edward Coles who announced his candidacy October 30, 1821, might have been expected to find greater favor in the sight of an antislavery man like Hooper Warren. Coles was a Virginian of the planter class who had served as private secretary to Madison and who had been sent on a special mission to Russia. By inheritance a slave owner, he had emigrated to Illinois that he might free his Negroes and establish them on land of their own in a free state. It is significant of a certain feeling for the dramatic in the man that he reserved the announcement of their freedom to his slaves to a beautiful morning in April as his boats were gliding down the Ohio below Pittsburg. Principle was the food on which his soul was nourished; in their cooler moments even his bitter enemies were compelled to admit his untarnished integrity. Withal there was about him a certain stiffness, a certain consciousness of his own virtue, possibly a tendency to pose. For some reason his personality seemed to grate on Hooper Warren, who consistently assailed him in the *Spectator* with a studied malice that was so obvious as to defeat its own end. He made clumsy mockery of Coles' somewhat awkward attempts to

[7] *Edwardsville Spectator*, April 10, 1821; *Illinois Intelligencer*, July 3, 1821.
[8] *Edwardsville Spectator*, May 22, November 6, 27, 1821; *Illinois Intelligencer*, July 31, 1821.

mingle familiarly with men. On the ground that Coles was register of the Edwardsville land office, Warren represented him as a federal appointee from without the state. He even questioned the sincerity of Coles' opposition to a convention and tried to fix on him the stigma of holding slaves in Missouri.[9]

The Edwards faction, unable to agree on a candidate of its own for governor, was apparently hostile not only to its old enemy, Phillips, but also to Coles and to a third candidate, James B. Moore. In the case of Coles at least the hostility was natural as Coles was a supporter of Edwards' enemy, Secretary William H. Crawford. Pope and other members of the faction endeavored to persuade Edwards to run; when he refused they considered John Reynolds. Finally Pope, having come to a decision in favor of some candidate, tried, much to Edwards' displeasure, to bind the party to his choice. Probably this candidate was Thomas C. Browne of the supreme court, who had been quietly making ready for some time but who announced his candidacy only at the end of the campaign. He did not gain the full support of the Edwards party, Edwards flatly refusing to take any part in the contest.[10]

Coles was elected by a narrow margin. He received 2,854 votes to 2,687 for Phillips, 2,443 for Browne, and 622 for Moore. Certainly the Edwards faction had not efficiently exerted itself for any candidate; and while there is little evidence in regard to the activity of their opponents it seems unlikely that the selection turned in any decisive fashion on factional alignments. Apparently the personality and opinions of the candidates played a controlling part.

Coles, evidently concluding that the bold course was the safe one, determined to force the fighting on the slavery issue. In his message to the assembly in December he pointed out the fact that slavery, contrary to the spirit of the northwest

9 *Edwardsville Spectator*, April 9, 1822.
10 Washburne, *Edwards Papers*, 190-192. This is a draft letter of Edwards which Washburne surmised was written to Governor Bond. Internal evidence shows without doubt it was to Pope.

Edward Coles

[From original owned by Chicago Historical Society]

ordinance, existed in the state and concluded that the provision of the act of cession protecting the French inhabitants could be regarded as having expired after the passage of forty years; he suggested the abolition of the institution, the repeal of the black code, and the passage of effectual laws against the kidnapping of free blacks. A majority of the senate committee to which the antislavery recommendations of the governor were referred — Risdon Moore and John Emmet — submitted a favorable report. The minority member, Conrad Will, dissented. The house committee returned an unfavorable report. Both these dissenting reports declared the abolition of the slavery existing in the state to be beyond the power of the legislature. The senate report argued that the convention of 1818 had been hampered by the provisions of the Ordinance of 1787 but that as a sovereign state Illinois could deal with the whole question in a new constitutional convention. This, the senate report concluded with clumsy irony, was the only way of settling the question that the governor had at heart.

The slavery advocates now openly set about submitting the question of a convention to popular vote. The senate offered but little opposition. There, on February 10, 1823, the resolution passed twelve to six. The canal bill was before the senate at the same time with the resolution for a convention, indeed it was passed with a negative vote of only three immediately after the passage of the convention resolution. In both houses the pro-convention group captured some votes by threatening the canal bill with destruction unless the convention resolution went through. They brought into play every form of petty politics. Sometimes they brought pressure on individual members by introducing bills that would if passed irritate their constituents. Sometimes they resorted to bargains on the location of county seats and the creation of new counties. Sometimes they drummed up among a recalcitrant member's constituents instructions in favor of a convention.

In the house the convention party tried a test vote on January 27 and found twenty-two affirmative and fourteen negative votes, the latter including William McFatridge and Thomas Rattan who finally voted for the convention. It was evident that the vote would be a close one, and on January 29 a resolution formerly presented by A. P. Field to the effect that the two-thirds vote requisite to pass the resolution was a two-thirds vote of both houses sitting together was reconsidered and passed. This device, however, can have been intended to serve only as a last resort.

The pro-convention leaders were suspicious, with good reason as it proved, of the loyalty of some who had hitherto voted with them, notably of Nicholas Hansen, the member from the Military Tract. Hansen they apparently hoped to keep in line, however, by threatening him with bills which would injure his district and through the fact that his name was on the list of commissioners in the canal bill. When the vote in the house of representatives was taken February 11 on the senate resolution for a convention, Hansen deserted; and the vote stood twenty-three to thirteen. Dumbfounded apparently by the reverse, the convention party moved to reconsider; but a vote of nineteen to sixteen sustained the chair in the obvious decision that on a vote lost for want of two-thirds, the motion to reconsider must come from a member of the minority. James Turney moved that the senate be requested to state the number voting for and against the resolution in that house, obviously an attempt to enforce the interpretation that two-thirds of both houses together would suffice. The legislature adjourned in confusion. That night a mob of legislators headed by a justice of the supreme court, furious at their defeat, groaned under the window of one of the anti-convention leaders, George Churchill, and burned Hansen in effigy.[11]

The convention leaders probably decided over night on the means to retrieve their defeat — the unseating of Hansen. At the beginning of the session Hansen's seat had been contested by John Shaw. Elections in Shaw's "Kingdom of Pike" were strange matters; in this particular one a dispute about the

[11] *Edwardsville Spectator,* February 15, March 29, 1823.

judges of election in one precinct had resulted in eighty-three votes for Shaw in a polling place set up by the electors and of twelve votes for Hansen in another one presided over by the regular judges of election. The returns for Shaw were thrown out; he filed notice of a contest but at Hansen's request he let it be held over for a few days and did not file it again until the legal time for filing had expired. The house committee on elections seated Hansen, very possibly because he was a bitter enemy of Edwards and could therefore be trusted to vote for Thomas for senator. Certainly inasmuch as they threw out Shaw's contest on the ground that it had been filed too late; and, since the delay occurred at Hansen's request and for his benefit, the equity of their procedure is not very clear. The seating of Hansen, however, as compared with his unseating on February 12 was the quintessence of justice and orderly procedure.[12]

On the twelfth of February, a day by a curious coincidence commemorative of a greater struggle with slavery, the general assembly convened for as strange a day's work as ever was done by an Anglo-Saxon parliament. The house by a division of twenty-one to thirteen ordered a reconsideration of the report, accepted two months before, that Hansen was entitled to a seat; it considered certain documents laid before it, notably an affidavit that to the affiants' belief a majority of the votes were cast for Shaw; and the conventionist members offered what reasons they could for the course they were about to take. By a vote of twenty-one to fourteen the name of Shaw was substituted for that of Hansen in the report. Shaw now took his seat, and Turney moved to reconsider an appeal from the decision of the chair on a motion for a reconsideration of the convention resolution. The decision was reversed, the reconsideration ordered; and the resolution for the convention passed twenty-four to twelve. It only remained to chastise

[12] Stevens, "The Shaw-Hansen Election Contest," in Illinois State Historical Society, *Journal*, 7 : 389 ff.; *Edwardsville Spectator*, February 15, March 9, 1823. I believe the evidence to the effect that Hansen was originally seated to gain his vote for Thomas is better than Mr. Stevens judges it.

Hansen; and his name, on Field's motion, was stricken out of the list of canal commissioners.[13]

Conventionists and anti-conventionists began immediately to organize for the eighteen months campaign before the people on the acceptance or rejection of the proposed call for a convention. The advocates of a convention held a meeting at Vandalia February 15 and appointed a committee to prepare an address and resolutions which defended the call of a convention on various grounds not connected with the slavery issue. On February 18, fifteen of the eighteen members of the assembly who voted against the convention held a meeting and adopted an address arraigning the methods of the majority and exposing their design of introducing slavery. The persons present agreed to subscribe each for a given number of copies of the *Spectator* provided Warren's loyalty to the cause were assured.[14]

The opponents of a convention pushed the work of local organization. On March 22 the "St. Clair Society for the prevention of slavery in the state of Illinois" was organized for the purpose of "disseminating light and knowledge on the subject of slavery, by cool and dispassionate reasoning, by circulating pamphlets, handbills, and other publications." A similar society was formed May 9 in Monroe possibly with but a small membership. In the next month an organization similar to that of St. Clair was formed in Edwardsville, though it did not specify the nature of the propaganda to be undertaken. On the fourth of July citizens of Morgan established a more elaborate organization apparently designed to support antislavery candidates for office.[15]

As the day of the election approached, the opponents of slavery held caucuses or conventions to nominate anti-conven-

---

[13] That Coles, as Hooper Warren insinuated, had bought Hansen over by a promise of the recordership of Fulton county is unlikely. The bargain could not possibly have been consummated after the consideration had been earned. *Edwardsville Spectator*, February 15, 1823.

[14] *Ibid.*, March 1, 1823.

[15] *Ibid.*, April 12, July 12, September 20, 1823; *Illinois Intelligencer*, July 26, 1823.

tion candidates. They drew the issue even in contests for local offices; and naturally in legislative elections they concerted measures to prevent divisions of the anti-conventionist forces and a possible recurrence of the events of 1823. In St. Clair county a convention made up of delegates elected in each township was called to nominate county and legislative candidates. A similar call was issued in Bond, Fayette, and Montgomery for the choice of a candidate for senator. All this the convention party denounced as caucus methods.

From the sources of information available the conventionists appear to have been slower in organizing than their opponents. In August a meeting in Madison county recommended the appointment of township committees to promote the cause of the convention; in October, 1823, and March, 1824, township party organization was adopted in White and Wayne counties. The anti-conventionists averred that on December 3, 1823, a convention meeting at Vandalia adopted a state organization consisting of a central committee of ten, and committees of five in each county, and of three in each township.[16]

The conventionists complained of the influence of the clergy which was generally thrown on the antislavery side. The Christian church conference located on the Wabash and a Baptist sect, the Friends of Humanity, both denounced slavery as a sin. The Methodist circuit riders and preachers assailed slavery and slaveholders to the point of provoking bitter retorts. Conventionists accused them of denouncing slavery in Illinois and stopping at the houses of slaveholders in Missouri and pronounced their real dislike of a convention due to the fear that it might exclude them from the legislature. The *Illinois Republican* was so prolific in abuse of this sort that Warren took occasion to brand it as hostile to the Methodists as a body. He believed further, he said, that the clergy of all denominations were zealous in opposition to the convention.

[16] *Edwardsville Spectator*, January 27, February 17, April 13, 1824; *Illinois Intelligencer*, November 1, December 6, 1823; *Illinois Gazette*, April 10, 1824.

Illinois tradition affirms that John Mason Peck labored assiduously against a convention though no contemporary evidence
of his activity appears.[17]

In newspaper publicity the resources of the two parties
were more evenly divided. For Henry Eddy's *Illinois Gazette*
the politic course was proslavery, and while the paper admitted
articles on both sides its guarded expressions of sympathy were
for the convention. Coles at the beginning of the struggle
suggested that Morris Birkbeck and Richard Flower establish
an anti-convention newspaper for eastern Illinois at Albion,
but the suggestion was never carried out. Coles had hopes
of the support of the Kaskaskia *Republican Advocate* till April
of 1823; but finally under the editorship of R. K. Fleming it
supported the convention, as did the *Illinois Republican* at
Edwardsville.[18]

The editors of the *Illinois Intelligencer*, William H. Brown
and William Berry, disagreed on the issue involved in the convention struggle. In order to force out the anti-conventionist
Brown, the assembly before adjournment voted the public
printing to Berry and Robert Blackwell. Under the new pub-
lishers the newspaper at once took up the cause of the
convention. A year later, however, with its purchase by Coles
and a coterie of anti-conventionists, David Blackwell replaced
his brother as editor; and the *Intelligencer* became an open
opponent of slavery.[19] The *Edwardsville Spectator* at the
beginning of the struggle pursued an anomalous course. Its
strictures on the Shaw-Hansen scandal were those rather of
an enemy of Edward Coles and Nicholas Hansen than of an
opponent of the convention. T. W. Smith hoped for a time
to win Warren over; but the anti-convention forces by promises
of financial support assured the newspaper's loyalty to the side
of freedom.

Coles further sought support from outside the state. His

17 *Edwardsville Spectator*, May 24, August 2, November 1, 22, 1823; *Illinois
Intelligencer*, May 17, July 5, August 23, 1823, May 17, 1824.
18 Washburne, *Edward Coles*, 178.
19 *Ibid.*, 167.

friendship with Nicholas Biddle introduced him to certain Philadelphia Quakers who supplied him with antislavery tracts for distribution by the thousand. These were forwarded to St. Louis merchants along with their goods and were thence forwarded to Coles. Their source apparently was never learned by the conventionists. Had it been there would doubtless have arisen a tremendous outcry against the interference of citizens of other states in the affairs of Illinois.[20]

The conventionists entered the controversy with their opponents under one serious handicap. They apparently judged it unwise to take an irrevocable position that the convention was designed to introduce slavery; yet they did not positively deny that some alteration in that direction was intended. There was an undercurrent of slavery sentiment noticeable in all their manifestoes. At the beginning, however, they emphasized the anti-conventionist opposition to submitting the question of a convention to the people, representing it as a denial of the popular right to alter and remodel the government at will. The anti-conventionists, they said, were unwilling to trust the people; they were contemners of instructions from their constituents; they were even federalists. On the other hand the anti-convention party argued that the convention which would be called would not carry out the will of the people. They pointed to the fact that under the existing system of representation, eight northern counties would have eight members in a convention and nine southern and eastern ones, with substantially the same number of voters, fifteen. Once the southern counties on indifferent grounds had secured a convention, their delegates in it could decide as they would the question of slavery and freedom.[21]

Meanwhile the conventionists were all things to all men. "They avow the object to be," said one writer, "to amend the particular defect which you may imagine the constitution to have. Thus if you should be in favor of removing the seat

[20] Washburne, *Edward Coles*, 154-164.
[21] *Illinois Intelligencer*, March 8, 29, May 31, 1823; *Edwardsville Spectator*, March 1, April 12, 1823; *Kaskaskia Republican*, April 20, 1824.

of government to Alton or to Carmi, to Edwardsville or to Palestine, Kaskaskia, Covington or [MS. torn] [be] assured that his particular wish will be effected by having a convention. If you have no other objection to the constitution but the county commissioners court and the council of revision, then these are the only alterations that will be made to it. If one is in favor of altering the constitution and appointing the judges for a term of years, he is assured that that is one of the principal objects to be effected; if on the other hand another should be opposed to it he will be assured there is no danger of such an alteration being adopted. If one is opposed to the extension of Slavery, he will be told that it is not contemplated, and that if it were to be attempted, it could not be effected. If on the other hand he should be in favor of making this a slave holding state, he is assured that that is the great and chief object in view."[22]   Such were the types of argument employed.   The antislavery party answered them by pointing out for instance that the constitutional provision regulating county commissioners was so elastic that it said nothing of the duties or pay of the commissioners, or by stating that Elias K. Kane of the convention party had himself been the sponsor for the council of revision.[23]

Where slavery, limited or unlimited, was the avowed motive for the convention, the arguments varied. In the neighborhood of the Gallatin saline, the *Illinois Gazette* printed articles dwelling on the advantage to accrue from the renewal of the supply of indentured Negroes, which otherwise under the existing constitution would be cut off in 1825. Starting from the propositions that it was vain to expect a sufficient supply of white labor to man the salt works, since not even enough to supply the saline with agricultural produce was forthcoming, and that the work in so warm a climate could be performed only by Negroes, they concluded that the welfare of the saline was bound up in slave labor, and that the pros-

22 *Edwardsville Spectator*, May 25, 1824.
23 *Ibid.*, March 2, April 13, 1824.

perity of the whole district depended on the salines. Such arguments were used to persuade the people of Gallatin that slavery was an object well worth buying at the expense of support to the canal, even though the latter would diminish the importance of their county as the gateway to Illinois.[24]

So far as the conventionists undertook to justify slavery in the abstract they relied on the current method of reasoning of the day — what may be called the diffusion argument. Admitting that the presence of slavery in America was a thing bitterly to be deplored, they proposed so far as was possible to ameliorate the situation by extending as widely as possible the area in which slaves were to be found. This would not only improve the material condition of the slaves by enabling their masters to keep them in a country where food was cheap but in the long run would tend to bring about their emancipation. Usually the conventionists claimed that their intention was at most only to introduce a limited slavery which in time would abolish itself. Sometimes they suggested provisions by which a man might hold a limited number of slaves for a term of years, the offspring of the slaves to be free at a certain age. Lest the state be overrun with free blacks, the freedmen were to be sent to Africa by that fashionable slavery specific, the Colonization Society.[25]

For this policy advantages both moral and material were claimed. Many slaveholders, it was said, who disapproved of the institution would be glad to avail themselves of so excellent a scheme. It would extend christianity among the Negroes, supply labor of a type adapted to clear the soil without suffering the sickness that impaired the strength of the white settlers and suited to the menial tasks of drawing water and making fires in the salt works, which Adolphus Frederick Hubbard had singled out as the duties prescribed to Negroes by the laws of nature. In the background of the minds of advocates of this

[24] *Illinois Intelligencer,* June 28, July 5, 1823; *Illinois Gazette,* July 5, 1823, January 10, 1824.
[25] *Kaskaskia Republican,* March 30, 1824; *Illinois Gazette,* October 11, December 20, 1823, January 10, April 17, 1824; *Illinois Intelligencer,* November 22, 1823.

benevolent scheme was often the idea that the philanthropic slaveholders who entered the state would buy lands and improvements from the pioneers then in possession and would with their wealth form a welcome addition to the upper classes of the population. The complacent smugness of such arguments which passed current in the *Gazette* particularly prompts a savage desire to let a sentence which was written in all seriousness stand as a caricature of them. After commenting on the fact that the great men of the state were all slaveholders the writer added: "Other strong inducements I have for the introduction of slavery into this state are, that in the sickly season, the sick could have more attention paid them — the community would flourish, our state would be more republican, and more populous — the condition of the slaves much ameliorated, and the several churches of Christ would be considerably enlarged."[26]

The antislavery writers in their range of arguments wellnigh ran the gamut. There is hardly a line of argument used by the abolitionists of later days but has its prototype in this period. The question of the validity of the slavery prohibition in the Ordinance of 1787 and of the guarantee in the Virginia deed of cession was debated at length.[27] The pretense of biblical authority for the institution was exposed by a keen analysis of the limited slavery of the Jewish law as revealed in the books of Moses. Slavery in itself was denounced as a sin and the parent of vices and sins; it was declared contrary to the fundamental principle enunciated by the Declaration of Independence that all men are created equal. Sketches descriptive of the misery of the slave appeared set in language appealing to the emotions as frankly as did *Uncle Tom's Cabin*. Above all the antislavery pamphleteers insisted that slavery was a moral issue and this more than a quarter century before the Lincoln-Douglas debates.[28] The following passage

[26] *Illinois Intelligencer,* April 26, 1823.
[27] See above p. 47-50.
[28] *Edwardsville Spectator,* July 12, August 16, 1823; *Illinois Gazette,* November 8, 1823.

is a startling analogy to a well-known memorandum of Lincoln's "Is it not quite as unjust, because some men are black, to say there is a natural distinction as to them; and that black men, because they are black, ought to be slaves . . . is it not the hight [sic] of arrogance to allege that because we have strong feelings and cultivated minds it would be great cru[el]ty to make slaves of us; but that because they are yet ignorant and uncultivated, it is no injury at all to them? Such a principle once admitted lays the foundation of a tyranny and injuce[sic] that have no end."[29]

On material grounds the opponents of slavery pointed out the flaws in the diffusion argument. The history of mankind and of the slave trade from Africa and from the old south was cited to show that no matter how great the drain from it a reservoir of population always filled again to its ancient level. Slavery in Illinois it was said would only increase the demand for slaves and provoke anew kidnapping and the slave trade. Nay furthermore as the cool climate of Illinois unfitted it for the slave crops but adapted it as a home for men, the state would be degraded to a breeding ground of slaves for the southern market!

To the man of today, however, the most powerfully convincing arguments against slavery were those which warned the free farmer of Illinois of the ruin that the introduction of the institution would bring upon him. Here the slavery penmen were face to face with overwhelming odds in the character of the combatants who opposed them. Confronting them was Morris Birkbeck, a man trained in the principles of human liberty, intellectually the descendant of well-nigh six generations of radicals who had labored for the people's freedom. The conventionists who opposed the petty tricks of political electioneering or addresses smacking of the college debating hall to the writings of Birkbeck were holding up a lath sword against the hammer of Thor. With a greater cause than Swift's to inspire him the author of the earlier letters of "Jonathan

[29] *Illinois Intelligencer,* May 21, 1824.

Freeman " may claim a comparison not discreditable with " the Drapier's " letters.   Birkbeck, knowing how to make a phrase of homely English do the work of a highly polished paragraph, in his " Jonathan Freeman " letters strove in simple language to inspire the small farmer who was dispirited by hard times to renew his faith in his ability to subdue the land and possess it without calling in slaveholders.

" I am a poor man, that is to say, I have no money — but I have a house to cover me and the rest of us, a stable for my horses, and a little barn, on a quarter of good land, paid up at the land office, with a middling fine clearing upon it. . . . We help our neighbors, who are generally as poor as ourselves; — some that are new-comers are not so well fixed.   They help us in turn, and as it is the fashion to be industrious, I discover that we are all by degrees growing wealthy — not in money, to be sure, but in truck.

" There is a great stir among the landjobbers and politicians to get slaves into the country, because, as they say, we are in great distress; and I have been thinking pretty much about how it would act with me and my neighbors. . . .

" I have lately seen people from Kentucky . . . are as bad off for money as we — some say worse. . . .   As money seems to be all we want, and they want it just as much as we do, I don't see how those Slave Gentry are to make it plenty."   He believed that farmers wanting to sell out would not be able to sell their improvements to slaveholders, for "they can get Congress land at a dollar and a quarter an acre.   It is men who come from free states with money in their pockets, and no work-hands about them, that buy improvements." [30]   As for the saline, white workmen would flock to it once the Negroes were excluded.   The scarcity of which the farmers complained was not a scarcity of the essentials of a healthy robust life, but merely a scarcity of the money to purchase luxuries.   Instead of repining because their produce brought little in the New

[30] *Edwardsville Spectator*, November 1, 1823. The slaveholder was an employer of Negro, not of white labor, and his money would be spent not in the state but in the east for luxuries.

Orleans market, they should learn to produce at home the articles of manufacture they required. In the wilderness they enjoyed plenty and liberty, and with that they should be content.

With equal effect Birkbeck pointed out the loss of social solidarity that would result if the slaveholder came in. "The planters are great men, and will ride about, mighty grand, with their umbrellas over their heads, when I and my boys are working, perhaps bare-headed, in the hot sun. Neighbors indeed! they would have all their own way, and rule over us like little kings: . . . but if we lacked to raise a building—or a dollar—the d—l a bit would they help us." [31] Freemen came from slave states because "it is impossible for free men to thrive by honest labor among slaveholders and slaves." The planter would not tax himself for free schools; but the farmer must suffer from the pilfering of negroes and ride patrol all night while his women shared with the planter's wife the dread of a slave insurrection. In a word Birkbeck succeeded in fitting the argument against slavery squarely to Illinois conditions.

In the election the proslavery men were routed. The vote was 4,972 for a convention and 6,640 against it. The conventionists polled their majorities in the counties of the south. Gallatin gave them 82 per cent, Pope, 69, Alexander, 60, Jackson, 66, Hamilton, 67, Jefferson, 70, Franklin, 60. They carried Wayne with 63 per cent of the votes, and Randolph with 55 per cent. On the other hand they either lost or won by insignificant margins in such counties as Union, Johnson, and White of the south, while the north central counties were decidedly against them by fair majorities and the northern counties by overwhelming ones. In Pike the anti-conventionists got 90 per cent, in Fulton, 92, in Morgan, 91, in Sangamon, 83, in Clark, 79, in Edgar, 99. In the group of eleven counties bordered on the north by St. Clair, Washington, Marion, Wayne, and White, casting 3,788 votes, 62 per cent of the

[31] *Edwardsville Spectator*, November 1, 1823.

vote was for slavery. In the nineteen counties to the north of this, out of 7,814 votes cast only 33 per cent was for slavery, and these figures are increased by the 51 per cent and 45 per cent cast in Fayette and Montgomery respectively.

It is unlikely that the two factions[32] that divided state politics were definitely aligned in the contest. The leaders of the anti-Edwards faction were actively for the convention. On the other side Cook was definitely aligned against it though he took no very active part in opposition, and Edwards, while remaining publicly noncommittal, privately confided to a few friends his opposition to the measure. Yet many loyal lieutenants of Edwards such as Henry Eddy and Leonard White were active conventionists. In view of the rapid changes of affiliation and the lack of data as to the factional alignments at different times it is impossible to say definitely how many of the conventionists or anti-conventionists were at the time active in either faction. After the election many anti-conventionists were found in Edwards ranks but many conventionists as well. As Peck remarked, after the election the question of the introduction of slavery in Illinois was at an end politically, though Edwards was not above trying to revive it for political effect. Future political movements and alliances had no relation to the position of parties in the convention struggle.

The two men who had been most closely associated in the struggle, Coles and Birkbeck, made no political advantage out of the triumph of their cause. Coles as a candidate for the senatorship in 1824 joined the coalition against Edwards only to see the prize fall to Elias Kent Kane, a proslavery man. Several of Coles' nominations to office were rejected by the senate, notably that of Birkbeck to be secretary of state, an office he had held in the interim. In his messages of 1824 and 1826 Coles reiterated his suggestion that the assembly provide by law for the abrogation of the remnants of slavery in the state and the repeal of the black code and adopt effective measures against kidnapping; but in spite of the antislavery attitude

[32] For discussion of these two political factions see below, p. 92 ff.

of the state long years passed before this was done. Coles' work in Illinois was finished. He wished to run for congress in 1828 and did run in 1830; but both times his ambition was disappointed. He left the state and its politics for a long, happy, and apparently uneventful life at Philadelphia.

The end of Birkbeck's career was a tragedy. The country of the Illinois had but poorly recompensed his high hopes. It had brought him financial losses, galling criticism, disappointment in love, and estrangement from his friends. He had performed with high efficiency the duties of secretary of state, but the enemies he had made by his war on slavery sought to wound him so far as they could by rejecting his nomination for the office. A few months later while swimming his horse over a swollen creek he was swept away to his death. Long since those most directly interested in preserving his memory have left the state, and his name has been practically forgotten in the commonwealth he served so well.

V. THE WAR ON NINIAN EDWARDS

THE question of slavery apart, Illinois politics for the first twelve years of statehood consisted of a struggle between personal factions. Till the rise of Jacksonian democracy national parties in the modern sense of the word were nonexistent; and in Illinois the divisions and disputes over the presidential aspirations of Crawford, Adams, Clay, Calhoun, and Jackson were secondary in interest to the contests between the state factions and at best served only to intensify their strife or to create cross divisional lines. At first sight political contests within the state are a maze of personal and factional rivalries. The clue lies in the existence of two factions, the Edwards and anti-Edwards, each a rather loose group of personal followings, in which disaffections, mutinies, and changes of side occurred with confusing rapidity.

In the case of the Edwards faction at least the bond of union was partly common business interests. During the constitutional convention in 1818 the attempts of Nathaniel Pope, Benjamin Stephenson, and others of the Edwards faction to secure the location of the state capital on one of their town sites reacted against Governor Ninian Edwards when he was candidate for the senate in 1819.[1] Stephenson, Edwards, and Theophilus W. Smith in 1820 were concerned in promoting an addition to Edwardsville. Both Stephenson and Edwards, along with William Kinney, and with Richard M. and James Johnson of Kentucky were interested in the Bank of Edwardsville. Thomas Hart Benton bitterly attacked the institution in the St. Louis newspapers; and, when in 1822 he assailed the national policy of leasing the lead mines to the Johnsons and others, it was Edwards who came to their support. The con-

[1] Buck, *Illinois in 1818*, p. 286-292.

duct of the Bank of Missouri toward the banks of Edwardsville and Shawneetown created a common bond of financial
interest between Edwards and John Marshall and John Caldwell of the Shawneetown bank; and both men politically were
his friends and supporters.[2]

The central figure in this party was the stately Ninian
Edwards, already a politician of note in Kentucky when in
1809 he was appointed governor of Illinois territory. Kindly,
charitable, generous, and at the same time pompous, overbear-
ing, and affected, he had many warm friends, many enemies
too, and perhaps many associates who humored his foibles
so long as doing so would promote their own advantage. The
quality of mental balance was almost completely lacking in
Edwards. By turns he was bold and overcautious, headstrong
and vacillating, now plunging rashly into an enterprise such as
the attack on Crawford, of which he had not counted the cost,
now hesitating between two courses and striving to follow both
when an irrevocable decision between them had to be made.
A mental shiftiness sometimes led him into equivocal positions
which he could justify only by elaborate explanations. Notably
in the Crawford imbroglio by piling up card houses of circumstantial evidence to prove his innocence of charges which he
should have been able to ignore or to deny flatly, he frittered
away his fair fame. His contemporaries, like students in these
latter days, doubtless grew weary of reiterations and of elaborate proofs of his abilities and integrity. Finally, trying to
hit on a course that would throw away none of his claims on
the various presidential candidates, he was swept away in the
flood of intolerant Jacksonism.

Aligned with the Edwards faction were Nathaniel Pope,
formerly delegate in congress and at the beginning of the state
period a federal judge, Daniel Pope Cook, his nephew, in a
year or two to become Edwards' son-in-law, Thomas C.
Browne, a justice of the state supreme court, and Leonard

[2] *Annals of Congress*, 17 congress, 1 session, 465-470; Washburne, *Edwards
Papers*, 156, 158.

White of Gallatin county.   Of the lesser men William Kinney,
Theophilus W. Smith, and E. J. West were soon to desert
the faction and ultimately to become leaders of the opposition.

Comparatively little of the methods and purposes of the
opposition party is known except from its opponents.   Of its
leaders, Jesse B. Thomas had begun his career with the bargain
of the Illinois country delegates that had led to the division of
Indiana territory.   John McLean from the eastern side of the
state was a man of considerable ability but with an irascible
temper which led him to bitter and vindictive outbursts against
enemies or false friends.   Joseph B. Phillips, till his removal
from the state after his defeat for governor, was another
member of the party; Shadrach Bond, a man of no great spirit
or ability, was soon by Kane's influence drawn from a position
of neutrality into the faction.[3]

Elias Kent Kane, who was apparently till his death in
December, 1835, the chief of the faction whenever he chose
to exert his influence, is the enigma of early Illinois politics.
In the case of every other man of prominence, the man, his
friends, or his enemies have left materials for a sketch or a
caricature of him.   Kane is a man in a mask.   Letters to and
from him, even from father and friends, newspaper puffs, the
epithets of enemies, a school boy's letter about him, survive;
but among them can be found not one human touch, not one
phrase that can endow the man with a living personality.   No
anecdotes that would characterize him have survived.   Cata-
logs of his political abilities, virtues, and vices can be found;
again and again is seen his influence at work; but from all these
can be drawn no picture of Kane himself.   It is known that he
was of a decayed aristocratic New York family, a graduate
of Yale who came to Illinois to seek his fortune.   Yet strangely
he seems to have taken no interest in the great enterprise that
in the days of his highest power Yale men undertook at Illinois
College.   The distinctive gift of his alma mater to her sons

[3] Washburne, *Edwards Papers*, 150.

[From original owned by Illinois State Historical Library]

has sometimes been said to be a certain reserve and convention of manner; and at the last one is compelled to dismiss Kane as so far typically a Yale man.

At the time of the institution of state government the two factions appear to have reached a compromise as to the disposition of offices. Shadrach Bond, who had belonged to neither faction, was elected governor without opposition; both sides had been anxious that he should withdraw from the congressional race in which McLean beat Cook by fourteen votes. In the legislature, Cook was elected attorney-general, and Thomas C. Browne and Joseph B. Phillips, judges of the supreme court by decisive majorities. Ninian Edwards was similarly elected to one senatorship, receiving thirty-two votes out of forty cast. Jesse B. Thomas of the opposite faction was elected to the other seat on the fourth ballot, by a majority of three over Leonard White, an Edwards man. In this election a bargain apparently had failed, and in the congressional election none can have existed. The fact, however, that Edwards, who drew the short term expiring in 1819, hesitated about announcing his candidacy for reëlection led to an attempt to defeat him by arousing jealousy among eastern Illinois members on the score that both senators were from the western part of the state. He was finally elected by a vote of twenty-three to nineteen.[4]

Edwards and Thomas carried their factional rivalries to the senate. They were soon at outs on the question of federal appointments in the state. Edwards, who fared the worse in the contest for registerships and receiverships, rather injured his standing by the energy of his protests. Jealous of interference with his power of appointment, President Monroe refused to entertain Edwards' proposal that he and Thomas be permitted each to select two of four officers for the new land offices. The president and the more staid part of official Washington appear to have been surprised and puzzled at the bitterness of

[4] *Senate Journal*, 1818, 1 session, 16, 28; Washburne, *Edwards Papers*, 149-150, 154.

the contest between the two factions.[5] "The local parties, in which you appear to have lived," wrote William Wirt to Edwards, "have kept you in a constant state of partisan warfare—which, of all conditions of human life, is best calculated to sharpen the observation of character, to whet the sagacity in the detection of hostile movements, even at a distance, and to fructify the invention in the adoption of countervailing manoeuvres. But when a man rises, as you have risen, above the horizon of this petty warfare, he ought to forget all local feuds. . . ."[6] Such was the counsel of a friend who had attained a mental poise such as Edwards never achieved. The advice was calculated to conditions of the political age that was passing rather than of that which was coming in; but Edwards might well have taken it to heart.

The rivalry between Edwards and Thomas was soon intensified by their affiliations in the presidential conflict. Thomas together with Thomas Hart Benton, whom Edwards had sought to defeat for the Missouri senatorship by running Cook's brother against him, espoused the cause of William H. Crawford. Daniel Pope Cook, who, as has been seen, had in 1819 and 1820 been elected to congress over the anti-Edwards leaders, McLean and Kane, apparently was inclined to favor Adams. Edwards was at first inclined in the same direction, but by his own account seeing that Calhoun had a better chance against Crawford, he transferred his allegiance to the war department.[7] Soon he and Cook were carrying on a dangerous and daring warfare against the redoubtable Crawford.

In the session of congress of 1821–1822 Cook began a vigorous attack on Crawford, the secretary of the treasury, for appointing Jesse B. Thomas to the lucrative task of examining western land offices. He pursued this in the house with a persistency that probably detracted from its effect, persevering even after a committee report exonerated Thomas and Craw-

[5] Crawford to Edwards, January 10, 1821, in Chicago Historical Society manuscripts; Washburne, *Edwards Papers*, 167, 181, 185.
[6] Washburne, *Edwards Papers*, 188-189.
[7] Adams, *Memoirs of John Quincy Adams*, 5: 304, 525.

ford of unconstitutional or improper conduct.[8] The attack was doubtless for the moment against Thomas rather than Crawford. The Calhoun leaders were anxious to see Thomas as a Crawford partisan defeated for reëlection to the senate; and Edwards was urged directly by Calhoun to secure his defeat even by a bargain. "The reëlection of Thomas," he wrote, "would have a very bad effect. You must run but one, and if necessary you ought to come to an understanding."[9] The Illinois papers of the Edwards faction attacked Thomas during the course of 1822, accusing him of trying to buy his election by promises of offices and charging that he was in opposition to Monroe and in alliance with Crawford.

The Edwards faction was not under strict enough discipline to agree on any one candidate to oppose Thomas. Pope, perhaps in the earlier part of the year, had endeavored to pledge the Edwards support to John Reynolds. Edwards was incensed that this should have been done without his knowledge; very likely at this time he had none too good an opinion of Reynolds' ability and integrity; and he was piqued at being pledged without his knowledge to support another Edwards' faction aspirant for the senatorship whom Pope proposed to get out of the way by that means. At the meeting of the assembly, Lockwood, White, and John Reynolds were all candidates on the Edwards side.[10] Reynolds tried to postpone the election in the hope that the charges brought against Thomas might gain weight or that the various persons to whom he was reported to have promised the same offices might grow suspicious. He also appealed to Edwards for unity in the faction and for efficient use of the patronage to fix wavering supporters, but with no result. Thomas, Kane, Bond, Joseph Kitchell, and McLean were united; and January 9, 1823,

[8] *Annals of Congress,* 17 congress, 1 session, 635-637, 829-831, 876, 897-898, 912-916; *Illinois Intelligencer,* May 4, 1822; *Edwardsville Spectator,* February 5, 1822.

[9] Edwards, *History of Illinois,* 493.

[10] Washburne, *Edwards Papers,* 192-203. This is a draft without an address. Washburne believed it was written to Bond, but a careful study of its contents leaves no doubt that it was to Pope.

Thomas was reëlected, receiving a majority of six over Reynolds, White, and Lockwood.

Meanwhile, Edwards and Cook had become directly involved in a contest with the secretary of the treasury. Crawford's financial policy toward the western states has been considered in a preceding chapter.[11] Here it may be recalled that he had undertaken to use the unstable banks of the west in collecting the revenue from the public lands in the more than unstable bank note currencies of that region. Statesmanlike as the measure was, it had resulted in losses to the government; and no doubt a politician so active as Crawford had not failed, where he could, to advance his political fortunes by his financial favors. On specific points this policy was attacked by Edwards and Cook, the latter securing in the house of representatives repeated calls on Crawford for the production of great masses of correspondence with agent banks. Edwards, by the use he endeavored to make of this material against Crawford, involved himself in what became known as the A. B. plot.

The A. B. plot had developed in 1823, when there appeared in the *Republican,* the Calhoun organ at Washington, a series of articles under the signature A. B. which not only attacked Crawford for malfeasance in his official relations with banks but further insinuated that, under a call made by the house the year before for correspondence relating to banks, certain letters had been withheld and crucial parts of another marked for omission when the correspondence should be printed. To weigh the testimony fully would require a chapter by itself; here it may be said that at best the evidence was far from proving conclusively bad faith on the part of anyone concerned and that the details alleged to have been suppressed were of no great importance. John Quincy Adams, by no means likely to be prejudiced in favor of Crawford, believed the design of the A. B. letters was to remove Joseph Gales and William W. Seaton, Crawford supporters, from their post of public print-

[11] See above, p. 53 ff.

ers.[12] An investigation, perhaps of a somewhat partisan cast, finally exonerated all accused in the A. B. letters. It was generally understood that Edwards was the author of the letters; and the fact that he had used information obtained in a semiofficial capacity as a basis for anonymous attacks on his political enemies seriously impaired his prestige with men like Adams and Monroe and was sedulously used against him by the partisans of Crawford.

Edwards' senatorial career indeed had not been especially gratifying or profitable to him. His financial interests had suffered by his absence from Illinois. His reputation for sobriety of judgment had been impaired not only by his supposed leadership in the A. B. plot, but possibly also by an occasional vehemence such as marked his attempt in 1820 to amend the land bill in the senate, an attempt which some senators considered indecorous. He had seen Thomas outstrip him in the race for preferment when in 1820 the latter received an appointment on the senate committee on the public lands. Perhaps on account of his ill health he was not active in the senate during the 1822–1823 session, frequently failing to answer to his name and presenting almost no memorials and petitions; in this session he was on no standing committee. During his term he had repeatedly considered resigning, for the first time in 1819, then in 1821 when in a huff at his discomfiture over appointments, again in 1822 when he resented Pope's attempts to dissuade him from resignation, and finally in 1823 when Calhoun entreated him to remain.[13] Early in 1824, however, he sought from Monroe the nomination as minister to Mexico. Monroe was at first inclined to refuse to consider him because of the A. B. affair. Cook was earnest in his efforts with Adams in behalf of his father-in-law, and Edwards obtained the nomination. For some time it seemed that the senate might reject it for the same reasons that had influenced Monroe in his

[12] Adams, *Memoirs of John Quincy Adams,* 6: 227-228, 296-297, 370-372.
[13] Washburne, *Edwards Papers,* 202-203; Edwards, *History of Illinois,* 496; *Annals of Congress,* 16 congress, 1 session, 9, 26.

opposition, but finally it confirmed the appointment. Edwards, however, was destined never to set out on the mission. A new outbreak of his feud with Crawford brought both men to a death grapple.

Edwards in his arraignment of Crawford for depositing the public money in banks where it proved a total loss had had to encounter the uncomfortable fact that he himself had been instrumental in securing a deposit for one of the defaulting institutions, the Bank of Edwardsville. He had asserted, however, that in the fall of 1819 he had disclaimed further responsibility for the bank in a newspaper publication, a copy of which he had sent to Crawford, and that further he had induced Benjamin Stephenson, in his capacity as receiver at Edwardsville, to write Crawford suggesting that for the present he had better not deposit further with himself as bank president. So Edwards had testified before a house committee in February of 1823. In view of the attacks previously made on him, it is not surprising that Crawford, in sending to congress a report containing a last installment of the correspondence demanded by the various calls, should have concluded with the statement that no such letter as Edwards described was to be found in the treasury files.

Edwards, on the point of departure from Washington when this report appeared, regarded it as an attempt to ruin his good name. Continuing on his journey toward Illinois, he sent to the house of representatives a communication with accompanying documents, recapitulating several of his former charges against Crawford and reiterating his statement as to the existence of the letter. At the Edwardsville land office he procured a copy of the rough draft of the letter in question and of another which referred to it. The house of representatives promptly recalled him to testify in an investigation. It seemed at the time that the presidential race was likely to be run with Crawford against the field; and his partisans realizing that Edwards' charges against him, if established, would ruin his chances, rallied around him. Edwards' old associates, on the other hand, hesitated to imperil themselves by defending him too openly; and he was left to fight almost single-handed against his enemies.

In this situation Edwards found himself committed to charges which were not susceptible of plain demonstration. The death of Stephenson had left no direct witness to the writing of the letter save Edwards. The existence of the draft letter in the Edwardsville office indorsed by Stephenson, but as it developed written in Edwards' own hand, was no positive proof that Stephenson had actually sent a letter casting doubts on the solvency of his bank, or that Crawford had received it. Edwards tried to meet the difficulty by deducing from the later letters by Crawford a fine-spun thread of proof that the letter had actually been received. Crawford's counsel before the committee were able to advance an interpretation at least as plausible in favor of their client; what was more important, by a comparison of dates and of the time taken by the mails they showed that it was impossible that the letter could have been taken into account in a letter which Edwards argued was a furtive answer to it. Edwards was reduced to the position of impeaching Crawford's veracity on his own word, plus a tenuous line of circumstantial evidence.

On the other specifications of his charge Edwards was equally unfortunate. In general they depended for proof on elaborate arguments drawn from intricate bodies of evidence, the sifting of which is wearisome to the scholar and inexpressibly dull to the lay reader. Edwards' proofs were sufficient to convince Crawford's enemies but not to silence his friends. Further Crawford's counsel by various witnesses, notably Senator James Noble of Indiana, sought to discredit Edwards' veracity by proving that when he feared that his nomination would be rejected by the senate he had denied to several persons the authorship of the A. B. letters. The stroke from the politicians' point of view was a masterly one. Instead of being content merely with turning aside Edwards' charges by controverting evidence and interpretation, they impugned the veracity of the man on whose unsupported evidence much of the charge was based.

In meeting this counter attack Edwards' intellectual habits betrayed him into his supreme error. Instead of taking the stand and denying on his oath the testimony against him, he devoted himself to building up by a long series of witnesses, letters, and affidavits a structure of circumstantial evidence designed to show that it was impossible that such conversations should have taken place, but in each instance falling a little short of demonstration. The committee, though made up in Crawford's interest, in exonerating him left a serious blemish on Edwards' reputation.

It is impossible to decide whether Edwards or Crawford had the major part of truth on his side. In view of Crawford's political situation it is impossible to accept implicitly the conclusion of a committee numbering several of his friends and allies. It is as easy to explain the facts regarding Stephenson's letters by supposing them to have been suppressed in Crawford's office as to explain them by supposing that Stephenson wrote the first letter to please Edwards, and the second to convince him the first had been sent, and actually forwarded neither. It is easy to believe that Crawford in his dealings with banks had shown political friends "undue favors," such as Edwards alleged. There are certain grave discrepancies in the testimony designed to fix on Edwards the denial of the A. B. letters. Finally one must remember that by their enemies at least many of Crawford's followers were accounted desperate and unscrupulous politicians.

On the other hand certain facts of Edwards' conduct point toward what was at least a moral obliquity in his character. Occasionally he seemed to attempt a suppression of facts. The affidavit which he secured to describe the draft of Stephenson's letter specifies that the draft was indorsed in Stephenson's hand but not that it was written in Edwards'. In the whole course of his narratives Edwards overemphasized the warning Crawford might have taken from his publication and from

Stephenson's letter, for both publication and letter were laborious in their attempts to shift responsibility without giving cause for real alarm. Edwards' conduct in the A. B. affair had not seemed to dissentients or even to friendly onlookers overscrupulous on the point of honor; further, several of his attacks on Crawford's dealing with specific banks were trivial and unfair. To dismiss Edwards with a clear character and to give him the verdict against Crawford is impossible.

Whatever be the conclusion as to Edwards' deserts there can be no doubt that for the time being he was brought to the verge of financial ruin. He had of course resigned his senatorship before accepting the Mexican appointment; and his detention to testify as to his charges against Crawford compelled him to resign that also. He was obliged to refund the portion of his salary which had been advanced him; and the sum he had already invested in his outfit proved almost a dead loss. He was prepared to dispose of his speculative landholdings at a heavy sacrifice, and he even professed himself willing to accept a county clerkship to support his family.[14]

Meanwhile Cook had upheld the political fortunes of the Edwards faction in Illinois against the ablest and most popular leaders of the opposition. In 1819 and 1822 he defeated McLean; in 1820, Kane; and in 1824, Bond: all by decisive pluralities. His tremendous personal popularity was the principal cause of his success. In 1819 and 1820, it was true, he had triumphed on the antislavery principle; but his opponents seemed able to devise no issue that would enable them to overcome his popularity. Charges that he had been guilty of improper use of his frank and of associating politically with federalists were of no avail. In 1822 James Hall, under the signature of *Brutus* attacked him in the *Illinois Gazette*, accusing him of assailing Crawford for bank policies that had helped the west in its need, but to no purpose. In 1824 the attempt on the part of Bond's friends to identify Cook with the anti-

[14] Washburne, *Edwards Papers*, 225-229, 230-231, 429; Adams, *Memoirs of John Quincy Adams*, 6:374-375.

convention party led the *Gazette* to remark that half the conventionists in eastern Illinois were for Cook and that for Bond to create a coalition between Cook's friends and the anti-convention party was suicidal. It is much more significant to find attacks circulating which represented Cook and Edwards as members of a reigning family.[15]   In years to come such charges had their effect.

One issue, however, had been raised against both Cook and Edwards as early as 1820 and was destined to annoy them both so long as they remained in politics. The accusation was made that from self-interest they had voted against a reduction of the price of public land in 1820. Edwards and Cook both declared that they had voted against the bill which reduced the price of public land from $2 to $1.25 an acre, because it also oppressed the west by abolishing the credit sales system. Edwards pointed to the fact that in the senate he had repeatedly endeavored to lower the price still more and to secure preëmptions to actual settlers, pressing his amendments with such vehemence that at last he had fallen in a swoon on the floor of the senate. Edwards must have known the futility of offering for the approval of eastern senators such radical price amendments as he did; the whole series that he proposed has a touch of buncombe to it. No doubt the reduction in price operated disastrously on men like Cook and Edwards with heavy speculative holdings, and it was said on fair authority that Edwards had written to his associate in speculation expressing his fear lest the measure pass. Of a piece with this charge was one brought against Cook in 1822 to the effect that he had opposed the creation of a new land office and of preëmption rights in the Sangamon country with a view to the possibility of his own family's monopolizing the land in case it were sold at Edwardsville.[16]   This charge was, however, effectively denied.

[15] *Illinois Gazette*, June 29, July 6, 1822; *Edwardsville Spectator*, July 18, 1820, July 27, 1822; *Illinois Intelligencer*, July 22, 1820, July 27, 1822; *Kaskaskia Republican*, April 20, 1824.
[16] *Illinois Gazette*, June 29, July 27, August 3, 1822; *Illinois Intelligencer*, July 27, 1822; Edwards, *History of Illinois*, 510, 517, 518.

Local issues, or local applications of national issues, predominated in congressional elections. Thus in his address to his constituents in 1824, Cook found but little room and no important place for the Monroe Doctrine and the slave trade. Instead he stressed the feasibility of an Illinois-Michigan canal, appropriations for the improvement of the Ohio and the Mississippi, the extension of the Cumberland road, a possible system of national internal improvements, a more liberal policy of relief to purchasers of public land and finally and most important the tariff. The tariff by virtue of the home market argument was made an important political issue in the west in the early twenties. Thus in 1824 Bond's avowed policy of encouragement of agriculture was set down in his party as opposition to protected manufactures.[17] Crawford was attacked in Illinois as hostile to internal improvements and protection, and it is not clear that as yet his friends ventured to join issue on the question. The appearance of the tariff as a sectional issue must be noted in this connection. About 1820, because of its interest in a protective tariff, the east was assailed for hostility to the west. In view of the future trend of politics toward a low tariff alliance between west and south, it is interesting to note the declarations of southern members that if oppressed by a high tariff the south could no longer afford to furnish the principal market for the livestock of the west. As yet, however, in the limited materials for Illinois history available, no answering echo can be detected.[18]

The presidential question was before the people of Illinois for nearly three years before the election of 1824. For some time, as nearly as one can determine, predilections of individuals often expressed by Fourth of July toasts in favor of one candidate or another determined their respective allegiances. As the election drew near, however, the field narrowed. Cal-

[17] *Illinois Gazette,* April 24, July 17, 1824. Cook on the tariff of 1824 voted generally for protection. *Annals of Congress,* 18 congress, 1 session, 1545, 2236, 2289-2294, 2310-2316, 2327-2330, 2337, 2338, 2627-2629.
[18] *Illinois Gazette,* June 3, 1820; *Annals of Congress,* 18 congress, 1 session, 1677.

houn withdrew from the race. Clay and Crawford, in spite of the fact that factional considerations would suggest Crawford's support by the anti-Edwards men, were believed to have little strength in one or another of the three electoral districts in which the state was divided. Later it was said that Kinney, Kane, McLean, and others of the anti-Edwards faction had favored Crawford. Accordingly the presidential election, though attracting fewer voters than the congressional election, became complicated by coalition candidates, trades, and rumors of trades.

In the third district, comprising southwestern Illinois, nothing remarkable occurred. In the first district a delegate convention nominated James Turney as a candidate for elector pledged to vote for either Jackson or Clay according to the turn of events. The *Intelligencer,* which favored Clay, warned his supporters not to be deceived as Clay actually was stronger than Jackson or Crawford, whom it regarded as the probable beneficiary of the movement. Finally Jackson, Adams, Clay, and Crawford electors were all run.[19]

In the second district a different set of problems presented themselves. The chief of them was the danger lest the Jackson vote be split among several electors and an Adams man be chosen. Henry Eddy was nominated as Jackson elector by a public meeting which his enemies stigmatized as a caucus. This and the statement that Eddy secretly favored Adams led Joseph M. Street to offer himself as elector pledged to vote for Jackson for president and some republican for vice president. The suspicion was openly expressed that he was a stalking horse to divide the Jackson vote and secure the election of a nominal Clay elector who would vote for Crawford. Both Jackson and Adams men denounced this scheme; and in parody of Street, an Adams man, A. G. S. Wight, offered himself as elector for "Crawford for President, and Joseph M. Street, or some well known Republican for Vice President."[20]

[19] *Illinois Intelligencer,* September 24, October 22, 1824.
[20] *Illinois Gazette,* October 16, 1824.

In view of the interpretations later put upon Cook's pledge to vote in the house for the man who had a majority of the vote in Illinois it is important to note the results. An Adams elector was chosen in the first district, and Jackson electors in the other two. In no case had the presence of two electors for the same candidate caused a serious split in the vote. In the state at large Adams had 1,542 votes; Jackson, 1,272; Clay, 1,047; and Crawford, 219. This estimate, however, does not include 629 votes cast in the first district for Turney, the Jackson and Clay elector. His vote given to either Jackson or Clay would have given either a plurality over Adams. On the other hand the *Edwardsville Spectator* in its abstract of the votes lists Turney's under "Crawford," and this undoubtedly represents the source of a portion of the vote. It is not surprising that Cook apparently considered that he had received no popular mandate and was at liberty to follow his personal inclinations which led him in the house of representatives to cast the vote of Illinois for Adams.

Six months later, and almost a year before the congressional election of 1826, Joseph Duncan offered himself as a rival candidate to Cook. Duncan had played a minor part in state politics for several years, serving as a senator in the legislature of 1824–1826; he can scarcely be classed with anti-Edwards faction. Intellectually he was by no means the peer of Cook, nor did his followers claim it; and it is not surprising that Cook and his friends hardly took his candidacy seriously. Duncan, however, had a fair military record. As a boy of seventeen serving as ensign it had fallen to him to be the first to give his vote in council of war for the defense of Fort Stephenson, one of the military successes of the War of 1812, whose memory was still green in the west. His military service and the fact that he was a farmer were made to contrast favorably with Cook's long career in public office; he had the hearty support of the anti-Edwards faction; and to improve his position, immediately after the adjournment of the legislature in 1826, he began a thorough canvass of the state.

It soon became apparent that the campaign against Cook was to be carried on by negation rather than assertion. Mutterings of discontent with his vote for Adams had appeared a full year before Duncan was held up to the people as " a citizen who has been weighed in the balance and not found wanting." Cook's friends soon concluded that this vote was a vulnerable point which must be defended. Sometimes they endeavored to explain Cook's conduct as according with his pledges. Sometimes they appealed to the voters to remember that Cook had differed with them but this once in six years. As a motive to forgiveness of this offense, if offense it were, they pleaded the influential position Cook had attained in congress and the great services that in virtue of it he had rendered and could still render to his constituents, notably on behalf of the canal.

A second vulnerable point in Cook's position was reached by the cry that the Edwards-Cook connection formed a reigning family. The public land vote of 1820 was brought out for use against both Cook and his father-in-law. To this charge Cook's supporters replied by attempting to demonstrate in the family relations of James M. and Joseph Duncan, their uncle R. K. McLaughlin, and David Blackwell a family dynasty similar to the Cook-Edwards-Pope alliance; but the attack was hardly as successful as that of their opponents, who could point to the fact as a graphic demonstration of their charge that while Cook was running for congress, Edwards was running for governor.[21]

Edwards had embarked on the campaign for the governorship in the hope of receiving a popular vindication from the charges made against him in his controversy with Crawford. In the 1824 legislature he had stood for reëlection to the senate and had been defeated for the unexpired term by John McLean who, in his turn, was beaten for the full term by Elias Kent Kane. In spite of the fact that the election left his enemies

[21] *Edwardsville Spectator*, May 27, June 30, July 7, 28, August 4, 1826; *Illinois Intelligencer*, January 25, June 29, August 3, 1826; *Illinois Gazette*, April 28, 1826.

quarrelling among themselves and that Lockwood and Browne of his faction were reëlected to the supreme court, the rebuff was a hard one; and he naturally listened to those of his friends who assured him that the people were anxious to prove their confidence in him by giving him an overwhelming vote for governor. R. M. Young assured him of a vote of five or more to one in the southwestern counties where the Jackson men were anxious to rebuke Crawford. Till the campaign of 1826 was near its climax Edwards retained his confidence that his vindication was to be by a flood of popular votes and could not understand why his opponent Thomas Sloo did not give up the contest unless he trusted to some bit of eleventh-hour chicanery.[22]

Edwards set forth on a state wide personal campaign. Everywhere his main theme was an arraignment of the financial mismanagement of the state in recent years. He assailed the legislature for paying out state paper at a third its face value and for issuing auditor's warrants at a similar depreciation. He took credit to himself for having secured annual sales for taxes of nonresidents' land as well as residents'; under the former system he averred nonresidents had deprived the people of Illinois of a currency by hoarding depreciated state paper to use in paying their taxes. "Such impositions as these," so ran his drafted speech, "upon a free, high-minded and independent people, I boldly assert have no parallels in the annals of free government, and they are only to be borne by that Christian charity. . . ."[23] One writer not disposed to be unfriendly to Edwards stated that sometimes his denunciations traveled even farther and covered the whole course of government from the halcyon days of his territorial rôle and "arraigned and charged at the bar of public opinion every man who has shared with yourself the confidence of the people." Edwards, it may be noted, denied this charge in its terms rather than in its spirit.[24] It would not be surprising if in oratorical

[22] Washburne, *Edwards Papers*, 237-239.
[23] Edwards, *History of Illinois*, 203-206, 213-214.
[24] *Illinois Intelligencer*, July 6, 1826.

enthusiasm he sometimes transgressed the bounds of his manuscript speech. Whether, as his opponents suggested, in each county he expressly exempted its delegations from his censures cannot be known.

Edwards' attacks on the legislature drew forth a retort which contributed powerfully to Cook's defeat and to the narrowness of his own plurality. Strangely enough it came from George Forquer, a man hitherto, and later, hand-in-glove with Edwards politically and even then inclined to favor him as against his opponent. Forquer was a man of hot and suspicious temper, quick to suspect and resent treachery on the part of a political associate; and possibly in a moment of irritation at Edwards' attacks on the legislature of which he had been a member and of distrust of Edwards' good faith toward himself, he published in the *Illinois Intelligencer* of July 6 an article signed "Tyro." In spite of the signature the blow was sped by the hand of a master of controversy, and it reached not only Edwards but the whole system of factional strife in politics which he personified.

"Tyro" pronounced that the attacks of Edwards on the legislature as a body merely to pave his own way to political power were enough to alienate all thinking men from him. Though politically able, he was by no means infallible; instead of seeking the office as a vindication he was pursuing it madly through ex-cathedra denunciations of measures and men. He should remember, "Tyro" added, that the days when the factional strife of the territorial parties could keep men in political subjection had departed. "The sycophants of territorial bondage have lost their influence and dwindled into contempt. The dazzling halo, with which the former exercise of lordly power, occasioned the ignorant to associate your name, is broken, and you now stand before them as an object of political charity — a naked, crumbling monument of a morbid ambition. A race of men, honorable in their views, pure in their feelings, with talents hereafter to be felt, are now in political embryo, who have not been tamed or degraded under the banners of either of the old parties that originated the territorial feuds, and which have ever since harassed the country with the most intolerant proscription." Forquer had discerned the fallacy that underlay the whole factional system — it imbued its adherents with the idea that the open and avowed end of politics was the gratification of a personal ambition. Under "Tyro's" analysis the absurdity of Edwards' seeking a public office to salve his honor of a thrust received in factional warfare is self-evident.

"On the first appearance of *Tyro*," wrote John Marshall after the election, "I anticipated the storm that was to follow. . . . I was not mistaken, it was a fatal storm. You must be aware now that the freedom with which you commented on the management of the finances, State Bank, &c., however just was nevertheless very impolitick. It arrayed almost every man that had been in the Legislature since 1821 and all the Bank and Circuit Court interest against you, which, by a little management aided by the cry of 'a family of rulers' was unfortunately brought to bear on Mr. Cook." [25]

The attempt to turn the politics of a state to the advantage of a personal faction had resulted fatally to the faction whose work first was made apparent to the people. Edwards was elected by a vote that considering the weakness of his opponent and the great expectations with which he had begun the contest was in itself a disgrace. He could muster but 6,280 votes against 5,833 for Sloo and 580 for Adolphus F. Hubbard, the butt and jest of Illinois politics. Joseph Duncan defeated Cook by a vote of 6,322 to 5,619 excluding 824 votes cast for James Turney.

Cook's defeat has usually been laid to popular resentment at his vote for Adams. But while the issue was raised in the campaign and while outside the state Cook's defeat was repeatedly assigned to it, the evidence that it was the deciding factor is by no means conclusive. Edwards asserted that it had not been, though his statement may be assigned to an

[25] Washburne, *Edwards Papers*, 255.

anxiety to convince Clay that he held the balance between the Jackson and administration forces in the state. Duncan, however, did not run as a Jackson man. Further, in 1826 Cook lost decisively but few Jackson counties on which his hold had not been precarious before, though in many instances he lost them by increased majorities. Not one of the Jackson counties that he lost in 1826 did he carry both in 1822 and 1824. Further he obtained decisive votes in several strong Jackson counties such as Pope, Gallatin, Edgar, Morgan, Greene, and Alexander. Pope county he carried by an increased majority and Gallatin and Alexander he had lost in 1824. Marshall's letter already cited is evidence against the accuracy of the assertion. Further the story that Cook's vote was the cause of his defeat tended to establish itself in Illinois history, since in 1830 the supporters of Kinney were anxious to prove Reynolds' apostasy to Jackson; and they argued that he had supported Cook in 1826, representing Cook as at that time defeated on the Jackson issue.

The explanations offered by friends who were in close touch with the situation were Cook's inability to stump the state, the reiterations of the old public land charge, and the use of the fact that father-in-law and son-in-law were at the same time running for the two highest offices in the gift of the people of Illinois.[26] Yet the historian may speculate whether in view of the letter of Marshall and the article by "Tyro" the causes mentioned were not symptoms of a cause rather than causes themselves. Their gravamen after all lies in the assumption that Edwards and Cook in their political course had been moved by their pecuniary interests and their personal ambitions. It was that against which "Tyro" had really protested, the governing of the state for the benefit of the leaders of a personal clique.

Finally one may note that Edwards and Cook assumed toward their constituents an attitude characteristic of the past

[26] Edwards, *History of Illinois*, 451; Washburne, *Edwards Papers*, 260-261; *Edwardsville Spectator*, July 7, September 29, 1826.

rather than the future. Edwards had pompously asserted that he was a candidate for office by the call of the people, and that anyone contesting with him must do so for sinister motives.[27] Cook's friends repeatedly urged the grants he had obtained at Washington and the further benefits that he as a member of ability and a friend to the administration could procure for the state. Yet in spite of apostrophes to the paramount abilities of Edwards and of promises of canal lands to be procured by Cook, the people of Illinois had voted in great numbers for men admittedly of narrow abilities who could promise little in the way of public services. The older political order was fading away, and Jacksonian democracy was on the horizon.

[27] *Illinois Intelligencer*, August 3, 1826.

VI.   THE RISE OF JACKSONIAN DEMOCRACY

THE first waves of the rising tide of westernism which found its expression in Jacksonian democracy had helped to undermine Cook's popularity in 1826. As year after year the tide rose the old factions of Illinois politics were to take note of it and to seek to turn it to their own political advantage or else to endeavor to evade its full force without traveling with it; but in the end the whole factional system of state politics was to be swept away by the flood tide of the new democracy. To understood fully the character and ideals of the movement on which Jackson rode triumphant through the latter part of his political career is to understand the history of the United States for two decades. Such an understanding is not easy to attain. Sometimes nearer, sometimes farther, from the heart of the movement was the chicanery and management of crafty politicians. The personnel changes: old leaders go over into opposition, and late converts take their places. Intellectually the movement develops and evolves so that the radical ideals of 1837 and 1840 to the Jackson men of 1824 would have appeared outlandish. Any estimate of Jacksonism must take careful account of the fact that it was an idea intensely alive and therefore intensely variable.

Perhaps the surest guide to the underlying elements of Jacksonism that persisted throughout the movement is the character of Jackson himself. That his character could divide men into worshippers and bitter critics was shown in the congressional investigation of the Seminole campaign during the session of 1818–1819, the first in which the state of Illinois had a voice. To men of one type of mind the raid into Spanish territory, the execution of Arbuthnot and Ambrister, and above all, Jackson's deliberate disregard of his orders in raising a company of Tennessee riflemen and mustering them into United States service, instead of calling on neighboring states for militia as he had been instructed, were alike characteristic of a "military chieftain" ruthless and lawless, the very counterpart of the men who have in Europe and South America made republican government a travesty on liberty.

On the other hand in the defenses of Jackson's character and conduct one catches an echo of the spirit of the American frontier—its directness and its disregard of all theories of action not corresponding with the facts of life. Jackson had been set the task of defending the frontier. He had taken the shortest and most direct way to do it, using the forces best suited to it, and not refraining from regard to the sensibilities of men who actually sympathized with the Indians. The means he had taken were neither humanitarian nor constitutional, but they were effective. Such a man to a west that had seen the doubts, hesitations, and failures of the Jeffersonian school seemed formed more nearly in the image of Washington and the revolutionary heroes.

The men who urged Jackson's claims to the presidential succession contrasted the claims of the man who had served his country in the field with the claims of those who had served her in congress or in the cabinet. They felt that the closet statesmen at Washington had disregarded Jackson's just claims because he was not one of themselves and had not been initiated into their methods of political finesse. The caucus which nominated Crawford must have seemed the very embodiment of such methods. The feeling culminated in 1825 when John Quincy Adams was elected president by the house of representatives, in spite of the fact that Jackson, of the four candidates, had received a plurality of electoral and possibly of popular votes. That the wirepullers should triumph over the plain soldier aroused intense indignation.[1] The cause of Jackson was associated by his friends with the broader cause of democracy. In the session of 1825–1826 a constitutional amendment

[1] *Annals of Congress*, 15 congress, 2 session, 256, 517, 529, 656, 689.

introduced in congress providing for a direct popular vote on the presidency put on record in the debate those who were willing to trust the people and those who were not. On one side were men who averred that the constitution of the United States did not permit of democracy and that a legislative training in statesmanship was an implied requisite for a holder of high office; men who defended the caucus because they believed that, if the congress did not eliminate a plurality of candidates before the election, the house or the senate would have to choose between them in the end; and finally, men who used the states' rights argument.[2] Everett stated bluntly what was perhaps in the minds of many, when he declared that a president elected by an overwhelming majority would be a dangerous one.

On the other side were those who believed that the people should nominate and elect the president directly, that he should be dependent on them for office and responsible to them for his acts.[3] This was the theory which was later to be so boldly asserted by Jackson in his claim to represent the popular will and which was exemplified by him in his war on the senate.

In Illinois the Jackson campaign of 1828 began December 9, 1826, when in the house of representatives A. P. Field offered a resolution indorsing Jackson and asserting that the election of Adams was by bargain and sale and contrary to the will of the majority. Three days later a motion to lay on the table till July 4, the usual way of killing a measure, was lost by a vote of 16 to 20. The counter-argument, as expounded by Alfred W. Cavarly, was that such action would prejudice the land grants for which the people of Illinois were petitioning congress, that it was unusual and could not be supported by any valid proof of the charges made. A compromise amendment offered by Thomas Reynolds which merely expressed confidence in Jackson was lost 18 to 18. Field finally moved to make the matter a mere nomination of Jackson, but his motion was

[2] Storrs, Archer, Stevenson, Ingersoll, and Mitchell of Tennessee.
[3] Saunders, Cambreleng, Drayton, Polk, Isacks, Lecompte, and Mitchell of South Carolina.

defeated 19 to 17. January 8, 1827, a motion to take up the resolution was lost 18 to 18 by a slightly different alignment of votes. On the last day of the session, with five Adams men and one Jackson supporter absent, a resolution declaring for Jackson passed 19 to 11. Such was the alignment of the house. Although no vote directly indicating the alignment was taken in the senate there was said to be an administration majority of 2.

Outside the legislature the movement in favor of Jackson was continued through the agency of county meetings. One was held at Belleville on March 8, which recommended Jackson as a candidate and urged the holding of similar meetings to take measures for his election. "They hope," was the comment of the administration organ, the *Intelligencer*, "by this mean, not only to discover their own strength but to give tone to public feeling; and if possible, induce a belief that Jackson is the strong candidate."[4]   In May, Kinney, West, T. W. Smith, and Kane were busy with a project to publish a Jackson newspaper in the state; and the next fall Fleming began printing the *Illinois Corrector* at Edwardsville. In the late fall and winter under the tutelage of the leaders district conventions to nominate electors were held; and in these as well as in the county meetings which elected delegates to them, resolutions were adopted denouncing Adams and praising Jackson. The *Illinois Gazette* asserted that the county meetings rarely consisted of over twelve or fifteen persons and that they were drummed up in county after county by political circuit riders like A. P. Field. Undoubtedly there was machinery at work, but in view of the results there must have been something more.[5]

In the political comment of the Illinois administration papers one notes surprise or even alarm at the lengths to which the Jackson enthusiasm was going. The *Intelligencer* com-

---

[4] *Illinois Intelligencer,* March 24, 1827.
[5] Kinney to Kane, May 12, 1827, in Kane manuscripts; *Illinois Intelligencer,* October 12, 1827, January 5, March 1, 29, May 10, June 21, 1828; *Illinois Gazette,* May 3, 17, 1828.

mented sarcastically on such ebullitions of enthusiasm as public meetings in which the planting of hickory trees was an important part of the exercises. It complained that New York had been lost to Adams by the votes of the riffraff. One Fourth of July orator of the preceding year had reminded his hearers that popular rights was the favorite theme of demagogues and that the fathers of the republic had equally opposed the despotism of a monarch and the licentiousness of the mob.[6] The *Intelligencer* clipped from *Niles Weekly Register* an editorial speculating as to why the election of a president should be fraught with so much more violence than the elections of senators, especially in view of the fact that the senate with its power of trial in cases of impeachments was by so much the more important branch of government! The enthusiasm for Jackson presaged to men of conservative mind the end of a stable and balanced political universe, in which sobriety, standing, and solid talents had governed.

Either side in the campaign freely barbed its arguments with abuse of the opposing candidate. For the Jackson forces the "corrupt bargain" between Clay and Adams by which Clay in return for the secretaryship of state was alleged to have thrown his forces to Adams did full duty in spite of the numerous refutations that were published. The South American policy of Adams and the alleged loss of the West India trade were duly considered, together with such matters as his lavish furnishing of the east room of the White House and his purchase of a billiard table — a piece of furniture that in the Illinois statutes figured only as a gaming device. In view of Clay's duel with Randolph, the accusation was made that the government at Washington was a "duelling administration!"[7]

For the reason that files of two Illinois administration newspapers have been preserved and almost no Jackson papers have been handed down, it is easier to outline the attack on Jackson than to state his defense. Efforts were made to prove

[6] Leonard Ross at Atlas. *Illinois Intelligencer*, August 4, 1827.
[7] *Ibid.*, November 4, 1826, August 11, September 8, 15, 1827.

that the real attempt at bargain and intrigue in 1825 had been in his favor. The statement that Jackson was a federalist in disguise was supported by the publication of his letter to Monroe in 1817 urging the latter to appoint federalists to office. Jackson himself was represented as a rowdy, a cock-fighter, a gambler, and a devotee of the code of honor.[8] Toward the end of the campaign his opponents fell back on such charges as that he was a Negro trader and a ferreter out of flaws in land titles.

Naturally in this campaign also Jackson was represented as a "Military Chieftain." A remark of Jefferson to Coles to the effect that the heavy popular vote for Jackson made him doubt the stability of free institutions was made to do duty in Illinois. His arbitrary conduct when New Orleans was under martial law was represented as an instance of his military violation of civil power. The incident most relied on, however, was his execution of six militiamen for what was represented as at the most a technical desertion after their term of service had expired.[9] For many a long year of his service in the democratic party Sidney Breese writhed under the charge that he had distributed "coffin handbills," with the coffins of the six depicted at the top and subscribed with doleful verse:

> He ordered Harris out to die,
>   And five poor fellows more!
> Young gallant men in prime of life,
>   To welter in their gore
>
> 'T was all in vain, John Harris prayed,
>   'T is past the soul's belief.
> Hard as a flint was Jackson's heart,
>   He would not grant relief
>
> .   .   .   .

[8] *Illinois Gazette*, June 7, 1828; *Illinois Intelligencer*, August 4, October 13, November 17, 1827, April 5, May 24, 1828.
[9] *Ibid.*, August 4, December 1, 1827.

Sure he will spare! Sure Jackson yet
Will all reprieve but one —
Oh hark! those shrieks! that cry of death!
The dreadful deed is done![10]

Besides all the personal issues there were issues of national policy at question in the election. The administration newspapers represented that the Adams policy of internal improvements and protection to manufactures was the policy preeminently adapted to the needs of the west. The insufficient market for western produce at New Orleans was a graphic argument for a system that would both enable manufactures to spring up on the soil of Illinois and furnish her with outlets to additional markets. Many of the Jackson men were disposed to agree with this estimate of the true interest of the west and to insist that Jackson also favored the policy. The administration papers forced the fighting on the tariff issue, a live national issue even at this early date, accusing the *Corrector* of hedging and vacillating on it.

The Adams internal improvement policy offered an issue even more vital to Illinois.[11] Edwards as early as 1825 had pointed out to Clay the strength that the administration would gain by the announcement of a project for a connection between western waters, the lakes, and the Atlantic. In the meetings in northern Illinois held to celebrate the passage of the canal bill of 1827 there were resolutions and speeches full of gratitude to Edwards, Cook, Adams, Clay, and the internal improvement policy. Calhoun's casting vote against the measure in 1826 and the unfriendliness to it of Jackson's friends were supposed to have seriously imperiled Jackson's chances. Consequently the *Intelligencer* laid its greatest emphasis on the importance of the internal improvement policy to Illinois. Toward the

[10] *Chicago Democrat*, April 29, 1840.
[11] *Illinois Intelligencer*, April 21, 1827; *Illinois Gazette*, February 23, 1828; Kimmel to Eddy, November 7, 1827, in Eddy manuscripts. The Jackson convention at Springfield resolved that it was convinced that its candidate, Andrew Jackson, was for protection and internal improvement. *Illinois Intelligencer*, May 10, 1828.

end of the campaign in an attempt to stir up sectional prejudice the administration papers represented anti-tariff and anti-internal improvement as policies dictated by the slave states.[12]

The supporters of Jackson endeavored to demonstrate Adams' hostility to western interests on another issue, that of the public lands. Ever since the spring of 1824 Benton had been urging a measure designed to remove the complaint that the United States arrested the development of the western states by disposing of its lands on terms too unfavorable to the purchasers. His graduation bill embodied the principle that the unsold public lands be each year reduced in price twenty-five cents an acre till they reached twenty-five cents, when if they did not find purchasers they should be ceded to the states. The measures also provided that when the price of public lands had reached fifty cents an acre, they should be donated to actual settlers in eighty acre tracts. Benton introduced this bill year by year, but it was not till 1826 that he was permitted even to speak on it. In that year, when in a propaganda for the measure he had secured a memorial from the Missouri legislature indorsing it, it was taken under the wing of the Jackson party in the state. In congress it received the support of Kane and Duncan, but roused the opposition of such men as Benton's colleague and rival, David Barton, who insisted it was an attempt to carry on the movement, frustrated in 1820, which had been throwing the public domain into the hands of speculators. It was defeated in 1828 in the senate, eleven Jackson senators, as the administration men pointed out, voting among the twenty-five opponents of the measure. The Jackson men, however, turned to Richard Rush's last report as secretary of the treasury in which he injudiciously urged protection to manufactures on the ground that it would keep population in the east where it could accumulate capital instead of spreading it thinly over the lands of the west. His further argument that the low price of the public lands acted

[12] Washburne, *Edwards Papers*, 240; *Illinois Gazette*, June 28, 1828; *Illinois Intelligencer*, March 17, August 4, November 3, 1827, July 5, 1828.

as a bounty on agriculture which should be supplemented by one on manufactures was, if anything, still more unfortunate. Both were used by the opposition to prove the sinister aspect of the whole Adams policy toward the west.[13]

The question of the public lands in Illinois politics followed a rather unusual course. First it must be noted that side by side with Benton's scheme in congress appeared the suggestions on the part of certain members that congress might well cede the public lands to the states in which they lay. This plan was usually based on an extreme theory of state sovereignty which proclaimed that, as the new states were admitted into congress on an equal footing with the old in all respects, it was preposterous that the federal government should control the soil in them, and accordingly declared that all compacts recognizing such a right were null and void. Benton had disclaimed any such implication in his measure; but the theory was enunciated by several westerners, such as Hendricks, who were well disposed to it. Tazewell indeed had in 1826 proposed a corresponding measure.[14] Other senators had favored the principle. But in Illinois, Edwards, who had declared in his message of 1826 that if the state did not receive the cession it must have classification and who in 1828 supported Forquer's rival proposal for a graduation based on a classification by value, came out in his 1828 message with a tediou and labored defense of the right of the states to the public lands based on doctrines of state sovereignty. This measure may have been an attempt to outbid his old enemies, Benton, Kane, and Duncan for popular support or it may have been, as his enemies suggested, designed in the interest of his own landholdings to stir up such animosity in the east as would ruin the chances of the graduation bill. Possibly, as Duff Green suggested, he hoped that the measure would be the basis of a coalition between the west and his old friends of Calhoun's party in the south. On public lands, tariff, and internal improvements in 1828–1829 it

[13] *Congressional Debates*, 1827-1828, p. 483-521, 614-629, 678, 2832 ff.
[14] *Ibid.*, 1827-1828, 152 ff., 625-629; *ibid.*, 1825-1826, p. 782.

was a question of alliances: would the west accept tariff and internal improvements and yield up the public lands policy to the jealousy of her growth harbored in the east, or would she ally herself with the south in return for free trade and a favorable land policy? The alternative was not clearly perceived in 1828; nor was it definitely recognized for some years; but in the large, so far as Illinois was concerned, the decision had been made.

The graduation policy as presented by Benton was a measure democratic in its intent. In spite of what was said by Barton and others one cannot help feeling that Benton was right in holding that speculation on a large scale in unimproved land was a hazardous business so long as so much wild land was still in government hands and that hitherto speculators had burnt their fingers in handling both public lands and military bounty lands.[15] Benton argued that the measure would give to the poor the opportunity by which they might rise to the position of useful citizens; he even argued that it was the duty of the government to settle the wild lands as expeditiously as might be, since men naturally had a right to the soil.

The tide flowed toward Jackson. Although the final vote —9,582 to 4,662—was overwhelmingly in Jackson's favor, the change in sentiment was by no means immediate or general throughout the state. On May 16, 1827, Joseph M. Street reported to Edwards from Shawneetown that the old Clay, Adams, and Crawford men were nearly all supporting the administration; and early in the next month he ascribed the weakness of Jackson to the bitter factional feeling in that section against Kinney and Smith. In a later letter he reported McLean much cooler toward Jackson. As late as August 15, 1827, one of Kane's correspondents believed that, while at that time Jackson had a majority in the state, in the end Adams would run very well. By February 22, 1828, Smith estimated that the Adams men had given up Illinois.

[15] *Congressional Debates*, 1825-1826, p. 720.

While the political issues of the future were brewing in the real Jackson movement, the leaders of the faction were watching events and planning that their personal interests should not suffer. Such old Crawford men as Kinney, Kane, T. W. Smith, Bond, and McLean had gone over to Jackson. By 1828–1829 the fervency and zeal of these converts for party regularity and proscription of their opponents was viewed by the older Jackson men, such as S. H. Kimmel and A. P. Field, with ill-concealed impatience.

On the other side Edwards was balancing on the political fence which divided the Jackson forces and the administration. On the one hand Duff Green was assuring him of Jackson's regard, his disposition to condone Cook's vote for Adams, and the certainty of Edwards' triumph if he only would come out for the constitutional amendment, which was the Jacksonian profession of faith. On the other hand, Edwards after his election took an independent if friendly tone toward Clay. While he did not hesitate to speak plainly on attacks against himself originating in administration sources, he declared that he could not, in view of the attitude of Jackson's friends toward the canal, expect the Jackson interest to predominate in Illinois. He explained the small plurality by which he had been elected by saying that he had made exertions to throw all his opponents on the Jackson side, so that he might eventually turn the balance either way. The hint to the administration was obvious. Edwards was supposed in 1827 to have come out for Jackson, but he supported a declared Adams man for congress in 1828, so that his position remained more or less equivocal.[16]

In state politics Edwards gathered what hope he could from the fact that the ranks of his opponents were disintegrating. The two senatorships to be filled in 1824 had sown discord. In the spring of that year Kane, Kinney, Sloo, and Kitchell all had their eyes on the prizes. McLean and Coles also stood forth as candidates. Kane apparently succeeded in

[16] Washburne, *Edwards Papers*, 256, 259.

combining the forces in support of McLean in order to beat Edwards who was hoping for a vindication by reëlection. On the third ballot McLean had thirty-one votes to nineteen for Edwards and two for Pope. A week later Kane was elected for the long term, beating Lockwood, McLean, Coles, and Sloo. McLean, who believed he had been tricked into entering the contest only to be humiliated, was furious and refused to be soothed by asservations that he had been reserved to cap the triumph of the coalition by beating Cook for congress. Another member of the coalition had to complain of similar treatment. In the election of justices of the supreme court, Wilson and Browne were confirmed, Lockwood and T. W. Smith elected, and John Reynolds frozen out. Exactly how the justices of the Edwards faction were elected is a problem. Reynolds very probably had been displaced by T. W. Smith's intrigues, and he did not hesitate to say that he had been the "whetstone" in the affair.[17]

The effect on the make-up of the factions of this intriguing is admirably described by a political observer of 1827 whose statements are corroborated by such independent evidences as exist. "Smith, Kinney, and West, are about to set up a Newspaper at Edwardsville — ostensibly for Jackson, but in fact to operate in State politics. Smith and Kinney want to be Senator and Governor. They go against Edwards, Thomas, but most especially and bitterly against McLean. *Party No. 2* consists of John Reynolds and Tom Reynolds the Beairs, etc., Jno Reynolds wants to be Senator — is inveterate against Smith, Edwards, Thomas and dont much like McLean. *Party No. 3* consists of Jesse B. Thomas *Solus* — the privates and officers yet to be enlisted. The Honorable Jesse is very bitter against Smith and Co., but more against McLean. He swears that McLean is a dishonest man and a dishonest politician — that he cant, and by G—— he *shant* be elected!

"I do not see how the above named men can ever again

[17] Kinney to Kane, April 10, 1824, in Kane manuscripts; McLean to Sloo, January 16, 1825, in Illinois State Historical Society, *Transactions*, 1911, p. 39; Reynolds to Cook, December 30, 1824, in Edwards manuscripts.

ımalgamate, at any rate they will not join with *Party No. 4* which consists of Jno McLean and his friends — Nor with *Party No. 5* which is composed of Edwards & Co.

"Depend upon it, my dear Sir," he continued, "these combinations which are going on in our State will ruin every man who is engaged in them. The people are beginning to complain loudly. Kinney is sinking faster than I ever saw any man, his violence disgusts even his friends. Thomas and Edwards are gone. Smith is universally feared, his ambition and his intriguing spirit alarm friends and foes. Lockwood and Wilson are greatly depreciated. All of these men must go down. McLean stands best, but his prospects are very doubtful. . . ."[18]

Other evidence attests the precarious condition of Edwards and his faction. It did not have control of the legislature chosen in 1826, and thereby all Edwards' assaults on the administration of the bank and finances were frustrated. In the legislative elections he was beaten. By the death of Cook in 1827 he lost a man of popularity and of recognized ability and what was worse a loyal comrade. There were none too many such left among Edwards' followers. Still he patiently worked away, seeking once more to attain victory by the old methods.

The senatorial election of 1828 was the point toward which all eyes turned. Thomas, who had not followed his old associates into the Jackson ranks, was out of it. His one hope had been a close contest with many candidates. By 1828 Edwards believed that Kane would succeed in bringing Reynolds, Bond, and Kinney to a bargain by which Smith would obtain the honor. Meanwhile Edwards, though not himself avowedly a candidate, kept himself informed of the probable disposition of candidates for the legislature in certain districts. Street believed Lockwood the only available candidate. Pope was anxious to run, being privately told by Smith and his followers that he was their second choice; but Edwards was provoked

[18] Hall to Sloo, June 3, 1827, in Illinois State Historical Society, *Transactions*, 1911, p. 41-42.

because Pope was not supporting Forquer against Duncan for congress. Accordingly he secretly appealed to McLean, suggesting that he support Forquer, promising in turn to support him for the senate even as against Pope and warning him that the combination behind Smith was planning to drive him out of state politics. McLean, however, apparently felt sure of his election and made no particular response to Edwards' overture, except by answering in a friendly tone after Forquer's defeat. He was elected senator unanimously, but his election redounded in the end to the benefit of the Kane group. Two years later Forquer lamented the fact that Kane by playing on McLean's violent likes and dislikes was able politically to do with the latter as he would.[19]

Meanwhile in a conference of his political associates at Vandalia Forquer late in 1827 had been put forward as a candidate for congress against Joseph Duncan. Breese and Coles had hoped for such indorsement from the group and each was correspondingly disappointed. On the other side, Kinney, Kane, West, Smith, and Reynolds supported Duncan as the Jackson candidate against Forquer, who was avowedly an Adams man. Forquer's friends tried to make the contest a personal comparison between the candidates, criticizing Duncan for various alleged oversights, blunders, and neglects that had hindered the state's interests. Further they tried to draw an issue between Benton's graduation scheme, reported to the house by Duncan, and a measure devised by Forquer for classifying public lands according to value, at one dollar, seventy-five cents, and fifty cents an acre with cession of all lands below the latter value to the state and immediate donations to actual settlers as compared with the eight years, during which they would have to wait under Benton's bill, after the land was brought into market. The expense of valuing the land was the obvious objection to this measure which Forquer's friends tried to explain away.[20]

[19] Washburne, *Edwards Papers*, 343, 353, 358, 360, 477.
[20] *Illinois Intelligencer*, July 5, 12, 26, 1828; *Illinois Gazette*, July 19, 1828; Forquer to Eddy, December 15, 1827, in Eddy manuscripts.

As contrasted with Edwards' and Cook's campaign of two years before, it is interesting to note the democratic and popular appeal made by Forquer. Against his opponent's claim to be a simple farmer whose shortcomings should be on that account condoned he set up the fact that he himself had been a mechanic. "Forquer, having been a mechanic," wrote Edwards to Eddy, "operates like a charm. . . . Our tickets should be . . . headed with the figure of a plow & plane, &c, '*For the peoples friend, who, like them, knows what it is to get his living by the sweat of his brow.*'"[21] Forquer's handicaps in other directions, however, were too many to be overcome thus even in the year of Jackson's election. The administration party was badly split between Edwards and anti-Edwards men, who had introduced their factional discords even in the chaos of Adams' election. Forquer lost many administration votes and by his own account received no real support from the great semi-independent feudatories of the Edwards group; and the fact that he was for Adams was used to turn the Jackson vote against him. In his defeat by a vote of 10,398 to 6,166 Edwards had suffered still another humiliating reverse.

The revolution of factions and Edwards' own restless political ambitions were next to bring him into alliance with John Reynolds, a man for whom he had hitherto scarcely concealed his contempt. Since Edwards had rebuffed Reynolds' senatorial aspirations in 1822–1823, the latter had gone over to the opposition, had in some way lost their support for reëlection to the supreme bench in 1824–1825, and had in 1826 supported Cook. In 1828, as has been seen, he was a satellite in the Kane constellation and had exchanged several broadsides of abuse with Edwards. During the following session he had endeavored to strike some bargain in regard to the senatorship with both Kinney and Smith in return for support for governor. Disappointed here he had turned to the

21 Edwards to Eddy, Election, August, 1828, in Eddy manuscripts; *Illinois Intelligencer*, July 12, 1828.

Edwards group, and in spite of the intention of the Jackson following to proscribe all Adams men, he had assisted together with McLean in electing Forquer attorney-general over McRoberts.[22]

Immediately after the legislative session he began his campaign. " I must stir or git beat. The people is with me," he wrote to Grant, February 7, 1829. Artfully emphasizing his Jackson affiliations he was nominated later in the fall by Jackson meetings. His circular set him forth as a child of the people, pitiful to the poor who suffered from taxation, and a friend to internal improvements and to a speedy distribution of the school fund for the benefit of the children then growing up in ignorance. So large were his promises that one irreverent critic suggested that, after promising internal improvements and lighter taxation to boot, it only remained to engage that the Mississippi run upstream one half the year and downstream the other for the special benefit of the river trade.[23]

By this time Reynolds had made his formal peace with Edwards, predicating his overtures on the practical ground that they had many friends in common and on the ideal one that it was necessary to unite to procure the good of the people. He again offered the senatorship bargain in general terms. Edwards in reply somewhat condescendingly accepted his overtures, stipulating that he have an authoritative voice in drawing the plan of the gubernatorial campaign — apparently planning to bring in his public land doctrines on Reynolds' shoulders to prepare for his own future political success with them.

The characters of John Reynolds and William Kinney, the two men who confronted each other as rivals in the race for the governorship, are an interesting contrast. John Reynolds, by virtue of a certain kindliness of spirit and a degree of cun-

[22] *Illinois Intelligencer,* January 9, February 20, June 12, July 10, 24, 1830; *Illinois Gazette,* January 17, December 12, 1829.
[23] *Galena Advertiser,* November 9, 30, December 28, 1829, January 11, February 15, 1830.

ning, was to shuffle his way through Illinois politics, getting much of what he wanted. He had been brought up in pioneer Illinois, had seen some ranger service in the War of 1812, and apparently in imitation of Edwards had adopted as a political asset the sobriquet of "The Old Ranger." He had had a narrow schooling in a primitive Tennessee academy termed by courtesy a college and had acquired some small classical learning which in certain circles he took care to display. Toward the end of his life he tried to carry on a learned correspondence with Joseph Gillespie, and at the end of a sophomoric composition on the traitor Count Julian and the ruin of the Visigothic kingdom, he begs his correspondent to write him his views on the pyramids of Egypt! The books which he wrote in the latter part of his life confirm the contemporary tradition of his mental slovenliness. His discourse couched in the shambling phrases of the pliant demagogue, while not ungrammatical, is strikingly unidiomatic. When he endeavored to cover his meanness of spirit with dignified or distant phrases, he is a pantaloon peeping from behind his mask. In politics, even in his seeking for office, he affected a transparent reserve. "I am in the hands of my friends," was his favorite phrase. Aided by his ability to avoid committing himself he pushed his way by means of factional politics, never hesitating to abandon old friends whom he no longer needed till at length in an age of sharply defined parties he discovered that the older political methods would no longer serve.

Kinney was the antithesis of Reynolds. He too was a product of frontier Illinois and had attained prosperity as a storekeeper. In that day his business did not seem incongruous with his calling as a Baptist minister. Hot-tempered, vehement, a good hater, a keen and open seeker for office, he exhibited in politics few of the conventional ministerial traits. He was far more straightforward, far more loyal to his friends than Reynolds. He was almost completely illiterate, but except in having his political addresses written for him, he made no effort to conceal the fact. His keen mother-wit was the source of a long series of shrewd characterizations of men and events, couched in rustic metaphor which often rises to the height of epigram. Genuinely trained in the world's culture he would have been the most remarkable man in the Illinois of his day.

Reynolds' plan of campaign was what might have been expected. He urged his friends to emphasize the contrast marked by his service as a ranger while Kinney stayed at home and speculated, until it was discovered that such comparisons called out derogatory comments on his own military services. In the neighborhood of the saline he saw to it that his policy of low saline rents to encourage large production was emphasized. He suggested that Kinney and the Reverend Zadoc Casey, candidate for lieutenant governor, be decried as ministers of the gospel who meddled with politics; he repeated the story that Jackson, solicited by Kinney for an office, told the latter that as a preacher he had an employment higher than any the president could confer and one which should demand his full attention. The tale was made to do duty in spite of Kinney's denial of its truth. In the attacks on Kinney directed by Edwards, Kinney's record on the state bank received important attention; and toward the end of the campaign Edwards insisted that it was necessary to inject the subject of the public lands more forcibly into the contest. Finally, as a last resort to remedy a "strange defection" among the Methodists, Edwards played on their old distrust of Kinney as a slavery advocate.[24]

The contest witnessed a use of the press by both sides to an extent previously unknown in state politics. Of the older papers, the *Illinois Intelligencer* under James Hall's editorship was frankly for Kinney on personal grounds, as Hall was an Adams man of 1828. Hall accordingly drew on himself much

[24] Reynolds to Eddy, July 13, 1830, Reynolds to Grant, June 1, 1830, in Eddy manuscripts; *Illinois Intelligencer*, April 3, 10, 17, 1830; *Illinois Gazette*, March 6, April 17, 1830; Edwards to Cyrus and B. F. Edwards, July 15, 1830, in Edwards manuscripts.

abuse ranging from charges that he was a bankrupt and a defaulter to ridicule of his publication, the *Western Souvenir*.[25]

The *Illinois Gazette* edited by A. F. Grant supported Reynolds; R. K. Fleming, who had edited a Jackson paper in 1828 but had been defeated for election as state printer, was employed under Breese's direction to print a Reynolds paper, the *Western* or *Kaskaskia Democrat*. Hooper Warren who had edited the *Sangamo Spectator* in Edwards' interest at Springfield moved to Galena and on July 20, 1829, began the publication of the *Galena Advertiser*. The *Miner's Journal* already in existence there finally threw its support to Kinney. At Springfield, S. C. Meredith in 1829 set up a Kinney paper directed by McRoberts, which Forquer vainly tried to capture under the noses of the opposition by inducements to Meredith. In the winter of the same year Forquer established the *Courier* there, ostensibly as a Jackson paper.[26]

That an Adams man should edit even secretly in Reynolds' interest a Jackson paper was an illustration of the anarchy, from the view of national politics, implicit in the factional alliance between the friends of Reynolds and Edwards. Old Jackson men in the Reynolds ranks, like S. H. Kimmel, McLean, and even Reynolds himself, had to urge the Adams men in the Edwards group either to refrain from attacks on Jackson or to say openly as little as might be on behalf of Reynolds. The Jackson contingent in the Reynolds party took the position that they were good Jackson men, often older and truer supporters of the Old Hero than were the new converts, and in no wise worthy of being read out of the party because they deprecated the proscription of Adams men in state politics or because they had not, like Kinney, been fortunate enough to gain the president's ear by misrepresentation.[27]

[25] *Illinois Intelligencer*, January 9, 1830; *Galena Advertiser*, July 27, 1829, January 25, March 29, 1830.
[26] *Illinois Intelligencer*, February 6, 20, April 3, September 29, 1830; Fleming to Kane, September 29, 1828, in Kane manuscripts; Washburne, *Edwards Papers*, 467.
[27] Kimmel to Grant, October 29, 1829, McLean to Grant, December 18, 1829, in Eddy manuscripts; Washburne, *Edwards Papers*, 432; *Illinois Gazette*,

The attitude of the two opposing camps is better understood in view of the fact that during 1829 a hot struggle for recognition and support from Washington had gone on between the two factions. Edwards through his brother-in-law, Duff Green, was in touch with the Calhoun party there; and apparently he was inclined for a time to speculate on participating, four years after 1828, in a contest in which Calhoun and Van Buren would be the contestants; but Duff Green warned him that Jackson would almost certainly be a candidate for reëlection. In May Green assured him that Jackson at length understood the state of parties in Illinois and was resolved to sustain Edwards and his friends. With this proof of Jackson's friendship to Edwards it is interesting to compare a letter of Hooper Warren of July 6, asking Edwards whether he wished the *Advertiser* to support Jackson in the new views of proscription and of opposition to the American system that had developed since Warren's last conference with Edwards. In Washington, Kinney with the aid of Kane and Duncan succeeded during the summer in persuading Jackson to recognize them in appointments. For the time Edwards' representative, Duff Green, believed that he had undeceived Jackson; but in November he had to admit that Duncan's influence with Samuel D. Ingham had prevailed against Edwards' candidates. Three months before Ingham had warned S. H. Kimmel that the administration would recognize no Jackson faction that had formed a coalition with Adams men. For the time Kinney appeared to have the indorsement of Washington.[28]

In the background of the Kinney-Reynolds contest were Edwards' perennial ambitions for election to the senate. Green had already pointed out to him that, if he came into the senate on his doctrine of the right of the state to the public lands, it might well be the ground of an alliance of the west

February 16, 1828, December 5, 26, 1829, April 3, 1830; *Illinois Intelligencer,* May 17, October 4, 1828. To impeach Reynolds' Jacksonism, the point was raised that Cook, whom he had supported in 1826, had been beaten because of his Adams vote. *Illinois Intelligencer,* May 22, 1830.

[28] Washburne, *Edwards Papers,* 379, 399, 427, 450; Ingham to Kinney, August 1, 1829, in Eddy manuscripts.

and Calhoun's friends in the south against the east. Toward
the end of the campaign Edwards brought the land issue into
the gubernatorial election. The opposition had already
revived the old story of Edwards' land speculations, and now
they opened up on him in full cry, maintaining that his measure
was designed to advance his own pecuniary interest by frustrating the west's hope of obtaining by moderate demands a
reasonable measure of relief. Kinney pronounced against
state ownership on the ground that the legislation would allow
the public domain to fall into the hands of wealthy speculators.[29]

Forquer was afraid that the intrusion of Edwards' senatorial ambitions into the election would result in Reynolds'
defeat. He impressed upon Edwards his belief that if he
appeared as an open contestant the forces of Kane, Duncan,
and Kinney would coalesce and bring about Reynolds' overthrow and that the opposition was trying to drag Edwards into
the campaign with that end in view. Edwards' friends had
met the charges of a bargain with Reynolds by assertions that
Edwards was not a candidate for the senatorship; but
Edwards, stung by an anonymous attack by Kane, prepared an
address to the people expressing a willingness to enter into a
contest with his antagonist. Forquer advised against its publication, however, until Edwards should have been openly
attacked by J. M. Duncan, lest its premature appearance would
mean defeat for both Reynolds and Edwards.

But the chief political factor in the campaign proved to
be Reynolds' own personality; his election was a triumph for
his policy of cautious campaigning designed to alienate as few
voters as possible. Further, it meant a passing triumph of
the older factional school of politics over the tendency to wage
local elections on national issues. After his election, the
governor prepared for publication in the newspapers an
unsigned leader announcing that his policy would be one of

[29] Washburne, *Edwards Papers,* 379, 427, 494; *Illinois Intelligencer,* June
12, 1830; *Illinois Gazette,* June 12, 1830; Jones to Browne, June 25, 1830, in
Eddy manuscripts.

moderation and not proscription. Reynolds, temporizing successfully with Jacksonism, had gained the full advantage to be derived both from anti-Jackson voters and from factional alliances. The conquest of Illinois politics by the Jackson party was delayed, but it was inevitable.

VII.   STATE POLITICS, 1830–1834

THE course of Illinois politics between the years 1818 and 1836 may stand as a warning to the superficial historian of the danger which attends an attempt to describe and classify political parties at different periods by the same terms or under the same categories. Not only is there danger of falling into the comparatively obvious error of using at too early a stage the terms whig and democrat but also the danger, less apparent, of attempting to explain state politics exclusively in terms of national issues and leaders.   The cautious student must recognize the fact that state factions differed from period to period, not only in alignment and personnel but in degrees of unity and cohesiveness.   Thus till 1826 it is easiest to explain Illinois politics in terms of two local factions.   By 1830 it becomes difficult to use this classification and after 1830 it is impossible.   For three or four years after that date it is necessary to describe politics in terms of individual cliques and followings, which at first used Jackson's name and then his measures as issues with which to embarrass their opponents. Only by degrees did the outlines of what are truly national parties emerge from the confusion.

The decay of the factional system in Illinois politics is illustrated in a series of letters from George Forquer in 1830 which when analyzed are an illuminating commentary on the political conditions of the time.   To Forquer the successful management of a campaign meant the bringing to bear in favor of his candidate all influences and groups in any way obligated to him and the keeping neutral of as many other groups and influences as possible.   "We must make Wilson and Lockwood and their friends fight with us. They shall not be indifferent any longer, and hold themselves like Pope, ready to dine with our enemies whilst our slain carcasses are yet bleeding. Embroil every man of them in the contest. . . . Could you write without attacking Kane, would it not be better? If you can whip his forces by killing off his generals, is it not the safest way to whip him too? Fix it so as to force him to attack as Duncan has done. They intend to have him in the scales. Give him no excuse to say he has been *dragged* into it. *They will drag him in.*"[1] In urging Edwards against openly challenging Kane to a contest for the senate, he wrote "Every man here when pushed for his real sentiments believes that Kinney is quite enough for us at one time. All agree that Kane and him at once against you and Reynolds and we are gone."[2]

The conditions in the Edwards faction made apparent by these letters were significant of the change that was taking place in it. The minor cliques of the older party, surrounding Samuel D. Lockwood, Thomas Mather, and William Wilson, secure in the spoils of past contests were slow to risk themselves in battle at the call of their old leader. T. W. Smith and Breese soon drifted away into independence. Outside the old Edwards ranks, Kane, Kinney, the Duncans, and Reynolds had each his little following, or rather a circle on which he was able to exert influence. The practical politicians counted on combinations of these cliques and influences rather than on the shadows of the two old factions. The times were ripe for the intrusion into politics of new rallying cries of wider appeal than personal popularity and for the creation of new parties. These came to pass through the introduction of national issues into state politics and of resulting national party divisions.

The disintegration of both factions is strikingly illustrated in the senatorial election of 1830. Kane and Kinney probably maintained something more than a benevolent neutrality toward each other on the governorship and senatorship. The death of McLean, however, left both senatorships vacant and caused Wilson, T. W. Smith, R. M. Young, and others to enter the field each with his personal following. Reynolds was

[1] Washburne, *Edwards Papers*, 519-520.   [2] *Ibid.*, 516-517.

thought to favor a coalition between Wilson and Young. William L. May, a member of the Springfield clique, suggested a coalition between Kane and Smith. The final result was the choice of Kane and John M. Robinson, a man from eastern Illinois of whom little is known at this time except that he was probably opposed to Kane. But while William C. Greenup gleefully announced to Kane that the Edwards forces were disintegrating so fast that both Edwards and Reynolds had offered to sign a recommendation for Kinney to be governor of Huron territory, Kane was apparently meditating a realignment. D. J. Baker believed that he had made tentative advances through him to Edwards. In January, 1831, Kane offered to support Edwards for congress in preference to Duncan. Duff Green through whom the offer was made believed that Edwards might in this way attain the leadership of the Illinois delegation.[3]

The secret of Kane's vacillation is perhaps to be found in the situation in national politics. As it reacted on the state it appeared primarily as a sheaf of personal rivalries. The Jackson party was split up into cliques. The power of Calhoun and of his mouthpiece, Duff Green of the *Telegraph* — still the official newspaper of the party — was waning. Calhoun was not the only aspirant for the power of Jackson when the Old Hero should be ready to relinquish it. Those who had formerly supported Crawford were now wavering between their allegiance to their former leader or to Van Buren. Kane's position was still uncertain, and even in 1831 Duff Green believed that Edwards might influence the whole Illinois delegation for Calhoun.[4]

[3] Rountree to Kane, February 15, 1830, Prentice to Kane, January 31, 1830, James M. Duncan to Kane, February 25, 1830, McRoberts to Kane, March 12, 1830, Greenup to Kane, November 3, 1830, May to Kane, October 21, 1830, D. Turney to Kane, October 15, 1830, in Kane manuscripts; Eddy to Grant, December 9-10, 1830, Breese to Browne, September 14, 1830, in Eddy manuscripts; Washburne, *Edwards Papers*, 557, 569.
[4] Edwards' information came partly through Duff Green, who believed Jackson would not run. Washburne, *Edwards Papers*, 488-489. Green wrote that he believed Kane, as soon as he thought it safe, would turn on him in Van Buren's interest. *Ibid.*, 552-554, 570.

Edwards was anxiously scanning the situation in Illinois which had become for a man of his type extremely difficult. His position was hard to maintain. For his strength he still had to rely in a measure on Adams and Clay men. Yet to oppose the cause of Jackson openly in a state wide canvass was to insure defeat. Edwards, still loyal to Calhoun, privately assured Jackson of his good will and desire for his reëlection, protesting bitterly, however, against the deciding voice that Kane and Kinney had in Illinois appointments. He assured Jackson that they were old Crawford men, that they were distributing offices among totally unworthy men of the same clique and were proscribing the original Jackson men. He even tried to inspire Jackson with the fear that they were plotting the union of diverse elements on Crawford against him, should he stand for a reëlection.

In 1831 at the last state wide election for a member of congress, Edwards had refused to run; and Duncan had won easily over Field and Breese, the one an avowed Jackson man and an opponent of Edwards' land policy, the other a supporter of that policy, constructively a Jacksonian if his land-bill past were forgotten, but otherwise with a whiggish tendency.

Edwards was near the end of his career. In 1832 with the state divided into congressional districts he entered the race in the first district at a late hour. Charles Dunn and Breese, the latter not without a trace of bad faith, were already in it along with Charles Slade. Edwards' belated entrance prevented him from stumping the district. Mather deserted his old leader, and the Adams and Clay men abandoned him because he was supporting Jackson. With a divided vote, Edwards was defeated by Slade.

As a matter of fact the opposition to Van Buren, disappointed in Calhoun, took up Richard M. Johnson for the vice presidency. As a western man, he was a candidate who could be favorably contrasted with Van Buren; and his candidacy could be made to take the form of a popular protest against the political management for which Van Buren had become notorious, especially as it was exemplified in the Baltimore convention, which it was claimed was a device to force on the country the candidate of a clique. The issue was sharply joined at a Jackson meeting held at Vandalia, January 2 and 3, 1832. McRoberts and Ewing after a vain attempt to adjourn the meeting *sine die* withdrew with their followers; and Field, John Dement, and Duncan remained to direct the Johnson men. An address was drawn up indorsing Johnson and protesting against appointing uninstructed delegates to Baltimore. Reynolds and Edwards lent the movement their support. On March 26, in spite of the protests of the *Illinois Advocate* that a Johnson indorsement would result in throwing the vote of the state to Clay, a Johnson convention met at Vandalia to appoint electors pledged to Jackson and Johnson. The personnel of the convention is most interesting. Some of the men in it, as James W. Stephenson, J. S. Hacker, and Dr. Early, emerged sound democrats. Others ended as whigs.[5]

The movement as might have been expected was unsuccessful. The nomination of Van Buren at Baltimore compelled a reasonable party regularity. Of the Johnson electors, three refused to serve, but before the election an attempt to reinstate the ticket was made. From the first the victory of Jackson and Van Buren in Illinois was assured. Even the whigs, while believing Illinois ready for a movement against Jackson and Van Buren, felt that Clay's land bill was too heavy a load for him to carry in Illinois and professed it wiser to support Wirt or McLean, whom it was thought Edwards would support.

With 1832 a new element of complexity appeared in the Illinois political situation which finally in connection with the older factional alignments and the personal issues of 1829–1832 caused the redistribution of partisans into whigs and democrats. Until that year, as nearly as one can judge, if a

[5] *Illinois Intelligencer,* January 21, 1832. John M. Robinson was for Johnson, Robinson to Grant, February 9, 1832, in Eddy manuscripts; Washburne, *Edwards Papers,* 579-580.

candidate was personally loyal to Jackson the voters were inclined to permit him considerable freedom of belief on what they considered the minor issues. Tests of party faith other than adherence to Jackson had not yet been devised. Thus in 1831 Duncan could avow his freedom from partisanship on political measures and still be supported by Jackson men.[6] But with 1832 and the years following, the demand that not only Jackson's name but also Jackson's measures be adopted caused a realignment among the factions.

Till 1832 national issues in general did not take a strong hold on the people or influence seriously the alignment of factions. With the Jacksonian policy of the removal of the Indians from the neighborhood of the settlements the west was heartily in sympathy, but no one was inclined to court defeat by opposing it. Edwards' public land policy was, of course, a prominent issue in 1830, 1831, and 1832; but it was hardly so expressed as to come into collision with any nationally proposed measure. When Clay prepared his distribution measure in 1832 even his friends were inclined to regard it as indefensible in Illinois.

On the tariff and internal improvements issues, the Clay-Adams men, if Breese is any criterion, were inclined to push the fighting. Breese came out boldly for protection and internal improvements and endeavored to force that issue against his rival, Coles. The year before he had suggested to Judge Thomas C. Browne that the *Gazette* publish an attack on Kane for his support of the president's internal improvements veto and possibly as a result had drawn from Kane a letter hedging on both the tariff and internal improvements, but indicating his opposition to a recharter. The newspapers occasionally raised the tariff question. These issues, however, till 1832 seemed not only to create little division among the factions but also to have aroused little interest among the people.[7]

[6] *Illinois Intelligencer,* July 16, 1831.
[7] *Ibid.,* December 4, 1830, May 21, September 16, 1831; Breese to Grant, June 22, 1831, and Breese to Browne, September 14, 1830, in Eddy manuscripts.

The election of 1832 saw a sharply drawn party division at least so far as the Clay element was concerned. Specifically they assailed Jackson for his policy against internal improvements and a protective tariff and for the danger to the country and especially to the currency of Illinois involved in his refusal to recharter the Bank of the United States. Indeed they apparently thought their best chance was to divide the Jackson men by supporting candidates favorable to their doctrinal position. The Jackson forces were none too well united on points of doctrine. The republican Jackson meeting at Vandalia, December 14, 1831, took no definite stand on the tariff question but laid the emphasis on Jackson's opposition to the "aristocratic doctrine" of vested interest in office, and his distinctly western attitude as friend to the settler and advocate of Indian removals.[8]

The issues steadily increased in national importance in the years following 1832. On the question of nullification Illinois had no doubts whatever. The senate spread Jackson's proclamation against the nullifiers on its journals and ordered 3,000 copies of it printed. Both houses joined in a resolution against the nullifiers. The removal of the bank deposits seemed at the outset to arouse no excitement in Illinois. The *Sangamo Journal* indeed avowed its belief that the people of southern Illinois gave themselves little concern about it and would not approve the call of a special session to charter a bank. It avowed also that the destruction of the bank had been the issue in 1832 and that Jackson was acting under a mandate from the people, however ill-considered a one it might be. Not till the spring of 1834 did the calling of meetings to approve or to protest begin.[9]

8 *Sangamo Journal*, December 8, 15, 22, 1831, January 5, August 2, September 22, October 27, 1832; for meeting at Vandalia see *Illinois Intelligencer*, February 18, 1832, and see also December 24, 1831. The *Vandalia Whig and Illinois Intelligencer* in its prospectus advocated Jackson's reëlection but pronounced for the whig measures. *Illinois Intelligencer*, March 3, 1832.

9 The only votes against the first resolution were cast by Davidson, Forquer, Mather, and Snyder; against the second were William B. Archer and Davidson. *Senate Journal*, 1832-1833, 1 session, 70; *Sangamo Journal*, October 26, November 2, 9, 1833. See protest of Gallatin in *Vandalia Whig*, April 3, 1834,

The two new elements described above, the personal rivalries between Jackson's would-be successors and the growing importance of national issues based on his measures, completed the breakdown of the older system of politics predicated on personal loyalty to Jackson and the older factional system. The flux was not fully completed for some years; not till 1836 can the rearrangements be regarded as the secessions of individuals and groups from one party to the other rather than as changes in the alignment of factions.

The best known change, that of Joseph Duncan, came with a certain dramatic quality and may be stated in detail both as typifying the forces at work and as being the pivot on which numerous other changes occurred. Duncan was certainly consulted by Kinney and Kane about the appointments by which they raised to power in Illinois their friends of the Crawford following. He had relied for his influence on his close accord with Secretary Samuel D. Ingham, a Calhoun man who fell in the cabinet reorganization. In 1830 the Kane followers suspected Duncan's loyalty to their chief in the senatorial contest, and Kane early in 1831 proposed to throw Duncan over and support Edwards. It is doubtful if the breach between them was ever closed. Personal ties doubtless were drawing Duncan away from his earlier alliance. Further he had maintained a policy of independence toward Jackson's measures for which in 1831 he had been criticized at home. He voted to pass the Mayville turnpike bill over Jackson's veto. Jackson's veto of the Wabash internal improvement measure doubtless irritated him more than his temperately worded letters indicate. Repeatedly in the session of 1833–1834 he voted against administration measures.[10]

Very possibly by 1833 he realized that he could no longer hope for national patronage and accordingly prepared to relinquish his seat in congress to seek a position of importance in state politics. Everything impelled him toward a change

and approval of Hillsboro and Danville in *ibid.,* February 27, June 12, April 13, 1834.

[10] *Congressional Debates,* 1833-1834, p. 2182, 2207, 2375, 2627, 2739.

of camps, and by 1833 the opposition to the administration in Illinois was prepared to accord him enthusiastic support. His candidacy for governor was announced early in 1833 by the *Vandalia Whig*, and the whig papers began a policy of keeping him before the public. "By keeping him constantly before them as an old public servant, against whom nothing is as yet alleged, and confirming by an occasional commendation in the newspapers the favorable standing he now occupies, they will be prepared for a formal annunciation when his friends think the proper time has come for it."[11] The Jackson-Van Buren party promptly prepared for war. They sent an agent into the state, if Duncan is to be believed, under pretext of examining land offices to stir up opposition to him. The *Advocate* at once declared war on him, and indicated the council of revision as the source of his candidacy. The council was at that time made up of Reynolds, Wilson, Lockwood, and T. W. Smith, most of them till recently Edwards' partisans.[12] The Jackson-Van Buren party began to canvass the list of available men to oppose him. First Berry was suggested, then Ewing; finally, November 27, the name of R. K. McLaughlin, Duncan's uncle, was proposed by a Coles county convention. A month later a Belleville meeting brought out Kinney — and on him the support of the Jacksonian or Van Buren party finally centered.[13]

Duncan by no means received the undivided support of the whig papers. For some reason the *Sangamo Journal* opposed his candidacy with asperity. It was accused by the *Shawnee-town Journal* of having been bought up by Slade and Kane with the federal printing to support Van Buren and oppose Duncan.[14] The *Sangamo Journal* had previously denounced

[11] Grant to Dement, June 26, 1833, in Eddy manuscripts; *Sangamo Journal*, February 9, 1833; *Illinois Advocate*, February 2, 1833.

[12] In February it was supposed that A. P. Field was grooming Richard M. Young for the race. Grant to Reynolds, February 6, 1834 and Reynolds to Grant, February 10, 1834, in Eddy manuscripts.

[13] The *Sangamo Journal*, March 30, 1833, denied Ewing's candidacy, and in the January 25, 1834 issue, expressed the opinion that Duncan would not run against his uncle. See also *Illinois Advocate*, December 7, 1833.

[14] *Shawneetown Journal* clipping in *Vandalia Whig*, April 3, 1834. The *Alton American* was inclined to believe the charge, see issue of April 14, 1834.

the *Banner* and the *Patriot* of Jacksonville for having permitted themselves to be influenced to suppress charges against Duncan's financial integrity. It charged the existence of a Jacksonville regency headed by Duncan which sheltered itself under Jackson's name though it was opposed to his principles. It countered the charges of the *Vandalia Whig* by the insinuation that Duncan had bought it to his support with a promise of the state printing, and by slurs on its opposition to Jackson. Certainly its opposition could not have taken a form more embarrassing to Duncan.[15]

In the spring of 1834 the *Sangamo Journal* gave enthusiastic support to the candidacy of General James D. Henry, the Illinois hero of the Black Hawk War. It is difficult to estimate exactly what was behind this movement. Henry was extolled as a man independent of party and as a mechanic; he was nominated by a series of county meetings, but the hopes of his supporters were destroyed by his sickness and death in the spring of 1834. Thereafter the *Sangamo Journal* inclined to the support of R. K. McLaughlin.

Of the four candidates McLaughlin offered his record as state treasurer and his former unflinching opposition to the state bank. James Adams' position in the campaign is not so clear; he was perennially a candidate and always an unsuccessful one. In spite of his later democratic affiliations the *Chicago Democrat* affected to believe that General Adams would be elected by the votes of the old Adams men, the stalwart Jackson votes being split between Kinney and McLaughlin and the "milk and cider" votes going to Duncan. Kinney based his hopes of office on his personality, his friends alleging that his errors were of the head and not of the heart. He was sentimentally pictured as a farmer and as a democrat in personal habits. The attacks he found it necessary to meet were mostly on his opposition to the canal and on his connection with the state bank. To the first charge the answer of his followers was a straight denial; to the second the claim that the Edwards-

[15] *Sangamo Journal,* February 1, April 19, 1834.

ville branch of the state bank with which he had been connected had really given relief to the public and had lost the state nothing. For the rest he relied on his undoubted allegiance to Jacksonism.[16]

Duncan of course had to stand or fall by his congressional record, so far as the voters understood it. The *Chicago Democrat* and the *Illinois Advocate*, assailing him as a deserter from Jacksonism, singled out his proposal for a bank and his other anti-administration votes. The *Alton Spectator* answered that he had stood firmly for his principles from the beginning on both internal improvements and the bank — it was Jackson who had departed from his. At a later time Duncan claimed that he had never, since 1830, used Jackson's name to carry his elections, being convinced that Jackson, his mind weakened by grief at the death of his wife, had been persuaded to drop his own principles and adopt Van Buren's.[17] Considering the political conditions in 1834 it is hard to see how any but the ignorant could have failed to see that Duncan was no longer in harmony with the federal administration. Possibly the lack of a specific renunciation of Jacksonism caused it to be taken for granted that he still made formal profession of faith. In 1834 that was still considered sufficient.

After the election, however, in spite of a few attempts by Jackson papers to regard his election as a Jackson success, there could be no doubt of his position. The *Sangamo Journal* judging him on his congressional record pronounced him an opposition man; an anti-administration toast proposed by him at a dinner after his election should have left no doubt of it; and the Jackson papers generally took the fact of his apostasy for granted.[18]

[16] *Alton American*, April 14, June 2, 1834; *Chicago Democrat*, July 23, 1834; *Illinois Advocate*, April 19, 1834; *Alton Spectator*, February 11, April 17, 1834. The *Alton Spectator* pointed out that both Kinney and Van Buren were hostile to the canal, June 5, 1834.
[17] *Chicago Democrat*, March 4, May 21, July 2, 23, 1834; *Alton Spectator*, July 1, 1834; letter in the *Sangamo Journal*, February 4, 1837.
[18] *Chicago Democrat*, August 27, September 17, November 12, 1834; *Sangamo Journal*, August 30, October 4, 18, December 6, 1834.

The story is told on doubtful authority that as Duncan was proceeding to Illinois to take his place as governor, he met Reynolds, then newly elected to congress; and after commenting on their exchange of offices, he was told by Reynolds that they were likewise changing political alignment, Duncan going over to the whig opposition while he himself had elected to stay by Old Hickory. Whether authentic or not the story shows an acute grasp of the political situation of the day. Duncan was passing through the zone of doubt in the direction of the opposition while Reynolds was traversing it in the opposite direction to a place in the Jackson-Van Buren ranks.

In 1834 in neither the congressional race of the third district between William L. May and Benjamin Mills nor in that of the second between Casey and William H. Davidson was the anti-Jackson line sharply drawn. Mills was in favor of R. M. Johnson for the succession as against May who advocated leaving the choice to a convention; but both made profession of faith in Jackson and both were supposed to be at the same time in favor of a bank. Similarly in the second district, Davidson while opposing the removal of the deposits from the bank and favoring its recharter was occasionally at least represented as pro-Jackson.[19] But in the first district Reynolds, while running as avowedly a Jackson man, courted the aid of the same knot of opposition men who were supporting Duncan for the governorship.

Reynolds claimed the support of A. F. Grant and Eddy at Shawneetown. A newspaper edited by R. W. Clarke was established there to support both Reynolds and Duncan. Friends of both men supported the enterprise by their subscriptions. The race began as a three-cornered one between Slade, Reynolds, and Adam W. Snyder, a partisan of Kinney. Slade had voted both for a recharter and against a restoration of deposits, votes which he had been able to reconcile to his own

[19] *Chicago Democrat,* May 7, 1834; *Alton American,* January 30, 1834; *Sangamo Journal,* February 8, June 7, 1834.

satisfaction by a process of casuistry but for which he was held
up to derision as a wobbler. In the election, however, he was
set down by his opponents as opposed to a bank. The death
of Slade left the decision between Reynolds and Snyder. Both
men, of course, were avowed Jackson men, but Snyder was in
favor of a United States Bank. His candidacy was under
especial patronage of the *St. Clair Gazette*. Reynolds proposed a bizarre scheme for a new bank and also a temporary
recharter of the old bank.[20] His expressed ideal was a modified United States Bank, " so that all parties will be satisfied."[21]
Reynolds was elected. As the death of Slade and the resignation of Duncan made necessary special elections to fill out their
unexpired terms, Reynolds and May each in his district offered
themselves for these also on the ground that the additional
terms would give them needed experience and acquaintance.
Reynolds delayed his announcement until he was sure that men
to whom he was under obligation did not offer themselves and
then pulled the wires necessary to make audible the voice of
public opinion soliciting him to become a candidate. Pierre
Menard became a candidate for the unexpired term in
Reynolds' district, and Pope appealed for support for him on
the ground of his benevolence and also because in spite of his
national republican affiliations his name had never been involved in the Jackson and anti-Jackson war.[22] Reynolds protested that the only result of Menard's entrance would be that
a Kinney partisan would beat him. He accused Pope of
already having gone over to Kinney. This was true in so far,
at least, that Pope had declined supporting him and had taken
up Snyder on the ground that Reynolds was "playing for all
the pockets," an art which indeed was the alpha and omega of
the politics of " John of Cahokia." Again he asked the help
of his Shawneetown friends, but not long after his election

[20] *Alton Spectator,* April 24, May 25, July 15, 1834; *Shawneetown Journal*
clipping in *Vandalia Whig,* April 24, 1834; Eddy to Clarke, April 26, 1834, in
Eddy manuscripts.
[21] Reynolds to Eddy, February 17, 1834, in Eddy manuscripts.
[22] " It is hoped that his name is a Talisman to neutralise the senseless noise
about Jackson-ism." Pope to Eddy, August 7, 1834, in Eddy manuscripts.

perceived the truth of Pope's warning that Reynolds was now "Ultra-Jackson and Anti-Bank."[23]

The process of political disintegration in Illinois had reached its height. Personal jealousies and factional rivalries, personal adherences to Jackson, Van Buren, Johnson, and differences over administration measures had thrown politics into confusion. The changes that had in four years taken place in the "Springfield clique" on account of the dominant Jacksonian powers in the state can be traced and are doubtless significant of what was passing elsewhere. In 1830 Forquer found that there was opposed to the Edwards faction in Sangamon county a knot of men probably headed by May, including A. G. Herndon, E. D. Taylor, and James Adams. About 1832, probably disgusted with the failure of the Edwards faction to follow their leader, Forquer accepted the support of the clique for the state senate. Two years later he succeeded May as register at Springfield when the latter resigned that office, to which he had been appointed through Kane's influence, to enter congress. It was later charged by the whigs that this was all a deliberate bargain, by which Forquer had sold himself; and it was also said that Peter Cartwright had made a bargain to support Duncan, the report alleging that John Calhoun, said to be another old opposition man, had bought him up by the promise of a surveyor generalship. In 1837–1838 the clique, headed as it was supposed by Forquer, read May out of the party altogether. Herndon, in 1835, disappointed of an office, was said to have joined the opposition.[24] Out of such personal rivalries and alliances cemented by national issues and national party allegiances was to arise a new political organization in Illinois based on broad and fundamental differences.

[23] Pope to Eddy, September 23, 1834, in Eddy manuscripts.
[24] *Sangamo Journal,* May 2, 1835, February 6, 13, June 18, July 16, 30, 1836; *Chicago Democrat,* August 12, 1835. Apparently a letter from May to Duncan existed as proof of the charge that Cartwright had made a bargain to support Duncan.

VIII. THE LAST OF THE INDIANS

ILLINOIS in 1830 presented that sharp dualism of development common to frontier societies. A small group of talented lawyers and jurists questing fortune in the west had brought with them the intellectual outlook of eastern cities; the towns of Illinois buzzed with political life. Affairs of state and nation, however, came only as whispers from afar off to the pioneer who, pushing out farther and farther from the tiny urban centers of the state, must single-handed win a home from forest wilds. He had, by this time, satisfied his most primitive wants. The replacement of the coonskin cap and leather breeches by store hat and homespun suit indicated the degree to which all material comforts had advanced; cabins were more substantial, clearings a little more extensive, settlements larger and closer together. Opportunities for mental and social development were still excessively meager. This poverty the pioneer felt keenly, if inarticulately; but at best he could enrich his life very slightly. A political campaign — with its sharp personal interests, its clashes, its victories, its eager seeking and jovial solicitation of the voter — formed a spot of vivid color in the drab months of the year. For the rest, the annual wolf-hunt, the house raising, the revival meeting must afford stimulus and diversion. Any news, any excitement, was welcomed. A wedding was an event seized upon and celebrated by the countryside for twenty-four hours; the report of a murder, the trial of a criminal was sufficient to draw an avid audience fifty miles.[1] Events like these broke, for a little, the isolation of the frontiersman's clearing — the clearing that was but a hole he himself had painfully cut out of the malaria infested forest.

[1] Nicolay and Hay, *Abraham Lincoln*, 1:39-41.

It was the forest, moreover, that concealed somewhere in its depths Indians — the great menace of the pioneer. To be sure, this menace was connected only remotely in his mind with the particular redskin who came begging at his door, whom he chased out of his cornfields or pursued after a raid on his hog pen; the latter was a creature to be dealt with good-naturedly, summarily, or sternly. One could usually drive a good bargain with him where peltries and a little whisky were concerned. When "Injuns" was whispered, however, its black magic called up not the image of these improvident, good-natured creatures, but that of a mounted gang of demons, who with wild whoops rode down upon a cabin "to imbrue their hands in the blood of innocent women and children."

This fear had not for many years been fed by direct experience. As settlements had thickened in the land, contact with the whites had broken down the independence of savagery and had robbed the Indian of the virility that had once made him a foe to be dreaded. Except on the outer fringes of settlement, knowledge of the Indian was identical with the legacy of horror tales treasured in each family. Combined with this fear, however, was hate, engendered by the War of 1812, that many settlers had brought with them when they emigrated to Illinois at the close of that conflict. Young, enterprising men, who in the campaigns of the preceding years had felt the lure of the untouched solitudes along the Mississippi, came pouring west to find a home on land that they felt should now be torn from the hostile Indian. It was this great increase in race hostility that brought about a new interpretation of Indian removal.[2] In response to it, Illinois extinguished Indian land

[2] Abel, "History of Indian Consolidation West of the Mississippi," in *Annual Report of the American Historical Association*, 1906, 1:233-412. Indian removal, when reduced to its simplest terms, was the exchange of tribal holdings within a state for unoccupied federal land in the far west. Originated by President Jefferson, the policy had had a vacillating and uncertain career under succeeding administrations. Indian removal was at times a method of lenient dealing, at times a means of harsh treatment of the aborigines. Gradually it became identified with democratic measures, as involving the doctrine of states rights, with an economic appeal to south and west alike. Jackson, with a westerner's hate of the Indian, had influenced Indian affairs since Monroe's administration; his own inauguration left no doubt of the future meaning of

titles with astonishing rapidity; small nomadic tribes made it easy for a man with the zeal of Ninian Edwards to render vast tracts clear of Indians far in advance of white population. To the pioneer, as well as to the politician and land speculator, Jackson's federal policy of removal of the Indians to some trans-Mississippi territory was a confirmation of their own conviction that the land belonged to the white man; they welcomed the means it supplied of ridding the country of the redskin.

Except for the episode of the so-called Winnebago War in 1827 which lasted only long enough to send panic through the frontier, most Illinoisans of the thirties had had no opportunity to express the peculiar complex of emotions that made up their feeling toward the aborigines. The Indians were far to the north and west of the settlements; for, although the population had by 1830 grown to over 157,000, it was confined to the south and central portions of the state along the wooded rivers and streams. The prairie country was still almost superstitiously avoided, and it was only the discovery of lead at Galena which caused a sudden spurt of immigration to cross the transverse barrier of the Illinois river. The whole of the north country was a trackless wilderness except to the fur trader and Indian; even to them much of it was unknown.

Practically all this land north of the Illinois had been ceded by the Sauk and Foxes to the federal government in 1804. In November of this year five of their chiefs and headmen had gone to St. Louis to endeavor to secure the release of a tribesman held there for the murder of a white man. It is possible that in the council preceding their departure, some instruction was given as to the sale of land. The Sauk and Foxes, small tribes, held much more land than they used, and they were envious of those tribes near them who were enjoying annuities from the government.[3] It is, however,

Indian removal. With the passage of the "force bill" in May, 1830, he committed the government to *forcible* removal of the Indian to the west.
[3] Drake, *Life and Adventures of Black Hawk*, 60.

a matter of conjecture only, as to whether the tribe had instructed a sale of some sort; but it is certain that the United States government has usually misapprehended the nature of the power exercised by the Indian headmen. They represented in no sense a centralized or autocratic power; what obedience they secured in civil matters was obtained through tact and persuasion, and the proved wisdom of their advice. Individual liberty was paramount in the Indians' scheme of things; coercion was unknown among them. A majority never bound the minority, however small, to regard its decision. In an evolved Indian government even Jeffersonian democracy would have been felt an irksome restraint. When this fundamental attitude of the Indian is borne in mind the difficulty of making and keeping any treaty is evident. In this instance the treaty was negotiated by William Henry Harrison who became popular with westerners for his success in securing land cessions; it was his custom to deal with factions and isolated bands by methods somewhat unscrupulous, though the practice was an invariable trouble breeder.[4] In this transaction he treated with five chiefs, away from home, on a mission which was, at least primarily, for a different purpose; while these headmen were befuddled by fire water, he concluded a treaty which, in return for an annuity of one thousand dollars, stripped the Sauk and Foxes of fifty million acres of land. This land, though overlapping into Wisconsin and Missouri, formed in Illinois the great triangular wedge between the Mississippi and Illinois river systems. By the terms of the treaty, however, the Sauk and Foxes were allowed to live and hunt upon the land so long as it was the property of the federal government.[5]

[4]Abel, "History of Indian Consolidation West of the Mississippi," in *Annual Report of the American Historical Association*, 1906, 1:267. Jefferson strongly disapproved of such methods and in May, 1805, he ordered Harrison to make explanations to certain threatening chiefs and to "counteract the effect of his own questionable methods."
[5]Thomas Forsythe, agent for the Sauk and Foxes, and for this reason knowing them better than any other white man, in 1832 wrote of this episode: "The Sauk and Fox nations were never consulted, nor had any hand in this treaty, nor knew anything about it. It was made and signed by two Sauk chiefs, one Fox chief and one warrior.

In 1816, 1822, and 1825 the Sauk of the Rock river country, without making any specific reference to its substance, unconditionally assented to and confirmed the treaty of 1804.[6] Black Hawk, a war chief who fought with the British in the War of 1812, acknowledged the land cession when he finally signed a treaty of peace in 1816, athough he later claimed that he was ignorant of its conditions.[7] The great village which had for a hundred years been the principal seat and burying ground of the Sauk was on the north side of Rock river near Rock Island, with that of the Foxes three miles away on the Mississippi.[8] Here they lived during the spring and summer months, while the women cultivated the great fertile cornfields, lying parallel with the Mississippi. The crops from these fields never failed; year after year they supplied the Indians bountifully with corn, beans, pumpkins, and squashes. The island across from them was a garden filled with strawberries, blackberries, plums, apples, and nuts; and the river abounded in fine fish. The uncultivated land about the villages afforded rich pasturage

"When the annuities were delivered to the Sauk and Fox nations of Indians, according to the treaty above referred to (amounting to $1000 per annum), the Indians always thought they were presents (as the annuity for the first twenty years was always paid in goods . . .), until I, as their Agent, convinced them of the contrary, in the summer of 1818. When the Indians heard that the goods delivered to them were annuities for land sold by them to the United States, they were astonished, and refused to accept of the goods, denying that they ever sold the lands as stated by me, their Agent. The Black Hawk in particular, who was present at the time, made a great noise about this land, and would never receive any part of the annuities from that time forward. He always denied the authority of Quash-quame and others to sell any part of their lands, and told the Indians not to receive any presents or annuities from any American — otherwise their lands would be claimed at some future day." Printed as appendix to Mrs. J. H. Kinzie, *Wau-Bun*, 383; Royce, *Indian Land Cessions in the United States*, 666 and map 16.

[6] *Ibid.*, 680.

[7] He says of the transaction, "Here, for the first time, I touched the goose quill to the treaty — not knowing, however, that by that act, I consented to give away my village. Had that been explained to me, I should have opposed it, and never would have signed their treaty.

"What do we know of the manner of the laws and customs of the white people? They might buy our bodies for dissection, and we would touch the goose quill to confirm it, without knowing what we are doing. This was the case with myself and people in touching the goose quill the first time." Black Hawk, *Autobiography*, 69.

[8] The Sauk had about eight hundred acres under cultivation.

for their horses, while hunting grounds and lead mines lay not far away.

Miners on their way to Galena observed this chosen spot, and about 1823, although the far fringe of settlements was still fifty miles away, squatters appeared to give the Indians their first experience of the white man as a neighbor. Apparently at the mercy of the red men, these daring forerunners were quite untouched by fear; in violation of both federal law and the provisions of the treaty of 1804, they at once began to take possession of the Indian cornfields. Of all the vast domain ceded to the whites, this particular region was the only part actually used by the Indians; but the newcomers, feeling that the land by right belonged to the white man, and relying on the support of both public and official opinion, worried themselves not at all over fine discriminations. They wanted the fields. They took them.

The Sauk and Foxes, though a spirited people, had killed no white man since the treaty of 1816; their meekness under the treatment of these whites is surprising. Each year the squatters encroached further upon their fields, continually fencing in greater portions. Indian women and children were severely whipped for venturing beyond the limits thus set, and boys and men were summarily chastised when the temper of the newcomers was aroused.[9]

The proximity of the whites quickly had its effect on the social organization of the red men. "Many of our people, instead of going to their old hunting grounds, where game was plenty, would go near to the settlements to hunt — and, instead of saving their skins to pay the trader for goods furnished them in the fall, would sell them to the settlers for whiskey! and return in the spring with their families, almost naked. . . ."[10] Each year only increased this unhappy condition. The most important Sauk chief, Keokuk, an able, eloquent, and

[9] Black Hawk was himself severely beaten on the suspicion of hog-stealing, an affront to his dignity that he never forgave. Black Hawk, *Autobiography*, 83-84.
[10] *Ibid.*, 81.

sagacious man, felt the futility of protesting at the advance of the whites. He decided, upon the advice of the Indian agent at Rock Island, that his people had better remove to their lands across the Mississippi, and all his influence was used to bring about the migration.

Black Hawk, a fighter from his youth, now an old war chief over sixty years of age, was by nature an active protestant. Having had but slight contact with the Americans, and that, unfortunately, of an untoward nature, he was quite frankly no friend of theirs. The British, however, had long ago secured and thereafter retained his friendship. He and his band made frequent trips to Canadian Malden, an unfailing source of presents and flattering words. This old man, his resentment easily roused and slowly quieted, disdained the counsel of Keokuk. His reaction in this matter may have been influenced by the fact that his own power waxed only in days of war; he was clearly jealous of Keokuk and the latter's sway over the people, and Keokuk's talk of removing roused the old warrior's contempt for his supineness. The faction opposing Keokuk's plan found a ready champion in Black Hawk, who at one stroke thus divided Keokuk's power and increased his own, and in addition opened a possibility of the Indians' standing their ground against the arrogant white neighbors to the end of retaining the beloved homeland. The struggle between the chiefs lasted two seasons; when Keokuk's eloquence finally persuaded the majority of the tribe to cross the river, Black Hawk and his band remained staunchly at their village.

In spite of his warlike nature, up to this time the old chief had in advice and action shown a paradoxical meekness and forbearance in dealing with the white intruders. For a long time he was concerned only with being allowed peaceably to remain in his village. These settlers, however, were bringing a biting realization of the full meaning of federal claims, and with the sharp goad of mistreatment he had become convinced that the treaty to which the whites so constantly referred was a fraud. Even to Black Hawk's simple standard, the thousand dollars annuity was too greatly disproportionate to the land involved. The only living signer of the treaty had always vigorously denied that he had ever so much as considered the sale of land north of Rock river, much less consented to it in a signed treaty. When Black Hawk told his story to the British agent at Malden, and later to General Cass, they affirmed that if it was true the whites could not remove him; and Black Hawk determined now to employ different tactics with the intruders. Almost simultaneously with his decision, however, the squatters, who for seven years had with increasing self-assurance been encroaching more and more daringly upon his homeland, took out preëmption rights over a few quarter sections of land which included most of the village, the graves, and the cornlands that time out of mind had belonged to the Sauks; the force of the provision in the treaty of 1804 that guaranteed the right of the Indians to live and hunt upon the land as long as it remained the property of the United States was thus cleverly evaded.

The squatters, now squatters no longer, but preëmptioners with legal property rights over part of the disputed land, at once ordered the Indians to remove — not from the land actually sold, but to the west side of the Mississippi. To their astonishment, fortified by advice of friends that the land had never been legally ceded, Black Hawk turned upon them and indignantly ordered them to leave the country. Strangers appropriating their fields, strangers plowing up the graves of their fathers, strangers in the homeland regarding the *Sauk* as intruders — these burning realities were dire fulfillment of the fear of white rapacity that had come upon him when first he learned that the yearly presents his people had been receiving were in reality payment for tribal lands. To Black Hawk it appeared incomprehensible that the Great Father should wink at the forcible seizure of this one small point of land when the whites had gained from his people such quantities beside. If such was the case, however, he proposed a stand against the aliens.

At this unexpected change of front the settlers fled in panic. In April, eight of them sent a memorial to Governor Reynolds setting forth their grievous wrongs at the hands of the Indians. It appeared that the Sauk on the Rock river had "threatened to kill them; that they acted in a most outrageous manner; threw down their fences, turned horses into their corn-fields, stole their potatoes, saying *the land was theirs and that they had not sold it,* . . . levelled deadly weapons at the citizens," and as a final outrage these Indians had gone "to a house, rolled out a barrel of whiskey, and destroyed it."[11] On April 30, thirty-seven settlers again asked protection from the Sauk, who it was claimed were acting in "an outrageous and menacing manner," and in May, receiving no reply, sent a personal delegation to the executive.

Governor Reynolds, from memorials, letters, and rumors was convinced of the imminent danger of an Indian war; in fact, he proclaimed Illinois in a state of "actual invasion" and called for volunteers.[12]

By June there were six hundred volunteers and ten companies of regulars in the field under General Edmund P. Gaines, marching across the northern wilderness. They were a comforting array to the terrified inhabitants. The Indians, dismayed by this menacing reply to their crude effort to secure justice, watched the demonstration of the assembled troops in front of their village on June 25; and during the night the whole band quietly withdrew to their lands in Iowa, so that the next day the troops entered an empty village. On June 30, 1831, General Gaines and Governor Reynolds were able to negotiate a treaty of capitulation and peace by which the Indians not only confirmed the ancient cession of 1804 but solemnly agreed never to cross to the eastern side of the

---

[11] Drake, *Life and Adventures of Black Hawk,* 100; Stevens, *Black Hawk War,* 80-85. Black Hawk avers that he pleaded with the whites to cease selling whisky, but that one man in particular persisted until he went with a party of Indians, rolled out a barrel and destroyed the liquor. "I did this for fear some of the whites might be killed by my people when drunk." Black Hawk, *Autobiography,* 89.

[12] *Sangamo Journal,* April 26, 1832.

Mississippi except by permission of the United States government.

The Indians, however, had left their growing crops in Illinois, and it was too late to plant anew in Iowa. By autumn they were out of provisions. One night a little company of their young men crossed the river to steal roasting ears from the crops they had left on their old lands. The whites fired upon them and complained loudly of the double offense of thieving and of violating the treaty. Much more startling was the daring of an expedition of Foxes, who went up the Mississippi to avenge upon the Menominee warriors the murder of eight Fox chiefs the previous year.[13] They fell upon a party of twenty-eight drunken braves encamped on an island opposite the fort at Prairie du Chien, and scalped and mutilated the whole band. This to the Indian code was only just reprisal; Black Hawk indignantly refused to deliver up any of his band for trial, especially since no such demand had been made of the Menominee the year before.

During this episode famine conditions continued. At the invitation of the Prophet, Black Hawk determined to cross the Mississippi the following spring and raise a crop with his friends, the Winnebago. He had a childlike conviction that so long as he showed no warlike inclinations and was not entering his old village, the government would not molest him. After his people had been strengthened by a year's plenty, he hoped to perfect the rosy, if somewhat nebulous, plans that he had formed from reports brought to him by Indian runners. They assured him that a powerful coalition of British, Winnebago, Ottawa, Chippewa, and Potawatomi stood ready to aid the Sauk and Foxes not only in regaining their village but in repaying the humiliation and injustice they had suffered from the Americans. The supreme importance of filling the stomachs of his band made the present consideration of war impossible. With naïve security in the thought of his present peaceful intentions, he with his four hundred warriors took their

[13] *Sangamo Journal*, May 3, 1832.

women, children, and belongings and in full view of Fort Armstrong, crossed the Mississippi in April, 1832, and started up Rock river toward the Winnebago country.[14]

General Henry Atkinson with a small company of regulars had recently been stationed at Fort Armstrong to enforce the demand of the Indian department for the Fox murderers of the Menominee. Upon news of the invasion, he sent an express ordering the band to return. Black Hawk, affronted at his preëmptory tone and protesting his peaceful mission of making corn, refused and continued to refuse when threatened with force.

Meanwhile, the news had spread, and Illinois was ablaze with excitement. Conditions in the state were ripe for an Indian war; a month after Governor Reynolds' fiery appeal, sixteen hundred volunteers rendezvoused at Beardstown. They were backwoodsmen, hardy, courageous, excellent marksmen and horsemen, who had progressed across a continent by the aid of rifle and ax—with an appeal to fisticuffs in case of personal difficulties. Their independence, their isolation, their whole habit of life, built on a proud consciousness of Anglo-Saxon and Jeffersonian tradition, produced the sharpest individualism. These men, starving for incident, heard in the call to arms a promise of a frolic more venturesome than a wolf hunt; it involved an appeal to the spirit of public service to hunt down and destroy a pest more deadly than wolves.[15] They themselves were unconscious of the tremendous psychic hold the savage had established over them in the form of a fear, which in the face of a threatened reverse would stampede them in frantic hysteria.

The troops had been gathered in from the fields. Willingly, even in the face of two successive bad seasons, they left

[14] "When the Black Hawk and party re-crossed to the east side of the Mississippi River in 1832, they numbered three hundred and sixty-eight men. They were hampered with many women and children, and had no intention to make war." Printed as appendix to Mrs. J. H. Kinzie, *Wau-Bun*, 385; Thwaites, "The Story of the Black Hawk War," *Wisconsin Historical Collections*, 12:230.

[15] In 1814 the territorial legislature offered fifty dollars to any citizen killing or taking a depredating Indian, while only two dollars was given for a wolf.

their plows, grabbed their rifles, and rode away to form themselves democratically into companies at the nearest crossroads.
They chose their officers as children form for a tug of war, by
standing in line behind the man of their choice.   Then, whooping, yelling, firing their guns in the air, they raced off to war.[16]
That such troops would be able to understand or submit
readily to discipline was not possible.   Allow the man whom
they had recently honored by electing captain — a man whom
they knew thoroughly as no better than themselves — allow
such a one to take advantage of his position to direct an action
undesirable to them?   Incomprehensible!   To the recently
elected captain this point of view seemed entirely reasonable.
With an active sense of political favors to come, he was not
the one to insist when thoroughly convinced that such insistence
would effect nothing but his own unpopularity.

The rollicking volunteers, divided into four regiments,
a spy battalion, and two odd battalions, marched to Fort Armstrong where, on the seventh of May, General Atkinson
assumed command.   It was at once agreed that General Samuel
Whiteside with the recruits should proceed about fifty miles
up Rock river to Prophetstown, there to rest until the ten
companies of infantry regulars from the fort with provisions
could follow in keel-boats.   The troops, arrived at Prophetstown, burned the vacant village by way of pastime and marched
on toward Dixon, with splendid improvidence abandoning
baggage trains and provisions in order to make better time.
Upon their arrival they found two independent battalions of
mounted volunteers under Major Isaiah Stillman, itching to
get into a scrimmage and display their prowess.   Accordingly,
Whiteside sent them to spy out the land farther up Rock river
and, if possible, to find the Indians.   On the fourteenth of
May, Stillman, with his men on the alert for a chance to scalp
a savage, encamped in a small grove of scrub oak completely
surrounded by open, undulating prairie.

[16] Wakefield, *History of the Black Hawk War*, 154; Nicolay and Hay,
Abraham Lincoln, 1:89.

The Indians were not far away. For a week Black Hawk had been in council with the Prophet and the Winnebago; and to his dismay he was learning that the fair promises of British and Indian aid awaiting him when he should require were empty. Hospitality even was not of the warmest. Black Hawk, himself an unsophisticated old fellow, was often the dupe of the wily and mischievous who had persuaded him into believing that which he secretly desired. Added to his own growing fear that his hopes were groundless came the sharper one that his people should discover the fruitlessness of their quest. Disturbing rumors of war preparations among the whites were brought him. With gathering apprehension he pushed on to Sycamore creek in the hope that his council there with the Potawatomi might bring forth something more hopeful. But the advice of Shabonee, the friend of the whites, was well heeded; Black Hawk could effect little. The Potawatomi were politely aloof; they had no corn to share, much less had they men. Only a handful of hotheads and jingoes listened to Black Hawk. The day of a sharp repulse to white aggression would never dawn; the story of British aid was false; and the Indians were now too well acquainted with buttered bread to risk plainer fare.

For Black Hawk the bubble had burst; he was defeated; he was now ready to return and make corn in Iowa. On the heels of his resolution came the news of an encampment of three hundred and forty soldiers only eight miles away. Here was a chance, with not too great a loss of dignity, to accede to the whites, and he immediately sent three young men under a flag of truce to arrange a council at one of the other camps. The Indians rode to Stillman's eager men, who, toward sunset, saw the approaching trucebearers nearly a mile away; awaiting no orders, many jumped upon their horses and ran the Indians in amid yells and imprecations. While their mission was being explained five other Indians whom Black Hawk had sent to watch the effect of his message were observed on a knoll about three-quarters of a mile away. The excitement in camp increased; first twenty men, then others, dashed away to bring in the newcomers. The Indians, seeing the headlong approach, wheeled to ride away. The whites fired; two of the Indians were killed; and when the camp heard the shots, one of the Indians who had accompanied the flag of truce was shot down in cold blood.[17]

With the shooting, it became impossible for the officers to exert any control over the raw and independent men. Here was the fun they had left home to find. Little groups continued to gallop away in an irregular stream over the darkening prairie to join their comrades who had been so fortunate as to be first in an Indian fracas.

In the bedlam of the camp, the two remaining Indians escaped; three of the party of five hurried to Black Hawk with the news of the reception given his flag of truce. Black Hawk was astounded. He had with him forty warriors only; but, seeing the pursuing riders approaching, he formed his men behind a clump of chaparral with a stirring appeal dearly to sell their lives in avenging their wantonly murdered comrades. When the foremost of Stillman's men was all but upon them the Indians burst from cover with a crackle of rifles — whooping, yelling, and dashing madly into the midst of the advance guard. That squad in one blinding flash realized its temerity; imagination peopled thickly the early darkness with blood-thirsty savages. With a yell of "Injuns! Injuns!" the troops wheeled and fled headlong toward camp — the whole force in a very madness of fear.[18]

The astonished Indians pursued, but it was impossible to come up with the flying foe. They had to satisfy themselves with dispatching those unfortunates who fell behind. The men did not stop when they reached camp but abandoning everything rushed on through toward Dixon. All night and the next day exhausted men came straggling into Atkinson's camp with fearful and wonderful tales of the fifteen hundred or

[17] Stevens, *Black Hawk War*, 132-133; *Sangamo Journal*, October 6, 1832.
[18] Captain Adams and a handful of men made a brave stand and fought till they fell. Stevens, *Black Hawk War*, 134.

two thousand Indians deployed about with diabolical military genius by General Black Hawk![19]   Each was convinced that the slaughter had been tremendous — that any not yet arrived in camp were slain.   The actual loss in fact was only eleven men, but the immediate effect on Indians and whites was tremendous.   Black Hawk, feeling that he had been precipitated into certain war, was elated by his success; the capture of precious provisions, blankets, saddlebags, and camp equipage now made it possible for him to think of carrying on hostilities. Sending out scouting parties to watch the movements of the whites, he removed his women and children to the swampy fastnesses of Lake Koshkonong, near the headwaters of Rock river in Wisconsin.   Leaving them here, he and his braves, with parties of recruits from the Winnebago and Potawatomi, descended on terrified northern Illinois to harass it with border warfare.

The panic that had arisen in Illinois at news of the Indians' first coming was as nothing compared to that which now swept over the state.   Everywhere on the frontier homes were hurriedly deserted, while families and whole settlements scuttled to forts.[20]   The frontier shivered with an apprehension which feverishly increased as stories of bushwhacking warfare began to come in.

Governor Reynolds at once issued a fresh levy for two thousand men.   This was necessary as the troops, completely disheartened by Stillman's disaster, clamored to be discharged. Many had enlisted for a few weeks only; though there was now direct need of their services a storm of protest arose from them in which the bad weather, the neglected fields, the lack of provisions, and the futility of further pursuit, all played a part as reasons for abandoning the enterprise.   The impossibility of carrying on a war with an unwilling militia as soldiery was only too apparent; late in May the governor mustered them out of service.   Three hundred rangers reën-

[19] *Sangamo Journal,* May 3, 14, 24, 1832.
[20] *Ibid.,* May 31, June 21, 1832.

listed at once so that the frontier might have some protection while a new army was being raised.[21]

During this interval, an irregular border warfare was carried on in which two hundred whites and about as many Indians lost their lives. News of the massacre at Indian creek where fifteen men, women, and children were slaughtered,[22] of the sharp skirmish on the Pecatonica where Major Henry Dodge and a gallant handful avenged five murdered whites, and of the desperate attack on Apple river fort hurried the army into service. In less than three weeks after Stillman's defeat thirty-two hundred mounted militiamen took the field under Atkinson. This force was divided into three brigades, with Generals Alexander Posey, Milton K. Alexander, and James D. Henry in command. Colonel Jacob Fry's rangers, Dodge's Michigan rangers, and the regular infantry completed the fighting force of four thousand men, or ten to one of the Indian strength.[23]

The real problem that faced these commanders was that of bringing to the consciousness of the unruly men under them a realizing sense of the necessity of obedience. Neither the disciplined companies of infantry under Atkinson nor the thousand regulars being rushed from the seaboard under General Winfield Scott could win the war against a mounted enemy, unwilling to make a stand. But a militia, however well-mounted and however intrepid, which refused to submit itself to discipline, would convert the war into a series of Stillman's runs.

In General James D. Henry, Illinois found the man for such troops. A blacksmith in civil life, his avocation had been the study of military tactics and memoirs. The narrow limits of the incident called the Black Hawk War afforded him the

[21] *Sangamo Journal*, May 24, 31, 1832; *Galenian*, June 13, 1832; Stevens, *Black Hawk War*, 141.

[22] *Sangamo Journal*, May 31, 1832.

[23] Thwaites, "Story of the Black Hawk War," in *Wisconsin Historical Collections*, 12:246. It is to be remembered that the description of the Wisconsin country is drawn from contemporary accounts of men suffering from the hardships of marches through a wilderness.

opportunity to display an alert tactical sense, a military judgment far above that of his colleagues, and, most important, a
power in handling men that in a few weeks turned obstinate
material into a trained army.

For some weeks, however, it was not evident that the
second campaign would be more fruitful than the first. Though
all advantages were with the whites, the army seemed unable
to apprehend how weak an enemy they were pursuing. Black
Hawk had no army — only a band of warriors heavily encumbered with the unaccustomed responsibility of women and
children. For more than a year they had been ill nourished,
and they had now been reduced to a literally starving condition. The rugged country through which they fled was quite
unknown to them; their guides, as ill-fortune pressed close,
deserted them. Though it was midsummer, these dreary
wastes of bogs, morasses, lakes, and pine forests yielded
neither game, fruit, nor fish. They lived on the bark of trees,
roots, and horseflesh.[24]   Black Hawk had selected this deso-
late country in the belief that the whites could not follow into
its fastnesses; but when Atkinson with the main army pursued
him to the headwaters of Rock river at Lake Koshkonong, he
was forced to flee onward, west and north in the hope that he
and his starving band might reach and cross the Mississippi
to safety.

The army, after the hopeful rush on the warm trail to
Koshkonong, only to find a hastily deserted camp, began to
flounder about in aimless marches and unsatisfactory explora-
tions. Spirits rapidly sank. Men grumbled that they could
wander forever in that hateful northern country and the Indians could remain that long a will o' the wisp. Sleeping
uneasily on their arms in fear of a night attack, being short
rationed for days at a time, wading hip deep through water
and mud, marching toward nothing but long stoppages — all
this they were enduring with never a sight of a hostile Indian!

[24] Drake, *Life and Adventures of Black Hawk,* 152; Black Hawk, *Autobiography,* 130.

The whole thing seemed ridiculously futile; Governor Reynolds and his staff with other prominent Illinoisians having had sufficient experience of war left for home. By the middle of July the volunteer force had been reduced one-half. Fatigue, delay, hardship, privation were not the frolic for which they had enlisted.[25]

Under these circumstances Atkinson fell back to Fort Koshkonong to await the return of Henry, Alexander, and Dodge who with their commands had been sent to Fort Winnebago for supplies. While there, these officers were positively assured that Black Hawk was encamped about thirty-five miles north of Atkinson. Elated at his proximity, they agreed to disobey orders and to march directly toward Black Hawk. Alexander, however, almost at once reported that his men refused to go. Henry, of different stuff, quelled a threatened mutiny among his officers and with Major Dodge started on a three days forced march over miles of treacherous swamps. Then, unexpectedly, they struck the broad, fresh trail of Black Hawk trying to escape by way of Four Lakes and the Wisconsin.

The men were rejuvenated. Tents, baggage, blankets, and even clothing were dumped in a pile in the wilderness; and the forced march continued. Here at last was a chance for real fighting and a speedy end to the war; there was no grumbling even when a terrific rain storm forced the men to travel over a hundred miles with nothing in their stomachs but a little wet flour and raw meat. They were hot on the trail, with the rear guard of the Indians only two or three miles in advance. Pots and kettles and all manner of Indian camp equipment lined the way. Exhausted old men, too ill to keep up with their flying bands, fell behind to disclose by their weakness the straits to which Black Hawk was reduced.[26]

---

[25] Reynolds, *My Own Times*, 251-252; Ford, *History of Illinois*, 132-135.
[26] Ford, *History of Illinois*, 139-146. Some half dozen of these old creatures, blind and infirm, were promptly shot and scalped by the whites. Thwaites, "Story of the Black Hawk War," in *Wisconsin Historical Collections*, 12:253; Wakefield, *History of the Black Hawk War*, 109-110.

Late in the afternoon of July twenty-first, the Indians came within a mile and a half of the Wisconsin river. To protect the crossing of the main body, a chosen war party of about fifty braves, directed by Black Hawk, made a stand on the bluffs. After a wild charge, the Indians fought lying down in the tall grass. The whites left their horses behind and, "with the most terrific yells that ever came from the head of mortals, except from the savages themselves," charged the position again and again with a heavy fire.[27] The fighting continued for a half hour with casualties about even, when the Indians began to retreat slowly toward the river. Henry, instead of following up this seeming advantage, did not pursue them into the unknown, marshy ground ahead. He knew that disaster would have met his men in the darkness, though the engagement itself had cost them only one life and eight wounded. There are varying accounts of the Indian loss, but this valiant stand of the weakened warriors accomplished its end; it kept the superior force of the whites at bay until the band crossed the Wisconsin.[28]

For the Indians, ugly misfortune was biting close; they realized it keenly. Just before the dawn of the day following the battle of Wisconsin Heights, the troops encamped on the battlefield were terrified to hear the shrill, eager tones of an Indian in a long harangue, which they supposed was addressed to a war party. The Indian guides and interpreters had left the army after the battle, and no one in camp understood the oration. Henry felt it necessary to quell the rising fear of his men by an address reminding them of their dauntlessness on the previous day, of the diabolical wickedness of the enemy, appealing to them to stand firm, and prophesying that they would again be successful. That the Indian's oration was a speech of surrender in which he confessed their starving condition, their inability to fight when encumbered by women and children, and their anxiety to be permitted peaceably to pass

---

[27] Wakefield, *History of the Black Hawk War*, 111.
[28] *Sangamo Journal*, September 1, 1832.

over the Mississippi, to do no more mischief, was not learned
till after the annihilation of the band at Bad Axe.[29]

A large party of women, children, and old men begged
canoes and rafts from the Winnebago and floated down the
Wisconsin, trusting that as noncombatants the garrison at
Fort Crawford would allow them to escape. But a party of
regulars from Prairie du Chien attacked them, capturing
thirty-two women and children; the rest of the party were
killed or drowned during the onslaught; and those who escaped
into the woods perished with hunger or were there massacred
by a band of three hundred Menominee allies under a staff of
white officers.[30]

Those of the Sauk who had no means of descending the
Wisconsin started out over the densely wooded hills and inter-
vening black swamps toward the Mississippi. "Many of our
people were compelled to go on foot, for want of horses,
which, in consequence of their having had nothing to eat for
a long time, caused our march to be very slow. At length we
arrived at the Mississippi, having lost some of our old men
and little children, who perished on the way from hunger."[31]

On the afternoon of the same day the steamboat *Warrior*
was seen approaching under the command of John Throck-
morton. Black Hawk, eager that no more of his miserable
band should die, told his braves not to shoot, hoisted a white
flag, and called out in the Winnebago tongue to send a little
canoe that he might go aboard and give himself up.[32] The
captain, though the message was translated to him, affected to
believe that the flag was a decoy and ordered them to send a
boat on board. This was impossible, because every boat the
Indians could secure was being used to carry a load across the

[29] Ford, *History of Illinois*, 146; Wakefield, *History of the Black Hawk
War*, 115-116, 134.

[30] Thwaites, "Story of the Black Hawk War," in *Wisconsin Historical
Collections*, 12:255; Black Hawk, *Autobiography*, 132.

[31] *Ibid.*, 133. Twenty-five warriors, wounded at Wisconsin Heights, also
died and marked the trail for the whites. Ford, *History of Illinois*, 146.

[32] *Sangamo Journal*, October 6, 1832.

Mississippi and all were far beyond call. The captain in writing an account of the incident, August 3, 1832, continues: "After about fifteen minutes delay, giving them time to remove a few of their women and children, we let slip a six-pounder, loaded with canister, followed by a severe fire of musketry; and if ever you saw straight blankets, you would have seen them there. . . . We fought them for about an hour or more until our wood began to fail. . . . This little fight cost them twenty-three killed, and of course a great many wounded. We never lost a man. . . ."[33]

Such was the reception of Black Hawk's last chance at surrender, for the army bringing destruction was close upon him. Following the battle of Wisconsin Heights Henry's command, in need of provisions, fell back to Blue Mounds whence the whole force under the command of Atkinson started in pursuit of the Indians. No effort was spared to make time over the toilsome way and the army was only twenty-four hours behind Black Hawk in reaching the river. Upon their approach, the Indians, in order to gain time for crossing, sent back about twenty men to intercept the army within a few miles of their camp. This party was to commence an attack and then retreat to the river three miles above the Indians. The ruse succeeded. The attacking party fired and then fell back before the charge of the whites; the army immediately began a hot pursuit.

Henry was bringing up the rear with the baggage; Atkinson, jealous that the Illinois militia and its commander rather than the regulars with their chief should have discovered the enemy and won a victory, had placed the recently victorious brigade in the rear and had left it without orders. Reaching the point of attack, Henry plainly saw the main trail leading lower down. His three hundred men were formed on foot and advanced upon the main body of three hundred Indians, who were taken completely by surprise. They fought des-

[33] Drake, *Life and Adventures of Black Hawk*, 153-154; Ford, *History of Illinois*, 156-157.

desperately; but in their famished condition they were no match for their opponents, who with bayonets fiercely forced them back from tree to tree toward the river. Women, with children clinging around their necks, plunged desperately into the river to be almost instantly drowned or picked off by sharpshooters.[34] Atkinson, hearing the din behind, returned a half hour later, and the slaughter proceeded more fiercely than ever. The steamboat *Warrior* came back to rake with canister the islands that some of the Indians had reached. Old men, women, and children alike were slain. "It was a horrid sight," wrote a participant, "to witness little children, wounded and suffering the most excruciating pain, although they were of the savage enemy, and the common enemy of the country." [35]

The massacre of the Bad Axe continued three hours. One hundred and fifty Indians were killed outright and as many more lost their lives by drowning. About fifty, mostly women and children, were taken prisoners. Three hundred Sauk succeeded, either before or during the battle, in reaching the Iowa side, to be there set upon by one hundred Sioux, sent out by General Atkinson; half of them were slain, and many others died of exhaustion and wounds before they could reach their friends in Keokuk's village. Thus by the second of August not more than one hundred and fifty of the band of nearly a thousand which crossed the Mississippi in April, lived to return to their lands in Iowa.

On August 7, 1832, General Winfield Scott, who had been delayed by the outbreak of cholera among his troops, arrived to assume command.[36] The following day he mustered the

[34] *Sangamo Journal,* October 6, 1832, September 7, 1833.

[35] He piously reflected, however, that " the Ruler of the Universe, He who takes vengeance on the guilty, did not design those guilty wretches to escape His vengeance for the horrid deeds they had done, which were of the most appalling nature. He here took just retribution for the many innocent lives those cruel savages had taken on our northern frontiers." Wakefield, *History of the Black Hawk War,* 132-133.

[36] *Sangamo Journal,* August 2, 1832. The asiatic cholera first reached this country in June, 1832, and broke out among Scott's detachment of troops while they were passing up the Great Lakes. It was so virulent that two of the four vessels proceeded no farther than Fort Gratiot; the others, after a period of delay reached Chicago in July. Fort Dearborn was converted into a hospital,

volunteers out of service. Black Hawk, with several of his prominent men, was taken prisoner and held as hostage for some months, during which time he was taken through the eastern states so that the white man's power might be fully impressed upon him. In June, 1833, he was released, and shorn of all power the old chief returned to the remnant of his people in Iowa. "Rock river," he said, "was a beautiful country. I loved my towns, my cornfields, and the home of my people. I fought for it. It is now yours. Keep it as we did." [37]

He was conquered; no other Indian in Illinois questioned the dominance of the white race. The north country was now ready for white possession.

where the pestilence raged violently for several days; checked there in August, it again broke out among the troops at Rock Island, to be finally arrested by removing the men to small camps on the Iowa side of the Mississippi. Quaife, *Chicago and the Old Northwest*, 328-337; Stevens, *Black Hawk War*, 242-249.

[37] *Ibid.*, 271; Quaife, *Chicago and the Old Northwest*, 337. Thwaites, "Story of the Black Hawk War," in *Wisconsin Historical Collections*, 12:264-265.

IX. THE SETTLEMENT OF THE NORTH

EVEN before the Indians had retreated from northern Illinois, the advance of settlers into that region began. This advance of population northward is one of the most significant facts in the history of the decade from 1830–1840. It influenced not only the character of the population through the type of immigrants who poured in, but also the demands of the state for public land legislation and the consequent course of political events. Further by making evident the need of better transportation the immigration provoked the internal improvement mania of 1837. The land speculator, as elsewhere in Illinois, seeing a future metropolis in his town site, turned to a railroad as the quickest means of realizing his vision; and what was of greater consequence of persuading others that it was a reality.

By 1830 it was evident that the tide of immigration was passing by the vacant lands of southern Illinois and turning to the north. Already in the rich bottoms of the Sangamon the pioneer stage had passed, and settlement was thickening in Sangamon and Morgan counties at a rate that was provoking the jealousy even of Madison and Greene, to say nothing of the counties to the south.[1] Throughout the Military Tract the population was beginning to spread; the southern end of the tract had been settled ever since the days when Shaw and Hansen had contested the throne of the kingdom of Pike; but now pioneers were moving north. Peoria on the Illinois river was laid out in 1826. In the same year an Ohio speculator plotted Lacon under the name of Columbia. When in 1826 a pioneer from Bond county settled near Magnolia his nearest

---

[1] *Alton Spectator*, November 23, June 25, 1833; *Sangamo Journal*, January 19, February 2, July 12, 1833.

neighbors were fur traders at Hennepin. In 1835 he sold out his holdings for $4,200 only to lose his profits in town lot speculation. In 1830 the county of Putnam, then including Bureau, Marshall, and most of Stark, had 700 inhabitants.[2] The town plots of Macomb and Monmouth dated from 1831. Rushville, in 1829 a hamlet of seven cabins, was incorporated in 1831 with 180 inhabitants.

The spread of population tells a part of the story.[3] In 1831 there were some ten thousand people in the southeastern part of the tract — Calhoun, Pike, Adams, Schuyler, and Fulton — and the increase of population to this day has necessitated the formation of but one additional county in that region. Elsewhere in the tract there were some two thousand inhabitants, most of them in Hancock, Knox, and Henry; north of them there was a straggling population. The Indian traders, Colonel George Davenport and Russell Farnham at the Sauk village, were the leaders of a few squatters, whose settlement later became Rock Island; and at Dixon's Ferry where the Peoria-Galena trail crossed the Rock there was a little settlement with a few others along the trail above it. By 1840 Knox county alone had seven thousand inhabitants, while the four counties just north and west, Jo Daviess, Whiteside, Carroll, and Rock Island, had together a population of some nine thousand persons.[4]

Another interesting means of visualizing the settlement of the north is found in the record of the public land sales, though one must be careful to make the proper allowance for the activity of the speculator. Illinois land sales for the period were very speculative in character, varying more from year to year than those in Missouri; in all the west the prevailing rule was large sales in one state in one year and in another the next. Thus in 1834 less land was sold in Illinois than in Ohio, Indiana, Alabama, Mississippi, or Michigan. In 1835 the

2 *Peoria Register,* April 1, 1837, May 5, August 25, September 8, 1838; Pooley, *Settlement of Illinois,* 380, 381.
3 *Ibid.,* 559.
4 *Sixth Census of the United States,* 376.

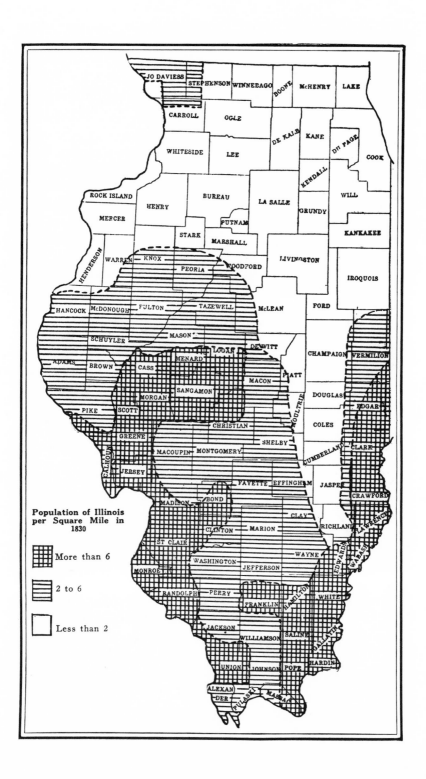

Population of Illinois
per Square Mile in
1830

More than 6

2 to 6

Less than 2

sales leaped from 354,013 acres to 2,096,623, outstripping Ohio, Indiana, Michigan, and Alabama. Illinois did not distance Mississippi till 1836. Again in 1836 Indiana outran Illinois.[5] As passing events drew the attention of the speculator now to this state, now to that, the sales rose to high figures, then fell to comparatively low ones. A glance at the table of sales reveals the fact that the boom of 1835–1837 was most evident in the western and central Illinois offices — Edwardsville, Springfield, and Quincy — and at Chicago. In the other Illinois offices the increase was more uniform, showing least in the ill-starred Vandalia district. In all the offices the sales reached their height in 1836, then showed a rapid decline and a more moderate rate of sales thereafter.

Before examining in detail the settlement of northern Illinois it is necessary to consider for a moment the unusual speculative conditions which existed in the Military Tract. This territory lying between the Illinois and the Mississippi rivers had been set aside for the location of military land warrants issued to soldiers in the War of 1812. By 1837, 17,075 patents had been issued for 2,831,840 acres of land.[6] This by no means included the whole which contained 3,500,000 acres. Further, all tracts much in excess of, or much less than, 160 acres had been excluded from selection. Accordingly the government still had considerable desirable land in the region. The greater part of the lands, however, passed into the hands of speculators. Some of it, forfeited for nonpayment of taxes, was snapped up by such Illinois magnates as Ninian Edwards. The general policy of speculators was to hold out for high prices. Romulus Riggs of Philadelphia, who affected a sentimental interest in the state and named his daughter for it, offered in 1837 two hundred and sixty-six quarter sections for sale at prices which S. H. Davis supposed would run from five to forty dollars an acre.[7] Davis pointed out that it was foolish

[5] *Executive Documents*, 24 congress, 2 session, number 6, p. 8, 11; *Senate Documents*, 25 congress, 3 session, number 11, p. 12, 16.
[6] *Executive Documents*, 25 congress, 2 session, number 83.
[7] *Peoria Register*, October 14, April 8, July 8, 1837.

to pay such prices when federal land of good quality could still be had for $1.25 an acre, especially in Peoria and Knox counties.[8]

During the same period the prices of town lots also showed the influence of the speculators' activity. In 1836 lots in Quincy sold as high as seventy-eight dollars a front foot. In April, 1837, desirable town lots in Monmouth were worth one thousand dollars. Less desirable ones were selling at the rate of seventy-five to one hundred dollars. In Peoria at the

A TABLE O|

	1820	1821	1822	1823	1824	1825	1826	1827	1828	1829
Shawneetown	2,392	3,329	2,050	1,253	2,278	1,357	2,086	3,340	4,512	8,14:
Kaskaskia	1,658	1,627	1,661	793	1,278	711	1,901	2,256	3,415	6,38:
Edwardsville	2,649	35,243	5,373	11,223	5,541	5,748	6,584	8,398	18,829	28,60:
Vandalia		9,227	2,205	640	614	895	1,472	1,743	3,591	19,40|
Palestine		954	16,474	7,903	11,936	10,323	12,915	9,466	20,537	47,22'
Springfield				38,720	22,339	26,767	56,122	33,398	45,206	86,49:
Quincy										
Danville										
Galena										
Chicago										
Totals	6,699	50,380	27,763	60,532	43,986	45,801	80,080	58,601	96,090	196,24

This table is compiled from the following sources : *Executive Documents*, 21 congress, 2 session, number 2, p. 57 ; *ibid.*, 23 congress, 2 session, number 3, p. 92 ; *ibid.*, 24 congress, 1 session, number 5, p. 10 ; *ibid.*, 24 congress, 2 session, number 6, p. 8 ; *ibid.*, 26 congress, 2 session, number 38, p. 10 ; *Senate Documents*, 23 congress, 1 session, number 9, p. 62 ; *ibid.*, 25 congress, 2 session, number 11, p. 13 ; *ibid.*, 25 congress, 3 session, number 17, p. 8 ; *ibid.*, 26 congress, 1 session, number 21, p. 13.

same time the best lots sold for one hundred dollars a front foot;[9] and in March, 1837, there were twelve or fourteen houses within sight on Kickapoo prairie when nine months before there was not a house.

In the Rock river country the effects of the boom of 1836–1837 were more apparent. On the way to Savanna in Carroll county, Dayton, Cleveland, Portland, Lyndon, and Union Grove had all been laid out in 1836, most of them then having from three to twelve houses, with lots selling at from ten to one hundred and twenty-five dollars. On the road to Galena,

[8] By 1838 land near Peoria cost from ten to thirty dollars an acre; land in the tract could then be had for three to five dollars an acre. *Peoria Register*, October 20, December 8, 1838.

[9] *Ibid.*, April 1, 1837.

Grand Detour and Dixon had been laid out in 1836.   In 1839 they were towns of fifty houses, and the most desirable lots in them and in Oregon were held at from four hundred to six hundred dollars.[10]

It was in the northeast, however, that the records of land sales indicate the highest prices and most rampant speculation. The price of unimproved land in the vicinity of Ottawa had in 1838 increased to three dollars an acre.   In the years 1835–1837 land speculation was focused at Chicago.   June 18, 1834,

SALES

	1831	1832	1833	1834	1835	1836	1837	1838	1839
0	20,523	17,624	28,936	6,904	10,299	160,430	100,977	54,102	97,858
0	11,186	17,417	29,235	15,196	19,870	156,738	105,405	90,303	149,108
0	100,350	80,713	92,261	124,302	345,794	503,572	111,823	42,789	58,904
2	43,174	8,021	21,615	20,207	29,165	127,345	183,891	109,516	178,239
3	54,872	23,773	22,043	22,135	38,376	285,025	144,744	106,547	143,123
3	99,496	59,996	109,642	66,804	478,976	480,837	104,388	68,835	29,999
	160	1,118	29,604	36,131	367,337	569,376	142,909	165,243	50,776
	9,647	13,710	26,901	62,331	155,784	277,023	67,323	35,690	35,240
					280,979	202,365	35,764	87,891	229,471
					370,043	436,992	15,618	17,640	160,154
8	339,408	122,372	360,237	354,010	2,096,623	3,199,703	1,012,842	778,556	1,132,872

the *Democrat* remarked the fact that seventy-five buildings had been erected in Chicago since spring.   By December the city had a population of 3,279.   Next year strangers were crowding in so fast that for want of accommodation they were sleeping on floors.   Provisions were scarce, and flour sold at twenty dollars a barrel.   It became necessary to meet the criticism of the envious east with assertions that prices of one hundred and fifty-five dollars a foot for town lots were based not on speculation but on the exigency of the business situation. Lots, that in the spring of 1835 sold for nine thousand dollars, by the end of the year were held at twenty-five thousand dollars; and rents were correspondingly exorbitant.[11]

The same effects of feverish speculation and settlement were to be seen to the south of the Illinois river.   In the narrative of a journey to the northeast of Springfield in 1837, Bloomington was noted as a town with six or eight stores,

[10] *Peoria Register,* May 25, June 1, 1839.
[11] *Chicago American,* August 15, 1835, January 2, July 9, 1836.

separated from Decatur by an almost unsettled country. Mackinaw had drawn together twenty-four houses and five stores, the existence of five or six mill "seats" within two or three miles being an attraction. Speculative town sites were scattered far and wide. Washington in Tazewell county, with three or four hundred inhabitants, had four stores, two blacksmith shops, one cabinet shop, a steam mill, four schools, and six liquor-selling establishments designated under various names.[12] The nucleus of a town was a mill to grind grain, a store to supply dry goods and hardware for the sustenance of the family and the supply of the farm, and a grocery or public house to supply wet goods for the comfort of the inner man.

A special feature of the settlement of the north was the coming of settlers in colonies or organized groups. As early as October, 1832, Simeon Francis, who was inclined to deprecate the tendency to form colonies, noted wagon trains passing through to Fulton county from Ohio and another company of emigrants from Vermont, which led him to comment on the advantages for the settler of prairie and timber country. Sometimes there was more of the speculative than of the group spirit in the movement, as when in 1839 it was rumored that six eastern capitalists were about to offer for sale to actual settlers forty thousand acres near Mt. Auburn in Christian county. This, however, was not a typical case. La Grange in Henry county was settled by a colony from New York and New England that bought twenty thousand acres, setting apart a quarter section for a town site.[13] In 1833 a caravan of fifty-two people from Vermont, New Hampshire, and northern New York, led by the Lyman brothers, came by wagon to settle in Sangamon county, the country having been previously explored by two of their number. A Connecticut colony established Rockwell in La Salle county. In 1836 three colonies were located, one at Tremont in Tazewell, one in Knox county,

[12] *Sangamo Journal*, June 10, September 9, 1837.
[13] *Ibid.*, October 11, 20, 1832. As early as 1834 there was a society in Massachusetts, the Old Colony Brotherhood, to promote emigration to Illinois. *Chicago Democrat*, November 12, 1834.

and one somewhere near Varna called Lyons. The founding of Weathersfield in Henry county by a colony from the Connecticut town of that name is of interest. The first settler came out to the purchase in October, 1836; in the next year, sixteen men were there, six with their families; by July of 1839 there was a population of one hundred. Each colonist had a quarter section of prairie, twenty acres of timber, and a village lot. In 1836 a New York colony settled at Galesburg on sixteen sections of which one thousand and four acres were reserved for a college. The purchaser of each eighty acres was allowed the free tuition of a youth at any time within the limit of twenty-five years in the institution which is now known as Knox College. In 1839 a Catholic colony was projected at Postville in Logan county.[14]

It remains to consider the broader economic principles underlying the progress of the individual settlers in the north. These are not so obscure as those effecting the settlement of southern and central Illinois in the preceding decade. In fact it is possible to describe the processes of home-making from abundant data collected almost on the spot by careful observers in so many specific instances as to make generalization possible.

The problem of the settler in this decade was to sustain himself on the land while he broke and fenced enough prairie to farm successfully. Instead of grubbing up the underbrush and planting his corn in the shadow of girdled trees as the earlier pioneer did, the later settler added to his field by breaking each year a little more of the tough prairie sod. When he himself did not own the oxen necessary for the work, he was able to hire it done at a fairly well-established price of $2.50 an acre. Similarly there were standard prices for fencing — usually $1.25 to $2.00 a hundred rails, a rate increasing with the distance it was necessary to haul them. At every turn whether for breaking prairie or hauling rails, the use of oxen was necessary and the man who located his farm on heavy

[14] *Peoria Register*, July 8, 1837, May 12, June 30, 1838, July 6, 1839; *Sangamo Journal*, January 23, 1836; Gale, *Brief History of Knox College, passim; Chicago Democrat*, May 22, 1839.

prairie at a distance from timber found himself penalized for his choice in dollars and cents.

The generally established principle for the location of a farm was that it must contain both prairie and timber, usually in a ratio of two to one. A man could, it is true, avoid the necessity of having timber of his own by helping himself from timber lots still belonging to the federal government or owned by nonresidents, but to some New England consciences the latter method if not the former seemed unethical. For the future development of a farm, however, the wise man held to the proper proportion of timber and prairie as essential. The speculator accordingly made haste where he could to seize on the timber at the edges of the great prairies, secure in his knowledge that those who were foolhardy enough to enter the adjacent untimbered land would in the end have to buy from him at his price.

Still, as the decade passed, men began to assume such risks. An observer in Tazewell county in 1837 noted with surprise that settlers had pushed out four or five miles into the prairie. Repeatedly it was proposed to plant timber on the prairies, or to use "stone coal" for fuel and to substitute sod fences or white thorn hedges for the usual rail fence. In 1839 the cost of putting a rail fence around a "forty" was from two to three hundred dollars, a rate which seemed to call for a more economical system of fencing. It was this need that caused the popularity of the Osage orange hedge which was advocated by Jonathan B. Turner. In the minds of most settlers, however, proximity to timber as to water was still essential.[15]

His selection of land once made, the settler's method of conquering it depended on whether or not he had money. If he had financial resources, he built a cabin for his family, bought or hired several yoke of oxen, and set to breaking prairie at a rate of twenty to forty acres a year, meanwhile buying grain to sustain his family and his oxen. His sod corn, however,

[15] *Sangamo Journal*, February 2, 1832; *Peoria Register*, August 11, 1838; *Chicago Democrat*, March 25, 1834.

raised on the newly broken prairie, unless the hogs got into it while it was still unfenced, produced perhaps fifty bushels an acre. Sometimes he came out alone in the spring to plant the first crop and brought his family in the fall. If on the other hand he had merely his own labor and a yoke of oxen, he easily found enough work to support his family, while in his spare moments he improved his own land. If he was a skilled carpenter or millwright, he was sure of good wages and he might rent a farm while waiting to develop his own claim. If the owner stocked his leasehold for him, the rent was half or two-thirds of the produce. If he stocked it himself, it was one-third. Meanwhile his wages, if he was industrious, at length enabled him to buy a claim and usually to enter it at government price when the land was put on sale.[16]

An integral part of this system was, as may be imagined, a recognition of the binding force of squatters' right. Long before the country was put on sale by the federal land officers, squatters had established claims on the most desirable combinations of timber, prairie, springs, and healthful sites. Such claims the rough and ready custom of the frontier accepted as valid, and another settler coming on the land was forced by public opinion to recognize the claim by buying off the occupying claimant. Except where extensive improvements had been made, the prices of such claims were not high; but the business was moderately profitable, and many pioneers made and sold one claim after another in their progress toward the sunset. This perennial squatter, so obnoxious to the eastern congressman, was defended by the westerner, because he was aiding in the development of the country by enabling the permanent settler to purchase even in the wilds a little grain, a few broken acres, and a cabin that, until other itinerant squatters had helped him to raise a better one, would shelter his family.[17]

Property rights so acquired and transferred were real bases of land titles and wealth, and there were exact rules to

[16] Peoria. Register, July 1, 1837, April 7, September 1, 29, 1838, June 15, 1839.
[17] Ibid., August 25, 1838.

govern them. Thus in the early days of the settlement of the north, laying four logs for the foundation of a cabin established a claim for the duration of a year. In order to keep off the claim jumper, it was necessary in 1837 to build a cabin sixteen or eighteen feet square or to break five acres of land. These improvements served to hold the claim for six months. In the Military Tract the usual claim was one hundred sixty to two hundred forty acres, but in the north three thousand acres could be so held, and even town sites were said to have been located on such claims.[18]

In the face of legislation and executive rulings framed by indignant eastern statesmen, such claims were maintained by force of public opinion, usually manifested in the settlers' meetings, which before each district was put on sale bound all settlers to hold together in support of each other's claims against outside bidders and sometimes even established boards of arbitration to decide disputes between claimants. Sometimes, in case settlement had preceded survey, these boards devised ways by which each man might make secure his improvements by a common bargain. Having once reached an agreement among themselves, the settlers attended sales in a body to exercise moral suasion on any rash outsider who dared to bid over the minimum for an "improvement." Under such circumstances scarcely a tract of land was struck off at ordinary sale at more than $1.25 an acre.[19]

The settlers were not able in the same way to guard themselves against usurious interest charges in case they had to borrow money to buy their claims. Frequently a sale was set at a time that seemed almost designed to give the money lender his opportunity, before crops were harvested or shortly after money had been put into improvements on assurances that the sales would not take place for a year. At such times short term loans brought ten per cent a month, thirty to fifty per cent a year, and thirty to forty per cent for two years. A

[18] *Peoria Register,* July 1, 1837, July 28, 1838.
[19] *Chicago American,* January 14, 1837; *Chicago Democrat,* March 9, May 4, July 20, 1836; *Executive Documents,* 25 congress, 3 session, number 241.

lesser annoyance was the seeming caprice of land office receivers in the designation of the bank notes which they would accept. Frequently it was charged that, by refusing to take the money brought to them, the receivers compelled the buyers to pay a brokerage of from two to five per cent to have it "shaved" by some local financier. Land office officials were often charged with trickery and with speculation in this and other ways.[20]

As has been said before the determination of the national public land policy turned on the fact that the economic interests of east and west and their theories of the purpose of the public domain were fundamentally different. To the easterner the public land was the heritage of the states, bought by the blood of their sons in the Revolution, and the pledge of national unity and good faith. To him as to Alexander Hamilton it was the source of a fund for public finance, not the future home of a great part of the American people.[21] Indeed as the easterner saw settlers flocking into the new lands of the west draining eastern towns of labor and leaving the farms in the old cradles of liberty to revert to wilderness, he sometimes did not attempt to conceal his dislike of western settlement and his desire to retard its progress. To the westerner who complained that settlement was too slow and who called for legislation to accelerate it, he listened with ill-concealed derision.

Against the squatter, that typical western figure, the easterner's wrath was especially aroused. He considered him a worthless trespasser on the public property, whose trespasses had repeatedly to be condoned by preëmption acts. Said Samuel A. Foot: "The disposal of the public lands has been, in this way, absolutely wrested from the Government, and monopolized by speculators and squatters; land system is virtually broken down, and we are gravely told, 'it is best for us

[20] *Peoria Register*, August 4, September 29, November 17, 1838; *Chicago American*, October 7, 18, 26, November 1, 1839; *Sangamo Journal*, June 25, July 30, 1836.
[21] *Congressional Debates*, 1830-1831, p. 471. Ohio was passing out of the ranks of the public land states. *Ibid.*, 1831-1832, p. 1452.

it should be so,' and nothing remains for us but to give the squatters preëmption rights; and, instead of legislating for them, we are to legislate after them, in full pursuit to the Rocky Mountains, or to the Pacific Ocean." [22] In the mind of the easterner the squatter was a prolific source of trouble with the Indians, equally galling to the humanitarian sentimentalists from districts that had not heard the war whoop since Queen Anne's War and to the thrifty public financiers. Of the squatter's lauded services as a pioneer of settlement, the eastern congressman was frankly skeptical.

On the other hand, to the westerner from the public land state the vacant national domain appeared as the source of freeholds for uncounted thousands, the basis of the majesty and power of great commonwealths. Only let the government unbar the gate and all this dream would speedily be realized. Meanwhile, so long as men without money had to squat without title upon the public domain and men with money had to limit the extent of their exploitation by the high government price of wild land, all these advantages were postponed. States sat with the greater portion of their lands under the control of a landlord who elected to keep it desert, yielding no revenue to the state, adding nothing to its population and wealth. The public land policy, that in the opinion of the easterner was draining the older states of population, to the mind of the westerner was locking up the west from settlement. The one trembled at the rapidity of change and development, the other fretted because he saw how much more rapid settlement might become under more liberal land laws.

The debate on Foot's resolution, which was designed to limit the sale of public lands by forcing the sale of those already on the market, apart from its significance in constitutional history, places the two points of view in sharp contrast. To the westerner it appeared that the Connecticut senator's inquiry, by stopping surveys, would leave only undesirable and picked over lands in the west, would cut off emigration to states like

22 *Congressional Debates*, 1829-1830, p. 443.

Illinois, and would close for many years to come the northern
half of its domain.[23]   Robert Y. Hayne had been quick to
point out to the west that its true friends lived in the south and
the debate resolved itself in its earlier phases into an argument
between Webster and Benton as to whether or not the traditional New England policy was to hamper the west.   Benton,
eschewing the internal improvements that the east proffered
the west through the American system, elected to stand fast
with the south in an alliance based on free trade and liberal
public land policy; and in its broader outlines that alliance
comprehends the history of the older democracy until the disaster of 1840.

The western land policy generally supported in congress
was that of Thomas Hart Benton.   It is true that in Illinois
politics Edwards' doctrine of the state's right to the public
lands persisted till 1833, and its revival in congress by a Missouri representative in 1839 merely embarrassed Benton and
the advocates of his policy by serving as a red rag to arouse
the east.   Clay cleverly sought to connect Edwards' policy
with Benton's.[24] "The Senator," he said, "modestly claimed
only an old smoked, rejected joint; but the stomach of his
Excellency yearned after the whole hog!"[25]   The outlines of
Benton's policy of graduation, the scaling down year by year
of the price of unsold land, and preëmption, the allowing of
special purchase privileges to actual settlers, has already been
outlined.   In general it may be said that preëmption measures
were intended to enable the small buyer to earn on the public
land enough to acquire title to a farm; graduation measures
by successive reductions of price were designed to bring onto
the market parts of the older west, such as southern Illinois,
that still were thinly settled.[26]

The east and the whig party, as the diminution of the

[23] *Congressional Debates*, 1829-1830, p. 4, 11, 23, 44, 60, 96.
[24] *Illinois Intelligencer*, April 16, May 21, 1831; *Illinois Advocate*, January 26, 1833; *Sangamo Journal*, April 19, 1823.
[25] *Congressional Debates*, 1831-1832, p. 1102.
[26] *Ibid.*, 1829-1830, p. 8.

public debt seemed about to force a new disposal of the public land revenue allotted to its discharge, were obliged to find a rival public land policy. They found it in the distribution measure first proposed in 1832 by Henry Clay, a westerner, but not a citizen of a public land state. Clay's policy proposed the distribution among the states of the revenue from the sale of the public land, with especially favorable consideration to western states. The measure was adroitly conceived that the west might be conciliated by the offered sop of hard cash. The east, its framers hoped, would welcome a measure which would postpone the necessity for reducing the price of the public lands and would prevent the immediate drain of factory operatives to cheap lands in the west. The supporters of the policy designed to enlist the aid of the old advocates of the American system by laying stress on the state works of internal improvement which the distributed funds might initiate. Above all, the measure was in their intent one step in the direction of federalization of power.

Distribution remained a standing whig policy for years to come, and Benton accepted its challenge. He avowed openly that distribution must be defeated before his measures could be adopted, and he once more summoned the south to an alliance with the west. A distribution measure was passed in 1833, however, but was vetoed by the president. Meanwhile there was passed a series of acts granting preëmptions for short terms of years — in 1830 for two years, in 1833 and in 1834.[27]

In 1835–1836 a further development in what may be called the western land policy took place under the initiative of Senator Robert J. Walker of Mississippi, a state still as much western as southern. The tremendous sales of 1834 and 1835 in Illinois had provoked the fear that the public domain would pass into the hands of speculators, and Walker to prevent it proposed a preëmption and graduation measure designed to

[27] *Congressional Debates,* 1829-1830, p. 11, 44; *ibid.,* 1831-1832, p. 785, 903, 1148, 1167; *ibid.,* 1836-1837, p. 789.

limit sales to actual settlers in quantities not exceeding a section. Emphatically this would have benefited the small farmer of the north rather than the planter of the south. Concerning this measure, Clay prophesied that if it were passed the public domain was gone. Even some of the western senators opposed it. Calhoun's alternative measure, which proposed to cede the lands to the several states for one-third their proceeds, procured him some passing popularity in the west.[28]

Distribution in the form of deposit with the states succeeded in congress in 1836, after it was apparent that a pure distribution measure could not be passed over Jackson's veto. Meanwhile the land speculator was becoming a more and more disturbing problem, and his ubiquity is revealed by his figuring as a type character in the newspapers of that day. Walker designed his suppression, as has been seen, through preëmption. Benton characteristically aimed at the same result by a proposal that only gold and silver be received in payment for lands; and this proposal was finally embodied in Jackson's specie circular, which, Benton pronounced, had itself served as a preëmption act.[29]

In Illinois as elsewhere the whigs and democrats took ground on the rival land policies, and Illinois elected to adopt the democratic policy. Benton's policy, in 1831 and 1832, found indorsement by the Illinois legislature and in public meetings.[30] Preëmption in 1834 was a popular measure. Duncan, however, voted for the distribution act of 1833, which met the opposition of the Illinois Jackson papers and politicians; the *Sangamo Journal* favored it. The issue was also drawn in the presidential campaign of 1836, the whigs advocating distribution as a measure which would give the state a fund for internal improvements. In 1837 the Illinois senate approved Walker's measure. Van Buren's first message, deprecating temporary preëmption acts as inducing a disregard

[28] *Congressional Debates,* 1835-1836, p. 1028, *ibid.,* 1836-1837, p. 663, 733; *Congressional Globe,* 25 congress, 3 session, appendix, 44 ff.
[29] *Ibid.,* 25 congress, 2 session, appendix, 291 ff.
[30] *House Journal,* 1832-1833, 1 session, 740.

for law, advocated graduation by quality; but the Illinois papers pointed out that this proposal showed no more friend-ship for the west than Clay's plan. Clay indeed, no longer "Harry of the West," suffered the consequences of his con-temptuous remarks on squatters which were noted down by R. M. Young for use against him in Illinois.[31]

In the end, the public land policy acted upon by these two opposing forces remained stationary. On the one side the whigs were never able to secure a full measure of distribution; on the other, while the democrats in 1841 secured a permanent preëmption measure, they never achieved graduation. Yet the democrats throughout had stood more or less consistently for the interests of the western settler and in their policy was the germ of the homestead legislation, that prevented the total eclipse of the small freehold domain in the west. Whether graduation would have assisted the penniless farm laborer, or whether it would only have depreciated the holdings of those who had already bought for the benefit of the new land specu-lators cannot be said. The democratic party, however, es-poused the policy that looked particularly to the development of the west; and it is significant that Illinois, generally indorse-ing that policy, gave its votes to the party that maintained it. On public lands, as on other matters, the party of Andrew Jackson was still the party of the west.

After a digression, in which has been noticed the influence of the settlement of northern and central Illinois on the state's political course, a return may be made to the consideration of a more obvious result from settlement — development of com-merce and the consequent demand for more adequate transportation. Indeed the great speculative public land sales of 1834–1837 may be regarded as the decisive cause of the more than speculative internal improvement scheme on which

[31] *Illinois Advocate,* October 5, 1833; *Alton Spectator,* December 28, 1833; *Alton American,* January 3, 1834; *Sangamo Journal,* August 10, 1833, March 12, April 2, June 25, July 2, July 16, 1836, May 10, 1838; *Chicago American,* Janu-ary 30, 1836; *Illinois State Register,* June 24, August 19, 1836; *Senate Journal,* 1835-1836, 1 session, 80, 85; *Congressional Globe,* 25 congress, 3 session, ap-pendix, 225.

the state embarked in 1837. That system and the state's later attempts to extricate itself from the ruin it brought divides the pioneer period of the state's history from the era of transition.

Some notice has already been paid to the meteoric rise of Chicago in the commercial field; but the city which showed the steadiest commercial development in the decade was Alton. Alton had been hampered at the beginning of its career by litigation over the title to its site, and its aspirations to rival St. Louis had led it into a long drawn out and fruitless struggle to procure the passage of the Cumberland road through it rather than through St. Louis. It had been some time before Alton succeeded in enlisting the full strength of Illinois on its side. By 1831, however, the city was making rapid progress in importance as a produce market. New England capital came to its support. Griggs, Manning, and Company offered St. Louis prices for produce, calling for forty thousand bushels of wheat and offering to execute commissions in the east at a charge of two and one-half per cent.[32] By 1835 there were at least three firms of commission and forwarding merchants in business in the city; beef, pork, lard, whisky, furs, flour, lead were coming in for export from Quincy and Galena as well as from Alton's natural hinterland. Apparently tributary to Alton were numerous small towns where storekeepers bought of its wholesale merchants and forwarded local produce to its market.

Business methods in Illinois were from the modern point of view somewhat rudimentary. Alton merchants sold old stocks of goods at auction to country merchants on long credit. Collections everywhere were slow, a favorite business principle being that in hard times one did better by not driving his debtor to extremities. Newspapers, it is true, preached the modern gospel that true advertising consists in setting forth your wares in such fashion as to create a desire for them; and they laid down the rule that the true index of a town's business was the newspaper advertising of its merchants. Yet even while they

---

[32] *Alton Spectator*, May 14, October 23, 1832, January 22, 27, 1833, December 31, 1835.

urged this precocious wisdom on their patrons, they felt it necessary to advise them to show civility and courtesy to their customers and to warn them to beware of expecting every man who was shown goods to purchase.[33]

Galena in 1830 was a typical mining town which had grown up between 1823 and 1829 with the rise of lead production from 335,130 pounds to 13,343,150. The population was migratory, the miners coming to work in the lead mines in summer and most of them returning south in winter. It was a typical bonanza town with wages as high as twenty-five dollars a month and speculatively high rents, until the fall in the price of lead in 1829 produced genuine hard times. Even in 1837 a two-story frame store rented for eight hundred dollars a year, and lots were held at two hundred dollars a foot. The federal government in 1829 was still the landlord, leasing the lead mines on shares which were hard to collect. In 1829 it provided for a sale of town lots to holders, which curiously enough aroused some local opposition. In the thirties a doctrine, which had considerable vogue, that the federal government could not constitutionally lease its land made the collection of rents almost impossible; and the commissioner of the general land office as well as the state legislature urged the sale of the mineral lands to private holders.[34]

The most significant natural development in transportation between 1830 and 1840 was the establishment of a network of communication lines radiating from Chicago. Chicago's career began as a distributing point for merchandise brought by the Great Lakes route. In 1831 Enoch C. March imported goods to St. Louis via Chicago at one-third less cost than by way of New Orleans. In 1833 O. Newberry shipped several hundred barrels of beef from Chicago to New York via Albany at a cost of only thirteen dollars a ton. In 1834 weekly ar-

[33] *Alton American*, December 13, 1833; *Galena Advertiser*, August 31, 1829; *Peoria Register*, May 26, 1838; *Sangamo Journal*, July 13, 1833.
[34] *Galena Advertiser*, July 20, August 3, September 14, November 9, 1829, February 8, 15, 1830; *Peoria Register*, October 21, 1837; *Illinois Intelligencer*, October 7, 1831; *Miner's Journal*, July 22, September 20, 1828; *Senate Documents*, 25 congress, 2 session, number 131.

rivals of steamers from Buffalo were advertised. In 1835, 255 sailing ships arrived at Chicago; in 1836, 49 steamboats and 383 sailing ships. By 1839 there was a full-fledged steamboat pool which divided profits according to tonnage. Chicago merchants, not content with three weeks time and aspiring for even quicker and cheaper transportation, hoped that the New York and Erie railroad would enable freight to be shipped through as early as March 10 while the Erie canal was still frozen. Once this railroad and those across Michigan were in operation, it was said New York and Chicago would be only seventy-four hours apart.[35] Even with the twelve to fourteen days which was the minimum time required for freight between Chicago and the east in 1839, there were great possibilities in supplying other Illinois markets; thus it was believed that Galena could get goods two months quicker and much cheaper by way of Chicago. For penetrating the central part of the state, there was the Illinois river which was navigable as far up as Peoria or even Ottawa. The bad roads above Peru, however, were a serious difficulty, in rendering it a route of commerce tributary to Chicago.

Indeed the Illinois river for a time seemed more likely to become the trunk line of a considerable transportation system tributary to the Mississippi. In 1828 steamers went up to Naples, in 1829 to Pekin, in 1830 to Peoria. In 1831 there were 186 steamer arrivals at Naples, 32 at Beardstown, and 17 at Peoria. In 1837 the *Peoria Register* advertised seven packets to ply between Peoria and St. Louis and one between Peoria and Pittsburg. Nevertheless there were serious difficulties. The bar at Beardstown was a particularly obstinate handicap. In even the most favorable seasons navigation was practically at an end in September. Even thus, Naples, Beardstown, and Peoria enjoyed direct commercial relations with the outside world at Pittsburg and New Orleans. In 1838 Peoria had a daily stage to Springfield which linked it

[35] *Illinois Advocate,* October 21, November 11, 1831; *Chicago Democrat,* June 4, 1834; *Alton Spectator,* July 9, 1833; *Chicago American,* September 26, November 21, December 5, 1835.

with Terre Haute and St. Louis, as well as triweekly stages to Galena, Ottawa, and Rushville and semiweekly ones to Oquawka.[86]

Even from the earlier settlements the smaller rivers of Illinois had served for the transportation of freight. The *Talisman's* trip up the Sangamon is well known. As early as 1829 flatboats with cargoes of lead descended the Pecatonica and the Rock. In 1836 a steamer ascended the Rock as far as Dixon and in 1838 as far as Rockford. In 1839 there was a St. Louis and Rock river packet.

The Mississippi, however, remained the state's most important transportation route, and the ease of its navigation brought prosperity to the towns along its banks. In 1839 Savanna, a town of two hundred fifty inhabitants, was sending four hundred tons of freight a year to Oregon, Rockford, Freeport, Beloit, and Elkhorn. In 1837 Monmouth imported from St. Louis through Oquawka. Alton and Galena have already been mentioned; Warsaw and Nauvoo belong to a later period.[87]

In the midst of wild land speculations, it was inevitable that calculations of the cost of bringing produce to market from some "Stone's Landing," portentously rechristened "Napoleon," should have an important part. Already fair transportation routes were in existence; the question was how to improve them. The federal government would improve the Mississippi; in a liberal mood it had already endowed the Illinois and Michigan water route that would allow Chicago merchants to take their toll of what passed in and out by the lakes. To improve such rivers as the Illinois and the Rock by state enterprise was feasible. Men were not content, however, with these comparatively modest improvements. Not only were the "Goose Runs" of Illinois to be improved into

[86] *Peoria Register*, July 1, 1837, April 7, September 15, December 8, 1838, July 27, August 17, 1839; *Chicago American*, July 6, August 31, 1839; *Chicago Democrat*, February 10, 1836; *Sangamo Journal*, February 9, 1832; *Illinois Intelligencer*, November 19, 1831.

[87] *Sangamo Journal*, November 28, 1835; *Peoria Register*, April 1, 1837, April 27, May 12, 1838, October 12, 1839.

"Columbus Rivers," but scarcely five years had passed since the railroad had demonstrated its practicability, before dreamers in Illinois were devising routes by which the new discovery might give fabulous values to the lands away from the water routes. A state wide mania for improved transportation ended in logrollings and bargains which initiated a state system of internal improvements based on calculations imperial enough to have originated in the brain of Beriah Sellers himself.

X. THE INTERNAL IMPROVEMENT SYSTEM

THE internal improvement scheme of 1837 is not only the opening of a new era in the state's history; it is also the climax of the former one. The various threads of the state's political and economic interests — the desire of southern Illinois for an equivalent to the Illinois and Michigan canal, the local rivalries over the location of the state capital, the aspirations of land speculators — all were woven together to produce the fabric of the internal improvement system. It can indeed be most easily explained if each thread be followed separately to the point where it intertwines with the others.

The problem of connecting the waters of the Great Lakes at Chicago with the Illinois river seemed enticingly simple. The Des Plaines branch of the Illinois flows south parallel to the lake shore and sometimes not ten miles away from it. Moreover the two branches of the Chicago river, uniting from north and south to flow into the lake, contribute to lessen even that distance. Between the south branch and the Des Plaines lay in dry weather a portage of no longer than three miles; and in the wet season a lake or slough five miles long and six to forty yards wide through which Mackinaw boats of six and eight tons could pass into the Illinois without a portage. So nearly even were the levels of the two rivers that the change of the breeze would float objects from the "lake" now into Lake Michigan, now into the Des Plaines. This route, unimproved as it was, was regularly followed by the fur traders of Mackinac.[1]

The engineering problem, though simple in appearance, was in reality extremely difficult. Since the bed of the Des Plaines was in 1819 estimated to be some two feet higher than

[1] *American State Papers, Miscellaneous*, 2:555.

the lake, a bed channel would simply have turned the waters of the river into the lake. To correct this difficulty[2] Major Stephen Long recommended the construction of two locks at the two ends of the slough; but the opinion was generally held that in the dry season there would not be enough water to operate them and that it would be necessary to construct the canal to a lower point, somewhere near the falls of the Des Plaines. There was of course also the possibility of using some other portage, for instance that to the Kankakee, or that from the St. Joseph or Maumee to the Wabash, all of which were enumerated in the engineers' report of 1819.

At the beginning Illinois was concerned rather with obtaining means to construct the canal than with the engineering problem involved. After some differences both houses of the second general assembly concurred in a resolution directing the congressional delegates to work for a grant of the two per cent fund reserved for roads and of a strip of land a section wide along the canal route to the Illinois river. At the next session of congress in accordance with a resolution offered by Cook, an act was passed granting a strip ninety feet wide on each side of the canal and reserving from sale the adjoining sections.

Meanwhile, the canal had become a subject of newspaper discussion apparently both as a political question and as a matter of sectional rivalry. In 1822 articles began to point out the importance of a route to market other than that through New Orleans.[3] For this very reason it was generally supposed that southeastern Illinois would be opposed to a project that would tax that region to destroy its monopoly of the route to market via the Mississippi. Opposition developed a second time in the general assembly of 1822–1823, when A. P. Field proposed once more to memoralize congress to apply the two per cent fund to digging the canal. A canal bill after vicissitudes apparently promoted by members representing constitu-

---

[2] *American State Papers, Miscellaneous*, 2: 555. Since the foregoing was written the full account of the Illinois and Michigan canal by J. W. Putnam has appeared. See also *Annals of Congress*, 17 congress, 1 session, 2586.

[3] *Illinois Intelligencer*, November 30, 1822.

encies of the Ohio and the Wabash rivers was finally passed, February 10, 1823. Curiously enough it was finally reported back to the house the same day with the convention resolutions, probably both as parts of the same bargain.[4]

As finally passed, the bill provided for five commissioners to lay out a route for a canal and to calculate its cost; it directed them further to bring to the attention of the governors of Indiana and Ohio the desirability of improving the Wabash and the Maumee rivers.[5] The commissioners tried in vain to get the services of New York canal engineers, but finally were content with Justus Post to whom later they added René Paul.

The legislature of 1825 determined to turn the enterprise over to a private corporation which it created, consisting of Coles, Bond, Post, Erasmus Brown, W. S. Hamilton, Joseph Duncan, and John Warnock, who were to receive all canal grants and complete a canal in ten years; they were permitted to charge a toll of one-half cent per ton per mile on tonnage of boats through it, three cents on Illinois produce or merchandise, six cents on foreign merchandise, and eight cents on all else. In fifty years the state might buy the canal for cost plus six per cent interest.

Congressman Cook could hardly have been expected to approve this scheme. His political opponents were in control of it; it was contrary to the solution at which he himself had been working — a generous congressional land grant. During the session of 1823–1824, he had attempted to unite the interests of the enterprise with those of similar ones in which other states might join and to secure a grant to the state of lands along the canal reserved from sale by the federal government.[6] In November of 1825, therefore, he published an address urging a repeal of the canal act. In part his argument was that the sum of money which it would finally be necessary to raise to purchase the canal would be huge. He, therefore, advised borrowing on the credit of the school lands and the

[4] *House Journal*, 1822-1823, 1 session, 262.
[5] *Laws of 1823*, p. 151.
[6] *Annals of Congress*, 18 congress, 1 session, 873, 1914.

three per cent school fund, or better still seeking aid from the government; in the latter case he possibly intended to combine the project with one for an armory on the Illinois or Fox river. By an optimistic calculation he sought to show that the probable increase of Illinois population and of traffic would enable the state to finance the canal from the tolls. He was on safer ground when he pointed out the danger to the state of placing such a transportation monopoly in private hands and of the chance that it would control the politics of the state. Cook's figures were attacked, but his argument against the monopoly was not destroyed. As the *Edwardsville Spectator* pointed out, his opponents had to admit that the terms of the act were too unfavorable to the state; yet it was impossible to interest investors on less favorable terms. The legislature, meeting in special session January, 1826, to redistrict the state, repealed the act, the senate voting fourteen to three.[7]

In congress a bill for a canal grant had been brought up in the session of 1825 and again in 1826. The *Intelligencer* alleged that it suffered from the jealousy of Mississippi and Louisiana members, who feared that trade would be deflected from New Orleans. Finally in 1827, the act was passed. It granted the state one-half the land to a depth of five sections on each side of the canal, reserving for the benefit of the United States all alternate sections; the canal was to be toll free to the United States government and was to be begun in five years and completed in twenty. The act may perhaps be regarded as a last triumph of the liberal internal improvement policy of the administration; it was certainly regarded as a triumph in Illinois.[8]

Two successive Illinois assemblies undertook to utilize the grant thus obtained. An act was passed in 1829 which provided for the biennial appointment by governor and senate of three commissioners, one of whom was to act as treasurer.

[7] *Illinois Intelligencer*, November 25, 1825; *Edwardsville Spectator*, December 3, 1825; *Senate Journal*, 1826, 2 session, 58.
[8] *Illinois Intelligencer*, March 25, 1825, April 21, 1827; *Congressional Debates*, 1826-1827, appendix, xviii.

They were to survey a route, to select the land granted by the United States, and to sell it in tracts or in town lots. They were to use the funds obtained as soon as practicable for the construction of a canal, four feet deep and forty feet wide at the surface. This act, which as can be seen was very loosely drawn, was amended in 1831 so as to increase the efficiency of the board.[9] It raised the question of the practicability of improving the navigation on the Illinois river below the Fox in lieu of the lower route of the canal, and also the question of the use of the Calumet as a feeder below the Chicago and the Des Plaines; but of greater importance it raised the more fundamental question whether a railroad might not serve the state better than a canal. The commissioners, in their report of November 22, 1831, recommended on professional advice the construction of a railroad instead of a canal. During the winter of 1832 they made inquiries in New York as to possible financial supplies but without eliciting any offer which the state could accept.

The canal project, after a period of quiescence during 1833, became a political issue of importance in 1834; and candidates for office gave the matter much attention. Some merely declared for the measure. Of those who were more specific, some advised the completion of the enterprise by a private company; others specifically declared against taxation for it. In the south there was some attempt to move for the construction of a canal from the Wabash to Alton as more advantageous; this proposition of course called forth angry protests from the north.[10]

There was much dissent from the current opinion that expense must be avoided at all hazards. The *Chicago Democrat* denounced the proposal to endow a New York company

9 *Laws of 1829*, p. 14; *Laws of 1831*, p. 39.

10 Alexander M. Jenkins, *Alton American*, June 2, 1834; Benjamin Roberts, *Illinois Advocate*, July 5, 1834; James Evans, *Sangamo Journal*, July 5, 1834; James Shepherd and James Adams, *ibid.*, July 12, 1834; William Alvey, *ibid.*, July 19, 1834; R. K. McLaughlin, *ibid.*, July 26, 1834; William B. Archer, *ibid.*, August 2, 1834; George Forquer, *ibid.*, June 25, 1834. Forquer's proposal comprised a scheme for purchase in ten years for cost less the value of canal lands.

with the canal lands and to allow it to construct a railroad instead of a canal. Would the people, it asked, in order to keep the state's skirts free of debt, hand over canal lands that in five years would be worth two millions?[11] It disagreed with the findings of James M. Bucklin, an engineer of prominence, who had been consulted by the commissioners in 1831 as to the relative desirability of a railroad, concluding that he had overestimated the cost of a canal. Governor Duncan clung obstinately to the idea of a canal planned on an elaborate scale. In his inaugural he urged that the state proceed boldly with the enterprise relying on additional federal grants. He presented the stock arguments for canals as against railroads — permanency and freedom from repair costs. They furnished avenues of trade, so he pointed out, by which farmers in defiance of monopoly might carry their own produce to market. With a view of future developments imperial in its scope he suggested at the outset a cut sufficiently wide for a steamboat canal, except on the summit level where the cut could later be widened; and since the tolls would yield, in his estimation, a revenue out of proportion to any sum the work could possibly cost, he urged the state to undertake the work on its own account. A similar light-hearted optimism had marked his attitude toward the project, when it was discussed in congress.[12]

In the legislative session of 1834–1835 the debates on the canal act turned on the question as to whether the faith of the state or merely the canal land and its resources were to be pledged to the enterprise. The argument of the opponents of state credit was that if the lands were as valuable as they appeared to be they should be sufficient to attract capital; but the proposers of the measure argued that capitalists were ignorant of the value of the lands. As the act was finally

[11] *Chicago Democrat,* April 30, November 19, December 17, 1834; *Sangamo Journal,* June 21, 1834.
[12] *House Journal,* 1834-1835, 1 session, 25; *Chicago Democrat,* December 17, 1834, January 21, 1835, indorsed Duncan's policy. *Sangamo Journal,* July 26, 1834.

passed, the credit of the state was not pledged. The division on the roll call was sharply north and south, giving some color to the charge of the *Chicago Democrat* that the southern part of the state was trying to retard the progress of the northern.[13]

The act of 1835 authorized the governor to negotiate a loan not to exceed $500,000 on the canal lands and toll for the construction of the canal. He was to appoint with the advice of the senate a canal board of five, distinctly an executive tool of the governor, to construct a canal forty-five feet wide and four deep. The method of construction was not prescribed. Ex-Governor Edward Coles found in the east that the fundamental objection of the capitalists to this loan was the failure to pledge the faith of the state for the payment of principal and interest. It was pointed out that interest would have to be paid either out of the loan or from sales of town lots, the sale of which was purely discretionary with the authorities; and that it would not be possible, in case of default, to take possession of the canal. Capitalists regarded the transaction as based too much on the pleasing prospect of a further federal grant which might not be forthcoming. The character of the security behind the loan made it impossible to float it in Europe, where five per cent loans had ultimately to find a market. The northern friends of the enterprise, accepting Coles' conclusions, declared for a special session to formulate a proposition more acceptable from the financial point of view.

Primarily for purposes of apportionment a special session of the legislature was held. Duncan was optimistic as usual in his message. He predicted that the sale of United States lands at Chicago showed that the lands and town lots owned by the state, not counting the additional grants that might be relied on from congress, were even then worth from one to three millions. "It is now no longer to be dreaded," pro-

13 *Chicago Democrat*, December 24, 1834; *Illinois Advocate*, February 4, 11, 1835; *House Journal*, 1834-1835, 1 session, 459. In advancing to the third reading, it was then amended by striking out the credit of the state and passed 40 to 12, p. 503. See also *ibid.*, 470, 472, 501.

ceeded Duncan, "that any reasonable sum of money borrowed for the purpose of constructing this canal, will become a charge on the State Treasury." He therefore advised a loan and the sale of lots at Chicago from time to time to pay the interest.[14] He still insisted on a steamboat canal.

The canal bill was drawn up by its supporters in Chicago and altered and corrected by George Forquer. According to whig accounts it was endangered and nearly defeated by the partisan efforts of the democrats to provide for the appointment of commissioners. The act as it was finally passed, largely through the influence of the whigs, provided for the negotiation by the governor of a loan on the credit of the state for $500,000, issuing for it a six per cent stock redeemable after 1860, with a provision that it should not be sold for less than par. The governor and senate were to appoint three commissioners, removable for cause, to hold office until January, 1837, after which they were to be appointed biennially as the legislature should direct.

The canal was to be of boat size and supplied with water from Lake Michigan and such other sources as the commissioners might decide. The commissioners were instructed to sell lots in Chicago and Ottawa on annual installments. The canal was to begin at or near Chicago on canal lands and terminate near the mouth of the little Vermilion on land owned by the state. The needed legislation had been obtained; but, as events showed, the difficulties had only begun. The fate of the various projects in the public improvement system began to be vitally connected with the interests of the various aspirants in the impending contest over the location of the state capital; and in the trades and bargains, by which local projects of one kind and the other were advanced, local and sectional interests were predominant. The state capital was originally located in the wilderness at Vandalia with the intent that the state and not private speculators should profit from the exploitation of

[14] Coles to Duncan, April 28, 1835 in *House Journal*, 1835-1836, 2 session, 14; Delafield to Coles, April 20, 1835 in *ibid.*, 19 ff.; *ibid.*, 8.

town lots; but population had not followed the seat of government. The town lot speculation had been a failure; the town was supposedly unhealthy, and its boarding houses were reputed expensive and poor. An agitation begun, as it was claimed, by legislative candidates from Sangamon and Morgan counties in 1832 looked toward a settlement of the question of the location of the capital, after the allotted twenty years at Vandalia had expired. As soon as this subject was broached in the legislature, complicated sectional alignments appeared. By clever maneuvering the Madison county members, it was claimed, defeated a proposal for a location by a board of commissioners and substituted one providing for a popular referendum on Jacksonville, Springfield, Alton, Vandalia, Peoria, and a town to be located at the geographical center of the state.[15]

As it was passed, the act was by no means to the taste of the people of Springfield. The amended bill had been carefully devised to break up the phalanx of the north. It was evident that with Peoria, Jacksonville, and the geographical center all to contend with, the chances of either Alton or Vandalia were brighter than Springfield's. The *Sangamo Journal* bewailed the fact that the choice must be a minority one. It protested that no one could determine where the geographical center was or what was its fitness; it depicted the reputed unhealthiness and the liability to summer malaria of Alton.[16] The *Alton Spectator* advised it to look at the matter philosophically, remembering that if any town had been left out, Springfield might well have been it.

In December the idea of a convention to overcome the effect of the act by uniting the northern politicians on some one location was discussed. A meeting at Springfield on January 4, 1834, called such a convention to meet at Rushville

[15] *Illinois Advocate*, October 29, 1834; *Alton American*, May 12, 1834; *House Journal*, 1832-1833, 1 session, 271; *Senate Journal*, 1832-1833, 1 session, 290.
[16] *Sangamo Journal*, May 9, June 1, July 20, 27, 1833. The *Journal* was especially angry with the grasping spirit of Alton, *ibid.*, January 11, 1834.

the first Monday in April. The meeting duly convened on April 7 with delegates present from Knox, McDonough, Sangamon, Hancock, Morgan, Macon, Tazewell, Adams, Warren, Putnam, Schuyler, Peoria, and Cook counties. An attempt was made by a Schuyler delegate to recommend a repeal of the law and the selection of Springfield by popular vote. A postponement was moved and the adoption of an address protesting against the multiplication of northern aspirants and recommending Springfield was secured by an overwhelming majority. The minority, however, from Peoria, Putnam, Tazewell, Knox, and Cook complained that the convention had organized at an unduly early hour, before all the delegates had arrived. They believed that designating any one northern place would unite the whole southern part of the state; rather than have that happen, they preferred that the act should be repealed.[17]

With a view to the vote, all the aspirants put forth their arguments for themselves and against their neighbors. A Vandalia meeting, July 3, protested against the unfairness of deciding the question six years before the expiration of the allotted time, as Vandalia was just beginning to develop and urged the unconstitutionality of the law. The board of trade of Alton, June 16, issued an address calling attention to that city's well-nigh year-round water communication which made it accessible from various parts of the state. The location of the capital there they urged would insure the location of the Cumberland road as the state wished it. It would enable Alton to rival St. Louis in earnest, for "the great city of the Northwest is yet to be reared on the banks of the Mississippi." Jacksonville could argue a large population, a college, and a reputation for culture; Springfield could claim a location near the center of the state. Peoria urged its facilities for manufacture, its location on the main routes of travel between Galena, Chicago, St. Louis, and the south, and its water con-

[17] *Sangamo Journal,* January 11, April 19, November 15, 1834; *Chicago Democrat,* April 23, 1834; *Illinois Advocate,* July 19, 1834; *Alton Spectator,* April 17, 24, 1834.

nection.[18]   Against Jacksonville and Springfield was alleged
their distance from navigable rivers. In the referendum vote
Alton was successful but by a narrow margin only.

The decisive struggle came in 1837. In Sangamon county
the legislative elections had resulted in the choice of nine
staunch whigs — the famous "Long Nine." They stood for
the unity of the county and a common effort to promote its
interests. In revenge for this complete overthrow the democratic opponents, John Calhoun and his friends, attempted to
defeat the Springfield project, some of them lobbying for
Peoria and some for Illiopolis, a town set near the center of
the state in which Duncan was said to be interested. In May
of 1837, Simeon Francis of the *Sangamo Journal* sardonically
noted that the town was represented only by a wolf trap, a fit
symbol of those trapped there.[19]   The measure for which the
Sangamon county members determined to work was a vote by
the general assembly — thus they could ultimately hope to
eliminate rivals that divided their vote. By a narrow margin
they carried their new act. On the vote that followed, Springfield was successful on the fourth ballot; and Vandalia at the
next session sought in vain to secure the repeal of the act. On
June 20, 1839, Governor Carlin issued his proclamation removing the capital to Springfield on or before July 4.

The means by which the Sangamon delegation achieved
their triumph were probably maneuvering and trading of the
frankest sort. Orville H. Browning in his somewhat pompous
way at a dinner in Springfield gave all praise to the delegation,
pronouncing that it was their "judicious management, their
ability, their gentlemanly deportment, their unassuming manners, their constant and untiring labor for your interests,"[20]
that had won Springfield her triumph. Stephen A. Douglas
more bluntly denying that he had traded his vote to the dele-

    [18] *Sangamo Journal*, July 27, 1833, June 21, 1834; *Alton Spectator*, July 1,
1834; *Chicago Democrat*, April 1, 1834.
    [19] *Sangamo Journal*, May 13, July 1, 1837; *House Journal*, 1836-1837, 1
session, 610, 613, 663, 702.
    [20] *Sangamo Journal*, July 29, 1837.

gation for a land office — and indeed he voted for Jacksonville to the last — declared the delegation had traded everything to obtain the capital. Peter Green of Clay county denied that the trade had been made of votes for the capital at Springfield for votes for a system of internal improvements for the south. But later when it was proposed to repeal the internal improvement system, Lincoln indignantly declared that a bargain had been made between the friends of the system and the friends of Springfield and that it was irrepealable. A casual examination of the legislative journals shows the Sangamon men always working for everyone's interest, voting for all additions to the system proposed, and splitting on motions to substitute one thing for another. Thus the sectional contest over the capital location led to the triumph of local interests in public improvement legislation.[21]

Meanwhile between 1829 and 1836 various local projects for internal improvements had been broached, discussed, expanded, all of them being based on more and more extravagant calculations of profits. The time was ripe for their friends to unite, and by bargains of one sort or another to commit the state to putting under construction a wild and fantastic system of internal improvements. At first such proposals had attracted but passing notice. Thus in 1829 the *Galena Advertiser* clipped an account of a projected railroad from Pittsburg to the head of steamboat navigation on the Illinois and thence to the Mississippi. In 1831 one or two meetings were held to urge a railroad from Lake Erie to the Mississippi. On December 28, 1832, a Jacksonville meeting, while indorsing the broad project, added a suggestion for a railroad from Jacksonville to the Illinois river. Abraham Lincoln in offering himself for the general assembly in 1832 suggested such a railroad with an extension to Springfield but concluded that the estimated cost, $290,000, was prohibitory. He judged it better to improve the navigation of the Sangamon, making it available for boats of twenty-five to thirty tons, and reënforced his

[21] *Illinois State Register,* July 20, 1838; *Sangamo Journal,* April 22, 1837.

statement with arguments based on his flatboat trip down the river.[22]

In 1834 the project took a form which provoked the hostility of the friends of the Illinois and Michigan canal. As then framed the transverse project involved a canal from the Wabash to the Mississippi to connect to the eastward with the projected series of canals to Lake Erie and Buffalo. In support of such a project it was argued that Lake Erie would be open much earlier in the spring than Huron and Michigan and that a circuit would be thereby avoided.[23]   Forquer in 1834 did not by any means reject the plan of an Illinois and Michigan canal. Instead of the transverse canal, he suggested a railroad via Danville, Decatur, Springfield, Beardstown, Rushville, and Quincy.[24]   The *Alton Spectator* sarcastically pronounced that Forquer's scheme had special reference to Springfield's ambitions for success in the capital election. The *Sangamo Journal* in turn pronounced that the thing that would really insure the position of Alton would be a railroad which would make it the depot and market of the Sangamon country.[25]

This last project gained favor in Springfield during 1835. In a meeting on May 25, Forquer elaborated the possible advantages to be gained from a vigorous enlistment of local support for the enterprise. He regarded such a railroad as only a step in the completion of a line to the Wabash and Erie canal, which should be accompanied by one to the Illinois and Mississippi rivers. He computed the total cost at $1,248,000

[22] *Galena Advertiser,* September 14, 1829; *Sangamo Journal,* January 5, March 15, 1832.
[23] *Sangamo Journal,* April 19, 1834. It stated the *Alton Spectator* and *Beardstown Chronicle* were favorable to the project. See *Alton Spectator,* April 24, 1834.
[24] *Sangamo Journal,* June 28, 1834. James Adams in his canvass for governor advocated a canal or railroad from the Wabash to the Mississippi. *Ibid.,* July 12, 1834. Representatives from Adams and Schuyler counties met on December 7, 1835, and urged a railroad from the Erie and Wabash canal to Quincy via Springfield and Jacksonville and also suggested a railroad to the Ohio via Vandalia. *Ibid.,* December 19, 1835. There was a meeting at Mackinaw to urge a railroad from the Wabash to the Illinois. *Ibid.* Ewing proposed this in his message of 1834. *House Journal,* 1834-1835, 1 session, 16.
[25] *Sangamo Journal,* April 25, 1835; *Alton Spectator,* August 26, 1834.

and estimated the tonnage as 45,000 annually, yielding $675,-
000 in freights. The return from the bonanza he calculated
at eighteen per cent, and he believed the farmers perfectly
warranted in pledging their farms for stock. Once these roads
and the Charleston-Memphis line, together with the Wabash-
Erie and Illinois-Michigan canals were completed, Springfield
would sit enthroned with markets on three distant seaboards
as her vassals. A railroad convention of delegates from Sangamon, Macon, Madison, and Macoupin was held a few weeks
later to push the Springfield-Alton railroad scheme.[26] The
cost of the Springfield and Alton railroad was estimated at
$500,000. But it was also estimated that the country would
provide for it 37,346 tons of freight a year—assuming that
each of 3,000 farms exported annually 100 bushels of wheat,
200 of corn, and 100 of oats, 12 hogs, and 5 cattle. Imports
would be 12,500 tons annually. The gross receipts from Sangamon county alone would yield $172,050 revenue annually, not
counting that of the three other favored counties. The mania
for calculations of imperial commercial enterprises was in
men's blood and had to run its course.

One section of the state began to vie with another in pursuing bubbles. In the fall of 1835 the project of the central
railroad began to take form. On October 28 the *Chicago
Democrat* printed a letter from Sidney Breese suggesting the
construction of a railroad from the junction of the canal with
the Illinois river to the mouth of the Ohio. Meetings in
support of such a project were held in Shelby county, October
19 and 20, and November 18; at Vandalia, October 26; and
at Decatur, November 11. A meeting in Jackson county,
December 2, deplored the comparative apathy of southern
Illinois in pushing her interests and warned her that by standing still she was losing position. It demanded support from
southern members to the central railroad project.[27] An act
for a two and a half million dollar corporation with a long

[26] *Chicago Democrat,* June 10, 1835; *Sangamo Journal,* April 25, May
22, 1835.
[27] *Illinois Advocate,* October 21, 28, December 17, 1835.

and impressive list of incorporators passed the assembly in 1836.

Several schemes, as might be imagined, centered on Chicago. One that attracted some interest in 1835 was for a railroad from Chicago to Vincennes. A federal land grant was asked for it, and the company was incorporated with three millions of capital to construct a railroad via Danville, Paris, and Palestine, to be begun in three years and completed in eight. There was provision for territorial location of directors and the road might be operated by steam or animal power. Next summer stock subscription books were opened.[28] In 1837 T. W. Smith and others petitioned congress for a right of way and a right to preëmpt in a ten-year credit a section on each side of the road. In return, they made the offer to carry the mails daily. At the time it was said that a million dollars of stock had been subscribed.

Inevitably various localities of the state came each to the conviction of the advisability of pooling local interests in internal improvements in a common stock. As early as 1830, Coles had prepared for the historical society of the state an excellent account of the state's physiography with reference to navigation and internal improvements; but such considerations were not to have the decisive voice in the laying out of public works. On November 2, 1833, the *Sangamo Journal* noticed the statement of a London paper that fifty million dollars of English capital could be lent to states desiring internal improvements or state banks. In 1834 several candidates garnished their announcements with statements for or against internal improvement systems.[29] Duncan in his inaugural message proposed the future improvement of the Illinois and Wabash channels on some such fashion, but like a good whig he looked for a possible change of heart on Jackson's part which would bring

[28] *House Journal*, 1834-1835, 1 session, 141; *Laws of 1835*, p. 88; *Chicago American*, September 26, 1835.
[29] *Illinois Intelligencer*, January 16, 1830; *Illinois Advocate*, June 26, July 5, 1834. Easton Whitten and Benjamin Roberts offer for the senate in Bond county against internal improvements in state money. James Evans offers for the governor. *Sangamo Journal*, July 5, 1834 declares for the system.

federal aid. The *Chicago Democrat,* clipping the *Peoria Champion,* on December 3, 1834, proposed as business for the legislature the following railroads, Chicago to the Wabash, Chicago to Galena, and Terre Haute to Quincy. In that session, however, internal improvements were regarded as possible rivals to the canal and as such for the moment to be discouraged.[30]

In 1835 the movement gained fresh impetus. Forquer's speech, already cited, bears its testimony to the fact. On October 16, Sidney Breese[31] pointed out a possible combination of internal improvement schemes which he thought might supply transportation both to the south and west. The scheme included a railroad on the route of the Illinois Central, for which the credit of the state might be pledged. From it, branches might radiate to the Wabash and the upper Mississippi. This prospect of juncture of the canal and the central railroad was considered by some as stretching the credit of the state too far. A member professed that in the next session he voted against the canal, not because he thought there was any danger in pledging the bulk of the stock for the canal, but because of a scheme to couple canal and railroad and borrow four millions for them.[32] Such a combination was proposed by a meeting at Ottawa, November 18.

Breese's plan was indorsed by a letter in the *Sangamo Journal* of November 28, 1835, which proposed also a railroad from Alton to Shawneetown to intersect the railroad from Louisville to New Orleans as well as a railroad from the Wabash and Erie canal to Quincy and from Springfield to

---

[30] Henry reported in the house, January 10, 1835, that it was necessary to put the whole energy of the state in the canal, and accordingly he moved the rejection of the petition for the improvement of the Illinois river. *House Journal,* 1834-1835, 1 session, 264. William J. Gatewood argued similarly on the incorporation of a railroad from Logansport to Quincy. Forquer argued on the other side that after all the south had gained from salines, the north might be entitled at least to an incorporation. The difficulty was caused by a squabble as to the terminus at Alton or Quincy. *Sangamo Journal,* January 17, 1835.

[31] *Sangamon Journal,* October 31, 1835.

[32] *Illinois Advocate,* December 2, 1835, January 16, 1836.

Alton. By way of financing these projects the author suggested a combination of land and stock aid and a private company. The editor of the paper commented that the novelty lay in the setting forth of a system for the whole state.

In the Illinois senate in the session of 1835–1836, Edwards offered a set of internal improvement resolutions in which he proposed that, to limit the impending multiplication of ineligible routes, the committee on internal improvements should report bills incorporating companies for railroads from the state line toward the Wabash and Erie canal through Danville, Decatur, and Springfield to Quincy; from the termination of the Illinois and Michigan canal through Bloomington to Decatur; and from Alton through Edwardsville and Equality to Shawneetown. He proposed state loans to these enterprises and a state subscription of one-third the capital stock in case the stockholders of a company had subscribed two-thirds. The right to buy out the company on terms was reserved to the state. A week later, he amended the resolution by providing that the line to Bloomington and Decatur serve to connect the canal with the Wabash and Mississippi and the Alton and Springfield railroads. His intention was to extend the road at a future time from Decatur via Springfield to Vandalia where it would connect with the Kaskaskia river which was to be made navigable, if it was possible to do so, by the use of future appropriations.[33] Edwards saw far enough into the defects, such as they were, of the haphazard system of granting charters that obtained in the 1836 session; but his positive argument for the concerted system which he outlined was singularly wanting in insight. The plan he proposed was merely building the railroads to connect the navigable rivers and to furnish communication between the small cities of that day.

Taken collectively the charters of 1836, which were passed at haphazard and usually with no opposition, are rather interesting. First it may be said that they varied widely in their

[33] *Senate Journal,* 1835-1836, 2 session, 154, 198.

provisions, probably in accord with the preconceptions of the lawyers who drew them up. Some of them contained provisions by which the state might take the properties over after a term of years, either at an appraised value, or at the original cost plus a fixed yearly interest, or for cost pluš cumulative interest. Several contained provisions allowing the legislature to regulate rates, if after a term of years the profits of the company exceeded a certain percentage. There were charters, however, which lacked one or many of these provisions. Most of them contained a forfeiture clause in the event the road was not duly begun, and some specified elaborately the rate at which construction must progress. Sometimes the charters were for limited periods; in other cases the only limitation was a power of legislative purchase in a term of years; sometimes there was not even that.[34] The Illinois Central was granted a monopoly limited by regulation of tolls and a right of purchase after twenty-five years.[35] On stock issues, the limitations devised often seemed rather intended to secure a wide distribution of stock than any other purpose. Sometimes the capital was specified in the charter, sometimes a specified increase was allowed, and sometimes a limit was placed upon the income. The sole limitation on the Mississippi, Springfield, and Carrollton railroad was that ten per cent of the stock be paid in. The Warsaw, Peoria, and Wabash was under practically no limitation whatever.[36] Some charters included provisions for reports to the legislature and others did not. Had the hopes of 1836 ever reached fruition, Illinois would have been covered with a railway system almost defying regulation.

The details of the various evanescent charters of the 1836 session are of comparatively little interest. They suggest in

[34] Charters of Mt. Carmel and Alton; Pekin, Bloomington, and Wabash; Belleville; Alton, Wabash and Erie; Rushville; Wabash and Mississippi; Central Branch Wabash; Wabash and Mississippi Union; Pekin and Tremont; and Mississippi, Springfield, and Carrollton railroads in *Laws of 1836*, p. 8, 12, 16, 18, 20, 21, 23, 36, 54, 63, 65, 89, 90.

[35] *Ibid.*, p. 129.

[36] *Ibid.*, p. 12, 76.

no great degree the railroads of the present. This is true in the main probably because they were centered commonly at Alton rather than at St. Louis. Of the projected lines, the Galena and Chicago Union, the Illinois Central line from La Salle to Cairo, and one from Danville to Meredosia suggesting the line of the Wabash are the only extensive lines which still persist.

The fateful legislative session of 1836–1837 was the logical result of the charters of 1836. With so many enterprises in the field, the feeble resources that would scarcely have sufficed a single enterprise were diffused among many. It is difficult in the case of most of the enterprises projected during 1836 to trace any successful prosecution of the task of organizing them. In the fall, Gallatin, Wayne, Sangamon, and probably other counties appointed delegates to a convention at Vandalia to decide what parts of the various lines had better be supported.[37]

In the Illinois legislative session of 1836–1837 the internal improvement system began with Douglas' resolutions. They specified the Illinois and Michigan canal, a railroad from the terminus of the canal to the mouth of the Ohio, a railroad from Quincy to the Wabash and Erie canal, the improvement of the Illinois and Wabash rivers, and surveys of other works. These were to be constructed at the state's expense on a loan of [blank in resolution] on the state's credit, and the debt was to be floated by sales from the lands of the Illinois and Michigan canal, that enterprise being compelled to forego its privileged position and take its chance with the other works. Three days later in the senate, Edwards proposed a joint inquiry by the internal improvement committee of the two houses as to the expediency of devising a system for the whole state, the interest on the loan to be paid from a part of the distribution fund. He left open the question of construction by chartered companies. Full reports were made, and in con-

[37] *Sangamo Journal,* February 13, August 27, November 26, 1836; *Illinois State Register,* December 8, 1836.

sequence both houses passed resolutions begging shamelessly for federal land grants.[38] The house internal improvement committee reported on January 9. It began with the usual appeal to the brilliant prospects of New York and the even greater opportunity before Illinois. It fortified itself by the fact that in the internal improvement convention the people had been represented and had spoken their mind. It offered a plan more conservative than the conventions — certainly in view of the huge sale of lands in the previous year and the oncoming flood of immigration none too radical. It cheerfully dispensed with inquiry into costs with the fact that the cost of constructing railways in Illinois was capable of exact estimate and that if the routes were surveyed first, the state could not hope to buy adjacent lands at the federal price.

Descending to particulars, it recommended a loan of eight millions in the hands of a board of fund commissioners. To meet this debt the state might count on twelve million acres of taxable land by 1842. The railroads were to be begun at intersections with navigable streams and important towns and to be extended in both directions from them. It estimated the cost of railroads at $8,000 a mile or less and it recommended the expenditure of $100,000 each on the Great Wabash, and the Illinois and Rock, $50,000 on the Kaskaskia and Little Wabash, $100,000 on the Great Western Mail route, $3,500,000 on the Illinois Central, $1,600,000 on the Southern Cross railroad, and $1,850,000 on the Northern Cross.[39] As finally passed the act added $150,000 to the appropriation for the Western Mail route, and added to the act provisions for a railroad, Bloomington to Mackinaw involving an expenditure of $350,000; one from Belleville to intersect the Alton and Mt. Carmel at $150,000; one from Lower Alton via Hillsboro to the Illinois Central railroad at $600,000; one from Peoria to Warsaw to cost $700,000; and a branch of the Illinois Central railroad from the point where

[38] *Senate Journal,* 1836-1837, 1 session, 87, 89, 127; *House Journal,* 1836-1837, 1 session, 36.

[39] *Ibid.,* 1836-1837, 1 session, 202.

a line from Hillsboro to Shelbyville would intersect it to the
Indiana state line. In addition, $200,000 was divided between
the unfortunate counties which obtained no other appropriations.

The procedure by which these amendments were added is
difficult to trace. The bill was reported to the house along
with the report; it was reported back on January 23. Several
attempted amendments were defeated, the Sangamon members
usually voting for additions. An attempt to condemn the whole
system by resolution was lost by a vote of 9 to 70, most of the
opposition being from Greene, the lower Military Tract, and
Egypt. A second attempt to obtain a referendum on it at the
next election was lost 20 to 59, the opposition again coming
from the Military Tract and from Egypt. The amendments
usually were supported by the members interested in the addition, the members from Sangamon and Morgan and the
irreconcilables who wished to kill the bill. The bill passed
January 31, by a vote of 61 to 25.[40]

February 16 the senate committee reported the bill with
amendments. In the senate two additions were voted down.
The Bloomington and Mackinaw railroad was added. William
O'Rear's proposal for a popular vote was lost 20 to 20. The
amendment for $200,000 to the counties not otherwise favored
was added here also and adopted 31 to 9. The third reading
was carried, 25 to 15 and the passage by a similar vote.[41]
The representatives of White county in the house February 23
spread on the journal of the house a protest against the measure as designed to do nothing but raise the value of town lots
in certain favored spots; and as saddling the state with a debt
the interest on which was ten times the ordinary revenue. It
pointed out that the locations of the railroad lines were made
not by any settled plan but rather as a result of logrolling. The
protesters pointed out especially the disaster that might result
from the method of financing by bank capital.[42]

[40] *House Journal*, 1836-1837, 1 session, 363, 366, 443.
[41] *Senate Journal*, 1836-1837, 1 session, 445, 452, 466, 474, 475, 487.
[42] *House Journal*, 1836-1837, 1 session, 680.

Two days later the council of revision returned the bill with objections. Judges Browne and Lockwood objected to certain mere technical provisions which could be easily altered. Smith in concurring especially declined any expression of opinion on the question of expediency which he left to the general assembly. Duncan took issue on the ground that such roads could be made in a free government only by citizens or corporations. He pointed out the danger of interference in elections of those in power over the system. The objections of Browne and Lockwood were at once obviated and the bill passed 53 to 20. On February 27 the senate adopted the house amendment and passed the bill 23 to 13.[43] The state had embarked on its mad speculation in haste; it was to have full seven years in which to repent at its leisure.

[43] *Senate Journal*, 1836-1837, 1 session, 529, 531.

XI. THE WRECK OF THE INTERNAL IMPROVE-
MENT SYSTEM, 1837–1842

A S SOON as the internal improvement system had been adopted by the legislature, the board prepared to begin construction with all possible speed. It divided the state into three districts each with a principal engineer. As the law prescribed the policy of working on the enterprises simultaneously in proportionate amounts, construction was allotted among them. Accordingly 105 miles were put under contract on the Northern Cross, 69½ miles on the Illinois Central, 24 on the Peoria and Warsaw, 15 on the Alton and Shawneetown, 38 on the Alton and Mt. Carmel, 33 on the Alton and Shelbyville, and 9¼ on the Bloomington and Pekin. The board estimated the mileage of the roads at 1,341¾ and their total cost at $11,470,444.50. It pointed out that this sum exceeded the original figure set because the roads were found to be longer than they had been estimated. By December of 1838 the commissioners of public works had drawn on the fund commissioners for $1,142,027.00.

There was needed no acute observer to predict from the manner of its inception the ill success of the internal improvement system. Not only were some of the commissioners guilty at least of neglect and mismanagement, if not of positive malversation, but the enterprises were from the first befogged in the atmosphere of logrolling and bargain, under which the system had been initiated by the legislature. This condition necessitated an equal attention to all the localities benefiting by the improvements and contributing their share to the bargain by which it was pushed into operation. Accordingly the provision requiring simultaneous construction on all the roads prevented the concentrating of effort to complete any one and install it as a revenue producer. Out of a piece of newspaper pseudoscience Governor Kinney evolved a phrase to describe the situation. Writing to the citizens of Peoria who had asked that part of the projected railroad in their vicinity should be put under contract, he expressed the following opinion: "Respecting the 25th section of the Internal Improvement Law, to which you refer me, it is idle to say that there is any thing therein contained as a positive injunction upon the Commissioners' that they should commence on each side of every navigable stream, and progress each way *at the same time,* and also at each principal town. You know that every town, in the eyes of them that inhabit it, is a principal one. Such a course of proceeding would cut upon the whole system of rail roads into so many parts, disjointed and disconnected one from the other for the time being, that it would appear in the attitude of a 'jointed snake,' which had been whipped into so many pieces that some of them would be decayed and rendered useless before they could crawl to each other's relief, and therefore bring the whole into disrepute at once." The jointed snake was a good analogy for the internal improvement system.[1]

The mania for internal improvement was not satisfied even by the system itself. Private enterprises flourished side by side with it. Thus at the time when the system was beginning its journey through the general assembly, there appeared in the *Sangamo Journal* the prospectus of the Beardstown and Sangamon canal. The thirty mile cut from Beardstown to Huron would at a cost of six thousand dollars a mile take the place of a river route of one hundred miles. A possible connection with the Wabash canal was set forth and the prospects of the vast quantities of produce from the Sangamon country and of deflected trade from the Ohio were held out to investors. The state was to be asked to subscribe one-third of the capital. Among the other projects was one for a railroad from Rock Island to Bloomington by way of Henne-

[1] *Sangamo Journal,* March 17, 1838.

pin. Inside and outside the system men were living in a gilded age.[2]

In a very especial sense, as has been seen, the internal improvement system was the offspring of southern Illinois, which hoped to regain the ground that it had lost to the northern portion of the state during the preceding fifteen years. The men of Egypt hoped that the numerous railroads projected might turn back the tide of emigration which had flowed either along the Great Lakes or through southern Indiana to the head waters of the Illinois river. The traveler in 1839 commented on the backwardness of the region between Mt. Vernon and Equality, where the old settlers were still living in their rude cabins with very few improvements; but he added that the internal improvement system had drawn new attention to the south. Middle Illinois in view of the interest of the south in the internal improvement system was inclined to be somewhat sarcastic about it. In the assembly of 1837 there was an amusing passage at arms between Peter Green of Clay county and William Lane of Greene. Mr. Green advocated a bill authorizing a state bounty on wolf scalps, only to be told by Mr. Lane that his earnestness was due to the large proportion of wolves to human beings in his county, especially in comparison with Greene. Lane assured him, however, that when the various railroads projected in Clay had been constructed the ringing of the engine bells would scare all the wolves into Greene county, where, no railroads having been projected, they might live in peace.[3]

The faith of southern Illinois was pinned especially to the Illinois Central railroad. Not only was it the center of the system, having as tributaries the various crossroads and branches, but it served to connect the outlet of the Illinois and Michigan canal with year-round river transportation on the Mississippi. What the central railroad was to the system in the mind of the south, Cairo was to the central railroad.

[2] *Illinois State Register*, September 15, 1837; *Sangamo Journal*, January 6, 1837, January 28, 1838; *Alton Telegraph*, May 9, December 8, 1838.
[3] *Sangamo Journal*, February 25, 1837.

Men foresaw the development of Cairo into a commercial metropolis central to all the union; for was it not possible that the great Charleston railroad might terminate, if not at Shawneetown, at least at Cairo, thus uniting the junction of the Ohio and Mississippi with the southern Atlantic seaboard? John Logan of Jackson county, in the Illinois legislature, painted an inspiring word picture of ocean going ships laden with the produce of the West Indies discharging their cargoes at the wharves of Cairo. Meanwhile, with just scorn he repelled the possibility that the rival village of Caledonia, a little further up the Ohio might hope to rival Cairo as the Venice of the New World.[4]

But while southern Illinois and other parts of the state especially interested were enthusiastic over the system, the program of improvements had met consistent opposition from the first. It had been a political issue in the campaign of 1838, the democrats claiming that the whig nominees, Edwards especially, were then, or had been, hostile to the system. The whigs it is true endeavored to disprove the assertion that Edwards had opposed improvements, but admitted that he preferred that they should be constructed by private enterprise rather than by the state. Thomas Carlin, the democratic nominee, declared in favor of the system, though he later believed its scope was out of all proportion to the resources available for its construction.[5]

Joseph Duncan, of course, was the most inveterate opponent of the whole program; and the tendency of the whigs, as a party, especially in view of the fact that their political opponents upheld the system, was toward opposition. The *Vandalia Free Press,* for instance, declared that, while it was not opposed to a judicious employment of internal improvements, it considered that the system as it had developed had been rashly and unwisely adopted and that with the cessation of federal

[4] *Illinois State Register,* December 22, 1837, December 13, 1838, March 8, 15, 1839.
[5] *Ibid.,* February 9, March 9, July 13, 1838; *Alton Telegraph,* March 7, 1838.

deposits with the state, it was a difficult problem to obtain the money with which to carry it out. The *Sangamo Journal* pointed out the hindrance that a currency of gold and silver, limited in amount, would impose upon the financing of such a scheme. In the summer the *Peoria Register* began the publication of a series of bitter attacks written by a certain E. Harkness. Harkness declared that all the enterprises could not yield a revenue equivalent to the yearly interest on the money expended. He maintained that in reality the state had little surplus produce to export, not enough indeed to supply the laborers on the works. Where, he asked, were the reasons for the railroads to Cairo? What was the use of a railroad beginning and ending on the Mississippi? Galena was the only town upon its route that was not a mere name. Harkness finally called upon the people to express immediately their disapprobation of the system and of the men who had framed it.[6]

Until the arguments of the opponents of the system were reënforced by actual failure of the state finances, they did not become effective. The clue to the legislation of the session of 1839 is suggested in a New York letter published in the *Peoria Register* January 19, 1839, in which the correspondent stated that while London was flooded with state stocks, the preference was given to those of free states engaged in internal improvement. If Illinois would face the question of direct taxation, she might with profit send a commission to London to borrow. Of course, the prospect of taxation caused a recurrence of attacks on the system. Defending it against O. H. Browning, W. J. Gatewood of Gallatin warned him that, if its progress was checked, southern Illinois would retaliate on the canal which in earlier years it had sustained. He urged that the statesmanlike attitude toward the question was not a calculation of profits and losses in money but rather a consideration of the matter in the broader aspect of the development of the state.

[6] *Illinois State Register*, July 14, 1837; *Alton Telegraph*, March 14, September 22, 1838; *Sangamo Journal*, October 21, 1837; *Peoria Register*, August 25, September 8, 22, 29, October 27, November 2, 1838.

Abraham Lincoln suggested, in lieu of taxation, financing the proposed improvements by a speculation in the unsold land of the federal government.[7]

The net result of the legislative session was an enlargement of the system rather than its curtailment. In an amendatory law certain further expenditures for additional work were allowed. For the rest, a general taxation law was passed. It levied twenty cents on each one hundred dollars of property in the state. Needless to say this provoked opposition of the bitterest sort. At first, the *State Register* was disposed to defend the act. It pointed out that the law really was a poor man's tax law, as it compelled speculators to list land at its true value and carried no poll tax provision. It defended the obnoxious provision requiring the filing under oath of one's statement as being optional with the assessor to require or not and insisted that the law was not passed necessarily to support the internal improvement system, and hence could not be directly connected with it. The state, it was said, had never taxed itself hitherto and as a result had been led into uncertain financial devices such as plundering the school fund and the making of the Wiggins' loan.[8]

The text of the foregoing comment was the proceedings of a meeting in Bond county which attacked both the internal improvement system and the revenue law. The report of the meeting, rather able in its way, mercilessly cut to pieces the specious promises and calculations of profit on which the system had originally been founded. It stated that to pay interest on the cost of the railroads centering at Alton, sixteen thousand wagonloads of freight must pass in and out of the city in each month. The *Register,* coming to see light by April, had ceased to defend the revenue law and was inclined to leave it to the people for their acceptance or rejection. The meeting in Bond county was followed by one in Hillsboro, at which A. P. Field was present. It urged a special session of the general assembly

[7] *Alton Telegraph,* January 26, 1839; *Illinois State Register,* February 19, March 15, 1839.
[8] *Ibid.,* March 29, 1839.

for the purpose of repealing the system.   The *Register* deprecated the demand on the ground that the cry for a special session was a whig device to break up the system and incidentally
to elect a whig to the United States senate.[9]

The opposition to the law spread fast.   In Bond county it
was proposed that the revenue law be defeated by the appointment of assessors who would refuse to serve.   In one county
after another, resolutions attacking the system were passed,
frequently calling for a special session to curtail or classify it.
The revenue law, too, was often included in such denunciation.
Furthermore the enterprise was often arraigned as a white ele-
phant foisted on the state by bargain and corruption, sure to
involve the state in hopeless debt.   Only occasionally was a
voice lifted in behalf of the system as it then stood.[10]

The whigs were generally in favor of calling a special
session.   So far as parties were aligned on the question, the
democrats were at first opposed to it, alleging their fear that
the whigs might take advantage of it to repeal the revenue law
or to engineer a *coup d'état* respecting the secretaryship of state
and the senatorship.   The whigs denied that they had any
such intention.   In the spring their papers were flatly for a
classification of the system, by which work would be continued
only on a part of it.   They pointed out that the democrats
were inconsistent in favoring classification of the system and
opposing a special session, for if a change were to be of any
avail whatever it must come immediately.   The democrats,
however, were by no means completely in favor of an alteration
of the system at this time.   Thus on June 21 the *State Register*
pronounced against classification reporting a scheme by which
the people might yearly decide what sum they must spend upon
improvements.   It pointed out the difficulty of satisfying by a
classification the jarring local interests and of deciding which

[9] *Alton Telegraph,* March 24, April 13, May 24, 1839; *Illinois State Register,*
May 29, 1835, April 5, 19, 1839.

[10] *Alton Telegraph,* May 11, 18, 1839; *Illinois State Register,* June 14, 1839;
Vandalia Whig, June 7, 1839; *Peoria Register,* June 15, July 6, 1839; *Sangamo
Journal,* June 28, July 26, 1839.

locality must suffer the abandonment of its pet enterprise. The same issue contained an illustration in point in the action of a meeting in Edgar county which would not consent to the classification if its own route was omitted.[11]

During the summer the two parties shifted their position on the question of a special session. In July, Carlin had offered as excuse for not calling one the fear that it might, like the previous session, extend the system instead of curtailing it. In September, the whig newspapers professed that in the present situation they could see no need for a special session, though they still inclined to favor classification. By November democratic meetings were declaring against the internal improvement system or urging its classification. When Carlin finally called a special session to meet on December 9 the *State Register* took to task the *Chicago Democrat* for opposing his action, adducing as reasons for the call the fact that the plans, even if they were not too extensive for 1837, were certainly too ambitious for 1839, and that the people generally desired a reduction of the system to a size proportionable to the state's hope of completing it. Possibly in this argument there was the desire ascribed to the *Register* by the *Journal* of embarrassing the "Long Nine" of Sangamon county by compelling them either to abandon their pledges or to oppose the will of their constituents. It was said at the beginning of the special session that Carlin was coming to the capital late so that his message might not be revised by the party leaders as it had been in 1838, when a proposal for classification had been omitted at the behest of the locofoco leaders. The democratic leaders at the beginning of the session were reported to have disclaimed any responsibility for the call of the assembly, and they left Carlin to state the reasons for it and to bear the brunt of the consequences of having called it.[12]

[11] *Chicago American*, May 29, September 5, October 2, 1839; *Sangamo Journal*, May 17, 24, June 14, July 19, 1839.
[12] *Illinois State Register*, November 9, 16, 1839; *Sangamo Journal*, December 16, 1838, May 24, July 19, September 23, November 15, 1839; *Alton Telegraph*, December 14, 1839.

In his message to the general assembly Carlin pronounced in favor of a classification of the internal improvement system and of the adoption of a more economical method of carrying it into effect. He ascribed the system in the first place to the spirit of speculation, " the natural offspring of an inflated paper circulating medium," that had affected not only individuals but even such conservative bodies as the general assembly. In spite of the fact that it was well understood that the system was the result of mutual concession and compromise and that its advantages were to be dispensed as equally as possible throughout the state, it was necessary to classify immediately. The localities with favorite improvements, which should be eliminated by the scheme of classification, must bear their loss with patriotism for the common good. The message detailed the progress of the financial negotiations in London for funds to support the system, which will be considered later. The session finally provided for the cessation of work upon the system and in effect by so doing brought about its permanent abandonment. Thenceforth the state was confronted with the problem of paying for the extravagance into which it had entered and from which it withdrew too early to obtain any considerable advantages.[13]

The attempt to obtain in exchange for state bonds the funds with which to carry on the internal improvement enterprise had begun in 1837, when Mather and Oakley, the fund commissioners, endeavored to negotiate a loan in New York. Finding no success there, they turned to the State Bank and to the Bank of Illinois. The State Bank agreed to take seventeen hundred and sixty-five bonds of one thousand dollars each and the Bank of Illinois nine hundred similar bonds. A second appeal to the New York market was more successful than the first. The commissioners sold a million dollars in state internal improvement stock to Nicholas Biddle, a similar amount to J. Irvine, and three or four blocks of one hundred thousand each

[13] *Illinois State Register,* January 4, 1840; *Alton Telegraph,* January 25, February 8, 1840; governor's message to legislature, January 8, 1845, in *House Journal,* 1839-1840, 2 session, 14.

to other capitalists. May 7, 1839, the fund commissioners, M. M. Rawlings and Charles Oakley, sold to John Delafield $283,000 in state bonds, interest on the bonds beginning May 7, 1839. Delafield, by the terms of the contract, was to pay for the bonds in five installments of fifty thousand dollars each on the first of December, February, March, April, and May, and one of thirty-three thousand dollars on June 1. The contract certainly was not favorable to the state. The committee also made some sales of bonds in smaller amounts to eastern banks and one more considerable to the contractor for the Northern Cross railway.

Having exhausted the possibilities of the New York money market the Illinois agents turned to London. On August 22, 1839, Rawlings and Oakley made a contract with John Wright and Company of London. By this contract, which was rather elaborately drawn, the Illinois agents agreed to turn over to Wright for sale $1,500,000 in state bonds in return for two advances and gave him the option on the flotation of a further sum to the amount of $4,000,000. The borrowers on behalf of the Illinois and Michigan canal, who had been working independently, had now reached the same point in their pursuit of money. Although the commissioners had disposed of a considerable number of bonds to federal and state banks, to private banks and investors, the terms were not advantageous to the state; and they too were obliged to seek money in London. On October 30, 1839, Reynolds and Young made an agreement with Wright and Company for the sale of a million dollars in canal bonds.[14]

No sooner had this series of loans been consummated than the whole financial house of cards began to fall. First the stages of the negotiations with the Wrights may be followed. There was a fatal difference of opinion as to the interpretation of the law prescribing that the Illinois bonds be sold at not less than par. The contract for a million in sterling bonds of the state had required Wright to advance but $250,000, and in

[14] *Reports General Assembly,* 1839-1840, house, 393.

return for this he was to be the state selling agent, deducting his commission from the proceeds. Further, the bonds were drawn at the face value of £225 but were to yield only $1,000 in the United States, although the exchange between London and Illinois might be as high as fourteen per cent. In remitting for interest and for final payment, therefore, the state would remit far more than the par value of the amounts due translated into American currency in Illinois. A senate committee declared the contract null and void, insisting that Wright was no better than a financial shark. The report was drawn in O. H. Browning's somewhat flowery style. "Well may we say of London," exclaimed he, "'the shark is there, and the shark's prey,— the spendthrift and the leech that sucks him.'"[15] Hacker retorted with a report from the committee of the senate on internal improvement, indulging in some rather cleverly put personal allusions derogatory to Browning.[16] The majority and minority of the house committee differed as to the legality of the sale of canal bonds, which Wright had been permitted to sell at 91 or over in London, retaining for himself any excess between 91 and 95 and above 95 dividing his profits with the state. A joint judiciary committee reported against the legality of the sale.[17]

Naturally such action by the Illinois general assembly did no good to the financial interests of the state in London. Whether Wright had intentionally misled the representatives of the state or whether he had merely been too sanguine in interpreting the contract and laws which they brought with them, it is not necessary to state. But the report of the Illinois committee compelled him for a time to cease his operations, even though the general assembly did not adopt the report recommending the disavowal of the contract. Carlin, under the circumstances, could not in February of 1840 see his way clear to continue the contract with Wright. The contractors on the canal, however, proposed to proceed with the work, if

[15] *Senate Journal,* 1839-1840, special session, 140.
[16] *Reports General Assembly,* 1839-1840, senate, 209.
[17] *Ibid.,* 1839-1840, house, 123, 149, 393.

they might receive canal bonds in payment which they could hypothecate with Wright, according to the terms of the contract which the legislature had not indorsed. Young, meanwhile, did not cease to urge on Carlin that the state contract with Wright be carried out. Finally, on May 1, Carlin yielded and confirmed the sale of the million canal bonds. Characteristically he protested to the last that it was not a sale at par within the meaning of the act.[18] But Carlin's hesitation and the attitude of the general assembly had done their work. It was too late to save Wright's position in London. Overloaded with the state's bonds and possibly suffering from the malignity of other houses opposed to dealing with Americans and the American states, in November of 1840 Wright became bankrupt. William F. Thornton, president of the board of commissioners, had previously on July 20 agreed to sell at a rate of 83 to Magniac, Smiths and Company £225,000 sterling in bonds belonging to the contractors,[19] and for a time that firm attended to the financial interests of the state.

In apportioning blame for the disaster to the Wrights it is impossible to avoid the conclusion that in a certain degree their misfortune was their own fault. The interpretation which they gave to the term "par" was certainly a forced one, and while in all probability in view of the way Illinois securities were marketed no better rates could have been obtained, they should have been more cautious; and even in spite of any representation made to them, they should have recognized the fact that they should have trusted their own judgment as to the terms of the loan rather than the judgment of such men as Young and Reynolds. At the same time the vacillation of Carlin and the general assembly at the critical moment undoubtedly contributed to rendering the financial position of the Wrights critical.

It was in the United States that the effect of the fund com-

---

[18] *Reports General Assembly*, 1840-1841, senate, 360, 362, 363, 364, 373, 374.
[19] *Ibid.*, 1840-1841, senate, 30 ff., 393.

missioners' policy was most apparent. The Atlantic Bank which had bought the public improvement bonds broke before the Illinois bonds had passed out of its hands, and these were ordered returned to the state's order. John Tillson and the other two fund commissioners worked at cross-purposes, and Tillson was accused of malfeasance. It is not easy to determine whether or not he was guilty, but certainly he was hoodwinked in at least one negotiation with the result that the security for fifty bonds sold became worthless. He had also private dealings with Delafield which may have affected his course as a public officer. The state's contract with Delafield soon led to a lawsuit devised to prevent him from disposing to innocent third parties of the state bonds of which he had gained possession. Governor Carlin had protested and rightly against the terms of Reynolds' contract with the United States Bank by which the state was compelled to pay principal and interest in London, thereby giving the bank at home a premium based on exchange. Furthermore, the use of various agencies for marketing the state bonds made it impossible for any financial house to deal in them successfully or to hold them for a favorable turn of the market. Again and again large customers of the state, like the Wrights, had to complain that parcels of bonds that had come on the market for small purchasers were being passed about at rates which spoiled the sale of larger holdings. In 1839 the canal commissioners began the issuance of checks to pay contractors on the canal; and by fall this method of financing was completely out of control.[20]

The problem of providing for interest on the state loan was becoming increasingly difficult. An act of the session of 1839–1840 provided for the payment of interest on canal bonds out of sales of canal lands.[21] The interest on state bonds held in London due in July, 1840, was paid out of £20,000 received from John Wright; and for the payment of interest

[20] *Reports General Assembly*, 1839-1840, senate, 370; house, 55; *ibid.*, 1840-1841, senate, 68.
[21] *Laws of 1840*, p. 80.

in the United States, Thornton borrowed $5,000 at home. Far more difficult was the problem of providing interest in January, 1841. In December the legislature passed an act allowing the hypothecation of bonds. But even with this proviso it was only by desperate effort that R. F. Barrett, the fund commissioner, succeeded in obtaining the money necessary for the interest. At the beginning of the session the assembly adopted a law levying a tax of ten cents on the hundred dollars for the interest on the loan and allowing the hypothecation of bonds to anticipate it, in spite of the protests of certain democrats at allowing banks to dictate the policy of the state in this particular. The interest for July, 1841, was obtained by John D. Whiteside as fund commissioner in return for the hypothecation with Charles Macalister and Henry Stebbins of 804 bonds, a proceeding which saddled the state for years to come with a dispute involving the question of the disposal of bonds to innocent third parties.[22]

Upon the abandonment of the internal improvement system the vital question was how the state might pay what it had already borrowed to construct that system rather than how the state might obtain funds to complete it. Interest in the question of internal improvement shifted to the attempt of persons interested in the Illinois and Michigan canal to engage the state to find the funds necessary to proceed with that work. In Cook county the canal question was an extremely important one in local politics. Thus in the summer of 1840, partly as a result of a disagreement in the democratic convention, it was urged, especially by the *Chicago American,* that the democratic ticket was anti-canal; and a canal ticket was nominated. The whigs nominated no candidates against them and apparently the ticket drew a good share of the whig support, the canal laborers alone being held responsible for the defeat of the canal ticket. John Pearson was elected senator over James Turney; Ebenezer Peck, Albert G. Leary, and Richard Murphy repre-

[22] *Reports General Assembly,* 1840-1841, senate, 327; *ibid.,* 1842-1843, senate, 75; *Laws of 1841,* p. 167; *Illinois State Register,* December 18, 23, 1840.

sentatives over W. B. Ogden, John M. Wilson, and G. A. O. Beaumont.[23]

The canal ticket, though defeated, had its revenge, for the canal delegation, as it was called, had no success in its attempt to push the interests of the canal in the legislature. The whig papers stated that the partisanship of the canal members alienated the friends of the canal in the general assembly and frustrated their attempts to secure a measure for its continuation. Pearson especially was accused of committing the unpardonable sin of interfering with the local measures of his fellow senators, and the fact that the Cook county delegation, worked for the election of a partisan canal commissioner disgusted the whigs, who would otherwise have been disposed to favor the canal. Whatever may have been the cause, the legislature finally adjourned without making any provision for the continuance of the work.[24] According to the *Alton Telegraph*, the canal members discovered that their party would not support them in behalf of the canal, and their partisanship drove away whig support in the senate. The vote on the question bears out this statement fairly well.[25]

Certainly, whether or not the canal delegation could have guided their enterprise more skillfully, there was great wrath in the north among both whigs and democrats. As the *Sangamo Journal* put it in commenting on the result of the session of 1840–1841, the delegation had upset the judiciary, turned out Thornton, the canal commissioner, elected Peck to an office, and as a result had stopped work on the canal by antagonizing its friends. The *State Register* had to take the *Chicago Democrat* to task for its attacks upon the legislature. The political

---

[23] *Belleville Advocate*, August 23, 1840; *Chicago American*, June 26, July 27, 30, August 5, 1840.

[24] *Alton Telegraph*, February 13, 1841; *Chicago American*, January 14, February 15, March 18, 1841; the contractors had proposed forming a corporation to contract with the canal commissioners for the completion of the canal. According to the *American* it appealed to the canal members to give this project a chance at success by refusing to caucus for the appointment of canal commissioners, warning them if they did so they would prejudice the whigs against the measure.

[25] *Alton Telegraph*, April 10, 1841.

careers of all members of the delegation except those already ensconced in office were at an end, an effect which possibly "Long John" Wentworth, whose views may be found in the *Chicago Democrat,* did not deplore. Certainly neither Leary, Murphy, Pearson, nor Peck ever again interfered with his political ambitions in the north.[26]

The canal region did its best to undo the fatal work of its delegation. Meetings were held in the north demanding a special session to devise a means for the continuance of work on the canal. The newspapers issued similar appeals and demands for the resignation of the canal members in the hope that more efficient ones might figure in the special session. Carlin, though he did not call a special session, was induced to make promises of issuance of state bonds for the continuation of work on the canal. The *Sangamo Journal* protested that the issue of bonds was impossible, declaring that the only relief would be by reverting to the method of a chartered company. Being on the line of the canal the *Chicago American* was of course in favor of Carlin's plan, but generally throughout the state the whigs opposed the hypothecation of bonds for the benefit of the canal or for any other purpose whatever. The reason is to be found perhaps in clippings from the *New York Herald* to the effect that the hypothecation of bonds to Macalister and Stebbins had ruined the credit of the state. The *Sangamo Journal* was inclined to think that, while the state would not repudiate and would ultimately pay all, the bondholders must be resigned to wait for a few years without interest until the restoration of prosperity under a whig administration in the nation would make it possible for Illinois to pay off her seventeen millions of debt.[27]

Eventually the hard times, the overwhelming debt, the difficulty of meeting even such taxes as were laid, produced throughout the state a cry for repudiation. In the general assembly of 1841 one member, describing conditions in his

[26] *Sangamo Journal,* March 26, 1841; *Illinois State Register,* March 19, 1841.
[27] *Sangamo Journal,* September 10, October 22, November 19, December 3, 17, 1841; *Alton Telegraph,* November 13, December 11, 1841.

neighborhood, declared that magistrates and constables were the only business men. In Bond county, a meeting to protest against additional taxation laid down the doctrine that the state was not morally bound to pay its debts. In Montgomery a nonpartisan meeting called for frugality in government, denounced the baleful results of government debts, and advanced the doctrine that there must be no taxation to pay principal or interest on debt except in so far as the people had received some return for it. In Scott county it was said that the bonds were bills of credit and as such unconstitutional and not binding upon the state.

Both whig and democratic papers denounced the doctrine of repudiation as stated by such extremists, but there was some sparring between the two parties in attempting each to force the other to a definite stand. First the *Sangamo Journal* declared that a proposed anti-repudiation article in the democratic state platform of 1841 had been tabled. On the other hand the *Register* declared that the *Journal* had come out for repudiation or for taxation sufficient to pay the debt; and the *Register* pronounced the people too honest for the one and too poor for the other. On December 16, the *Alton Telegraph* declared the *Battle Axe* to be the only paper in the state in favor of repudiation; but by November 13, it had declared that the payment of interest should stop unless the bondholders would take still more bonds at par. It pointed out truly enough the fact that Illinois bonds had been hypothecated at thirty-three cents on the dollar, while Indiana bonds on which the interest even was not paid were sold at a higher rate. It believed that the legislature, refusing longer to issue state bonds unless creditors would take them at par, should levy as heavy a tax as possible for their ultimate payment.[28]

The payment of the July, 1841, interest was the last attempt to keep the state's finances solvent. From that time the state defaulted on her interest, and her bonds fell far below

[28] *Illinois State Register,* October 29, November 5, 1841; *Sangamo Journal,* December 24, 1841.

par. The financial situation sank into deeper and deeper confusion. No proper accounts were kept, and the progress of
the various fund commissioners in settling with the state's
debtors, such as Delafield and the New York banks, multiplied
the intricacy of the situation. The party jealousies which had
hampered and biased the work of the state's financial officers
from the beginning continued in political squabbles, such as
that one on the canal route between the friends of Thornton
and of Isaac N. Morris. The taxation law of 1841 was used
by surrounding states as an argument by which to attract emigrants from Illinois to their own borders. The oft repeated
statement that Illinois was a ruined state was heard on every
hand. The railroad lines which had been intended to make
her the commercial center of the union were abandoned, finding
employment only where thrifty farmers used their rights of
way to grow beans.[29]

In the maze of proposals, or appeals for relief, that came
from all sides, not much can be seen in 1842 but the claims of
personal, factional, sectional, or party interest. In 1842 there
was a recrudescence of repudiation sentiment which was, however, generally frowned upon. County meetings here and there
demanded strict economy in the legislature in the way of salaries and the elimination of such time-wasting devices as
committees of the whole and allowing members to speak more
than one hour on a question. From the line of the canal emanated various proposals for continuing that work, which still
went on. Sometimes these implied obtaining a larger federal
land grant, the sale of canal lots and lands, or the use of the
distribution fund. The people of southern Illinois rather believed that the distribution fund should go to rehabilitate the
school fund. Various schemes for the system as a whole were
proposed. The *Chicago American* of May 11, 1842, published
a plan calling for drastic economy, a revision of local government in the interest of economical administration, and taxation

---

[29] *Alton Telegraph,* August 27, 1842; *Illinois State Register,* February 4,
August 26, 1842; *Chicago American,* June 14, July 27, 1842.

to pay the interest on the bonds; for the property itself the newspaper went back to the old idea of 1836 of construction by chartered companies, to whose stock the state should subscribe. The *State Register* on behalf of Gatewood contended with the *Telegraph* for the honor of the authorship of a scheme, the crux of which was to dispose of the state lands at the generous estimate of $20 an acre. The *Telegraph* and the *Register* were unable also to agree as to the amount of the debt, the *Register* insisting that for practical purposes the bonds sold by the bank, the appropriated school fund, the federal deposit, and all bonds irregularly issued should be deducted to the amount of six million. Another proposal was that the state sell its property for bonds and scrip; the distribution fund according to this proposal was to go to the school fund. The *Sangamo Journal* published a letter which offered the solution of a tax of thirty cents on the hundred to be directed to payment of the state debt, using the proceeds of state lands and the distribution fund for expenses of government. This letter further suggested dividing the debt pro rata to real and personal property throughout the state and exempting from its shares of the debt each tract which paid the share thus alloted to it.[30] The very extravagance of these schemes is eloquent of the hopelessness of the situation, as it appeared to men of the time.

As the political situation stood at the outset of the gubernatorial campaign of 1842, it was to Joseph Duncan that the question naturally presented itself for decision. He had opposed the system in the beginning, and now running for office as an elder statesman it was for him to find the state a solution. But Duncan's mind could supply him with nothing but negatives. He would not issue more bonds or hypothecate them, and he would seek additional land grants for the canal, but beyond that apparently he could not go. He proposed to sell off all state properties and bank stock, taking state indebtedness in return. Like most whigs, he apparently thought the only

[30] *Sangamo Journal,* March 25, April 1, 1842; *Alton Telegraph,* January 8, 29, August 13, 1842; *Chicago American,* December 1, 1841; *Illinois State Register,* February 25, March 25, May 27, 1842.

possible solution was the return of his party to power and an enlargement under their direction of the field of the federal government. He relied on federal measures, banks, tariffs, distribution, and the resulting prosperity. To face the problem as one for the state to solve by application to it of her own abilities and of her own slender resources was a step beyond Duncan. The answer of Illinois had to be made in other terms than advocacy of federal legislation, and it was to be made through a man of very different type from Duncan.[31]

[31] *Sangamo Journal,* March 4, July 22, 1842; *Alton Telegraph,* July 2, 1842.

XII. THE STRUGGLE FOR PARTY REGULARITY, 1834–1838

OUT of the presidential contest in Illinois in 1835–1836, emerged the forms of the whig and democratic parties; out of the struggle over the subtreasury and the specie circular in 1837–1839 came a close alignment of the parties on party measures. Between 1835 and 1839 the doctrine of the necessity of party regularity was forced on the democratic party, and that party became a closely organized body with accepted principles. No longer could a man be saved politically by the name of Jackson unless he did the works of Jackson.

Nationally Van Buren was the candidate of the followers of Jackson who were beginning to term themselves democrats. The old Clay-Adams men mustered around candidates with a local appeal such as Webster or William Henry Harrison, hoping thus to beat the Van Buren forces in detail and throw the election into the house of representatives. The followers of Hugh Lawson White of Tennessee occupied a somewhat different position. Practically, they were allies of the opposition to Van Buren. They professed, however, that they were really Jackson men, loyal to their past professions of faith, but unable to swallow the personality and methods of Van Buren; and they were inclined to repel indignantly the charges of their opponents that they were deserters to the Clay-Adams party of 1828 and 1832.

The contest for the presidency in Illinois seemed at the outset of the campaign to be between Van Buren and White, and the supporters of each sought for all the aid they might derive from the great name of Jackson. There could be no doubt of Jackson's support of Van Buren; and accordingly the followers of White in their claims were compelled to argue that they were the true original Jackson men and that they held fast to the principles that Jackson had held and abandoned. Behind this willingness of even his opponents to trade on the traditions of Jacksonism there was, of course, an intention to play over the game that had elected Duncan governor in 1834 and to consolidate the anti-Jackson vote on an ostensibly Jackson candidate. This purpose the *Sangamo Journal* unwittingly revealed by its remark that Van Buren would run no stronger in Illinois than Kinney, for his party was Kinney's.

The Van Buren men naturally argued that White was a renegade from Jackson and his principles and a nullifier, seduced by Clay to follow out the scheme of splitting the nation between various candidates only to elect a whig in the house or senate. Accordingly they insisted on the need of conventions to insure party unity and on the necessity of party regularity. The Van Buren men, notably the congressmen, sought to bring this about, as the whigs claimed, by using national patronage to build up an Albany regency in Illinois. The *Sangamo Journal* pronounced that this was the intent of every appointment made during the past six months. It repeatedly accused the Springfield clique, May, Forquer, Calhoun, and Cartwright, some of them late converts to Jacksonism, of seeking to read out of the party on account of their loyalty to White such old time Jackson men as Bowling Green and A. G. Herndon. This in a nutshell was the White argument.

The number of Jackson leaders who supported White may be roughly estimated by a consideration of certain votes in the Illinois assembly on political resolutions in 1835–1836. On December 19, 1835, by a vote of thirteen to twelve the senate passed resolutions attacking Van Buren as an old federalist and a former opposer of Jackson, and nominating White with a disclaimer of the intervention of caucus or convention. On January 15, eleven members spread on the journal a protest against the truth of the resolutions and the expediency of bringing them forward.[1] The fact that on December 12 a

---

[1] *Senate Journal,* 1835-1836, 2 session, 76, 256.

resolution instructing the state's senators to vote to expunge the censure of Jackson passed by a vote of fifteen to ten affords an opportunity to gauge the amount of Jackson strength for White. Benjamin Bond, Levin Lane, and James A. White-side voted both for expunging and for the White resolution; and they may be set down as the measure of the Jackson-White strength.[2] Applying a similar test of the house, only three men who voted for expunging voted for a resolution deprecating conventions. Only four, Peter Butler, Thomas Hunt, Thomas Trower, and Milton Carpenter voted for expunging and against a preamble attacking White's supporters as nullifiers and federalists. Whatever may have been the alignment of the rank and file the leaders were certainly not seriously divided.

The opposition had to learn that it was not always possible in a national election to play the same game that had elected Duncan in 1834 — running a candidate who could be posed as a Jackson man and at the same time receive a solid whig vote. Their electoral ticket was assailed by the enemy on the ground that it was hand-picked and that too in Sangamon county.[3] As a partial concession to the complaints of friends in the north that the Military Tract was unrepresented, Bowling Green, a Jackson man of 1832, resigned; and to succeed him Colonel A. G. S. Wight was named. By whom was he nominated, the democrats asked at once.[4] The remainder of the ticket was composed of James A. Whiteside, Benjamin Bond, and Levin Lane, the three men who had voted for both the expunging and the White resolutions; the fifth man, John Henry, had stood firmly against both expunging and against the convention system.[5]

2 *Senate Journal*, 1835-1836, 2 session, 30, 78; *House Journal*, 1835-1836, 2 session, 63, 211, 233, 235.
3 *Chicago Democrat*, January 20, February 17, 24, 1836. The *Galena Gazette* and the *Jacksonville News* condemned the ticket as hand-picked in Sangamon.
4 *Sangamo Journal*, March 26, April 16, 1836; *Chicago Democrat*, May 4, 1836.
5 He repeatedly introduced anti-convention resolutions. *House Journal*, 1835-1836, 2 session, 27, 63, 234.

But even if Jackson men could support White, who had apostasized only on the bank question and by his attempt to rescind rather than to expunge, it was not to be expected that they could with equal facility support Harrison who had scarcely a tinge of Jacksonism. The democrats can hardly be blamed for regarding the question as to whether the White electors should vote for Harrison if Van Buren could so be defeated as one which would strip the White electors who consented to do this of even the pretense to Jacksonism. Bond, however, pledged himself to vote for Harrison in such a contingency, and the *Sangamo Journal* professed to be satisfied that the others would do the same.[6]

The Harrison movement appeared to gain ground as the campaign went on. There had always been an undercurrent of sentiment in Illinois in his favor. The *Mt. Carmel Sentinel* had favored him at first, though it had forsaken him for White without insisting on a convention. The *Chicago American* in 1835 had leaned toward him. In the fall of 1836, the *American* and the *Sentinel* were supporting him and the *Telegraph* was friendly to his candidacy. The democrats had perhaps foreseen this, as ever since February their newspapers had been firing occasional shots aimed in Harrison's direction. The first Harrison meeting in the state, according to the *Register*, was held in Madison county on August 13, 1836. Harrison was set forward as the friend of the west, the friend of the small farmer, the first to propose the sale of public lands in small tracts. As a western candidate he aroused enthusiasm such as could not be called forth by White who was accused of being the candidate of the nullifiers and the cloak for Calhoun's desire to organize the south on a sectional basis. Their alleged purposes seemed the logical fulfillment not merely of the *Sangamo Journal's* sneers at Carpenter, a legislative candidate, as an advocate of Negro suffrage, but also of the attacks on Van Buren for support of a similar measure in the New York

---

[6] *Chicago American*, September 17, 1836; *Sangamo Journal*, October 8, 15, 1836.

convention and on Richard M. Johnson, the vice presidential candidate, as an "amalgamator." White whiggism in Illinois wore a distinctly southern and proslavery cast. At this stage indeed the *Journal* distinctly criticized John Quincy Adams. It is therefore not surprising to find Lincoln and Dan Stone, the two signers of the memorable antislavery protest of 1837, participants in a meeting to celebrate the anniversary of the battle of the Thames.[7]

The democratic attacks on Harrison followed the same line as in 1840 — criticism of his military career and services especially as compared with those of Johnson, the slayer of Tecumseh, of his civil and military incompetence, of his federalism, of his vote to sell men out to service in satisfaction of fines. The story that the women of Chillicothe, in derogation of his military qualities, presented him with a petticoat was dragged out, not for the last time.[8]

The democrats in Illinois found Van Buren a rather heavy load to carry. It is significant that they rarely attempted an appeal to the personality or measures of the man himself. Instead they preached assiduously the necessity of union against the measures to divide the party and by that division secure the triumph of the "monster" and of its tool, the usurping senate. Especially before the Baltimore convention, which the opposition declared a political trick to foist Van Buren on the country, they emphasized the necessity for unity in the party and for the support of measures rather than of men.[9] "Resolved," ran one set of resolutions, "That the cry of *'no party,' 'proscription,' 'Office holders,' 'Kitchen Cabinet'* and *'Magician'* are terms 'invented by knaves, and made current among fools.'"[10]

[7] *Chicago American,* October 24, 1835, September 10, November 5, 1836; *Sangamo Journal,* April 16, May 28, July 9, October 8, 22, 29, 1836; *Alton Telegraph,* April 6, 1836; *Chicago Democrat,* February 24, April 20, July 27, 1836; *Illinois State Register,* June 3, September 2, 1836; *Illinois Advocate,* May 27, June 3, 1835.
[8] *Chicago Democrat,* July 27, October 26, 1836.
[9] *Illinois Advocate,* May 6, June 3, 1835.
[10] Meeting at Danville, May 16, in *Illinois Advocate,* June 10, 1835.

In general the democrats were glad to fall back on Jackson and use his mantle to cover the man professing to be his successor. The story told by a whig editor that a man of some intelligence from central Illinois had been convinced by democratic asseverations that Jackson had reared Van Buren from a youth in Tennessee to succeed him is doubtless exaggerated, but there is an element of truth in the situation it suggests. At best the democrats were able to do no more to make their candidate lifelike than to paint his countenance into the portrait of the conventional statesman of the day.

The whigs, however, in the twelve years between 1832 and 1844 when they had Van Buren for an opponent, sketched, deepened, retouched, and fixed a portrait that was as vivid as it was unflattering. Under their brush "little Matty" stood forth, outwardly a foppish, simpering, snobbish dandy, the antithesis of everything virile, the opponent of every measure desired by the west, and withal a tricky, shrewd political intriguer who had gained the ear of the great Jackson in his decay and had won his support to measures alien to the principles of the days of his strength, and all to satisfy Machiavellian ambitions that in the ordinary course of events would have been chimerical and preposterous.[11]

In this portrait there was most obvious justification so far as Van Buren's attitude toward the west was concerned. He had voted against western internal improvements, against the Cumberland road, the Illinois and Michigan canal grant, and the reduction of the price of the public lands. Here the contrast of his record with Harrison's was marked.[12] Against Van Buren there were brought other charges. There were stories that he was in friendly communication with the pope, that he was lending the public money to speculators, that he had opposed the War of 1812, had opposed white manhood suffrage, and advocated Negro suffrage in the New York

[11] *Sangamo Journal,* January 12, 1832, said that Jackson was formerly for internal improvements and tariff, and Van Buren had won him from them.
[12] *Chicago American,* November 5, 1836; *Sangamo Journal,* October 15, 1836.

convention.   He was twitted with his Crawford connections and his attacks on Jackson in 1824.[13]

The whigs attempted to make Van Buren's personality the issue and they were rather inclined to avoid any other.   Of course, they ventured occasional attacks on the bank policy of the administration; the *Alton Telegraph* believed that the specie circular would turn the hearts of Illinois away from Jackson.   But usually they declined meeting the democrats on the issues of Jackson's administration.   The senate whig resolutions of 1836 deal with a theory of the federalist origin of the democratic party rather than with real political issues.[14]

One exception there is.   The whigs stood firmly as the opponents of the convention, the caucus, and party regularity. It was on these issues that John Henry forced the fighting on the house resolutions.   At this point a plausible attack was made on the convention system as Van Buren's own system of fraud, trickery, and deceit by which the despicable Amos Kendall had brought about his nomination.   The whigs insisted that from the Baltimore convention down to the lowest county caucus such bodies were packed with officeholders for a selfish and corrupt purpose.[15]   In spite of all the efforts of the supporters of White and the whigs, Van Buren in 1836 was successful in both state and nation.

The final flux in the casting of the democratic party was the currency and banking question which was at its crisis in the years 1837–1840.   Under the older system, the regulation of the note issue of state banks, the regulation of exchange, the care of all government funds were intrusted to the United States Bank.   That bank Jackson had instinctively distrusted as the self-appointed regulator of the currency of the country,

[13] *Chicago American*, July 23, 30, November 5, 1836; *Sangamo Journal*, June 4, July 16, 30, 1836.

[14] *Senate Journal*, 1835-1836, 2 session, 76.   *Alton Telegraph*, November 16, 1836; *Illinois Advocate*, May 6, 1835, gives address of democratic convention rehearsing and indorsing Jackson's measures, and proving Van Buren a supporter of them.

[15] *Chicago American*, June 20, 1835; *Sangamo Journal*, June 13, September 19, 1835, February 20, 1836.

a private institution powerful enough to dictate to the government. In the name of the people he had made war on the "monster," had refused it a recharter, and had removed the government deposits from its keeping. In spite of the protest of the financial interests of the country, exemplified in the censure spread on the journal of the senate in 1834 and expunged in 1836 at the behest of Jackson and Benton, Jackson had continued on his course and, abandoning the use of a national fiscal agent, had deposited the funds of the government in selected state banks throughout the union. Despite the attacks of the opposition on the pet banks, as unsafe depositories chosen by favor, Jackson pressed on in his course, the democrats loyally following after him. They accused the United States Bank of using its power to oppress the state banks and by first expanding and then sharply contracting its credits of making financial stringencies in which a public clamoring for relief might be led to demand its recharter. In 1835 the democratic convention declared that two years experience with state banks showed them to be as useful to the government as the United States Bank had been.[16]

The situation, however, when viewed otherwise than through political spectacles was far from encouraging. By legislation in 1834 against small bank notes, repeated by proclamation in 1835, the general government sought to force specie into circulation as the customary medium of small transactions. Moreover, by 1836, the issues of state bank notes, no longer controlled by the United States Bank and encouraged by the deposits of government funds, were reaching startling figures — more startling still was their apparent tendency not to find a place in the commercial business of the country, but instead to be used for purchases of the public lands. Credit by means of bank notes had been expanded far beyond the needs of the legitimate transactions of business, simply because these fruits of overexpansion could be used to procure public lands. To save the public lands of the nation from passing

[16] *Illinois Advocate*, May 6, 1835; *Chicago American*, April 23, 1836.

into the hands of speculators Jackson issued the much criticized
specie circular, forbidding the reception of anything but specie
and notes of specie paying banks, immediately in the case of
large purchases and in the near future in the case of small ones.
Jackson's last official act in 1837 was to pocket an act repealing
the circular, which the whig papers duly catalogued as one
final example of the president's willingness to subordinate
to his whim the welfare of the country. As the panic of
1837 gathered force they characterized the circular as the
gambler's throw on which the outgoing administration
depended for resources to keep it until Van Buren could
take office.[17]

The panic of 1837 dashed to fragments the system of state
banks which had replaced the United States Bank and which
Jackson had sought to control by the specie circular. The
roots of that panic perhaps lay partly in the accordance by
English banks and exporters of excessive credits to our merchants; partly no doubt, in the era of unrestricted banking that
followed the war on the United States Bank. The democrats
insisted on the first reason, and asked if Jackson was responsible for the panic in Europe as well as for that in the United
States. But the whigs laid the whole at the door of Jackson's
financial policy. In his message addressed to the special session
of the legislature of 1837 Duncan denounced the whole panic
as due to the destruction of the United States Bank, the creation
of state banks, and the attempt of the executive to bolster up
his'mistake by a cry for an exclusively specie currency. Duncan
only gave official expression to what had filled the whig papers
for months; the whigs gleefully professed their belief that
Van Buren's party was ruined never to rise again.[18]

The *Illinois State Register* loyally stood to its guns, but
as the whigs sarcastically pointed out it was for some time at a
loss as to what it should profess as the true democratic creed.
In June it came forth with a declaration that the true remedy

[17]*Alton Telegraph*, March 22, April 26, 1837.
[18]*Senate Journal*, 1837, special session, 7; *Illinois State Register*, July 15,
1837; *Sangamo Journal*, June 3, 1837.

was a control by the government of its funds through its own officers and a divorce from all banks, and to this issue it clung and tried to hold the whigs. The *Sangamo Journal* on the contrary amused itself by listing the democratic papers that disclaimed any intention of establishing an exclusively metallic currency and rather sought to force that issue. It argued that the establishment of the *Madisonian* at Washington under William Allen's editorship implied Van Buren's desire for support in abandoning the kitchen cabinet, the locofocos, and the Jackson financial policy.[19]

If the democratic doctrine was fixed, its acceptance by congress was less certain. The *Journal* rejoiced and the *Register* raged over the election of Allen as public printer in preference to Francis P. Blair of the *Globe*. When it became apparent even to the *Register* that Casey, May, and Snyder, the Illinois representatives, had all voted for Allen, it could no longer apologize for their vote to table the subtreasury bill on the ground that they were waiting to know the will of their constituents. As early as October 6, it had had its doubts of May and Snyder; and now it denounced all three on the ground that their delay to seek the will of their constituents was all a fraud; and it branded them as members of the little knot of twelve Jackson men who had betrayed the cause of democracy at the very moment when the issue was self-government or government by banks.[20]

Judging by the attitude of its representatives in congress Illinois democracy was divided on the financial measures. Richard M. Young and John M. Robinson, the senators, who had both been of suspected orthodoxy in the past, were staunch

[19] *Illinois State Register,* May 20, June 2, 10, August 25, September 1, 1837; it claimed in the last named issue that the *Jacksonville Patriot, Sangamo Journal,* and *Alton Telegraph* were opposing the divorce. *Sangamo Journal,* July 29, August 19, 1837; the latter issue enumerated the *Globe, Alton Spectator, Quincy Argus, Jacksonville News, Danville Enquirer,* and *Chicago Democrat.*

[20] *Illinois State Register,* September 22, October 27, November 4, 10, 17, 1837; *Sangamo Journal,* September 25, October 7, 1837; *Congressional Globe,* 25 congress, 1 session, 73, 96, 103, 117. For the resolution that it was inexpedient to charter a United States Bank, May voted in the negative; Robinson and Young both voted for the subtreasury.

supporters of the administration's policy; Zadoc Casey and Adam W. Snyder though supposedly orthodox were undecided; and William L. May, hitherto the democratic, even the Van Buren leader in the state, was openly opposed to the whole fiscal program. The newspapers of Illinois, however, were generally locofoco, as the whigs would have said, and supported the subtreasury; and public meetings, probably under the spur of the party management, were beginning to indorse it.[21]

As an interlude in the struggle for party regularity on the fiscal issue came an attempt to use the issue to drive May out of the party. May and Forquer, whose janglings and jealousies had repeatedly been satirized by the *Sangamo Journal,* had finally broken company late in 1836. Forquer, so the *Journal* declared, deserted the Van Buren candidates, May, McRoberts, and Ewing, and threw his support to Richard M. Young, whose past was strongly tinged to say the least with whiggism and who had courted and obtained whig support by professing himself to be a Jackson man for prudential reasons only. Young on his part accused May of promising support for congress to both George W. P. Maxwell and Douglas in return for aid in sending him to the senate. As early as April, 1837, the *Journal* predicted that May would be read out of the party by the Springfield junto. In July the *Illinois Republican* was attacking May for his votes in the last session on the distribution of the surplus and the repeal of the specie circular. The *Journal* believed that Forquer was planning the ruin of Casey and Reynolds as well as of May.[22]

Others than Forquer, however, were destined to reap the reward of the plot, if plot there was. At the time when his control of the party was apparently the strongest, he disappeared from Illinois politics; in another year he died of consumption. Douglas and Young, however, continued their

[21] *Illinois State Register,* October 20, November 10, December 9, 1837.
[22] *Sangamo Journal,* November 5, 19, December 17, 24, 1836, April 22, May 27, July 8, 15, 29, August 5, November 5, 1837; *Illinois State Register,* August 4, 1837; *Chicago Democrat,* August 16, 1837.

war upon May. Douglas devoted himself to drumming up delegates to a convention at Peoria to nominate himself for May's place; and the *Chicago Democrat,* scenting a plot for Douglas' personal aggrandizement, began to shift its ground a little. The *Journal* praised May's course in congress but advised him not to be a candidate again, thus leaving the field clear for a whig to beat the nominee of the Peoria convention on the issue of radicalism and conservatism.[23]

The factional disorder in the democratic party for the moment offered a magnificent chance for the whigs to disrupt it. May drew up a powerful defense of his course in congress, pronouncing that against the subtreasury initiated three years before by an obscure congressman the authority of the sages of the past was for the use of banks as depositories for the government funds. He denounced the measures of the specie circular as calculated to retard the growth of the west and as having been three times rejected by congress. While justifying the old war on the bank because of its known interference in politics, he admitted that Jackson's party had not given the country a currency as good as that of the old bank. He defended his vote for Allen on the old ground of his Jacksonism. May thus took a strong position on which an attack might once again split the party. The whigs were eager to complete the work. The *Journal* praised all three of the representatives for their stand against locofocoism. A. P. Field begged the whigs to support Snyder if the democrats tried to beat him with a convention nominee. The democrats had the difficult task of attacking May for his financial votes without driving Snyder and Casey and their following out of the party with him. The whigs prophesied that the locofoco anti-bank doctrines would disgust true Jackson men. Kinney and Reynolds were believed to be unorthodox on the bank and subtreasury. It might well be regarded as doubtful if the "conservatives," like May, might not succeed in establish-

[23] *Sangamo Journal,* October 14, December 2, 1837; *Chicago Democrat,* August 16, 1837.

ing themselves as a party in Illinois even if they did not wrest from their opponents control of the older organization.[24]

Unfortunately for the conservatives the locofocos controlled all the orthodox democratic newspapers in Illinois except May's *Backwoodsman* and the Shawneetown *Voice and Journal*. Thus they were handicapped by having their day in court in the columns of the whig papers. The radical democrats with an instinctive political wisdom which they frequently displayed in Illinois politics took issue frankly on the subtreasury, despite the whig cry of "purse and sword," and their accusation that the administration's doctrine was to be forced on Illinois by the influence of officeholders. The *Register* on the other hand discreetly indorsed the repeal of the specie circular on the ground that the measure had after all fulfilled its usefulness and that it was now a discrimination in favor of the east against the west. Slowly the party in Illinois was forced into line. Snyder between March and June of 1838 turned to support the subtreasury, discreetly declining a reëlection. Some of the whigs even advocated supporting him for governor in preference to Edwards, if he cared to run.[25]

It was harder for the democrats to deal with Casey than with Snyder. June 1, 1838, the *Register* attempted an apology for Casey's irregular course on the old ground of awaiting instructions. It professed that it had suggested a convention in his district only for fear that a Van Buren man would run against him and thereby elect a whig. It admitted the validity of Casey's reason for refusing to submit to a convention — that his candidacy was announced before a convention had been projected. It came to the conclusion, humiliating for the party of conventions, that conventions were new things in Illinois, that one might injure the party, and that, since Casey had the administration's indorsement, perhaps a convention would

---

[24] *Sangamo Journal,* November 18, December 2, 1837, January 20, 1838; *Alton Telegraph,* December 20, 1837.
[25] *Sangamo Journal,* April 21, May 19, June 30, July 14, 20; *Congressional Globe,* 25 congress, 2 session, 213; *Illinois State Register,* February 9, 1838, June 1, 29, 1838.

be inexpedient after all.[26]   The secret was that Casey's strength in his district was so great that neither McRoberts nor Breese dared to run against him.

After Casey's vote against the subtreasury in 1838, however, the *Register* was forced to denounce him for his duplicity in deceiving the party on his position, and in selling himself to the bank.   It attempted in vain to induce McRoberts to run against him and on Casey's reëlection it had to admit him as a democrat, sound on all points except the subtreasury and entitled to credit for having at last deserted the *Madisonian*.[27]

It was only, however, by means of extraordinary personal popularity such as Casey's that one could defy the mandate of the party.   The use of the convention as a means of enforcing regularity and submission to the will of the party had really been eminently successful in its purpose, even though it meant submission to the will of the master manipulators like Douglas. Its value became strikingly apparent in the campaign for the governorship in 1838.   Late in 1837 a party convention had nominated for governor J. W. Stephenson, and for lieutenant governor, J. S. Hacker.   The whigs claimed that Stephenson had been nominated only because Reynolds, Kinney, Casey, and Snyder, the best men of the party, were all under suspicion of heterodoxy.   The choice could not have been more unfortunate.   "Stephenson is a defaulter to the amount of 40,000," wrote Field to Eddy.   "Say nothing about it to nobody.   We will modestly set on foot an inquiry by our papers.   They will of course deny it & then May has the Documents to prove the facts."   In fact, May's *Backwoodsman* was the first to open fire, whig papers at first affecting to believe that the story was a democratic trick.   The democratic newspapers were soon divided into contending camps, mainly on the question whether Stephenson's alleged default was not a load too heavy for his party to carry.   The *Register*, the *Chicago*, the *Galena*, and *Ottawa Democrats*, and the *Shawneetown Voice* stood by him.

[26] *Illinois State Register,* June 1, 1838.
[27] *Ibid.,* July 13, 27, August 3, 31, 1838.

The *Belleville News, Quincy Argus, Alton Spectator,* and *Illinois Standard* approved him, while the *Illinois Republican* remained on the fence. According to the *Journal,* however, a caucus at Springfield decided that he must be dropped as too heavy a load for Douglas to carry in the congressional race.[28] A new convention assembled and chose Thomas Carlin of Quincy as the candidate for governor. He was a man of honesty, but ignorant, and his choice seemed to point to a compromise in the ranks of the party. He was probably orthodox on the bank question, but he had been friendly to May after the attack on him had begun; and he was supported by the *Backwoodsman.*[29] His opponent in the convention was Breese, who apparently was one of the leaders of the faction attacking May.[30] The Belleville group, Reynolds, Gustave Koerner, W. C. Kinney, and Shields united in supporting Snyder. It was claimed that Carlin's victory was due to a bargain with McRoberts, and that the representation at the convention was small—three counties in the north, five in the center, nine in the south, and two in the east.[31] The nomination, however, was carried successfully into an election. The convention system of party organization, though sorely tried, had produced a degree of unity in the party that could hardly have been attained otherwise. It is little wonder that clever whig politicians like Lincoln, who were not too much wedded to the traditions of the past, came to look on the system with envy and to press its adoption in their own ranks.

[28] *Sangamo Journal,* January 20, 22, March 3, May 12, 1838; *Illinois State Register,* May 11, 1838, stated that Hacker resigned. Field to Eddy, January 22, 1838, in Eddy manuscripts.

[29] *Sangamo Journal,* May 12, July 28, 1838.

[30] Field to Eddy, January 22, 1838, in Eddy manuscripts; he was said to be back of the movement to run against Snyder.

[31] *Illinois State Register,* June 8, 1838; *Sangamo Journal,* June 16, 1838.

XIII. THE WHIG AND DEMOCRATIC PARTIES;
THE CONVENTION SYSTEM

IN THE decade between 1830 and 1840 the democratic party developed the idea of party regularity and devised the convention as a means of attaining it. To comprehend the character of this innovation one must first contrast it with the system it displaced. At the time of the admission of Illinois to the union the complete triumph of the republican party had for the time put an end to bipartisan politics; the political game turned around the ambitions of political leaders, the rivalries of political cliques, and the adaptation of political measures to the supposed interests of various sections of the nation. With the rise of Andrew Jackson, there came out of the confusion a party which obligated its members to loyalty to Jackson, the vindicator of the popular will. But as the "Old Hero" took his self-willed course in politics and expected those who professed to be his friends to support him in one measure after another, his partisans soon came to amplify the obligations of personal loyalty until it included support of Jackson's measures as well; and this new test they added as a sequel to the old shibboleth of personal allegiance.

So long as the political methods of the older day remained it was difficult to enforce any such test. The idea that one man should stand forth as a party candidate for an office was as unfamiliar to the politicians of the twenties as was the existence of national parties themselves. It often happened that a man was persuaded not to run for an office lest he jeopardize the chances of a friend who was also a candidate; but except where personal or factional considerations intervened, men felt free to present themselves as candidates for office as they would. Sometimes various polite devices intervened to bring the candidate and the people together. It often happened that a few voters, actuated by friendship, or by unwillingness to offend a rich man or a notorious bully, signed a newspaper notice or attended a public meeting summoning a coy politician to permit the use of his name.[1] The politicians of the day were expert in the arts of aiding a candidacy by putting forward or withholding other candidates and by forming elaborate combinations to sap the strength of a dangerous rival. Under such a system it was so difficult for the people to express clearly by their votes support or disapproval of the acts or political opinions of candidates that a bare profession of Jacksonism carried Duncan through election after election, whether in congress the Jackson measures enjoyed his support or not.

To combat such situations, the ideas of party regularity and of the use of the convention were worked out in the democratic party. As the theory was stated after 1835 in set after set of resolutions, politics in the United States was based on differences of principle as to government. The triumph of principles, rather than the triumph of any particular leader, was the end to be sought. "Without a frequent interchange of political sentiment, expressed by the people, and repeated by their delegates, properly authorized, the democracy cannot insure that success in their elections, which the purity and integrity of their principles, entitle them to claim."[2] The democrats saw that victory for their principles could be won only by centering the vote of the party on one man pledged to their support and by frowning on the candidacy of any rivals, as likely to divide the vote of the party and allow a minority in opposition united on one candidate to win. The means to this end was the convention; whether district, county, state, or national, it could state the principles of the party, choose a candidate to exem-

[1] *Illinois Advocate*, November 11, 1835; *Chicago Democrat*, February 25, 1834.
[2] *Illinois Advocate*, December 17, 1835.

plify them, and call upon the rank and file of the party to support him loyally.[3]

Its originators adduced many a truth in favor of the system. Not only did it tend to the triumph of just principles of government, but it was essentially democratic. Theoretically at least, it rested on a series of representations of the people, from the primary meeting in the district up to the national convention. Applied to national nominations, the convention was insurance against choice by a caucus or by the house voting by states—the dilemma of the statesman of 1824–1825. Further, since the representative assemblages were made up of incorruptible patriots, wealth and influence could have no part in their actions as they could under the old system of private nominations.[4] Under the convention system, in theory at least, the nomination sought the patriot purest in political life and most orthodox in principle.

Of course the practice in many cases scarcely corresponded to the theory. In the case of the Baltimore convention that nominated Van Buren for the presidency, the intention obviously was to rally the whole strength of the party to a man who unquestionably was not the choice of a large part of it. In that convention the vote of Illinois and Kentucky was cast by a man who had no authorization from the party in either state to represent it. If the convention lessened the influence of the man of wealth, it increased the influence of the man clever in political manipulation. Under the convention system poor young men who were at the same time shrewd politicians frequently rose to power. The political career of Stephen A. Douglas who boasted that he had introduced the convention system in Illinois was a typical example of such political shrewdness.[5] Yet even from such a result democracy may have been the gainer.

The adoption of the convention system in Illinois was not

[3] *Illinois Advocate,* April 15, 22, June 3, November 18, December 17, 1835; *Chicago Democrat,* May 27, 1835.
[4] *Illinois Advocate,* September 2, 1835; *Chicago Democrat,* July 15, 1835.
[5] *Sangamo Journal,* May 16, June 13, July 11, 1835, May 7, 1836.

the work of a day even in the democratic party. Thus in 1832 the cry that Johnson's claims to the vice presidency be submitted to the national convention was met by the nomination of electors pledged to Jackson and Johnson. In 1835 the alleged lack of time was set forth as a reason why Illinois should content itself with county meetings indorsing in advance the work to be done by the Baltimore convention. Nevertheless a democratic state convention was held which nominated delegates instructed for Van Buren and Johnson, and a long series of county meetings was induced to indorse the work of the convention.

Opposition was naturally aroused. A legislative nominating convention, held at Ottawa in the northern district in 1834, drew forth protests against it as a snap convention and caused the nomination of rival candidates. In the fall of 1835 Ebenezer Peck's proposal to nominate state officers in a convention called to nominate electors and his advocacy of extending throughout the state "the wholesome system of conventions" aroused protests. W. J. Gatewood strenuously opposed the system. The Greene county convention in 1836 resolved to let all who wished run for county offices. Southern Illinois was slow to adopt the idea of the convention as an enforcer of party regularity.[6]

The whigs at first criticized the convention system for what often enough it undoubtedly was, a devise of political manipulators to kill off candidates opposed to them. John Henry in the legislative session of 1835–1836 offered resolutions which declared that the application of the convention system to state and county offices was anti-republican. He drew an illuminating contrast between the new conventions, managed to whip the party into line in the interest of such cliques as the Albany regency, and the older public nomination meetings.[7]

[6] *Sangamo Journal,* March 1, April 5, 1832, April 18, May 2, 1835, February 6, 13, March 26, 1836; *Illinois Advocate,* March 9, 23, 1832, April 1, 15, 22, May 6, 1835; *Chicago Democrat,* March 4, 18, 21, May 21, 28, June 25, 1834.
[7] *House Journal,* 1835-1836, 2 session, 27; *Sangamo Journal,* January 30, 1836.

The principle of exclusion and regularity was the crux of the distinction between the older and newer system.

Some of the proceedings of early conventions afforded the whigs legitimate material for their satire. The *Chicago Democrat* one year argued for conventions, and the next, disgruntled at the local nominee for the legislature, refused to be bound by a convention nomination on the ground that as the convention had not harmonized public sentiment, its decision was not binding on the party. William L. May was nominated for congress in 1836 by a state convention at Peoria, consisting, as the *Sangamo Journal* averred, of twelve persons representing five out of twenty-three counties, chosen in primary meetings aggregating some twenty persons. Next year, with Douglas in control, conditions were changed; and a convention dominated by an over-representation, so it was said, of Sangamon and Morgan delegates nominated Douglas at Peoria. May protested that where a plurality of popular votes would elect, the action of a convention was not binding. The *Sangamo Journal* believed the affair had made the Military Tract ready to give up conventions and declared they were in such bad odor that Casey and Ewing would not consent to be nominated by them.[8]

Still the convention idea spread and with it went the organization of counties and districts by committees to call meetings and to correspond.[9] The system was applied to nominations in both county and state. Conventions of all grades adopted resolutions and addresses defining the path of the party. With all its faults, with all its abuses, the convention did its work well for the democratic party. It brought unity; it ended the possibility of such campaigns as Duncan's in 1834; and at least twice, in 1838 and 1842, it enabled the party to perform

[8] *Sangamo Journal,* April 30, May 14, July 2, 1836, September 2, October 21, November 25, December 9, 1837, January 13, August 4, 1838; *Chicago American,* July 4, August 1, 1835, July 23, 30, 1836; *Chicago Democrat,* July 8, 1835, July 20, 1836.

[9] *Illinois Advocate,* June 3, September 16, 30, December 2, 1835; *Chicago Democrat,* June 10, 1835, February 24, 1836; *Illinois State Register,* July 22, 1837, May 18, 1838.

the delicate maneuver of replacing one candidate with another under the enemies' fire without throwing the ranks into confusion. The whigs made no use of the convention corresponding to that of their opponents. They scarcely used it except for such matters as the nomination of electors. They drew their skirts carefully aside from the defilement of anything like caucus dictation. They came in time to use conventions for congressional and legislative nominations, but they shrank from a broader application of the system. There was always trepidation in the ranks when a convention seemed to be necessary to decide between state candidates and a feeling of relief when by the adjuration of newspapers and other persuaders, all but one withdrew, doubtless often leaving as much ill-feeling as a hard-fought convention battle would have left.[10]

Because the convention system proved satisfactory to the democratic party it does not follow that the whigs could have used it with equal success. The difference between whig and democrat was more than a mere difference in name and more than a difference of opinion on important questions of public policy. The difference was fundamental, it came from the inmost nature and marked diametrically opposite viewpoints. Barring accident and self-seeking a whig was a whig and a democrat a democrat because he had a certain well-defined attitude toward the world outside himself.

"I have been seeking and obtaining information upon the subject of your Bank Directory at this place," wrote William Thomas from Jacksonville to Henry Eddy in 1838,[11] "we can furnish as good a Directory as can be found in Illinois but we cannot divide the power between parties as is desirable, because all of our solvent business men in Town are opposed

<hr/>

[10] *Sangamo Journal*, September 1, 22, 29, 1832, February 20, 1836, December 23, 1837; *Alton Telegraph*, June 28, July 5, 1837, March 28, 1838; *Chicago American*, July 26, 31, August 2, 22, 1839; *Peoria Register*, December 9, 1837.
[11] William Thomas to Eddy, January 4, 1838, in Eddy manuscripts; see also *Chicago Democrat*, August 16, 1837. It remarked that of the emigration to northern Illinois the laborers were democrats and the speculators and claim jumpers whigs.

to the Administration. We have but two solvent merchants in Town as exceptions; they are doing small business." Generally speaking the foregoing passage may serve as a guide in a rough and ready division of political Illinois between the whigs and the democrats. The development of the actual alignment of individual politicians, the shifting and alteration of personal factions cannot so be generalized. The important fact to keep in mind is that in the decade between 1830 and 1840 two distinct groups of ideas developed into opposing political platforms and philosophies; and the passage quoted at the head of this paragraph may serve as a useful criterion to determine the location of the line of demarcation. It must be remembered that both these schools of political thought developed gradually and that while the turn and emphasis given their various doctrines were governed by local conditions in Illinois, the doctrines themselves came from without, growing in importance as they found a response in the minds of the natives.

Of these, the whig political philosophy is hardest to derive from the utterances of its Illinois exponents. Unlike their democratic opponents, they were not given to stating broad principles. In their case it is necessary to presuppose a rarely expressed affection and prejudice for the stability and permanence of the political institutions as they supposedly had existed and operated in the days of the fathers. Looking toward the past as they did, they were sentimentalists rather than idealists; their first great political victory was won on a sentimental appeal for a return to the measures and the political purity of the past and for the election of a man who seemed one of the last links to the days of the Revolutionary heroes.

The presence of this atmosphere of sentiment and conservatism would imply to the European student of politics a bourgeois party constituency. Paradoxical as the idea may seem, the business man, accustomed to do his work through a complex of human relationships is, however cynical, a good deal of a sentimentalist. Certainly the whig party in its specific measures appeared as a business man's party. In a fit of frank analysis of political parties in Illinois in 1839, the *Sangamo Journal*,[12] a whig organ, averred that among the whigs were to be found a "large proportion of the mercantile class — the shifting, bustling, speculating class whose wealth and fortunes enable them to court pleasure or enjoyment, or repose." It admitted that this class, comprising as it did bank directors and borrowers at banks, would find a common interest in the welfare of banking institutions. In its measures — banks, protection, internal improvements — the whig party was the party of the business classes and of those within their sphere of influence.[13]

Since the storm of innovation that was breaking on the country was forced on congress by the overpowering influence of the executive supported by a strongly organized party machine, the principles of the whigs naturally opposed the use of executive power and patronage for party purposes and sustained the legislature in its old standing and power against the assaults of the executive branch. It was for this reason that the whigs fought desperately the expunging resolution as calculated to destroy the independence of the senate. "Destroy public confidence in the Senate," wrote Governor Duncan in transmitting to the Illinois senators their legislative instructions to vote for the expunging resolution, "let the Legislature rebuke them for warning the people, that a new, dangerous and unconstitutional power had been asserted by a co-ordinate and powerful branch of the government — let the right be fully established that any power or person, except the immediate constituents of each separate member of Congress, shall have authority to call their acts in question — or that a man at the head of our government, at whose command six thousand bayonets will bristle in an instant, surrounded immediately and remotely, by one hundred thousand organized office holders, and numerous partisan office seekers, ready to obey his will — shall have authority to protest against, interrupt or question

[12] *Sangamo Journal*, February 16, 1839.
[13] In another light this appears in the complaint of democratic papers, that whig merchants would not advertise in them.

any of the acts of the peoples' Representatives, who are sitting in the presence of this mighty power, unarmed and unprotected, and who should look alone to the approbation of their constituents and the ballot box for all favor and all rebukes; in a word, let the Senate of the United States lose its independence by the loss of public confidence . . . and you must perceive that all power will soon be centered in one man; and that our march to despotism is inevitable." [14] With a somewhat similar feeling the whigs were occasionally disposed to question the right of instruction, arguing it as absurd that a legislature constitutionally empowered to elect senators every six years should by this device elect them whenever it would.[15] Senators took an oath to maintain the constitution, not to obey their constituents. It was precisely on this article in the whig creed, the guarantee of constitutional stability through the independence of the legislature, that the democratic attack began. Thus in 1835 the democrats branded the avowed attempt of the whigs to throw the election into the house of representatives as an endeavor to defeat the will of the nation.[16] They quoted, too, the alleged remarks of Tristram Burgess that he wished all future presidential elections might take place in the house of representatives so that no candidate could ride in on a wave of popularity and unseat republican institutions.[17] Exaggerated charges of the same sort accused the whigs of desiring a property qualification for voters and a president elected for life. Democratic papers fed their readers with clippings accusing the United States Bank of buying up newspapers, and portraying the rowdyism and violence of whigs in the east. As indicated elsewhere the reputed hostility of eastern whigs to

[14] *Sangamo Journal,* March 5, 1836.
[15] *Alton Telegraph,* April 6, 1836. This theory of the independence of the legislature is probably the abstract expression of the impatience of many congressmen personally strong in their districts at attempts to dragoon them into party ranks by stirring up trouble for them at home. A favorite cry of the whigs was election of men on their merits, not for their party affiliations. For example see *Chicago American,* June 20, 1835.
[16] *Illinois State Register,* November 9, 1838. The whigs it was said, like English tories, scorned instructions, *Illinois Advocate,* December 23, 1835.
[17] *Ibid.,* May 20, 1835.

removal of the Indians, to graduation, to preëmption, and to squatters was a heavy load for their party in the west to bear. More generally of course, they had to bear the imputation of aristocracy and of being friends to the rich. The democrats labored to show that the whigs were the spiritual descendants of the federalist party, just as the whigs labored to enumerate the many federalists who had been baptised democrats in good standing. Challenged to define federalism, one democratic editor strung together the following familiar political catch phrases of the day—believes in the Bank of the United States, that no vulgar democrat is fit for office, talks of the huge paws of the farmers, is for Daniel Webster or any other available candidate, fills people with Jack Downing froth and lies instead of facts relating to the prosperity of the country. The sketch of the whig, as the locofoco affected to see him, could not be improved on.[18]

Among the whigs there was always a strong undercurrent of native American sentiment which the democrats, intent on securing the foreign vote, were not slow to bring to the surface. In most instances where it appeared overtly in Illinois this sentiment was expressed in the very judicious question as to whether newly arrived immigrants to the United States should be permitted to vote. The conservative *Backwoodsman*, probably under May's tutelage, in 1838 denounced the practice of allowing the "Irish of the canal zone" who had been six months in Illinois to vote whether naturalized or not. It pronounced that if foreigners were not to rule the United States, the question of foreign votes must be decided. By 1839 the native born democrats of Joliet had been forced to join the whigs against the Irish. At the same time the Irish vote in Cook county was said to be a half of the total.[19]

[18] *Chicago American,* April 22, 1837, advocated a property qualification and barring out foreign voters. *Sangamo Journal,* February 2, 1839, on behalf of the whigs disclaimed a similar belief. *Illinois State Register* May 25, 1838, *Chicago Democrat,* May 21, November 5, 1834, January 15, 1838; *Illinois Advocate,* July 29, 1835.

[19] *Peoria Register,* October 20, 1838; *Chicago American,* July 11, 1835, August 3, 12, 1839; *Sangamo Journal,* September 1, 1838, January 5, 1839, clips

This issue leads to another one on which whigs and democrats joined battle, that of religious observances. The whigs as the party of conservatism were naturally sticklers for observance of religious forms. The tendency, of course, does not appear strongly in their own prints, though the *Chicago American* did clip an article accusing Tammany Hall of atheism. But the *Chicago Democrat* complained that the *American* was charging it with deistical opinions in order to secure the subscriptions and the advertising of the pious. The whigs were inclined to be emphatically Protestant and were accused, in connection with Nativist attacks, of being anti-Catholic. Most interesting of all, toward the end of 1833, an attack was made on Duncan, then on the verge of turning whig, alleging that he had come to represent the interests of the bank aristocracy and the national church aristocracy, especially of the Presbyterian church and the clique centering around Illinois College.[20]

So far as in this period the whigs succeeded in basing their opposition to the administration on fundamental political principles they did it by pointing out the danger to free institutions of the growth of the executive power. The lines on which this attack was developed have already been indicated. In its milder forms it appeared as a suggestion that Van Buren was planning to found a dynasty — clipped out of the whole cloth of a silly article in a London paper. The people were reminded of the rarity with which earlier presidents had used the veto.

the *Backwoodsman.* This material appeared at the time the whigs were much exercised at the canal vote being thrown to Douglas against Stuart. The *Quincy Argus* declared the whole difficulty was that they had not voted whig; clipping in *Illinois State Register,* September 28, 1838. At this time the German vote in contradistinction to the Irish was said to be whig, *ibid.,* October 19, 1838. Gustave Koerner on behalf of his German fellow-citizens addressed an inquiry as to the belief in native Americanism. It was answered with a letter favoring a liberal encouragement to immigration, *ibid.,* July 6, 1838. During the summer of 1835 the *Chicago American* evinced a sharp hostility to immigrant voters, especially in its clips, July 11, August 8; it attacked Van Buren because of his supposed willingness to let immigrants vote, June 20, 1835.

[20] *Chicago American,* June 20, July 11, 1835; *Chicago Democrat,* extra, March 25, 1835; *Illinois Advocate,* December 28, 1833, November 11, 1835. A basis of the charge was the fact that Duncan had refused to vote for R. M. Johnson's Sunday mail report. A resolution approving it had passed the Illinois senate unanimously January 17, 1831, *Senate, Journal,* 1830-1831, 1 session, 262.

After 1832 they excused the defection of old-time Jackson men by claiming that Jackson himself had abandoned his principles, on the use of the patronage, on internal improvements, and on the independence of the judiciary and of the senate. In 1839 the *Alton Telegraph* characterized the modern democrat as a man willing to bolt his principles to order and who thus had come to swallow the whole Hartford convention.[21]

There was much truth in the whig strictures for democratic principles were in a continual process of evolution, in the course of which reversals were frequent. Jackson had come into power as supposedly the friend of tariff and internal improvements, the foe of a second presidential term, and of the use of political patronage, yet on all these points the vigorous old man had seen or been made to see new light. But he had also come in as a protest against the refusal of the house of representatives, in exercising its constitutional right of election, to regard the expression of the popular will. That he was the vindicator of that will Andrew Jackson never forgot. He was the first of American presidents to grasp the fact that he might make himself the representative of the people. It was in the name of the people of the United States that he made war on the bank. Beyond any other in American history his figure, aged, but not senile, vibrant, passionate, masterful, has the eternal vigor of the will of the people.

There were men in America able to catch the inspiration and to enumerate the principles of a new democracy, the moving force in the war of the people against the moneyed interests. Illinois newspapers copied into their columns George Bancroft's address to democratic men of Massachusetts, claiming that the doctrine of the sovereignty of the people was opposed to the doctrine of the whigs which in its defiance of the populace and its faith in special privileges, harks back to the principles of their predecessors, the whigs of 1688. Coupled with this doctrine of the sovereignty of the people necessarily went a

[21] *Sangamo Journal*, December 18, 1831, October 20, 1832; *Alton Telegraph*, April 6, August 10, 1839.

limitation of what their servants in congress could do, a denial of the power of congress to grant special privileges to corporations, or by tariff or internal improvement to confer on any section of the country benefits in which the whole was not a sharer. Hence strict constitutional construction; "The world is too much governed" was the motto which the *Globe* set at the head of its column. It was accompanied by a repudiation of the doctrine that corporate rights are irrepealable. The whigs believed that these principles of the democrats were anarchistic, and they summarized their opponents' general principles as agrarianism, Fanny Wrightism (free love), and finally the supreme term of abuse, locofocoism.[22]

These were the fundamental principles of the democratic party. Whoever attempts to discover that they were consistently carried out, that they were in many, very many, cases more than stalking horses for coming politicians, whoever seeks to find in many of their caucuses and conventions anything but knavery and sharp politics will be disappointed. But the ideal was always there; the principle that the democrats stood for the rights of the many against the few, for the rights of man against the rights of property remained to mold into a different and more ideal frame the principles of some, at least, of those who professed them.[23]

Their translation into measures of interest in Illinois internal affairs indicates why the practical interests of Illinois would tend to bring the state to the support of the democrats. To Illinois, protection for its almost purely agricultural products was unnecessary. The United States Bank and its place in the financial life of the country was a thing capable of being visualized only by a few. And when panic descended on the country the people of Illinois, the rank and file not being hard hit, accepted the theory that the bank had deliberately brought

[22] *Illinois Advocate*, November 25, 1835; *Chicago Democrat*, June 3, 1835, May 4, 18, 1836; *Sangamo Journal*, December 16, 1837. The whigs argued that the credit system was really the democratic system, as it enabled the man with little money to get ahead.

[23] See the resolutions readopted at the state convention of 1838, *Illinois State Register*, June 8, 1838.

it on. The issue of internal improvements by federal aid was more tempting; but the canal grant was assured; in the thirties the democratic principles were still liberal enough to authorize grants for the improvements of the great rivers; and the only whig proposal, the distribution bill, was ominous of an eastern public land policy. To the west the vital questions were as yet those of the Indians and the public lands—and on both of these questions they naturally accepted the leadership of the men with western vision, Jackson and Benton.

XIV. THE PASSING OF THE OLD DEMOCRACY

THE democratic party in Illinois had scarcely completed its physical growth before its deterioration began. It had achieved unity and coherence and had become a distinct entity; but meanwhile in the union at large the party was rapidly changing; old rallying cries were forgotten, and others hitherto comparatively unimportant were stressed. The bank and the tariff sank to subordinate places, and slavery and its protection became the exemplification and end of states rights doctrine. The party was becoming less and less western and more and more southern. Its members in Illinois, rallying behind the old party name, were slow to see that nationally in its ideals and ends the party was not what it had been. The overthrow of the party in the election of 1840 marked the beginning of the end of the old democracy in the nation; and though they were still victorious in Illinois the democrats were soon to perceive that a change in their national relations had taken place.

The campaign in which Harrison was elected over Van Buren was one of the strangest in American politics. A party presenting an essentially sound financial policy exemplified in its recent record was swept away by opponents who scarcely joined issue with it save to caricature its views and who placed their chief reliance on a pageantry and enthusiasm essentially sentimental in their appeal. Not only was the contest and its aftermath one of the most picturesque in American annals, but it was with reference to the political habits of the parties and the nation one of the most significant.

On issues the position of the democratic party in 1840 should have been strong. Van Buren by the boldest and most statesmanlike measure of his career had brought his party finally to accept the subtreasury as against any bank. The county meetings and conventions in 1839–1840 generally declared for the subtreasury and the divorce of banks and government, often with a fling at banks in general as founded on special privilege, often with a reference to the danger of moneyed oligarchies and paper money mills and sometimes with an indorsement of Benton's specie currency policy.[1] With similar unanimity they attacked the whig bills barring office-holders from participation in elections and approved the repeal of the salt tax. Again they recurred to their old doctrine that the whigs were really federalists in the hope of placing on them the stigma of an unpatriotic past.

The whigs, on the other hand, attacked the subtreasury with a vehemence that as their opponents complained occa-sionally ignored the nature of the institution. It is true that they frequently argued for the necessity of a bank, a paper currency, and a credit system, maintaining that the prevailing hard times were due to the destruction of the paper circulating medium of the country; they argued with some plausibility that the credit system instead of being aristocratic in essence was really democratic inasmuch as it enabled the man without capital of his own to get a start in life on borrowed money. But they also argued that the democratic ideal was to reduce the wages of labor and the price of staple commodities to star-vation rates — eleven pence a day wages and sixteen cents a bushel for wheat; they even went so far as to draw conclusions from the supposed fact that the subtreasury was the institution of the autocratic countries of Europe and hence unsuited to the free air of America. They raked up a scheme for a terri-torial army proposed by Joel R. Poinsett, the secretary of war, and prophesied the direst consequences to American freedom when by its adoption and by the institution of the subtreasury both the purse and the sword would rest in the hands of one man. They condemned the subtreasury as a fertile source of

[1] *Illinois State Register,* August 31, November 9, 16, 23, 30, December 7, 21, 1839, January 4, April 3, 1840.

defalcations on the part of the various officers with public money in their charge. "The Saviour of the world," said Abraham Lincoln, "chose twelve disciples, and even one of that small number, selected by superhuman wisdom, turned out a traitor and a devil. ·And, it may not be improper here to add, that Judas carried the bag—was the Sub Treasurer of the Saviour and his disciples."[2]

However, in the heat of the campaign the fiercest fighting centered about the personality of the rival candidates. The whigs assailed Van Buren for having forced the subtreasury scheme through after repeated rejections by congress, recalling the fact that Jackson had never favored it. In this as in his candidacy for a second term, they declared, Van Buren had departed from the principles espoused by Jackson in the days of his strength. In the wake of the democratic policy they predicted the advent of free trade and as its corollary, direct taxation, the rising power of the president fortified by the use of the patronage, the army, the funds of the subtreasury, and the general perversion of the ways of the fathers. It would have been well had their attack gone no further. The old charges of 1836, however, accusing Van Buren of foppery, of voting for a limited franchise, and for allowing the vote to free negroes also appeared. Congressman Charles Ogle gained much temporary fame by a speech widely circulated in different versions, in which he commented on the luxurious furnishings provided for the president's house at the public expense and made rather clever demagogic use of French menus and bills written in French for the materials for certain pieces of furniture such as taborets, which he pointed out had their place in the ceremonial of European courts. Occasionally a paper deemed worthy of circulation an absurd story from an absurd London newspaper to the effect that Van Buren was planning to establish a dynasty on the throne of the United States. Under these circumstances the visit of "Prince John"

[2] *Sangamo Journal,* March 6, 20, April 3, 10, May 29, July 10, October 30, 1840; *Chicago American,* May 29, July 1, 10, August 20, 1840; *Alton Telegraph,* February 8, September 5, 1840.

Van Buren to the court of England was a portent fraught with dire meaning.[3]

In Illinois especially the old theme of Van Buren's hostility to the west was made to do duty, reënforced in this instance by Van Buren's refusal to support schemes for internal improvement in the west, the abandonment of work on the Cumberland road and the lake harbors, and the sale of the machinery pertaining to them. This it was said by the whigs was the price that Van Buren was paying for Calhoun's support. In contradistinction to such policies the whig papers cited Clay's last distribution bill, which they calculated would have aided the state's credit in a marked degree.[4]

The democrats tried in vain to counter with effect on the character of Harrison. They rang the charges on the fact that as a young man he had joined what was called an abolition society; they used once more the old charge that he had voted to sell white men into slavery. They twisted his words to make it apparent that in 1798 he had been a black cockade federalist of the Adams school. They assailed his military career at its most vulnerable points. They maintained with some truth that he was a manufactured candidate designed to catch the votes of the west. They told again and again the story that a committee at his home at North Bend had him in charge and that he was kept in a cage; a charge which the whigs insisted in interpreting in a more or less literal sense and in repelling with scorn.[5]

The fatal blunder of the democrats in scornfully referring to Harrison as a log cabin and hard cider candidate gave the whig leaders their inspiration. By the rarest stroke of political

[3] *Sangamo Journal*, April 10, July 3, August 2, 21, 1840; *Chicago American*, April 20, May 2, 8, July 16, August 18, September 23, 1840; *Illinois State Register*, September 25, October 2, 1840; *Belleville Advocate*, September 5, 1840.

[4] *Sangamo Journal*, October 12, 1839, January 24, July 10, October 16, 1840; *Chicago American*, April 17, August 13, September 24, October 28, December 29, 1840.

[5] *Illinois State Register*, January 21, February 21, March 6, 13, April 17, May 8, 22, 29, September 28, 1840; *Sangamo Journal*, January 28, March 13, 1840; *Belleville Advocate*, April 4, 11, 18, May 2, August 29, September 12, October 10, 1840; *Chicago American*, June 10, October 15, 1840; *Chicago Democrat*, April 13, 25, 1840.

genius they took Harrison, a man, good, pious, well-meaning, but one who had never displayed brilliant ability either in politics or in war and represented him as a man of a stature comparable to the heroes of the Revolution, a man whose political virtues would bring back the golden age of the past. The veteran of the Revolution was told that Harrison had received his first commission from the hands of George Washington. The farmer of the west was reminded that in a double sense he owed his farm to the man who had at once secured the passage of the law for the sale of small tracts and had protected the frontier from the Indians. As monster rallies were held on the old battlefields of the west, now centers of a teeming population, the sentimental appeal for the man whose active life had spanned this marvellous progress, who had represented the whole Northwest Territory in congress and who had been the backwoods governor of what were now three prosperous states was well-nigh irresistible.

The sentiment found expression in political pageantry on a scale hitherto undreamed of. There was rough horseplay enough in the manner of college freshmen; as for instance when a delegation from Chicago setting out to a monster whig rally at Springfield captured an enemy banner in the form of the derisive petticoat and bore its trophy with it in triumph. There was much carolling of whig songs, which seemed to the democrats the only answers their opponents made to challenges on the serious issues of the campaign. The whigs, abandoning all discussion, swung along in unreasoning subjection to the refrain

> Without a why or a wherefore
> We'll go for Harrison therefore.

Yet there was a deeper meaning to all this seeming frivolity. In the delegations that set out to the monster whig rallies, camping out at night on their way in the log cabins set up in the cities long past the pioneer stage, in which banker, merchant, and mechanic toasted Harrison in mugs of hard cider, one catches the spirit of a sort of national feast of tabernacles, a commemoration of the hardships and privations by which the west had been won. East and west alike at outs with the administration, but unable to agree on any set of measures, found common cause in the sentimental dream that with the election of Harrison the political virtues of the fathers and the golden age might come once more.

With the whigs one monster rally followed another. At one in McDonough there were said to have been present 2,500 men and 500 women; at Galena 2,486 men and 340 women; at Carlinville 3,000 persons.[6] The greatest of all was reported to have been that at Springfield which called together some fifteen thousand attendants who paraded by county delegations with banners and special floats. In reply the democrats could only allege that these were drunken and disorderly meetings, but they protested with more truth that the whigs were making an appeal frankly to the passions. The whigs retorted that the personal weakness of Van Buren in the state necessitated using the great name of Jackson at every turn in an appeal essentially perhaps as sentimental as their own. The whigs wisely refrained from attacking Jackson, rather professing a belief that the old Jackson men would vote for Harrison.[7]

In spite of all, however, the whigs did not carry Illinois. They attributed their vote, a little short of a majority, to the fraudulent ballots cast along the line of the canal; but the democrats were as quick to respond with countercharges of fraud and wholesale colonization. The whigs were able to rejoice, however, over a series of victories from the carrying of Maine to the final success, which was celebrated with firing of cannon for the Harrison states. Chicago celebrated with a barbecue at "Walter Newberry's enclosed lot, corner of Clarke and North Water."[8]

---

[6] *Sangamo Journal,* July 17, August 2, 1840.
[7] *Sangamo Journal,* January 10, June 5, 1840; *Chicago American,* June 10, 1840; *Chicago Democrat,* April 29, May 20, 1840.
[8] *Illinois State Register,* October 16, 23, 1840; *Alton Telegraph,* October 31, 1840; *Chicago American,* September 18, November 23, 25, December 4, 1840.

With that election much passed out of American politics. It was the last on which the shadow of the aggression of slave power in the west did not fall heavily. It saw the overthrow of the older democratic party. That party under an uninspiring leader had ranged itself for battle behind measures following naturally from the principles of democracy that it professed and it had been smitten hip and thigh. The sober second thought to which the democrats appealed turned the tide in their favor at the next election, but thenceforth it became increasingly apparent that southern politicians had taken the party out of pawn and that the vigor of its creed had departed.

The whigs did well to rejoice while they might for one of the most ironical instances of retributive justice in politics that history affords was about to overtake them. They had by the nomination of Harrison and Tyler sought to gather together the various elements that had in ten years past split off from the Jacksonian party. They had, therefore, made no attempt to formulate a national platform of principles which would have to hold bank and tariff whigs side by side with Virginia abstractionists like Tyler who prided themselves on their votes for the force bill. When the aged Harrison sank into the grave a month after inauguration, almost with his last breath, so the democrats believed, protesting against the policy of removals forced upon him in violation of his pledges, the whigs were face to face with a man on whose loyalty they had no hold. The party platform had been indefinite on the political issues. True in Illinois, they had argued for a national bank, but they did not stand firmly arrayed for it, contenting themselves with finding fault with their opponents rather than proposing measures of their own. Therefore they could not justly hold Tyler bound to the execution of their program.

Previously the whigs had been in high feather. They had occasionally warned the people that too much in the way of a revival of business must not be expected until whig measures could be inaugurated, but they gloated over the prospect of a United States Bank and of a retaliation on the democrats by a policy of removals that ostensibly sparing the worthy among their opponents in office would in effect spare few or none. It was true that the democrats complained that Harrison's inaugural address was no more specific on bank or tariff than previous party pronouncements had been but the whig papers asserted that his sentiments on the supremacy of the legislature, the veto, and officeholders' interference in politics would restore the halcyon days of Washington.[9]

It was not at first apparent that the death of Harrison and the accession of Tyler had brought about any marked change. Democratic papers set about appropriating for their own use the last of the sentiment and glamour that had enveloped Harrison by insinuating that the importunity of whig office seekers for removals had hastened his death and that the last words of his delirium, "Sir, I wish you to understand the true principles of the Constitution. I wish them carried out. I ask nothing more," represented a last appeal against the force that was driving him to the violation of his preëlection pledges. Indeed Tyler's early removals caused renewed wails from the democrats. The *Belleville Advocate* expressed a lingering hope that Tyler might be consistent with his strict constructionist principles and oppose a bank; but the *State Register* pronounced his message a jumble of federalism, democracy, whiggery, and locofocoism.[10]

The successive bank vetoes at the special session of congress sent politics spinning like a teetotum. The *Alton Telegraph,* while deprecating the burning of the president in effigy by indignant whigs at Jacksonville, was disposed to call for instructions to Tyler to resign. The *Sangamo Journal* was at best inclined to say little, and when it spoke, spoke in sorrow rather than anger. It protested that it could see no cause for locofoco rejoicing, for Tyler had approved the repeal of the subtreasury and the loan, bankrupt, and distribution bills. How could even locofocos take pleasure in the ruin of their

9 *Chicago American,* December 14, 1840, February 27, March 16, 1841.
10 *Illinois State Register,* May 19, 1841; *Belleville Advocate,* April 23, May 15, 29, June 26, 1841.

PASSING OF THE OLD DEMOCRACY 273

country? "The Log Cabins had been blown up," true enough, and pork and beef were selling at two cents a pound! The democratic papers triumphantly proclaimed that Tyler had followed his conscience. The *State Register* defended his integrity, averring that while the whigs had made the bank an issue in Illinois and had been beaten on it they had not made it so throughout the nation. The democratic county meetings throughout the state in the fall of 1841, while condemning the whig repeal of the subtreasury, tariff, and distribution measures and occasionally censuring Tyler for his share in them, were disposed to give the president full praise for his veto of the bank.[11]

The whigs, unable like the democrats to wait for action on the part of their opponents, rallied slowly. On the bank scheme proposed in Tyler's fall message, the whig papers were not enthusiastic. The general consensus of their opinion as collected by the *Sangamo Journal* was "half a loaf is better than no bread." The *Sangamo Journal*, inspired, as William Walters of the *State Register* insinuated, by hopes of obtaining the post-office printing, was inclined to be friendly to the administration. The whigs attempted to attribute the hard times to the specie standard. In the winter of 1842 they wished to revive the tariff issue. In part their propaganda, founded as it was on the danger of competition to southern cotton in British markets by East Indian cotton, was manifestly designed to win the south to the whigs. Most of the arguments seemed hardly adapted to western consumption with the possible exception of the home market argument and the fact that American wheat was taxed in England. They taunted the democrats with fearing to join issue on the question, and in fact the democratic papers had little to say till after Tyler's veto.[12]

[11] *Alton Telegraph*, August 28, September 4, 25, 1841; *Illinois State Register*, September 3, October 1, 1841; *Sangamo Journal*, September 3, 17, 24, October 29, 1841; *Belleville Advocate*, September 3, November 11, 25, 1841.
[12] *Sangamo Journal*, January 6, February 4, April 8, 15, December 22, 1842; *Chicago American*, January 14, 21, February 11, 26, April 20, September 16, 1842; *Illinois State Register*, January 14, October 7, 1842; *Belleville Advocate*, December 23, 1841, August 18, October 13, 1842.

In the midst of the confusion, party lines for a time were almost erased. Clay and his friends had in the name of the whigs excommunicated John Tyler, but for a time the mighty Webster remained in Tyler's cabinet. Tyler was able to count on many former democrats as well who rallied for a time to his standard. Charles Prentice persuaded William Walters of the *Illinois State Register* by dreams of controlling the patronage in the state to make overtures to Tyler, which Prentice used to persuade Tyler of his control of the party in Illinois. A longing for the patronage caused many whigs and democrats to come as near to Tyler as their consciences would permit.[13]

In the whig party the Clay men were the irreconcilables. The attitude which the party assumed toward Webster is instructive. Immediately after the vetoes, the *Telegraph* was inclined to criticize him for not resigning and the *Journal* to palliate his remaining in office. By the fall of 1842, however, whig papers were generally attacking him openly. The democratic papers during the congressional campaign of 1843 were inclined to diagnose the situation as Clay with his measures of assumption, bank, distribution, and tariff, as against Tyler and Webster, again the old Webster of 1818, the opponent of bank, tariff, and the American system. The *Telegraph* served notice on Webster that to run against Clay would insure his defeat and political ruin. By December the *Register* had decided that the Clay plan was to use Webster to elect Clay and then drop him, and that accordingly the Illinois whig leaders had ceased to attack him. Thus the question of the assumption of state debts by the national government, manifestly Clay's American system under another form, was advanced by the whigs late in 1842 for the congressional campaign, the *Telegraph* coming out for it openly, and the *American* at first hanging back. The *Register* pronounced it the plan of J. Horsley Palmer of Palmer, Dent, and McKillop, the great London financiers. In the fall of 1843 the whig state

13 *Alton Telegraph,* October 2, 9, 1841; *Belleville Advocate,* December 1, 1841; *Chicago American,* March 29, December 20, 1841, March 12, 16, October 4, 12, 1842; *Sangamo Journal,* October 1, 1841.

convention pronounced the issues to be protection, distribution, and a bank, and declared the party was united behind Clay.[14]

The possibility of an independent Tyler movement in the campaign of 1844 was not disposed of till the opening of the campaign. In 1843 Tyler had attempted to rally the office-holders to the *Madisonian*. In April the *Register* had assailed Isaac Hill for going over to Tyler, declaring that as a third candidate Tyler could not get thirty votes in Illinois and pronouncing his best course to be to seek to unite his former political associates. But at the same time Walters through Prentice was coöperating with Tyler to get whig officeholders replaced by democrats. In the spring of 1844, A. G. Herndon, Archibald Job, G. Elkin, and S. R. Rowan were active for Tyler on the Texas issue, but finally the issue was transferred to the Polk armory.[15] Ebenezer Peck represented it as the last attempt of the desperate Tyler men to get away from the tariff and currency issues.

The democrats had been at a loss as to their candidate. James Buchanan, Lewis Cass, and Thomas Benton had been suggested at different times. In August of 1842 the *Chicago American* thought they were about to take up Calhoun. In the summer of 1842 when Van Buren came to Chicago on what the *American* considered an electioneering visit, it urged the whigs to refrain from all but the ordinary civilities to him; Judge Henry Brown, who was given to reminiscences of New York, gave a picture of him lounging in dandified fashion about Albany. Some one placed a barrel of stale cabbage in the public square in possible reference to Van Buren's Dutch ancestry, but no further unpleasantness occurred.[16]

For a time there was a boom of moderate proportions for R. M. Johnson. The *Belleville Advocate*, Reynolds' paper,

[14] *Illinois State Register*, March 3, June 2, 16, 23, December 8, 1843; *Alton Telegraph*, November 12, 1842, April 15, December 23, 1843; *Chicago American*, March 15, July 21, 1842.

[15] *Alton Telegraph*, April 22, 1843; *Sangamo Journal*, January 25, April 11, May 30, June 13, July 14, 1844; *Illinois State Register*, April 7, 1843.

[16] *Chicago American*, December 11, 1841, March 18, June 23, 24, July 8, August 6, 1842.

came out for him in 1841 as the friend of the west and the advocate of reduction of the price of public lands. In May of 1843 he visited Belleville where the *Advocate* had not ceased to work for him. It insisted that he would get five votes in Illinois to one for any other democratic candidate. Only the *Galena Sentinel,* however, came to the support of the *Advocate.* Johnson's candidacy, however, was thought to be linked by Reynolds with his own as the anti-convention candidate for congress against Lyman Trumbull, Shields, or Koerner. The *Advocate* complained that the county conventions were packed against Johnson resolutions, and in Illinois his candidacy was practically at an end.[17]

By the late fall of 1843 the opinion of the state had crystallized in favor of Van Buren. The *Register* came out for him, September 22, the *Democrat,* December 20; and a series of county meetings had previously declared for him. The *Register* was accused of supporting Van Buren after having been bought off by Benton from its previous support of Johnson. Possibly too the *Register* had a slight inclination toward Calhoun.[18]

The democrats at the beginning of the campaign, began their restatements of principles in such form as has already been indicated. They began too a series of bitter attacks on Clay for his insolent reference in 1820 to the workers of the north as white slaves, for his contemptuous remarks about squatters and his opposition to liberal land policies. His part in the Graves-Cilley duel and his general violence of character were all brought out, even to the alleged "corrupt bargain." The party made the bank and the tariff its more serious issues. The whigs in their pre-convention campaign assailed Van Buren on the old issues of 1836 and 1840 — his hostility to the west, the standing army of 1839. The issues made by their conventions were usually protection, distribution, a bank, one term.

[17] *Belleville Advocate,* September 17, 1841, May 18, 23, December 21, 28, 1843; *Alton Telegraph,* September 9, 1843.
[18] *Illinois State Register,* April 28, June 16, November 24, December 1, 1843, February 16, 1844; *Belleville Advocate,* November 2, 30, 1843.

The democrats contended they were trying for a hurrah campaign like that of 1840, and evidenced their use of shingles for purpose of applause.[19]

A first result of the nomination of Polk instead of Van Buren at Baltimore was to overset all the whig preparations. The whigs had to change their position in the face of the enemy, hastily alleging against Polk his vote against the Cumberland road and his descent from tories, and finally using such stories as the famous Roorback. This last consisted in an incident of Featherstonhaugh's travels which was revamped into a description of a gang of slaves being marched south to be sold, each branded " J. K. P." This thrilling tale professed to be extracted from the travels of the Baron von Roorback, a mythical German nobleman whose name has found immortality as an American political catchword.

Otherwise the issues were narrowed to banks, a tariff, and the annexation of Texas; and in all these the democrats had the superior position.[20] Polk was easily successful in Illinois and successful by a narrow margin in the nation.

Yet the party was actually far from unanimous. The democratic papers had been quick to recover from their involuntary start of surprise at Polk's nomination and to multiply virtues in him and arguments for his election. Yet the *Register* lately alleged that a faction in Illinois guided by Benton had fought desperately against him. Once his course on the Texas and Oregon questions and on river and harbor improvement had become clear, that same faction in the democracy repudiated him and the newer southern democracy he represented.

[19] *Illinois State Register,* December 8, 1843, April 5, May 10, 31, 1844; *Belleville Advocate,* May 2, 9, 1844; *Chicago Democrat,* March 27, May 1, 15, 1844; *Sangamo Journal,* March 7, April 11, 1844.
[20] *Alton Telegraph,* October 5, 26, 1844; *Vandalia Free Press,* July 20, 1844; *Chicago Democrat,* August 28, October 16, 1844.

XV. STATE POLITICS, 1840–1847

SETTING aside national politics and party maneuverings for advantage on the issues arising from the internal improvement system, the springs of political life between 1839 and 1846 are to be found in a series of political quarrels and rivalries ending in the expulsion from active politics one after another of the older political leaders. True enough there were state issues proper in 1839–1840; but these speedily became incrusted with personal and factional rivalries. To trace this whole series of squabbles would be insufferably tedious. If the events be studied, however, as clashes between certain striking characters—Ebenezer Peck, T. W. Smith, William Walters, John Reynolds, and John Wentworth—they may engage the reader's attention.

The fact that the whigs were in an unfortunate situation on two state issues explains their failure to carry Illinois for Harrison in 1840. One of these issues arose from the so-called "life office" controversy in which they were on the unpopular side of a question that might be treated as one of fundamental political principle. The office of secretary of state had been held by A. P. Field since his appointment by Governor Edwards in the days when he was an "original Jackson man." The passage of time, however, had wrought miracles in party alignments, and in 1838 Field was a whig too inveterate for the democrats to endure in office. When Governor Carlin attempted, however, to choose a secretary of state more congenial politically to his associates, Field, always of a pugnacious disposition, refused to be ousted, pointing out that the constitution of the state failed to specify the term for which the secretary of state was to be chosen. Accordingly the whig senate, with the assistance of a few democrats, supported him

278

in standing upon his so-called rights. The governor's nominations were rejected; but after the legislature had adjourned, the governor's appointee, John A. McClernand, sued for the office. Two justices of the supreme court, Samuel D. Lockwood and William Wilson, held that while the term of the office was not for life the tenure under the constitution, until the senate should alter it, was dependent only on good behavior. Thomas C. Browne, a third justice, because he was related to McClernand did not give his opinion, and Theophilus W. Smith dissented.

Politicians were quick to take advantage of the issue. The democratic papers argued that it was beyond the constitutional power of the legislature to fix the term of an officer appointed by the governor and accordingly removable by him with the consent of the body that concurred in the appointment.[1] They recalled the story that on a former occasion Elias Kent Kane, the virtual author of the constitution, had declared it the intention of the convention that the governor should have power to remove. The state democratic convention accused the whigs of favoring a life tenure of office, adding to the accusation an attack on the " federalist " judges and senate. The topic was prescribed to the local conventions by a democratic circular issued by the state committee, October 10, 1839; and it figured duly in their resolutions.[2] The final result was that no law was passed and that the right of governor and senate to remove was vindicated.

Before the life office question had been settled, another politico-constitutional question had been injected into state politics; and, though the democrats were far from being in so favorable a position on it, in the end it gave the whigs no real advantage. A test case as to the right of aliens to vote, which Governor Ford declared to have been made up by two whigs and which the court itself at one time believed to be fictitious,

[1] *Illinois State Register,* August 17, 24, 31, September 28, December 14, 25, 1839.
[2] *Ibid.,* November 2, 9, 23, 30, December 7, 21, 1839, April 3, 1840.

appeared on the calendar of the circuit court at Galena. It was there decided on the principle that the provision of the constitution giving the franchise to free male inhabitants of specified age and color did not serve to include unnaturalized aliens even though they had fulfilled the time required for residence. The case was carried up to the supreme court in 1839 and argued in December. It came up again in June when according to Ford, Judge Smith privately suggested to the lawyers for the alien side a flaw in the record, which postponed the decision until after the election of 1840. Meanwhile the democratic leaders in the general assembly had planned such a legislative reorganization of the judiciary as might for the future at least secure them from any partisan decisions favoring the whigs.

The justices of the supreme court took the alarm and handed down this decision on the case at the December term, 1840. Judge Smith in the longest opinion decided the case squarely on the question of the right of the alien to vote whether naturalized or not. Judges Lockwood and Wilson in their decisions were more obscure. They concurred in the reversal of the lower court's decision but solely, as nearly as one can judge, on the ground that the law left the clerk no power to inquire whether the voter were an alien or not.

The assembly did not wait for the supreme court. On December 10, 1840, Snyder introduced into the senate a bill for the reorganization of the judiciary. After a prolonged debate the bill passed the senate by a vote of twenty-two to seventeen. On February 1 the house adopted it by a vote of forty-five to forty. In neither the house nor the senate were the democrats able to cast their full party vote for the measure.

As passed the measure provided for the appointment of five additional justices of the supreme court who with the four judges already sitting were to perform the duties of the nine circuits of the state and incidentally insure a democratic majority in the court. On February 8 the council of revision returned the measure with its objections signed only by the members of the supreme court. The three whig members instanced the terms of the measure and the fact that the circuit judges would be so overworked that cases would accumulate on the dockets. Smith dissented on the ground that the act was unconstitutional as retroactive and that it was subversive of private right as well as of public faith to the displaced circuit judges. On the reconsideration of the bill in the senate, E. D. Baker attempted, as nearly as one can determine, to start a filibuster, but was promptly declared out of order when he attempted to read documents or to have them read by the clerk and finally gave up. The bill passed the same day twenty-three to sixteen.[3] In the house the whigs, as they had done before, tried to obtain a popular referendum on the question, but failed. On the same day, the bill repassed by a vote of forty-six to forty-three.

The judiciary bill had far reaching effects on the democratic party. McClernand and Trumbull made the measure a test of party faith and bitterly denounced such men as S. G. Hicks and A. C. Leary of Cook who voted against it. The political ruin which the measure indirectly brought upon that insatiable Tammany politician, Theophilus W. Smith, is a better story. Smith had originally suggested to the democratic lawyers the flaw in the record which they had been able to use to postpone the decision of the alien case till after they had used the alien votes in the presidential election of the same year. At that time he had told the democrats that the whig justices were about to decide the case on constitutional grounds that would bar aliens from the right to vote. But in February of 1841 he issued with the other three justices a statement denying that the decision given out in December differed from that which they had reached in June. The various democratic leaders thereupon published their assertions that Smith had assured them to the contrary in June, and there is no particular reason to doubt their testimony. Smith, who in spite of his denial

[3] *Illinois State Register,* February 12, 1841.

probably had senatorial aspirations in the summer of 1840, had been disappointed in the election of McRoberts as senator,[4] and his wrath against his old associates was bitter. It was reported a year later that he had engaged to fight a duel with McClernand. The *State Register* declared that Smith was planning to establish at Springfield a newspaper, *The Jeffersonian Democrat,* ostensibly democratic but whose true object was to wreck the party. The *Register* charged that the paper would profess democracy but advocate whig measures and, while supporting the presidential candidate of the party, would oppose its nominee for governor. In August of 1842 the *Register* published a long attack on Smith, accusing him of heading a riot in Chicago during the election of 1840, of drunkenness, of nepotism, and of harassing the politicians who had favored the judiciary bill. The *Register* which published the article and the *Chicago Democrat* which clipped it were made defendants in libel suits by Smith on some of the charges in this attack. Smith's erratic conduct led some to believe that his mind was affected. Under a cloud mostly of his own raising, he resigned in December, 1842, from the supreme court and ended his long political career.[5]

Similarly the judiciary bill resulted in a turn in the political fortunes of another democratic politician, Ebenezer Peck. Peck was one of the ablest and at the same time one of the most abused of the democratic party leaders. The whigs were never tired of recalling the fact that while an American citizen he had gone to Canada, had become a king's counselor, and had, if report was true, done work for the government in the suppression of revolt and discontent before he came to Illinois about 1835 to preach the pure doctrine of democracy, conventional, undefiled, and regular. He had done yeoman service in the election of 1840 and now perhaps was claiming his reward. As a result, the whigs insinuated, of his conversion

[4] *Chicago American,* September 15, 1840, February 6, June 6, 1841; *Illinois State Register,* February 5, 1841; *Alton Telegraph,* June 26, 1841.
[5] *Illinois State Register,* March 12, 1841, August 26, December 2, 1842; *Chicago American,* March 11, 1841; *Chicago Democrat,* November 30, 1842.

to the support of the judiciary bill, for which, however, he had uniformly voted, the new supreme court, consisting, beside the former justices, of Sidney Breese, Thomas Ford, W. B. Scates, S. H. Treat, and S. A. Douglas, elected him clerk of the supreme court in the place of J. M. Duncan. There were but five justices present at the election and four of them voted for Peck. Even many of the democratic papers had nothing good to say of the appointment of the "midnight clerk," and Peck with his friends of the *State Register* and the Springfield clique found enemies ready to assail them on all sides.[6]

Notable among the enemies whom the Springfield clique had to encounter was "Long John" Wentworth, editor of the *Chicago Democrat* and for many years the leader of his party in the city. He had come to the state to seek his political fortune in 1836, and if Peck is to be believed had begun his career with Peck's financial support and patronage. Peck professed a very poor opinion of him; if it was real, like many others he understood Wentworth's political ability too late. Throughout 1842 Wentworth with the *Ottawa Free Trader* and *Carrolton Advocate,* waged open war on Peck, the *Register,* and the clique. For a time he hoped to secure in the legislature the defeat of Walters for public printer. In the legislature the clique was triumphant in the elections of 1842–1843. It defeated R. M. Young for senator, Walters alleging that he had Tyler leanings and was of doubtful orthodoxy, and elected Sidney Breese as a result, it was claimed, of a bargain by which the latter had withdrawn from the gubernatorial race of 1842.[7]

Walters was elected public printer, and for the three vacant seats in the supreme court left by the resignations of Ford, Breese, and Theophilus W. Smith there were chosen Young in

[6] *Sangamo Journal,* August 7, 1840, March 19, 26, 1841; *Chicago American,* June 27, July 14, 18, 24, September 18, 1840, March 17, 1841; *Illinois State Register,* May 7, July 16, 1841.

[7] *Alton Telegraph,* October 1, December 24, 1842; *Sangamo Journal,* November 11, 1842; *Illinois State Register,* November 4, 1842; *Chicago Democrat,* October 5, 19, November 30, December 14, 1842; *Belleville Advocate,* November 17, 1842.

the northern circuit, James Semple, and J. M. Robinson. Wentworth was much aggrieved at the placing of southern men in positions in the northern part of the state, asserting that the south would not permit a similar proceeding.

The rise to political prominence of such men as Wentworth had been preceded by the elimination of the politicians of the past decade. The congressional elections of 1841 especially had marked the end of an era. Of the three successful candidates the career of each had run its course with his election in this year. In the looseness of their party affiliations they typified the passing democratic régime in Illinois. In the first district that old political war horse John Reynolds had little difficulty in beating Henry L. Webb. Webb was a man of little ability and his candidacy was supported by the *Alton Telegraph* only after it felt assured that no stronger whig could be induced to run. Stephen R. Rowan had offered himself as a kind of independent candidate appealing especially to whig votes. Reynolds attacked him in spite of his three votes for Jackson and two for Van Buren as being for a bank, distribution, and the repeal of the subtreasury. The *Alton Telegraph* on the other side refused to consider Rowan's professions genuine in view of his political past; and finally, after in vain trying to bring Reynolds' blunders as financial agent for the state into the campaign, he did actually withdraw in favor of Webb. On the day of election Reynolds received 8,046 votes to 4,829 for Webb and 171 for Rowan.[8]

In the second district Zadoc Casey with a very nondescript record in congress was barely successful over Stinson H. Anderson, receiving 7,121 votes to 6,949 for his opponent. Casey had finally been read out of the party by the *State Register* which pronounced him no better than a whig, evidencing his declaration for a United States Bank, his course on the subtreasury, and his somewhat underhanded attempt to secure the speakership of the house. The whigs were disposed to give

[8] *Alton Telegraph*, April 17, May 15, 22, June 14, July 10, 17, 31, 1841; *Belleville Advocate*, April 17, July 3, 23, 1841; *Illinois State Register*, May 28, 1841; *Sangamo Journal*, June 4, 1841.

him support on the ground assigned by the *Sangamo Journal* that he was sound on at least one whig measure.[9]

In the north, John T. Stuart made his last successful run for congress. The democrats, according to their opponents, made a desperate attempt to defeat him by inducing some whig to run against him. The *Alton Telegraph* indeed felt it necessary to threaten R. F. Barrett with an exposure in case he ventured to fulfill the desire of the democrats by running against Stuart. James H. Ralston opposed him as the democratic candidate. The *State Register* reproved the *Chicago Democrat* for lukewarmness in his behalf, alleging that Wentworth had opposed the holding of a congressional convention in the district and had to the last endeavored to bring about the nomination of some favorite of his own. Wentworth professed to believe that anyone of half a dozen men might have successfully run against Stuart and concluded that it might have been better after all to have held a convention. At an earlier time, Thomas Ford had been considered as a possible candidate in the district. Stuart's victory was not imposing, for he received but 21,698 votes as against 19,553 for Ralston and 470 for Frederick Collins.[10]

Before the congressional race was over, the contest for the governorship had begun. At the end of 1840 O. H. Fellows, Edwards, Lincoln, Browning, Eddy, William Fithian, W. F. Thornton, and Joseph Duncan were all mentioned for the whig nomination. At the meeting of the legislature, however, the whig members reached a practical conclusion to run Duncan on his past record on the bank, internal improvements, and the canal. The question whether a state convention was necessary to reach an agreement as to the candidate, or whether the old method of compromise and of bringing influence to bear to induce rival candidates to withdraw might not be successfully

[9] *Illinois State Register,* June 11, July 9, 23, November 12, 1841; *Sangamo Journal,* May 21, August 20, 1841.
[10] *Alton Telegraph,* June 19, 1841; *Sangamo Journal,* May 7, June 4, August 20, 1841; *Chicago American,* January 29, 1841; *Illinois State Register,* August 13, 1841; *Chicago Democrat,* September 11, 1841.

applied, arose as soon as it appeared the party was not unanimous for him. The *Peoria Register* and the *Chicago American* had favored the candidacy of Thornton; and the *Shawneetown Republican* and the *Kaskaskia Republican* were for William H. Davidson, a candidate who on account of his anticanal record was not acceptable to the northern part of the state. Toward the end of the summer the *Fulton Telegraph* suggested the name of Abraham Lincoln, but the *Sangamo Journal* did not believe that Lincoln desired the office, since it would take four of the best years of his life from his practice and he had already been noted for the sacrifices he had made for party principles. The whigs issued a call for a convention to. meet the third Monday in December, signed by J. F. Speed, A. G. Henry, Lincoln, E. D. Baker, and May. Early in November, Davidson withdrew from the contest for the nomination, and the whigs at once entertained hopes that this move might render a convention unnecessary. The dislike of southern Illinois for conventions was advanced as a reason why it was especially desirable to avoid holding one if possible. The whig central committee accordingly withdrew the call for the convention, the democratic papers insinuating that it was at the command of the Springfield junto.[11] If one can judge by the later comments on the campaign by such whigs as Lincoln the harmony in the party in favor of Duncan was mainly on the surface.

While Duncan was being chosen by the whig members of the state legislature, Adam W. Snyder was being selected by the democrats. An opposition to him developed, partly based on the fact of his uncertain course on the measures that were the tests of party faith in 1837. A. G. Herndon wrote letters to the *State Register* signed "A Slashergaff," in which Robinson was in this particular favorably contrasted with Snyder; and in the fall Robinson was informally suggested as a candidate. Then, too, there was real hostility to Snyder exhibited, so the *State Register* claimed, by the *Chicago Democrat* on the

[11] *Chicago American,* January 13, 1841; *Alton Telegraph,* February 13, July 3, 10, 31, November 13, December 11, 1841; *Illinois State Register,* February 19, 1841; *Sangamo Journal,* October 15, 22, 29, November 26, 1841.

ground of his supposed attitude toward the canal. Utterances came emphatically from northern Illinois that it would support no man who was not unqualifiedly in favor of the completion of the canal. Finally Snyder, albeit in somewhat uncertain and equivocal fashion, declared in favor of the canal; and as the time of the convention approached, opposition to him died away. He was nominated on the first ballot, receiving 148 votes to 11 cast for M. K. Alexander, who had not, however, been put in nomination. According to the whigs the inner circle of the democratic party had decided that William A. Richardson should be run for lieutenant governor; it took four ballots in the convention, however, before John Moore was finally nominated. The *Quincy Herald* was rather loath to accept Snyder, apparently in view of his declaration for the canal; but there was no help for it.[12]

In Snyder southern Illinois had imposed on the party its gubernatorial candidate, but the chances of life and death were to render frustrate its advantage. As early as February reports of Snyder's serious illness began to circulate. By the end of April it was known that he was too ill to take the stump as the democratic papers were demanding, and on May 14 he was dead. Immediately the southern democrats began to move to secure the appointment of a man from that section as his successor. Reynolds was mentioned, but the telegraph had not yet revolutionized convention and nomination methods, and it was doubtful if his assent to a candidacy for the nomination could have been obtained in time to enable him to return from Washington for an effective campaign. Even so, his friends manufactured some support for him in Scott, Shelby, Williamson, and Gallatin counties.

The movement in favor of Breese was much stronger than that for Reynolds and developed much earlier. He was nominated by a meeting at Vandalia, and by the *Belleville Advocate* and by the *Illinois Sentinel*. It was said that the whole of the

[12] *Illinois State Register,* July 16, October 15, 22, 29, December 17, 29, 31, 1841; *Alton Telegraph,* January 22, 1842; *Sangamo Journal,* November 12, December 17, 1841; *Belleville Advocate,* October 15, 21, November, *passim.*

Wabash country was in favor of his candidacy, the *Wabash Republican*, the *Mt. Carmel Republican*, and a meeting in Effingham county all declaring for him. Breese expressed his willingness to run, provided it was possible to concentrate the approval of the party by county nominations and the support of democratic papers. Finally he withdrew in favor of Ford.[13]

Meanwhile northern Illinois with the assistance of the *State Register* had secured the acceptance of Thomas Ford as the candidate of the party, disregarding the claim of the south for a southern man. The *Register* on May 27 declared its belief that Ford was as good a candidate as could be selected and might as well be accepted in view of the fact that there was not time to hold another convention and that the consent of Reynolds could not be obtained in time. The *Chicago Democrat* also favored Ford's nomination. The *Chicago American* declared that a meeting at Springfield which formally assumed to nominate him was a packed one, only four counties out of the twenty represented in it lying below Vandalia. In the face of the *Chicago Democrat's* denials it insisted that the nomination of Ford had been arranged before Snyder's death by a clique of northern officeholders and office seekers, without allowing the southern part of the state any voice in the matter.[14]

As in 1838, the whigs were now to find that their introductory campaign work was almost worthless. Snyder's record was well known and offered openings to attack from various angles. Putting aside his supposed reliance on Mormon votes and his somewhat uncertain attitude on the canal, his opponents could say that he had tried to evade payment of a debt owed to the first state bank on the plea that the bank was unconstitutional and hence could have no existence sufficient to collect debts due to it. His course in congress in the critical years,

13 *Chicago American*, February 17, April 29, May 11, 23, June 6, 7, 15, 18, July 14, 1842; *Illinois State Register*, May 27, July 8, 1842; *Belleville Advocate*, May 26, June 2, 9, 1842.
14 *Illinois State Register*, May 27, 1842; *Chicago American*, June 2, 14, 30, 1842.

1837–1839, could be made to appear equivocal and had so been branded by such democrats as McRoberts and A. G. Herndon. The *Chicago American* indeed, on April 4, had remarked that democrats of the old school would support Duncan rather than Snyder.[15]

All efforts at collecting evidence against Snyder had been thrown away. The whigs had now on short notice to find material with which to assail Ford, and they made hard work or it. The best they could do was to denominate him a judge who had used his position to make political capital. The *Chicago Democrat* ran a cut of a dolefully long face representing Duncan when he heard that Ford had consented to run. The *Chicago American*, which had praised Ford's efficiency and integrity as a judge before it contemplated his entrance into politics, was now compelled to have recourse to hints of dangerous ambition on his part. His past as an Adams man was of course dragged out against him with the old charge of circulating coffin handbills. Whig papers remarked with great glee on what they alleged were Ford's discomfitures on the stump at the hands of Duncan. They tried in northern Illinois also to identify Duncan as the canal candidate, claiming that at Mt. Carmel Ford had declared that he was opposed to involving the credit of the state one cent more for the benefit of the enterprise; further that he had repeatedly tried in the southern part of the state to represent Duncan as the canal candidate to the latter's discredit.[16]

More worthy of note was the attempt to use against Ford the widespread movement in northern Illinois for union with the territory of Wisconsin in accord with the original plan for the division of the northwest territory. This agitation was probably due to despair at the overwhelming weight of debt that the state internal improvement system had apparently irrevocably imposed on Illinois. During 1842, and even

[15] *Chicago Democrat*, February 9, 1842; *Chicago American*, January 11, 28, 29, March 2, April 4, 11, 13, May 9, 11, 1842.
[16] *Chicago Democrat*, June 8, 1842; *Chicago American*, June 30, July 2, 16, 22, 25, 26, 27, August 1, 1842; *Illinois State Register*, July 29, 1842.

before that, meetings were held in one after another of the northern counties involved. Ogle, Stephenson, Jo Daviess declared for the union with Wisconsin by overwhelming majorities; in Stephenson it was said to be five hundred to one. In 1840 there had been in several counties a movement for a convention to consider sending delegates to sit in union with the people of Wisconsin. In 1842 Governor Doty warned Governor Carlin against making any selections of land on what, according to the people of Wisconsin, was the soil of their territory and under the jurisdiction of Illinois only from accidental and temporary conditions. The fact that Ford in southern Illinois opposed annexation was used duly against him in the north by the *Chicago American,* which professed to believe that the people of the north would sooner vote for an opponent like Duncan than for a traitor to their interests like Ford.[17]

For the rest the campaign centered on Joseph Duncan, as was inevitable in view of his long and checkered career in Illinois politics. The whigs were able once more to exhibit the finer points of his record — the boyish enthusiasm of the young officer of seventeen, the piety of the mature man, the long political career in congress and in the state, at least outwardly statesmanlike. On the other hand, all the devious things so readily to be found in the career of any man who has striven to become rich by means of speculation, were mercilessly pointed out by the democrats. Whether their case was good in all instances — in many it certainly was not — the explanation of many a shift and device of such a record, if not disgraceful, was sure to be embarrassing. The *Chicago Democrat* did not stop with advising Duncan to campaign with a plat of Illiopolis, the town site that had once aspired to be the capital of the state. Discarding such stories as the one that he had extorted from the people of Meredosia a part of their town site in return for his services to them in congress, and that he had negotiated for

[17] *Chicago American,* June 25, 1840, June 24, July 9, 18, 19, 23, 28, 1842; *Sangamo Journal,* February 4, 1842; *Alton Telegraph,* June 25, 1842; *Chicago Democrat,* March 23, 1840, August 10, 1842.

Thomas Ford

the location of an internal improvement railroad thither —
stories the latter of which at least is disproved by Duncan's
assertion that in spite of his opposition to the whole scheme of
internal improvements, that system, touching town after town
in which he was interested, seemed almost designed to buy his
support — still other matters remained. He had certainly
borrowed heavily from the State Bank, even though no proof
except assertion existed that his borrowing had influenced his
official conduct toward it. Finally there was the matter of the
defalcation of his brother-in-law, William J. Linn, receiver at
Vandalia; Duncan had been a surety for Linn, and if Walters
of the *State Register* may be believed — though Ford was
inclined to doubt the hypothesis — Duncan had procured from
Linn for his own security a mortgage on all his property, leaving the other bondsmen helpless. Walters was ready to avow
graver charges against Duncan to the effect that the fruits of
Linn's defalcations had assisted in Duncan's speculations in
Illiopolis and Michigan City. There is far from enough evidence to convict Duncan of trickery or dishonesty, but the
whole situation was one that to a man of a delicate sense of
honor would have been intolerable.[18]

Although the democrats were unsuccessful in fixing upon
Duncan the responsibility for the State Bank failure and for
the collapse of the internal improvement system, so far as the
bank was concerned they could state truthfully that he had at
least called a special session of the legislature in 1837 to
authorize its suspension and that his alternative to the internal
improvement system — construction by chartered companies
to the stock of which the state should subscribe — might have
been even more disastrous to the state than the system finally
inaugurated, since in that case the state would have given up
any chance for profits.[19]

[18] *Chicago American*, March 14, 28, April 26, June 10, July 22, 1842; *Illinois State Register*, May 13, June 17, July 1, 8, 22, 1842; *Alton Telegraph*, April 2, May 14, June 11, 1842.

[19] *Belleville Advocate*, May 5, 12, 1842; *Sangamo Journal*, April 15, 1842; *Illinois State Register*, April 8, 29, 1842; *Chicago American*, February 19, April 7, May 7, 18, 19, July 18, 1842.

Finally the democrats were prepared to take more decisive positions on national issues than their opponents. The whigs in vain protested against having the campaign fought on the national issues rather than on that of democratic misrule in the state; in vain they protested at having the hard times so evident within the state contrasted with their promises in 1840. Moreover Duncan, not realizing, as indeed he never did realize, that the school of politics founded on faction and personal influence in which he had grown up had, with the newer political order, gone, never to return, attempted to avoid taking a hard and fast stand on national issues; in a day when the worship of Jackson had passed even among the democrats he persisted in representing himself as a Jackson man, thereby only causing democrats to produce the caustic attacks on Jackson from some of his messages as governor, and northern whigs to refuse to support a renegade. After the election indeed the whigs attempted to explain their defeat by saying that the whig vote had not turned out, that in certain counties no attempt had been made to get it out. This attitude is an amazing contrast to the appeals for union on party lines and the warnings of the danger of split tickets that emanated to the democratic party from the *Chicago Democrat* and the *Belleville Advocate*.[20]

Evidence is not wanting to indicate that the weakness of Duncan's showing—he received but 39,020 votes, to 46,507 for Ford—was due to the fact that the party had never fairly united on him. The statement already cited[21] shows that such was the case even among men who called themselves whigs and adds as one reason for the lack of unity that Duncan had been nominated by the *Telegraph* and *Journal* without consulting the whigs of the northern part of the state. This is borne out in the implied comment on the conduct of the affair in the manifesto for party organization promulgated later by Lincoln,

[20] *Belleville Advocate,* June 30, 1842, July 14, 1843; *Chicago American,* May 26, July 14, 25, 26, August 30, 1842; *Illinois State Register,* May 20, 1842; *Chicago Democrat,* March 16, June 8, August 3, 1842; *Chicago Daily Journal,* January 20, 1845; *Sangamo Journal,* August 12, 1842.

[21] *Chicago Daily Journal,* January 20, 1845, and *Alton Telegraph,* May 13, 1843.

S. T. Logan, and Blackwell. Duncan's answer was the answer of the man dwelling to the last in the political atmosphere of his youth in which close party alignment had been well-nigh the mark of the beast. Once again he reiterated the political ideas of his younger days as the only means of safety and honor for the whigs; but to the new practical politicians like Lincoln, quick to perceive the advantage of the democratic party discipline and party unity, that course led only to defeat.

The new complications introduced into state politics by the redistricting of the state in 1843 for the seven congressional seats to which it was entitled contributed still more to bring forward new men. Walters in the *State Register* opposed the scheme of apportionment finally agreed on, arguing that on the basis of the vote of 1840 it made three districts safely whig; and he advocated the election of congressmen by the state at large instead of by districts, arguing that such a scheme would make for party unity. Possibly Walters foresaw what actually was the result, that the localizing tendency in the distribution of political power was to make it less easy to exercise control from the center.[22]

The democrats set about their work in the congressional districts eager for victory. In the seventh district, centering at Springfield and strongly whig, they nerved themselves with the cry that the district, formerly democratic, had been lost through the breaking of the ranks in the White movement of 1836. The democrats urged the use of the convention system as the device which had rescued northern Illinois from the whigs in 1841. The main interest, however, lay in the three-cornered struggle for the whig nomination between John J. Hardin, Edward D. Baker, and Lincoln. According to the *State Register,* in the contest at the whig mass meeting at Springfield between Baker and Lincoln, Baker polled his votes early, obtained the lead, and then called on Lincoln to withdraw, which the latter did. Later the *Register* declared that

---

[22] *Illinois State Register,* February 3, March 17, 1843; *Alton Telegraph,* January 28, 1842.

Sangamon county was kept in the whig column by the manipulations of the whigs who kept careful lists of the voters, knew how they voted, and brought influence to bear accordingly. Hardin, according to the *Register,* in spite of the attempts of the whigs of the junto at Springfield to sidetrack him, was the candidate and won handily, polling 6,230 votes to James A. McDougall's 5,357.[23]

Elsewhere the democrats were successful. In the fifth district which included the Military Tract, Douglas defeated Orville H. Browning by a vote of 8,641 to 8,180. In the fourth or Chicago district, Wentworth beat his opponents by a comfortable margin, polling 7,552 votes to 5,931 for Giles Spring and 1,167 for John Henderson. In the sixth, northwestern Illinois, Hoge beat Walker 7,706 votes to 7,222, the scale being tipped by the vote in Hancock, where Hoge polled 2,088 votes to Walker's 733. In the third district in eastern Illinois the democratic congressional committee addressed queries to the various democratic candidates as to their views and their readiness to submit to a convention. Of the candidates answering, Berry, Wickliffe Kitchell, and Orlando B. Ficklin all showed themselves reasonably orthodox, though Ficklin was inclined to dodge the question of the subtreasury. This apparently did not hinder his nomination on the fifth ballot. Ficklin beat Justin Harlan 6,425 to 5,528.

In the second district McClernand as convention nominee beat Zadoc Casey 6,364 to 3,629. Casey was still trying to play between whigs and democrats, and both expressed pleasure at his defeat. "Zadoc Casey," was Wentworth's comment, "the democrat, the whig, the conservative, the all-things-to-all men, is now beaten for the first time in his life and badly beaten too."[24]

In the first district the election was marked by the beginning

[23] *Illinois State Register,* March 24, April 14, June 9, 16, August 18, 1843.

[24] *Ibid.,* April 28, May 12, June 2, July 14, 21, 1843; *Belleville Advocate,* April 6, May 4, 1843. The *Belleville Advocate* had declared, April 6, that it believed the race lay between Berry, Forman, and Kitchell, with French and Ficklin as possibilities. See also *Chicago Democrat,* August 23, 1843; *Alton Telegraph,* August 26, 1843.

of an open feud in the democratic party that was to last with the utmost bitterness through three elections and end in the political overthrow of John Reynolds, the oldest and shiftiest politician in the state. John of Cahokia was a candidate for renomination, arguing to his constituents that, taken in its strictest sense, the doctrine of rotation in office did not compel them to abandon a candidate who had served them well. The position of parties as it disclosed itself in the campaign for the nomination was as follows. On one side were Reynolds and Trumbull who on account of Trumbull's difficulty with Ford were both bitterly hostile to the governor and the so-called Springfield clique. On the other was the triumvirate of Shields, Koerner, and William H. Bissell, all destined to achieve prominence in national politics. There was a warm contest for delegates to the congressional district convention, complicated by factional differences of opinion as to the proper methods of apportionment — differences too nice to dwell upon here, but responsible for the turning of the majority in a closely divided convention of some twenty odd delegates. As a result Reynolds and Trumbull, if one accepts the account of their friends, feeling that they had no chance before the convention as it was organized, withdrew or declined to allow their names to be presented. Accordingly on the first ballot, Robert Smith was nominated, receiving fourteen votes to eleven for Shields and two for Reynolds. In spite of the fact that Shields was apparently inclined to sulk and that the *Repository,* a supposedly democratic newspaper, kept up a hot fire on Reynolds during the campaign, and in spite of the fact that the whigs continually assailed Smith as a shifty Yankee speculator, the latter was elected. The *Alton Telegraph* attributed the result to a whig convention which had divided rather than united the party.[25]

The congressmen elected in 1843 naturally came up for a reëlection in 1844. In most of the districts there was no

[25] *Belleville Advocate,* March 30, June 8, 29, 1843; *Alton Telegraph,* July 15, August 26, 1843; *Farmers and Mechanics Repository,* July 15, 22, 1843.

change. Baker in the seventh district was nominated by a convention in place of Hardin who, according to the *Sangamo Journal,* declined a reëlection. The most interesting struggle, however, came in the first district where a second campaign in the war of John Reynolds against his foes was about to open. During the past year Reynolds' *Belleville Advocate* had waged relentless war on Walters, Ford, and the clique. Reynolds insisted that Smith had pledged himself in 1843 not to be a candidate for reëlection and, after a series of more or less veiled depreciations of conventions and attacks on the convention system, prepared to run independently. The old party quarrels broke forth again. The *Springfield Times* was declared by the *Sangamo Journal* to represent the southern Illinois end of the party as against Ford and the northern; and along with the *Kaskaskia Republican,* it took Reynolds' side against his opponents. The *Belleville Advocate* declared that the *Register* had conspired with the *Telegraph* and the *Sangamo Journal* to beat Reynolds and Trumbull and to rally a conservative party. The *Register* declared early in January that the *Times* apparently intended to support Reynolds and the whigs; by July, however, the *Belleville Advocate* was demanding that the *Times* keep out of the congressional fight and its attitude is impossible of diagnosis.[26]

Reynolds meanwhile struggled on. He repelled the declarations of his opponents that he was a whig insisting that he was against whig measures and only opposed assailing the whigs themselves with reproaches. He appealed to the voters on the ground of his long residence in the state, claiming that he was "acting democratic" before many of his present opponents were born. He asked them if the new settlers should be permitted to drive off the old settlers, and why, other things being equal, an old resident should not be preferred, once more bringing to notice that he had been a "ranger" thirty years before. All was to no purpose. The attacks of his opponents

[26] *Chicago Democrat,* May 28, 1845; *Belleville Advocate,* January 1, 18, 25, February 1, April 25, May 2, 9, 16, 30, June 6, July 4, 1844; *Illinois State Register,* December 8, 1843; *Sangamo Journal,* February 6, May 16, 1844.

and especially those of Koerner and W. C. Kinney in the *St. Clair Banner* did not relax. Reynolds after a long life of political shiftiness was at last pinned squarely on the point of party organization. He had run his last political race. He did not poll even five thousand votes out of 13,091 cast; and he carried only one county, Pulaski.[27]

Convention or no convention, Reynolds' day was done. In 1846 there was a new dispute as to the apportionment in a district convention, which after Smith's name had been withdrawn nominated Reynolds' ally, Trumbull, for congress. Smith was not to be beaten, however, as he had beaten Reynolds. County meetings began to call on him to run and to repudiate Trumbull. Smith finally issued an address to his constituents in a somewhat humble tone appealing to them not to stigmatize him alone among the delegation and pointing out his opportunities to be of more service than a new member. The whigs when he declared his intention to run independently decided apparently to support him, the *Journal* advising it, and the *Telegraph* favoring him decidedly in its news columns. Probably this was the result of a belief that Smith was not so extreme in his views as Trumbull, though as the *Advocate* suggested, it may have been the result of a bargain. The *State Register* was inclined at this time to take Trumbull's side and to plead for party regularity; the fact that the *Advocate* claimed that Ford and the clique were supporting Trumbull may indicate that the *Register* was no longer with the so-called clique. Smith beat Trumbull by two thousand votes.[28]

The next victim to the partisanship that obtained in the democratic politics in Illinois was Walters of the *State Register*, who with that more or less vague body defined as the "Springfield clique" challenged the congressional delegation and went down in the fight. The congressional delegation in the matter of patronage speedily reached the habit of acting

---

[27] *Belleville Advocate*, June 6, 27, August 1, 8, 1844.
[28] *Alton Telegraph*, May 2, June 13, 27, July 25, 1846; *Belleville Advocate*, May 7, 14, 28, June 18, 25, July 2, 9, 16, 29, 1846; *Sangamo Journal*, July 16, 1846; *Illinois State Register*, May 8, June 19, July 17, 1846.

together. According to Wentworth in 1845 the Springfield group, including members of the legislature then in session, had apportioned the good things among themselves and had then written letters of recommendation for applicants with the greatest freedom. According to him, further, the men at Springfield in order to facilitate the multiplication of promises were in the habit of sending the letter of recommendation to the applicant instead of the president. Finally President Polk insisted that the congressional delegation should agree on all offices before appointments were made. The *State Register* began a war on the delegation pointing out the danger of the concentration of political power in their hands in case the rule laid down by Polk were to be established. In part this discord arose over a new attempt, in the last session of the legislature, by John S. Zieber, Louis M. Booth of the *Quincy Herald*, and Kinney to oust Walters from the public printing office. The *Register* was speedily at swords' points with several of the most prominent democratic papers of the state. The *Quincy Herald*, the *St. Clair Banner*, the *Randolph County Record, Peoria Free Press, Illinois Gazette, Warsaw Signal*, and *Chicago Democrat* all set upon it. At Chicago, Walters could count on help against Wentworth from the *Chicago Democrat Advocate*, apparently controlled by I. N. Arnold who was aggrieved at the appointment of Mark Skinner as United States district attorney for Illinois. In the war on the congressmen, the *Register* had at first tried to draw Douglas in against them; but Douglas sharply declined to be separated from his colleagues and repelled the attacks against their efficiency and ability, notably for the loss of the school fund, which the *Register* was sending out against them. Walters was soon as bitter against Douglas as he had been against the others.[29]

The whigs insinuated their belief that the attempt to set Douglas against the rest of the delegation was an attempt to

[29] *Chicago Democrat,* January 1, 8, 22, February 19, April 2, September 24, 1845; *Illinois State Register,* April 4, May 2, June 6, July 11, 18, August 9, 22, November 7, 1845; *Sangamo Journal,* April 10, August 21, 1845; *Alton Telegraph,* January 18, May 10, 1845; *Chicago Daily Journal,* January 19, 1846.

weaken him so that he might be out of Ford's way in the race for the senate. Ford denied any such attempt, however, and the *Chicago Democrat* and other papers disclaimed any intention of being so easily lured into a quarrel with Ford. The situation cleared up slowly. In the fall the attack on Ford was continued by the *Jackson Standard,* edited at Jacksonville by J. S. Roberts, which accused Ford of using his office to elevate himself to the senate and to secure a governor favorable to his pretensions. Ford came out with an absolute denial, calling on his appointees to state if there had been a bargain in the case of any one of them. This attack as it seemed to the *State Register* was the result of a bargain between Douglas, McClernand, and Wentworth by which the two men first named were to be senators in order, Trumbull, governor, as an especial rebuke to Ford, and Lewis W. Ross of Fulton, lieutenant governor, to clear Richardson's way toward Douglas' seat in congress. In January the *Register* was compelled to admit that in view of a letter from Douglas to E. D. Taylor the charge of a bargain was groundless.[30]

Walters' career as a free lance had impaired the influence of his paper and ruined him politically. The winter had seen more bickering on his part with the delegation.[31] George R. Weber, his junior partner on the *Register,* had withdrawn in the preceding August. In June, 1846, Charles H. Lanphier assumed the duties of editor, Walters having volunteered for the Mexican War. A month later Walters died at St. Louis at the age of forty-four. His career was typical of many an Illinois journalist. He had been in his youth editor of the *Wilmingtonian* in Delaware, had then been one of Duff Green's subordinates in Washington, and had taken part in a kind of labor demonstration against Green, whom he afterwards claimed was in a plot to control the newspapers of the country financially, running them by his apprentices. He had then come

[30] *Chicago Democrat,* July 9, 23, October 8, 21, 1845; *Alton Telegraph,* July 19, October 18, 1845; *Sangamo Journal,* August 7, 1845; *Illinois State Register,* October 17, 31, November 7, 1845, January 23, 1846.
[31] *Illinois State Register,* February 20, March 13, 20, 1846.

to Illinois where he had preached democratic principles with some ability; he had become hopelessly involved financially by his liability on Linn's bond, had intrigued for the public printing, played partisan politics, and bandied back and forth coarse accusations of drunkenness with his rival, Simeon Francis of the *Sangamo Journal*. There was nothing extraordinary in the course of his life and just enough promise of something better in it to lend a touch of pathos to its end.

Another political journalist affords an instructive contrast with Walters. The early part of John Wentworth's career has already been sketched. It was, and continued to be, a series of quarrels with political rivals in the Chicago district in which Wentworth demonstrated an amazing capacity at retaining an unbreakable hold on the voters. In the campaign of 1846 Wentworth had against him in Lake county a paper edited by Aristides B. Wynkoop, a democrat with abolitionist tendencies, which did not belie its name. The *Little Fort Porcupine* began a series of attacks on the democratic clique in Lake county allied with and dependent on Wentworth, accusing them of spoils politics, and malfeasance in office. Its animus against Wentworth was open and apparent in every number, but the *Democrat* gave it comparatively little attention. The *Chicago Journal*, June 13, 1846, remarked that so long as it advanced Wentworth's financial interests in Little Fort he cared little for its attacks.[32]

Specifically, however, it assailed Wentworth with a number of charges which the whig papers were not slow to use against him. It called him to account for alleged shortcomings in securing good things for the district in the way of harbor improvements, his vote for Texas without an equivalent for the north, and held him up to execration as a laughingstock in Washington and an intriguer at home. Wentworth was accused not merely of such venial sins in pursuit of votes as riding the circuit under pretense of practicing law to keep his fences

[32] *Little Fort Porcupine*, 1845, 1846, *passim; Chicago Democrat,* June 30, July 28, 1846.

in repair, of flooding the district with franked documents, and of using the *Chicago Democrat* to puff him shamelessly, but also of prowling around the haunts of vice and immorality. He was accused of using conventions to cement his power, packing them with officeholders and then preaching party regularity. He was accused even of the worse political vice of disloyalty, of beating men for appointments and then none the less asking and securing their political support.[33] The political ghosts of Peck, of Leary, of Murphy, of Arnold, all sometime prominent in the district, were raised to accuse him of ingratitude. Such attacks recurred in campaign after campaign against the editor of the *Democrat*.

In return Wentworth usually warned his supporters to beware of split tickets and of alleged democratic tickets from which his name had been omitted. He retailed as former roorbacks told against him that he had fallen from his horse and been killed and that while still unmarried he beat his wife and child. He made merry about alleged democratic handbills appearing against him.[34] Hard hitting, astute, sometimes cynically frank, he held absolute sway in the northern district.

In spite of the acrimonious prelude, the gubernatorial contest of 1846 was a comparatively quiet affair. Among the democrats there were numerous pronouncements against banks without any very obvious statements to the contrary for them to combat. Trumbull, Scates, Cavarly, and McConnell were all proposed for the office, but finally the choice of the convention fell on Augustus C. French, an eastern Illinois man. The gossip had been that the Springfield clique had favored Calhoun as against Trumbull, and the nomination of French was represented as a compromise of good omen for the party.[35]

The only hope of the whigs had been apparently that Hardin, or possibly Lincoln, might be willing to run for gov-

[33] *Chicago Daily Journal*, March 4, 6, 8, 13, May 5, June 23, July 29, 30, 1846.

[34] *Chicago Democrat*, July 28, August 4, September 8, 1846.

[35] *Illinois State Register*, August 22, October 3, September 26, 1845, January 30, 1846; *Belleville Advocate*, March 14, 1846; *Chicago Daily Journal*, December 19, 1845, January 29, 1846.

ernor. When Hardin declined they were generally unenthu-
siastic. In April the *Telegraph* talked for a while of the need
of a close and compact whig organization, recognizing that
organization and not numbers was the true strength of the
democrats; and it urged a state convention; on a convention
the *Sangamo Journal* was not inclined to be enthusiastic, hoping
the whigs could agree without one. The *Telegraph* was
inclined to think the convention unimportant providing that
unity in that or in some other way was assured, even the suggestion was put forward by the *Sangamo Journal* that a nomination be made by a central committee on the basis of letters
written to it by whigs. George T. M. Davis of the *Telegraph*,
disagreed with this policy of his senior editor, claiming that at
Springfield in the winter the whigs had concluded to run no
one and to let the democrats for want of opposition quarrel
among themselves. Finally when the nominations were made
by a meeting at Peoria, the *Chicago Journal* put them at the
head of its columns but refused to consider their strength or
failure any criterion of the democratic strength in the state.
The *State Register* insinuated that the whigs were only nominating to keep up the organization. With the exception of a
few slurs at French as "Mrs. French's husband," a medi-
ocre man with a taste for drawing the long bow in accounts
of his exploits, the whigs did but little.[36] At the close of the
period of the first constitution the party that still called itself
democratic controlled Illinois.

    [36] *Belleville Advocate,* June 31, 1846; *Alton Telegraph,* July 26, August 9,
December 27, 1845, April 18, 25, May 2, 9, 16, 30, 1846; *Sangamo Journal,*
November 6, 1845, April 23, 1846; *Chicago Daily Journal,* March 24, December
13, 1845, April 20, July 15, 1846; *Illinois State Register,* June 16, 1846.

XVI. STATE AND PRIVATE BANKING, 1830–1845

IN SPITE of the fiasco of the first State Bank ten years had not passed since that institution had reached the height of its career when a new State Bank was created which had a history at least as unfortunate as that of the old bank. The state's second venture into the field of banking, like everything else in the political and economic life of the state in the period, was in the end connected intimately with internal improvement plans, although for years before the adoption of the internal improvement system, the establishment of a new State Bank had been urged on grounds both financial and political.

The beginnings of agitation for a State Bank may be traced to the belief that since the nation by the mouth of Andrew Jackson had rejected a national bank, state banks must arise to supply its place. In 1830–1831 and 1832–1833 bills for the establishment of a bank had been introduced into the general assembly. In the winter of 1832 a movement in Springfield for a bank to be run on capital borrowed by the state was sanctioned by so good a Jackson man as May; and in the senate of that year, when the bank bill was defeated by one vote, such democrats as Ewing, John Grammar, and Will voted in the affirmative.[1] In the fall of 1833 the *Illinois State Register* suggested a bank with capital to be paid in specie so as to escape dependence upon the note issues of banks of other states. The *Alton Spectator* believed, however, that before granting a charter it was necessary to allay the popular prejudices attaching to the idea of a State Bank. On March 18, 1834, it pronounced against a State Bank. The *Alton American* had on the day before declared for the bank on the

---

[1] *Sangamo Journal,* November 23, 1832, February 9, 1833; *Senate Journal,* 1832-1833, 1 session, 579.

ground of its possible assistance to business. The *Sangamo Journal* declared that the winding up of affairs of the United States Bank made necessary the establishment of an institution to supply currency in the place of that withdrawn from circulation, if the state were not to be overrun with the paper of other states.[2]

The session of 1834–1835 saw the inauguration of the new bank. W. L. D. Ewing, acting governor for the last part of Reynold's term, in his message to the legislature advocated a bank for the reason given by the *Sangamo Journal;* but Duncan, the new governor, was disposed to deprecate such a measure. The legislature set about putting the suggestions into law. By a margin of one vote in the house a measure was passed creating a bank with a capital of $1,500,000, of which $100,000 might be subscribed by the state and the remainder by individuals, preference over nonresidents and corporations being given to residents and small subscribers. The act required ten per cent of the capital to be paid in specie. When $250,000 in specie had been obtained from payments for stock or by borrowing, the bank was authorized to begin business. There were provisions which required the bank to liquidate, if for a period of ten days it refused to pay specie for its notes, and which imposed a ten per cent penalty for the time during which payment was deferred.[3]

The stock of the new bank being several times oversubscribed, the commissioners in charge of the subscription lists met in May to prorate the stock. Governor Ford relates that in spite of precaution taken to prevent such a contingency, Godfrey, Gilman and Company, John Tillson, Thomas Mather, T. W. Smith, and Samuel Wiggins succeeded in placing large blocks of the stock in the hands of eastern capitalists by using the names of Illinois citizens on subscription blanks for small amounts. In the meeting there was a sharp contest

[2] *Illinois State Register*, November 30, 1833; *Illinois Advocate*, December 30, 1833; *Alton Spectator*, December 7, 1833; *Alton American*, April 4, 1834; *Sangamo Journal*, December 13, 1834.
[3] *House Journal*, 1834-1835, 1 session, 14-15, 33, 510.

whether or not an attempt should be made to go behind the records of the subscription books. Finally, after much jockeying and maneuvering for position they decided by a vote of eight to seven not to go behind the books. Benjamin Godfrey, W. S. Gilman, Mather, and Tillson voted in the majority. Subscriptions standing in the names of foreigners and corporations were stricken off the list, and subscriptions of residents were cut to one thousand dollars and then prorated. Ford seems incorrectly to ascribe a share in these proceedings to Smith. When finally the bank was organized, Griggs, Weld and Company, Wiggins, Gilman, and M. J. Williams owned 7,539 shares, and eleven other persons 3,948 shares, an overwhelming majority of the stock.

The bank opened under the presidency of Mather; and, beside the head office at Springfield, branches were established at Vandalia, Galena, Jacksonville, Alton, and Chicago. Under the laws of 1836 additional branches were opened at Danville, Quincy, Belleville, and Mt. Carmel. In 1836, in return for a supplementary act which interpreted a provision in the first charter allowing an issue of an additional million of capital by the bank and extended to sixty days the term for which the bank could suspend payment on notes without invalidating its charter, the bank agreed to take over the payment of the famous Wiggins' loan. A large block of the additional shares issued came into Wiggins' hands.[4]

The State Bank meanwhile had been maneuvering to be chosen as United States depository, but it had encountered political difficulties. The sponsors for the bank had sought in vain to induce Reuben M. Whitney, the special examiner of depositories, to use his influence in their behalf. Secretary of the Treasury Levi Woodbury hesitated. He was informed that the bank was in the control of whigs and that to recognize it would give a check to the loyal friends of the administration in Illinois. Woodbury finally indicated his unfavorable atti-

[4] Dowrie, *Development of Banking in Illinois,* 65-67, 71; *Illinois Advocate,* June 10, 1835.

tude toward the application, specifying as reasons for the unfair allotment of stock the alleged unconstitutionality of the bank as being a State Bank only in name and its custom of not redeeming the notes of one branch at every other.[5] In all these charges there was much of truth.

Meanwhile 1837, the year of the internal improvement mania, drew on. In view of the liberal dividends paid by the State Bank it appeared to the advocates of internal improvement an ideal means of financing their ambitious project without subjecting themselves to the unpopularity sure to arise from an application of increased taxation. Accordingly the stock of the State Bank was increased by a $2,000,000 state subscription, which was to be paid for by an issue of state bonds at not less than par. Of these enough were to be sold to make the necessary cash payment on the stock. The state placed five additional directors of its own on the board, which hitherto had consisted of nine members.[6]

Meanwhile a similar subscription for a million was made to the old Bank of Illinois at Shawneetown, which had been revived in 1835. The bank had remained quiescent since its suspension in 1823, had started into life again in 1834, and in 1835 had had its charter extended to 1857. A committee in 1837 reported that the bank was well managed and that practically all its notes had been redeemed when it had ceased to discount in 1822–1823. It was in 1837 doing a legitimate business in buying bills of exchange on New Orleans issued against shipments of produce at one per cent discount and in selling exchange on Philadelphia and New Orleans at one per cent premium.[7]

The panic of 1837, which had such disastrous effects on the internal improvement system, began by putting into difficulties the banks upon which the system was based. Late in

[5] Dowrie, *Development of Banking in Illinois*, 72-73, 75 *passim; Sangamo Journal*, January 23, 1836.
[6] *Laws of 1837*, p. 18.
[7] Dowrie, *Development of Banking in Illinois*, 64; *Senate Journal*, 1836-1837, 1 session, 356.

May the banks suspended payments. Governor Duncan was persuaded to call a special session of the assembly to legalize the suspension of payments by the State Bank and to prevent the consequent forfeiture of its charter. This the assembly proceeded to do with certain limitations upon the business which the bank might perform during the period of suspension. It provided for relief to the bank's debtors during the time of suspension and limited to the amount of the capital paid in the amount of notes that the bank might issue. Finally, it prohibited dividends until payments were resumed.[8]

Partly perhaps as a result of local dissatisfaction with the banks' curtailment, partly with a view to the national political situation, almost immediately on the suspension of payments a hostility to all banks became vocal in the democratic party. For instance, some ten votes in the senate were cast against the bank's suspension measure. The *Sangamo Journal,* which justified the suspension on account of the financial relations of state and banks, was quick to mark this hostility and to call attention to its inconsistency with the democrats' responsibility for the creation and use of the banks; it proclaimed that the democrats were now declaring for a metallic currency. Shields used similar arguments against the antibank men in the democratic party, declaring that the men who had formerly employed the bank stock speculation to avoid the necessity of taxation for internal improvements were now claiming to be opposed to the bank on principle. He urged the necessity of giving the bank time in order to avoid involving the state and its citizens in ruin and declared that the ultras in his party were playing into the hands of the whigs. "The ultra democrats," he said, "are opposed to state institutions, they want specie. The ultra whigs are opposed to state institutions, they want a National Bank."[9]

The opposition to the bank in the democratic party was not convinced. Semple, for instance, who claimed he had

[8] 2 *Laws of 1837,* p. 6.
[9] *Senate Journal,* 1837, special session, 71; *Illinois State Register,* August 4, 1837.

always been opposed to banking institutions denounced banks as enabling the rich to grow richer by issuing three dollars in notes for one in specie and by enjoying corporate privileges. Jackson, he said, whatever might be said or inferred to the contrary, had never recommended the establishment of a bank. The *Sangamo Journal*, October 28, declared its belief that Kinney, Reynolds, Ewing, Shields, and Wyatt were against the locofoco doctrine of the *Chicago Democrat* and the *Jacksonville News* — the destruction of all banks. Resolutions denouncing banks that did not pay specie and urging the overthrow of all banks began at this time to make their appearance in the proceedings of county meetings.[10]

For a year and a half, however, the banks drew comparatively little attention. Nevertheless the clouds were thickening about the State Bank. In May of 1839 the *Chicago Democrat* published an article accusing it of financing pork and land speculations through the relatives and friends of its directors, as well as heavy lead speculation at Galena. The *Sangamo Journal* defended the bank, arguing that it had brought into the state a considerable amount of foreign capital which it would have held there but for the undeveloped resources of Illinois and the baleful effects of that democratic whimsy of specie currency.[11]

In the democratic county conventions held in the fall of 1839, perhaps in response to the pulling of wires at Springfield, resolution after resolution was passed demanding the divorce of state and bank and the reducing of the banks to a proper subordination to the will of the people. These resolutions warned the public against the danger of monied oligarchies, going so far as to declare against all banks, and pointed with alarm to bank influence in the government of the state. The Bank of Illinois, for its abstention from speculation and its endeavor to serve the people, had found favor in the eyes

[10] *Sangamo Journal*, October 28, November 18, December 9, 1837; *Illinois State Register*, August 14, December 1, 1837; *Chicago Democrat*, August 16, 1837.
[11] *Sangamo Journal*, August 23, September 6, 1839; *Chicago Democrat*, May 1, 1839.

of the *Register* at least; but R. F. Barrett, himself accused of speculation with funds of the State Bank, declined an appointment as state director in it on the ground that no system of management could restore the credit of the bank and regain the support of the public.[12]

In his message to the special session called to consider what was to be done with the internal improvement system, Governor Carlin was very severe upon banks in general and the State Bank in particular. He pronounced the incorporation of fiscal institutions to regulate the finances of the country contrary to the genius of a free people; he declared that the channels of business ought not to be filled up and controlled by a circulating medium susceptible of expansion and contraction at the pleasure of a few. He pointed to the danger of inflation and the resulting high prices and to the distress caused by the pressure of the bank on its creditors. He denounced the suspension whether legalized or not. Finally he invited a legislative investigation as to whether the bank legitimately tried to serve the business and public interests of the state or whether it had been of service solely to speculators.[13]

The legislative investigation forced even the friends of the bank to admit that a sorry condition of affairs existed. It was found that Wiggins had been allowed to use his bank stock as collateral for a loan with which to meet the payments due on it; it was found that the cashier of the Chicago branch had loaned considerable sums to pork speculators while accommodation was denied to others. Moreover it was discovered that the bank had lent its aid to ambitious schemes for building up in Illinois a commercial metropolis to rival St. Louis.

The commercial aspirations of Alton have already been noticed. They centered in the activities of firms of New England men, such as Godfrey, Gilman and Company, and of New England houses like Griggs, Weld and Company of

[12] *Illinois State Register,* September 28, November 23, 30, December 25, 1839; *Sangamo Journal,* December 10, 1839, January 21, 1840.
[13] *Senate Journal,* 1839-1840, special session, 17.

Boston. Godfrey and Gilman, by virtue of their influence as large stockholders in the bank had secured discounts and loans in one form or another to the amount of some $800,000. They had used these sums largely in attempts to turn the lead trade of the upper Mississippi from St. Louis to Alton. They had endeavored to operate a corner in lead as well as to make extensive purchases of smelters. The bank through other agencies too had come very near to buying and selling lead speculatively. Much of this speculative business not even the friends of the bank could condone.[14]

For a time the whig newspapers informed their readers that the locofocos designed to destroy the State Bank and to establish in its stead a political one guided by Ebenezer Peck and Theophilus W. Smith. Soon, however, they came to believe that the locofocos, finding that the whigs would not interfere to arrest their affected fury against the bank, were taking more moderate counsel rather than shoulder the responsibility of its destruction. The *Register* especially printed articles urging moderate courses, lest for the sake of antibank principles the country be ruined. Finally the legislature allowed the bank to continue its suspension, until the close of the next session of the legislature, under certain limitations including the obligations to accept its notes in payment of all debts due it.[15]

The wording of this grace was such as to enable the opponents of the bank to curtail the benefits which the institution might legitimately have expected from it. In order if possible to meet the problem of providing for the interest on the state debt, Governor Carlin in the fall of 1840 summoned the new general assembly in special session two weeks before the regular day of meeting. The democrats elected to believe that this special session must necessarily terminate before the day on which the regular session would begin. Accordingly the end of the next session of the legislature would fall not in February

[14] Dowrie, *Development of Banking in Illinois*, 90 ff.
[15] *Sangamo Journal*, January 7, 21, 1840; *Illinois State Register*, December 25, 1839; *Alton Telegraph*, December 28, 1839.

as might have been expected, but in December. A resolution was pushed through both houses of the legislature for *sine die* adjournment, as the whigs claimed from the malevolence of Theophilus W. Smith. The whigs in the house strove to prevent adjournment by absenting themselves in such number as to prevent a quorum. As a last desperate resort, Abraham Lincoln, Joseph Gillespie, and Asahel Gridley inscribed a defenestration on the annals of Illinois by jumping out of the statehouse window, an expedient worthy of better things than the twitting Hardin later gave Lincoln on the subject.[16] The assembly adjourned. The legislators considered themselves ill used when the governor declined to waste a second message on them in their new session. The State Bank resumed payments, hoping that other banks would live up to an agreement to resume on the fifteenth of January.[17]

The democrats, in spite of the whig charge that a clique among them desired the destruction of the bank that there might be reared a structure of six millions in its stead, affected — at least some of them — to claim that the bank had been frightened by false fire and that adjournment had been taken on the grounds of purest constitutional practice with no reference to the bank whatever. The bank's refusal to finance the state further or to cash salary warrants soon caused the democrats to look with sympathy on its plight; and they ultimately legalized its suspension till other banks in the south and west should resume and even allowed it to issue notes of one dollar, two dollars, and three dollars. A minority of some fourteen democrats in the house, and ten in the senate served to pass the bill.[18]

The State Bank under the suspension act went on its way; it increased instead of reducing its note issue; it made loans to directors and began work on an expensive banking house.

[16] *Illinois State Register,* December 18, 1840.
[17] Dowrie, *Development of Banking in Illinois,* 97-98; *Illinois State Register,* December 11, 1840, January 1, 1841; *Chicago American,* December 10, 1840; *Belleville Advocate,* December 12, 1840.
[18] *Chicago American,* December 10, 12, 26, 1840; *Illinois State Register,* December 11, 1840, January 1, 1841; *Sangamo Journal,* December 11, 1840.

Throughout 1841 and the earlier months of 1842 democratic attacks on the bank redoubled. Suspensions, nonliability of stockholders, the unholy alliance of bank and state were all attacked in heated resolutions. The *State Register* the week after praising the Bank of Illinois for its judicious course declared against all banks. The *Belleville Advocate* repeatedly urged farmers to take only gold and silver in payment for their produce. The whigs, affecting to resign themselves to the fate of the State Bank, devoted themselves to fixing on their opponents the responsibility for its crimes and misman-agement, looking only to a national bank for relief. At times the *Chicago American* was as keenly critical as the *Democrat,* which had to explain the defects of the bank management under democratic administration as the fault of easy virtued demo-crats who were sufficient in numbers when allied with the whigs to give the bank control in the legislature. By the early sum-mer both whigs and democrats agreed on the general proposi-tion that the banks must resume or forfeit their charters. The stock of the State Bank a year before had fallen to thirty-seven cents on the dollar. In February of 1842 the credit of its notes in Illinois declined, and in April they fell to forty-four cents on the dollar.[19]

Meanwhile it was thought that the Shawneetown bank might extricate itself from its difficulties and resume; but it passed the day set for resumption, June 15, 1842, and its notes, which on May 14 had been within six or seven per cent of par at Chicago, were a month later at ten per cent discount. John Marshall, who as president had conducted the bank's affairs with skill, refused a reëlection in January, 1843. The notes of the Bank of Cairo, representing another revival of a terri-torial charter which had furnished in 1840 a very large share of the small note currency and which apparently was then on

---

[19] *Chicago Democrat,* February 9, June 8, October 19, 1842; *Belleville Advo-cate,* January 27, March 3, 10, April 28, September 22, 1842; *Illinois State Register,* April 8, May 6, 13, 1842; *Chicago American,* March 10, 19, April 2, 7, 13, 25, 1842; *Alton Telegraph,* July 16, 1842; Dowrie, *Development of Bank-ing in Illinois,* 99, 101.

a sound basis, by 1841 had begun to depreciate; and by December, apparently after it had been rumored that the Wrights were interested in the bank, the notes were unsalable in both Chicago and St. Louis. The charter was repealed in 1843, but the bank was not liquidated for twenty years thereafter.[20]

The fate of the State Bank and Bank of Illinois was rendered inevitable by the fact that they were linked with the disastrous state internal improvement system. Compelled to pay dividends on stock paid for by bonds selling in 1840 and 1841 at all manner of discounts, their burden was a heavy one. Bad banking only hastened the inevitable result.

With the fall of the banks the currency of the state, which had hitherto consisted largely of bank notes, fell into apparently hopeless confusion. In the fall of 1842, state offices finally refused to accept State Bank paper for taxes. In July, it was said business was very near a specie basis in both Chicago and St. Louis. In September the *American* declared that at Chicago little was in circulation beside specie and notes of the State Bank of Indiana and the Wisconsin Marine and Fire Insurance Company. The latter concern, whose guiding spirit was George Smith, a canny Scotchman, for many years gave Chicago a sound paper currency almost in defiance of the law.[21]

When the State Bank came up for final judgment in the assembly of 1842–1843, two different points of view were evident. There were certain radicals who were opposed to all banks and all corporate privileges on principle and advocated repeal of the bank charter. The radicals won over Governor Carlin to their side and induced him to recommend the repeal in his last message. This action seriously hampered his successor, Ford, who rejected the proposal on grounds both of the state's financial advantage and of the bad effect on

---

[20] *Chicago American,* September 11, 1840, January 13, December 10, 1841, March 22, April 19, May 4, 14, 18, June 29, 1842; Dowrie, *Development of Banking in Illinois,* 126-128.

[21] *Chicago American,* July 12, 27, August 27, 1842; Dowrie, *Development of Banking in Illinois,* 129.

European capitalists that such a violation of vested right would produce. Instead he proposed a compromise by which the state bonds should be withdrawn dollar for dollar in return for the surrender of the state's stock.[22] Governor Ford with the support of McClernand and Douglas forced a bill through the house of representatives adopting the project, by a vote of one hundred and seven to four. Peck and Trumbull—in the hope of receiverships if the bank were smashed, according to the *Alton Telegraph*—demanded more violent measures; but their agitation merely served to draw on Trumbull the fire of McClernand at its hottest. They made Ralston their agent in the senate to oppose the bill; but the only result was to give the latter the opportunity to sit for his portrait in Ford's history, the governor drawing the picture with his pen dipped in the sharpest caustic. The act passed, and the bank began what was to be a long period of liquidation. The bonds of the state, turned over almost immediately, were burned by the governor before the statehouse, as a symbol of the state's decision. But this was only the beginning of a process the end of which lies far outside the period of this volume.[23]

The Bank of Illinois was compelled to accept liquidation of a similar sort, but it was allowed a year to pay up the second half of the million of indebtedness to the state in exchange for state stock. In the second payment, it attempted to include certain of the bonds hypothecated to Macalister and Stebbins; this resulted in a controversy and finally the acceptance of the bonds by the state at forty-eight cents on the dollar. Ultimately the only creditors to suffer a total loss were the private stockholders in the bank.[24]

Thereafter at least until the close of the period, the doc-

[22] On investigation it was found that the State Bank held $2,100,000 in state bonds which could be set off against a sum some fifty thousand dollars larger, made up of the following items: bonds $1,686,000, scrip $17,534.50, advance for current expenses $292,373.17, advance for fund commissioners $156,496.42.
[23] *Alton Telegraph*, December 31, 1842; Dowrie, *Development of Banking in Illinois*, 13, 166 ff.; Ford, *History of Illinois*, 307 *passim*; *Illinois State Register*, January 6, 1843; *Sangamo Journal*, February 2, 1843.
[24] Dowrie, *Development of Banking in Illinois*, 124-126.

trine of the democratic party was against further incorporation
of state banks, against the connection of state or nation with
a bank, and, as phrased by certain ultra-radicals, against anything but a gold and silver currency. Antibank utterances were
bandied back and forth in the party meeting and journals with
a view, as Ford sarcastically remarked, to the obtaining of
personal popularity at a cheap rate. Nevertheless in the party
there was a tendency on the part of more moderate men to
recognize the inevitableness of some form of banking institution. The *State Register* had occasionally to meet charges
that it secretly desired the establishment of banks. And there
was in the democratic party, as the constitutional convention of
1847 was to demonstrate, a strong element inclined to temper
its utterances regarding the iniquities of all banks. The next
chapter of banking in the state, however, remains to be written
in the succeeding volume.[25]

[25] *Illinois State Register,* February 3, August 18, 1843, February 9, October
11, 1844; *Belleville Advocate,* August 1, 16, 1843, January 1, 1844, November
29, 1845; *Chicago Democrat,* July 10, 1844, February 23, 1846; Ford, *History
of Illinois,* 297.

XVII. THE INTERNAL IMPROVEMENT SYSTEM: THE SOLUTION

TO COMPLETE the story of the internal improvement system so rashly inaugurated by the state of Illinois in 1837 it remains to give an account of the means by which the state was finally extricated from the seemingly hopeless position into which its general assembly had thrown it. With the story of the salvation of the state is inseparably connected the name of Thomas Ford. Thomas Ford, seventh elected governor of Illinois, had had an obscure political career until the time he was elected to the position of chief executive. Poverty had hampered him in his political ambitions as it had hampered his half-brother, George Forquer, compelling them both to serve for years as stout henchmen to other leaders. Forquer had been embittered by his overlong apprenticeship in politics, and Ford probably suffered from a similar cause. He was a lawyer of no mean ability and had served with honor as circuit judge before he became governor. At the end of his term as governor he set himself to write a history of Illinois, one of the two or three remarkable books written in the state during the formative period. Ford undertook the task of explaining the political tendencies and habits of the Illinois of his day, in particular, of explaining for the benefit of future generations the seemingly inexplicable devotion of the people of the state to the kind of partisan politics exemplified by Peck. With this ideal before him, Ford produced a book that only the disillusioned cynicism with which it is written has held back from recognition as one of the clearest and most subtle analyses of American politics. Being one of the earliest of books on the philosophy of American history, it should no longer be neglected and dismissed as merely an old book of state history.

At Ford's inauguration the state stood at the point where a decision must be made with reference to internal improvements. Carlin, passing off the stage as governor, sent a farewell message to the general assembly that is no more than a sigh of "'Tis a' a muddle." Like the good locofoco he was he attributed the whole internal improvement scheme to the baleful effect of paper money. He detailed in meager, bewildered paragraphs the steps of the state's downfall; he told the legislature that their duty was to provide for the payment of the interest on eleven millions of debt, some $670,000. He denounced as impracticable the raising of any money from the sale of state lands; and as arguments against taxation to discharge the interest he pleaded a declining tax roll, a disappearing circulating medium and popular disapproval. Thus abandoning all hope of paying the interest on the debt, he told the general assembly that it must plan to reduce the principle by surrendering the state lands to the bondholders in case they cared to take them. He recommended the rejection of the state's share of the distribution fund on grounds of principle and stammered his way to the close alike of his message and of his official career.

No stronger contrast to this message can be imagined than the inaugural of Ford. By the openness and sincerity with which it discussed the state's plight it carried conviction of the honesty of its statements and proposals. The frankness with which it coupled the admission of the justness of the state debt with the need for patience on the part of the creditors, if the state ever were to be able to pay all, showed that the backwoods judge had found instinctively the method of address that wins the confidence and support of men of affairs.

"The whole amount of the State debt," wrote Ford, "excluding interest now due, may be put down at the sum of fifteen millions one hundred and eighty-seven thousand three hundred and forty-eight dollars and seventy-one cents; which sum, from the best information which I can obtain, appears to be composed of the following items:

Bonds negotiated on account of the Canal........................$3,747,000.00
Scrip and certificates of indebtedness issued to contractors by the
    Canal Board 689,408.00
Bonds negotiated on account of the system of internal improvements. 5,085,444.00
Scrip issued to contractors on account of internal improvements..... 929,305.53
Bonds issued to and purchased by the State Bank on account of State
    stock 1,765,000.00
Bonds issued to and purchased by the Bank of Illinois on account of
    State stock 900,000.00
Bonds issued on account of the State House at Springfield.......... 121,000.00
Due the government of the United States, when called for, on account
    of surplus revenue deposited in the State Treasury............ 477,919.00
A portion of this sum, by act of the General Assembly, was added
    to the school fund, and consequently, by our present law, we
    are indebted to the school fund on that account in the sum of... 335,592.00
Due the school, college and seminary funds for money borrowed by
    act of the General Assembly, to assist in paying the current ex-
    penses of the State...................................... 472,492.18
Due the State Bank of Illinois for paying Auditor's warrants and
    interest on the same..................................... 294,190.00
To the Bank of Illinois at Shawneetown on settlement.............. 369,998.00

"Upon the whole of this sum, except so much as is due to the school, college and seminary funds, and so much as is due to the United States on account of surplus revenue deposited, interest is now due from the first day of July, 1841. It has hitherto been supposed, that the profits of the State stock in the two banks would be amply sufficient to pay interest, not only on the sum paid in bonds, amounting to two million six hundred and sixty-five thousand dollars, but also on the further sum of three hundred thirty-five thousand and five-hundred ninety-two dollars, part of the surplus revenue, first added to the school fund and then converted into bank stock. But the failure of those banks, and their present precarious situation, renders it almost certain that if we continue our connection with them the amount of bonds paid in will be nearly a total loss, and consequently that sum will form one of the demands upon which interest will have to be provided in future. Those banks have not for a long time past, as far as I am informed, declared or paid any dividends in favor of the State; consequently, the interest provided by law to be paid to the several counties on the sum of $335,592, part of the surplus revenue added to the school fund, has formed a demand on the State Treasury and has been paid out of the ordinary revenues derived from taxes. I cannot believe that it was the intention of former legislatures to make this a permanent demand upon the treasury, to be raised by taxation. It must undoubtedly have been supposed by our predecessors that the profits of banking would be fully sufficient to meet the appropriation. I, therefore, submit to the General Assembly whether the State is any longer bound to pay interest on that sum, unless it can be derived from the profits of the investment.

"Many persons suppose, and I think with great probability, that an arrangement can be made with the two banks, by which the State can get back the two million six hundred and sixty-five thousand dollars in bonds, which have been issued to them." [1]

At the outset Ford declared that the people of Illinois did not believe in repudiation. He pointed out that even in 1841 they had in good faith done their best through their general assembly to raise a sufficient fund for interest. He dismissed as impossible the sale of state lands and property or the tax of one and one-half cents on the dollar necessary to meet the interest on the state's debt. "The main thing with which the world can justly reproach us is, that we were visionary and reckless; that without sober deliberation, we jumped headlong into ambitious schemes of public aggrandizement, which were not justifiable by our resources. Nor are our original creditors free from reproach, on the same account.

"They as men of intelligence, sufficient for the proper management of large capital, ought as well as ourselves, to have foreseen our future want of ability, and the constant catastrophe which our common error has produced." He pointed out that while a single year's tax at a rate sufficing to pay the interest might be raised, that it could not be repeated, and that the creditors would be left if they insisted upon such a measure, to deal with a depopulated and ruined state. "If our creditors are ever to be paid, it will not be by the mere

[1] *House Journal*, 1842-1843, 1 session, 39-51; *Senate Journal*, 1842-1843, 1 session, 33-44.

territory composing the State, nor by the abstract thing called State sovereignty, but by the people who may be here, the inhabitants of the land; and how are they to be paid if we depopulate our country?"

Having thus stated to the creditors the argument against taxation to the hilt, Ford stated the true remedy. "Let it be known in the first place that no oppressive and exterminating taxation is to be resorted to; in the second, we must convince our creditors and the world, that the disgrace of repudiation is not countenanced. . . . I would, therefore, recommend to the General Assembly to speak on this subject in the most decisive manner, so as to give every assurance that in due time, we will tax ourselves according to our ability, to pay our debts. The consequence will be, that our creditors, who are persons of power and influence, instead of reproaching us and getting up a moral crusade against us, as against a confederated band of unprincipled swindlers, with a view to coerce us to our duty, will be directly interested in doing us all the good in their power." Wiser words had not been spoken since the system began.

Ford suggested that immediately the creditors be offered at a fair valuation all the landed property of the state to diminish the debt by so much. Meanwhile he urged the completion of the canal as sure to enhance greatly the value of a portion of the state land. He recommended that the canal, now five-eighths completed be pushed to completion as a lock canal. With a series of sound recommendations for state finance the document concluded. In its twelve pages Ford had carried conviction to his hearers.

Inaugurated by such a message the work of the general assembly was fruitful. It passed acts for the winding up of the State Bank and of the Bank of Illinois, providing in each case for the surrender to the state of the bonds which they held in exchange for the surrender of the stock in the institution owned by the state. The general assembly further provided for the sale of all state lands and property acquired in connection with the internal improvement system to be paid for in evidences of state indebtedness or in gold and silver with the intention that a part of the state indebtedness might thus be liquidated. Unfortunately the assembly reduced the tax rate to twenty cents on the hundred; further it provided for the issue of warrants in return for the surrender of the Macalister and Stebbins bonds, but years passed before this act resulted in the final settlement of the controversy. Further the legislature passed a resolution disclaiming any intention of repudiation. Most important, however, it passed an act for the completion of the Illinois and Michigan canal. By it the governor was authorized to negotiate on the credit of the canal and its appurtenances a loan of $1,600,000 from holders of canal bonds or from others. The canal property was to be made over to trustees elected by the subscribers as security for the payment of the loan and bonds, with the proviso that bonds were not to be sold till after the completion of the canal which would be within three years after the act went into operation. Meanwhile, the trustees were to operate it for the benefit of the subscribers and other bondholders until the indebtedness to them was fully paid. The governor was authorized to negotiate the terms except that he might not pledge the state's faith for the payment of the bonds.

In his history of Illinois [2] Ford gives the credit for devising originally the scheme of completing the canal to Justin Butterfield of Chicago, who in the summer of 1842 had succeeded in interesting several of the large capitalists among the state's eastern creditors in the device which was proposed. Undoubtedly, however, Ford must be given the credit for adopting the scheme and for stating it officially in the clearest possible manner as he presented it in his first message.[3]

These measures did not pass without sectional and partisan opposition. Southern members like McClernand denounced the measures as calculated to tax southern Illinois for the

---

[2] Ford, *History of Illinois*, 295.
[3] *Laws of 1843*, p. 21, 30, 54, 191, 231 ff.

benefit of the northern counties; Ficklin protested against the payment of the Macalister and Stebbins debt by taxation. It was the *Alton Telegraph* that kept up the most consistent, concerted, and malevolent attack on the program by which Ford sought to rescue the state finances. It declared that it was criminal for Illinois to borrow another dollar until her debts were reduced. It served notice that it would expose any garbled statement of state finances, naturally thereby doing what it could to diminish the confidence of the foreign investors whose aid was so necessary for the initiation of the schemes. It showed the cloven hoof by declaring in the end for assumption of state debts by the national government as the only means out of the difficulty. It asked if Oakley and Ryan, on their pilgrimage to the English bondholders, would tell them that the democrats had repudiated the Macalister and Stebbins bonds and repealed the charter of the Bank of Illinois. It declared frankly that foreign capitalists were justified in hesitating to lend the state more money. Similar statements came from the east; the democrats might well wonder if the opposition to the measure was not further inspired by a desire to induce the state in desperation to adopt federal assumption and distribution and with these measures the political party that favored them.[4]

In pursuance of the act for the completion of the canal Ford appointed Oakley and Ryan commissioners of the state to the bondholders. They found themselves much hampered by the reduction in the rate of taxation by the legislature at the last session, finding it difficult to give the bondholders satisfactory assurance in view of it that the state could from that time be trusted to fulfill its obligations. They procured a considerable subscription, however, amounting to a million and a half in the United States and sold about two millions of the bonds in England at rates of thirty-two to forty per cent, on the terms that twelve and a half per cent be paid at once and

[4] *Chicago Democrat*, March 21, October 11, 1843; *Illinois State Register*, March 17, 24, 1843; *Alton Telegraph*, February 4, 1843.

that the remainder should be forthcoming only in case the next legislature provided for the future payment of a part of the accruing interest and a gradual payment of the arrears the terms that twelve and a half per cent be paid at once and of it. The subscription, however, could not be completed and accordingly was not binding. Baring Brothers and Magniac, Jardine and Company, in London, interested themselves in behalf of the state's proposal.[5] They requested Abbott Lawrence, W. Sturgis, and T. W. Ward of Boston to choose agents to examine into the canal situation in Illinois and in the United States and to report to them as to the feasibility and security of the whole scheme. Perhaps unfortunately they chose as commissioners Captain William H. Swift and John Davis, the latter a whig politician of Massachusetts who boasted the sobriquet of "honest."

Davis and Swift visited Illinois in the late fall of 1843 and produced a long report, somewhat prosy reading, in which after professing extreme caution on every point they inclined to favor the proposition; and so they reported to the English bondholders. Unfortunately the suspicion of political motives entered here. Probably at the suggestion of Abbott Lawrence, Davis was summoned to England by the English bankers interested; and the subscription to the loan was delayed. The democrats, including Michael Ryan, one of the commissioners, were inclined to believe that it was a piece of politics to attempt to frustrate the settlement of the debts of Illinois in order that in the presidential election of 1844 the whigs might have one more argument for assumption of state debts. The English bankers concerned denied any such motive, without doubt sincerely; but it is far from clear that some of the wealthy whigs of New England who were their trusted advisers on American affairs were equally innocent.[6] Whatever may have been the reason the negotiations hung fire until the legislative

[5] *Reports General Assembly*, 1844–1845, senate, 90 ff., 129 ff.
[6] *Chicago Democrat*, November 27, December 25, 1844, September 24, 1845; the charge appeared originally in the *New York Journal of Commerce*. *Reports General Assembly*, 1844-1845, senate, 133.

session of 1844–1845. There the crucial question was as to whether the state would comply with the demand of the bond-holders for additional taxation.

Once more the word repudiation was current and perhaps somewhat less generally in men's minds. Various measures were suggested in the course of the session. Orval Sexton of Gallatin proposed that the canal law of 1843 be repealed and work on the canal be stopped, and that for the payment of the debt the state rely on a sinking fund. He proposed a pro-viso to the interest bill allowing the legislature to repeal it at will terming the act " real cane break, hunting shirt " democracy.[7] There were on various hands complaints of the dictation of the bondholders and statements that their demand for the levy of an insignificant tax out of all proportion to the $1,600,000 loan was absurd. In addition there were expres-sions of dread at the danger to Illinois of her entanglement in a perpetual monopoly. Alfred W. Cavarly was for complet-ing the canal by taxation and by the issue of scrip due in three years. Richard Yates declared for refunding the internal improvement and statehouse debt at three per cent, for relying on taxation to raise the interest and for the use of any surplus for a sinking fund. There were counsels even more eloquent of blank despair. Fithian proposed turning over to the state's creditors its property and one or two millions more in bonds on which the interest was actually to be paid. George H. Hanson of Coles was firm in the belief that further taxation would ruin the state past all repair and that it would never be able to pay.[8]

The measure which was finally passed provided for a mill tax in 1845 increasing in 1846 to a mill and a half and there-after remaining at that figure, which was to be sacredly devoted to the payment of the interest on the debts of the state except-ing that on the bonds hypothecated with Macalister and Stebbins. A new canal act repeating the provisions of that of

[7] *Sangamo Journal*, February 27, 1845; *Alton Telegraph*, January 25, 1845.
[8] *Sangamo Journal*, March 6, 13, 1845; *Belleville Advocate*, January 16, 23, 1845; *Chicago Daily Journal*, January 13, 16, 1845.

the previous session completed the necessary legislation. Northern Illinois was wild with joy; public meetings thanked the various men concerned, Oakley, Ryan, Davis, Leavitt, and the governor. The *Chicago Journal* headed the news with "Joyful News!!! Get out your Spades and Go to Digging!!" The vote on the interest bill had been twenty-one to twenty in the senate and in the house sixty-six to thirty-nine on a test vote.[9]

At one time the democratic papers of the north were inclined to attempt to set the whigs down as repudiators. In general the whigs were nearer the mark in declaring that the true enemies of the state's rehabilitation were the southern democrats, though Davis of the *Alton Telegraph* now as heretofore was inclined to criticize viciously.[10] It was probably true, however, that some of the whig papers were inclined to believe that in the failure of their proposal, the distribution act, the democratic measure was fair game.[11] As a matter of fact proportionately more whigs than democrats voted for the measure in both houses. The real significance of the vote is to be sought from another angle. If we except a little block of votes in Hancock and Adams and a few scattered votes in the south, the vote on the measure was sectional. The valleys of the Illinois and the Rock were for the measure, and southern and eastern Illinois against it.

Here ends the internal improvement question as an issue vital to the life of the state. There were still to be squabbles between the trustees appointed by the state and the trustees appointed by the bondholders. Whig papers claimed that the price of Augustus C. French's nomination as governor had been the removal of Jacob Fry as trustee, and they denounced savagely his appointment of Oakley. Oakley soon became involved in an open quarrel with the other trustees whom he

[9] *Chicago Daily Journal*, March 3, 7, 1845; *Laws of 1845*, p. 31, 44; *Senate Journal*, 1844-1845, 1 session, 400; *House Journal*, 1844-1845, 1 session, 577.
[10] *Illinois State Register*, March 14, 1845; *Alton Telegraph*, February 8, 22, 1845; *Chicago Daily Journal*, January 25, March 8, 12, 22, 1845; *Chicago Democrat*, February 5, 1845.
[11] *Sangamo Journal*, January 2, 1845.

accused of incompetence, nonresidence, and the taking of excessive salaries. An attempt on his part to get William Gooding removed as engineer failed in a bondholders' meeting.[12] The session of the legislature of 1847 saw a series of laws designed to complete the refunding of the state debt. One authorized the issue of new bonds in exchange for the old, as well as of certificates for the payment of interest then in arrears, the certificates to bear interest after 1856 and to be redeemable after 1876. A second act authorized a settlement with Macalister and Stebbins. A third provided for the issue in exchange for canal scrip of Illinois and Michigan canal bonds and for the accrued interest of certificates of indebtedness of noninterest-bearing certificates receivable for canal lots and lands hitherto sold.

Here may be concluded the tedious story of the financial devices and arrangements by which Illinois in sober earnest succeeded in extricating itself from its financial embarrassment. The tale of such devices cannot be made so interesting to the reader of history as can the account of the party alliances and the bargaining mania by which the state at first plunged itself into the internal improvement system. Yet, for the student of the politics of the state the contrast between the two is instructive. Between the Illinois of 1837 and the Illinois of 1847–1848 there was all the difference between light-hearted reckless youth and sober responsible manhood. The state by democratic machinery of government had chosen a man to extricate it from the result of its errors and headlong extravagance. In doing so Illinois had learned and learned much, and had acquired poise and balance. Undertaking in the end the payment of her debt the state acquired the respect of the world and acquired also political experience and judgment which were to fit it for active and efficient participation in the great affairs of the union during the next twenty years.

[12] *Chicago Daily Journal,* December 19, 1846, January 25, February 2, 8, September 20, 1847; *Chicago Democrat,* July 20, November 19, 1847; *Illinois State Register,* June 17, 1847.

XVIII. THE SPLIT OF THE DEMOCRATIC PARTY, 1846–1848

THE events of President Polk's administration made it plain that the old Jacksonian democracy had disappeared, and that in the party that ostensibly represented it, the interests of the south appeared to dictate the decision on every issue. Texas and Oregon had been coupled in the expansionist democratic platform of 1844. But no sooner was Polk in the saddle than excellent reasons were found for compromising the north's controversy with Great Britain over Oregon and pressing the south's interest in Texas to the extreme of war with Mexico. Finally the doctrine of strict construction was so applied to appropriations for river and harbor improvements that the outraged north found itself cut off from the fruits of federal bounty apparently at least essential to its very commercial existence. So at least the north argued. The student of history would hardly admit, *in toto*, the north's indictment of the motives of the southern statesmen in the party; but the fact remains that northern democrats believed or professed to believe them and that the Oregon and river and harbor questions were sufficient to cause in the democratic party in Illinois and in the nation a division having a slavery and antislavery cast.

In its propaganda for the annexation of Texas the south since 1843 had been able to count on support in southern Illinois. John Reynolds especially had taken Texas under his tutelage, arguing that it would be a necessary counterset to Iowa and Wisconsin, and the southern Illinois democratic papers followed him in advocating annexation frankly on proslavery grounds. The division on the question in the state was as much sectional as political, the *Chicago Democrat* having little to say on the question, the whig papers, such as the *Telegraph* and the *Chicago Journal,* handling it severely as an iniquitous southern scheme and a sop to the slave power.[1] After the presidential election was decided and during the 1844–1845 session of congress the various papers maintained their former attitudes toward the measure, the *Belleville Advocate* enthusiastically approving, the *Chicago Journal* bitterly hostile, and the others saying as little as possible. Actual hostilities within the state, however, began only when 1845–1846 saw the administration's surrender of the alleged rights of the north in Oregon.

Illinois' interest in Oregon, like that of its neighbor state, Missouri, and of the latter's political prophet, Thomas Hart Benton, was on account of its geographical outlook most lively. Semple claimed that the first all-Oregon meeting held in the United States had been held under his promotion at Alton in 1842. Anger over England's bullying attitude on the McLeod affair and the Maine boundary added fuel to the flame. The whig papers, though some of them, such as the *Telegraph,* were outspoken, occasionally entered a mild dissent against too violent a policy. When in the presidential contest of 1844 the cry of "54° 40′ or fight" had triumphed, the Illinois democrats affected to fear lest before they could take office their opponents would compromise the rights of the United States — for had it not been such secretaries of state as Adams, Clay, and Webster who had yielded the rights of the United States on Texas, Maine, and on Oregon itself?[2]

In Illinois the democrats were vociferous in their resolution that, if needs must, 54° 40′ be submitted to the arbitrament of the sword. Both whigs and democrats made a possible naval war on the lakes an argument for the construction of a ship canal at the Illinois-Michigan portage as an essential measure

[1] *Belleville Advocate,* November 9, 1843, May 16, 1844; *Illinois State Register,* May 24, 31, June 14, 1844; *Alton Telegraph,* August 31, October 12, 1844; *Chicago Journal,* July 27, 1844.
[2] *Belleville Advocate,* February 27, November 4, 1841, December 29, 1842, January 9, 1845; *Chicago American,* April 25, 1842; *Alton Telegraph,* November 12, 1842; *Illinois State Register,* February 17, March 24, April 14, 1843.

of preparedness, and writings of Lieutenant Maury on the subject under the name of "Harry Bluff" were widely copied and commented on.[3] By fall however, the whig papers declared their belief that the democratic administration in the end would back down—a forecast verified by Polk's first offer of a compromise on the 49° line.

Polk's withdrawal from 54° 40' threw into a quandary Illinois democrats with northern sympathies who wished to remain loyal to the party. John Wentworth, the Chicago congressman, was especially hard beset. Along with Stephen A. Douglas, Joseph P. Hoge, John A. McClernand, and Robert Smith of Illinois he voted among the "immortal ten" who declared that the Oregon question was no longer a subject for compromise. In debate Wentworth, Ficklin, and Douglas insisted that Oregon and Texas had been linked by the Baltimore convention and that the faith of the party was pledged to achieve both. In the state the county meetings held in the early winter, while not taking direct issue with Polk, urged the maintenance of a claim to all Oregon, and the state convention resolved that since the proffered compromise of 49° had been rejected, congress should dissolve joint occupancy.

The senate's delay in adopting the resolution giving notice for termination of the joint occupancy added new fuel to the fire. The *State Register* was confounded, solemnly warning the southern democrats that this offense would never be forgiven by the west. A meeting of voters in St. Clair county resolved that they would not support for office anyone who submitted to a compromise on 49°. They proposed William Allen of Ohio as the next president. Wentworth warned the southern democrats that their course on the Texas and Oregon question was fatally weakening the party in the north.[4]

In March and early April, 1846, the democrats still clung

[3] *Belleville Advocate*, April 17, May 22, 1845; *Little Fort Porcupine*, May 21, 1845; *Chicago Democrat*, October 18, 1845.
[4] *Illinois State Register*, January 30, 1846; *Belleville Advocate*, April 11, 1846; *Chicago Democrat*, April 3, 1846.

to the hope that 49° had been offered for the last time and that thenceforth the nation would stand firm on the 54° 40′ line. Both whigs and democrats for the moment believed war imminent. The county meetings and conventions held in McLean, Livingston, Vermilion, Lake, De Kalb, and Champaign, while not censuring Polk and while even praising him, insisted on 54° 40′. On April 1, however, the *Chicago Democrat* printed a letter from Wentworth admitting the 49° men controlled the senate. The *State Register* was very bitter in its comment. The *Galena Jeffersonian*, the *Chicago Journal* remarked, had read Polk out of the party on the subject, but predicted that the 54° 40′ men in Egypt would soon tack. The whigs, while far from united on the question, had avoided committing themselves unfavorably.[5] In the democratic party, on the other hand, the question had created a bitter feeling between the northern and southern wings of the party.

The ill-feeling aroused by the prospective settlement of Oregon on the basis of 49° was stirred up to fever heat by the violation of northern interests caused by Polk's veto of the river and harbor bill, and here too the measure divided the party in the state against itself. For years democrats interested in federal internal improvements had had to steer a careful course to avoid the implications of the growing strict construction doctrines of the party. In Illinois the difficulty was complicated by the fact that the interests of the various parts of the state were diverse and even conflicting. While Wentworth was interested primarily in the lakes, Ficklin and Robert Smith were anxious for the continuance of the Cumberland road, and McClernand and Smith for the improvement of navigation on the Ohio and Mississippi; and on grounds of principle they voted repeatedly against bills for the improvement of the lake harbors. From lack of unity, the seven Illinois congressmen that took their seats for the first time in 1843–1844 were not able to achieve the results that might have been

5 *Chicago Daily Journal*, April 5, July 6, 18, 1846; *Belleville Advocate*, March 14, April 4, 25, May 21, August 6, 1846; *Illinois State Register*, March 27, 1846; *Chicago Democrat*, May 26, June 16, 1846.

expected and in the end only produced jealousies and divisions in the party through the state.

In session after session the same divergencies of interest divided the Illinois members.   Thus in 1844 Wentworth and Douglas labored hard to prove constitutional in the western river and harbor bill the Illinois river appropriation — a crucial item from the strict constructionist viewpoint.   Finally McClernand, Robert Smith, and Ficklin voted against the bill, the two former alleging constitutional grounds and meager appropriations for the Ohio.   This vote drew down on Smith the censure of the *Belleville Advocate*.   Wentworth too was much exercised that Ficklin, Hoge, McClernand, and Smith voted against the eastern harbor bill; he believed complaisance in that direction to be a fertile source of votes for western measures.   He feared that Tyler's veto of the eastern bill would cause retaliation on the west, believing the veto to be the work of men who desired to divide east and west.[6]

When in the 1844–1845 session a similar sectional war in congress ended in the pocketing of the river and harbor bill, the western internal improvement men sought to persuade the south of its community of interest with the west in internal improvement.   The Memphis convention, largely attended by Illinois whigs and democrats, represented an attempt to bring about such a union, on the policy of the improvement of north and south transportation routes through the great valley for needs of peace or of war.   The west, from the fact that its commerce passed out through the Gulf of Mexico, was reminded of the value of coast defenses and lighthouses in Florida as well as of similar improvements on the lakes.   The convention urged the ship canal from Lake Michigan to the Illinois river, the completion of the Cumberland road to Fort Smith, Arkansas, improvement of lakes, harbors, and northern rivers, a military road from Memphis to Texas, and an armory

[6] *Congressional Globe,* 28 congress, 1 session, 568; *Belleville Advocate,* May 16, June 6, July 18, 1846; *Chicago Democrat,* August 14, 1844, declared the exertion of Wentworth among others induced Tyler not to veto the "western harbor bill; " *ibid.,* October 21, 1845.

at Fort Massac. The campaign for these and for the ship canal was committed to the charge of committees of Illinois men, whigs and democrats. McClernand thought the movement calculated especially to give southern Illinois the impetus for the lack of which its growth had been retarded.[7] If question of constitutional principle did not again intervene, the democratic party saw an opportunity once more to be in complete accord.

The session of congress of 1845–1846 presented to the democratic party the crucial test of its newly found unity. The Cumberland road project was again brought forward by Ficklin. Breese, however, opposed land donations for it; and the measure, to the wrath of the *Sangamo Journal* was killed by constitutional arguments despite the attempt of its friends to demonstrate it as an implied compact between the federal government and the new states.[8] Meanwhile Wentworth devoted himself especially to the river and harbor bill. He was afraid that amendments might be added that would transcend Polk's conservative constitutional scruples. One of the items that he feared was the Cumberland road, another the Louisville and Portland canal and still another the ship canal to the Illinois river.[9] The latter project was in danger continually because according to Wentworth the Indiana delegation was determined that any communication of the sort must come through their state. Whenever the Illinois river was inserted in the bill, they at once added the Wabash. Wentworth complained that its enemies always sought to kill the bill by dragging in rivers and harbors of their own or by including such projects as that of the Tennessee river, sure to be vetoed.

It was on the east emphatically that Wentworth placed his reliance for the securing of the appropriations. He hoped to

[7] *Alton Telegraph*, June 21, 28, 1845; *Chicago Democrat*, June 25, July 23, 1845; *Belleville Advocate*, October 11, December 6, 1845; *Illinois State Register*, June 20, September 5, October 21, 1845.
[8] *Congressional Globe*, 29 congress, 1 session, 84, 195, 383, 600, 615, 622; *Alton Telegraph*, January 31, April 18, 1846; *Sangamo Journal*, April 23, 1846.
[9] *Congressional Globe*, 29 congress, 1 session, 354; *Alton Telegraph*, March 21, 1846.

unite the Illinois and Indiana members to vote for an appropriation for Lake Champlain to conciliate the New Yorkers, whom he presumed were the friends of western internal improvements. As always he insisted that the opponents of better lake harbors resided in the west and south, not in the east. Late in February he hoped that the bill would have clear sailing, but then came the attacks on strict construction grounds from such men as R. Barnwell Rhett. In April the *Chicago Democrat* despondingly remarked that the improvement of the lakes would be defeated between the whigs, who would vote for anything to revive Clay's old system, and the southern men who, to kill the bill, would vote for any amendment.[10]

The whig papers of Illinois were inclined to regard the affair as none of theirs. They predicted the veto of the measure, saying that Polk as a result of the party straddle on interstate improvements had not been pledged. The *Telegraph* gave Wentworth full credit for his efforts for the measure, especially his success in retaining the St. Louis harbor, while declaring that an appropriation for the Cumberland road or the Illinois river would defeat the bill. The *Chicago Journal,* nearer home, declared that Wentworth had done his best but was devoid of influence; and after the veto of the measure the whig newspapers joined in denouncing Polk.[11]

In addition to his troubles in Washington, Wentworth again had the handicap of a divided congressional delegation and a divided party at home. When Polk vetoed the bill on constitutional grounds, McClernand was one of his confidants; and both he and Ficklin voted against it. The *State Register* was unsympathetic; as early as April 3, in 1846, it regretted that the Mississippi appropriations were in a bill with so many unsound items; and it approved Polk's veto saying that if he

---

[10] *Chicago Democrat,* February 23, March 11, 30, 1846; *Alton Telegraph,* March 14, 1846; *Congressional Globe,* 29 congress, 1 session, 438, 479, 485, 493, 496, 506, 516, 522, 527.
[11] *Chicago Daily Journal,* March 19, 28, May 26, 1846; *Alton Telegraph,* April 4, 1846.

erred, he erred on the side of safety. In various sections of the state the party presses took the same ground. In the Military Tract the *Pike County Sentinel* and the *Quincy Herald* approved the veto. The *Charleston Globe,* in eastern Illinois, and the *Wabash Democrat,* at Shawneetown, opposed a river and harbor convention. On this movement, the *Register* was inclined to look askance and the *Washington Union,* whether from personal spite at Wentworth, from sectional jealousy, or from disdain of logrolling, openly attacked it.[12] Polk could count on support for his act in a state whose material interests he had injured.

The veto made Wentworth's position as a good party man extremely difficult. To his constituents he had to admit that it was of no avail during the remainder of Polk's term to hope for river and harbor appropriations. Henceforth he said if the people wanted harbors they must elect "northern" men to congress. The whig papers went further in expressing popular disgust. They denounced Polk as a traitor to his party on the tariff, Oregon, and the river and harbor bill. The *Chicago Journal* commented sarcastically on the sale of the harbor machinery at Chicago, denouncing Polk's treachery and his economizing at the expense of human lives. The ships in the harbor half-masted their colors when the news arrived. In the river counties the cant term for snags became Polk stalks, and a sandbar at the mouth of the Chicago harbor was named Mount Polk.[13]

Out of the indignation in the sections and parties interested in internal improvements came an extra-partisan movement of protest culminating in the river and harbor convention of 1847. Loose construction in the direction of internal improvements

[12] *Congressional Globe,* 29 congress, 1 session, 530; *Illinois State Register,* April 3, August 21, September 4, October 9, 1846; *Chicago Daily Journal,* October 14, 1846; *Chicago Democrat,* July 2, 1847; *Little Fort Porcupine,* November 3, 1846.
[13] *Chicago Democrat,* April 18, 1846; *Chicago Daily Journal,* August 10, 11, 12, 19, November 17, 1846, May 13, 1847; *Sangamo Journal,* August 20, 1846; *Alton Telegraph,* August 28, November 6, 1846. The *Chicago Democrat,* November 13, 1846, professed to see in the veto the cause of inroads made by the whigs on the democratic strength in the lake congressional districts.

SPLIT OF DEMOCRATIC PARTY   335

emphatically was good whig doctrine, and domestic indignation in the localities affected chimed in with whig principles. The first call for a convention by the *Buffalo Commercial* was welcomed by whig papers and by the democratic ones concerned by their local interests. The *Chicago Journal*, September 15, suggested that it be held July 4, 1847, at Chicago. The *Chicago Democrat* hesitated for several weeks and finally pronounced for it. The convention, held at Chicago, decided that both whigs and democrats should apply to every candidate the test of loyalty to river and harbor appropriations.[14]

Wentworth, however deeply provoked as he was, was not yet ready to abandon the party. Again and again he protested that river and harbor appropriations were good democratic doctrines despite Polk and grandfather Ritchie, the "Nous Verrons" of the *Washington Union*.[15] Wentworth had led an assault in congress the previous session on the tea and coffee taxes proposed by the administration; and he and Douglas, who certainly was not warm in the fight on rivers and harbors, joined in a bitter war on Thomas Ritchie, the editor of the "organ." In the face of the south Wentworth flaunted the doctrine of the Wilmot proviso—yet at the same time he professed his willingness to support the nominee of the Baltimore convention. Wentworth manifestly, even while making war on the administration, was determined not to break with his party.

Undoubtedly, however, by his repeated assaults upon the administration and its policies he was wreaking a vengeance on the leaders of his party past his power to undo. Through the patient work of years in the columns of the *Chicago Democrat* he had acquired personal influence over the farmers of northern Illinois that one rival after another had tried in vain to shake. Yet the men whom year in and year out he had trained in the democratic principles of the older school were not men to

[14] *Chicago Daily Journal*, September 9, 15, 24, 1846; *Chicago Democrat*, September 29, 1846, July 13, 1847.
[15] *Ibid.*, July 30, 1847.

forget; they refused to follow Wentworth when he pronounced the nomination of northern men like Cass sufficient of a solace for the wrongs of the north on Oregon and Texas, on river and harbor vetoes, and on the aggressions of the slave power that the older democracy had tolerated, half conscious that it violated its principles. Abolition had gained ground rapidly in the north during late years, and the time.was inevitably coming when the cumulative effort of southern aggressions would open the eyes of the northwest to the fact that " democrat " no longer meant what it had in the thirties. It was Wentworth's part in politics to state the premises, but only at the last to accept the inevitable conclusions that flowed from them. In 1847 he had denounced the policies that to the end of the " Old South " were to dominate the democratic party, but till 1856 he called himself a democrat.

At the outset of the campaign of 1848 the whigs at every point had the tactical advantage. The public land question during the administration of Tyler and Polk, so far as Illinois was concerned, had been burning itself out. In the spring of 1841 whigs and democrats in the state set off against each other the distribution bill of the whigs and the land cession scheme of Calhoun. The democratic papers, of course, opposed the whig distribution bill which passed through congress in the special session of 1841. The bill itself, however, contained a provision suspending its operation while import duties in excess of twenty cents on the dollar were in existence. A bill repealing this proviso was pocketed by Tyler in 1842, so that for all practical purposes the bill was a dead letter except in the preëmption provisions about which the whigs cared the least. Land cession measures were intermittently brought forward by Illinois congressmen in 1844 and 1845–1846. In 1846 a graduation measure was brought forward, argued at great length with little originality and finally defeated on a petition by eastern members who voted to lay it on the table in retaliation for the votes of western congressmen against the eastern harbor bill. A graduation bill was introduced at the next session but came to nothing.[16] With lands being sold off rapidly Illinois was fast ceasing to be a public land state, and her interest in a liberal land policy and in the party that had prómoted it was becoming correspondingly less.

The war with Mexico, too, was far more advantageous from the point of view of party politics to the whigs than to the democrats. At the outset the best the *Register* could do was to attempt to fix on various whigs and whig organs the charge of opposition to the war carried to unpatriotic extremes, but the attempt was not very successful. It early expressed the desire of a speedy peace with Mexico in which Mexico might under the guise of a sale compound her debts to the United States by the cession of territory in a moderate amount. It assailed the whigs severely for trying to make the war out to be a war of conquest, although at other times it preached the doctrine of manifest destiny for the extension ultimately of the territory of the United States not merely to California but to Darien and the Canadas. The obstinacy of the Mexicans in refusing to admit that they had succumbed to the manifest destiny of Anglo-Saxonism compelled the democrats to look forward to a long and obstinate war to bring them to terms; and such abortive measures as Polk's safe-conduct to Santa Anna into Mexico, which only permitted him to become the arch leader of the opposition there, were much better campaign material for the whigs than for the democrats. By the summer of 1847 the *Belleville Advocate* was compelled to admit that an occupation of extensive territory was necessary for an indefinite period before it might be hoped that Mexico would listen to reason. A war with no apparent end is not an attractive plank in the platform of an American party.[17]

[16] *Sangamo Journal,* May 21, 28, September 17, 1841; *Alton Telegraph,* April 24, 1841; *Illinois State Register,* August 27, 1841; *Belleville Advocate,* October 8, 1841; *Congressional Globe,* 28 congress, 1 session, 443, 28 congress, 2 session, 66, 29 congress, 1 session, 172, 29 congress, 2 session, 41, 200, 528; *Chicago Democrat,* July 21, August 18, 1846.

[17] *Illinois State Register,* June 26, July 10, 24, 31, August 14, November 6, 1846; *Belleville Advocate,* October 29, December 31, 1846, June 3, October 14, November 4, December 2, 1847.

It was with every tactical advantage that the whigs approached the election of 1848. As the *Alton Telegraph* outlined the situation, the administration had tried to cover up its retreat on the Oregon question with a "little war" only to find Mexico unexplainably obstinate, and further had made the mistake of not drawing generously enough on the enthusiasm and patriotism of the country to strike a decisive blow. On larger issues the paper a year before had pointed out that at the time the democrats were committed by their acts to the ultra stand on the tariff and slavery and must expect the defection to the whigs from their own or from third party banners of tariff democrats, native Americans, and abolitionists. The cry of democracy and the name of Jackson would no longer serve to hold the true democrats in line, and the locofocos would find themselves left alone. The whigs need only take issue fairly on the tariff and the subtreasury.[18]

Curiously the whigs at first were inclined to pass over the advantage they might enjoy in running the hero of Buena Vista as their candidate. In the summer of 1847 the *Chicago Journal* seemed to incline strongly in the direction of Henry Clay as the old and trusted exponent of whig principles who alone could rescue the nation from the crisis to which the policy of the administration both foreign and domestic had brought it. G. T. M. Davis, one of the two editors of the *Alton Telegraph*, took a similar stand late in 1847, claiming that Zachary Taylor in view of his treatment of the volunteers was not entitled to the support of the whigs, and further that they were on the verge of a mistake such as that of 1840. John Bailhache, the other editor, was inclined to agree with his colleague in regard to Clay, though fearing that his speech against the war and conquest had lessened his chances in the west. The *Telegraph*, however, took exception to the action of an unin‑ structed high convention in nominating Taylor, professing that he had lost very much in popularity in the last six months

18 *Alton Telegraph*, September 11, November 20, 1846, October 15, 1847; *Sangamo Journal*, May 7, 1846.

by his refusal to accept a party nomination and by the luster of Scott's triumphs; but Bailhache professed his willingness to support Taylor. The Taylor movement indeed was one that had begun in the preceding spring. The *Sangamo Journal* had come out for him on April 8, 1847. The *Quincy Whig* and the *Morgan Journal* had both declared for him a few days later. The *Chicago Journal* and the *Alton Telegraph* during the spring had both praised Taylor to the skies without coming out specifically in his favor.[19]   By the fall the democratic papers were predicting that Taylor would be eliminated in favor of Clay or some similar candidate, but finally they inclined to the belief that the Illinois whigs would acquiesce in his choice.

With a military hero as a candidate, with the favorable position on every issue, with their opponents torn by personal and sectional feuds as well as divided on political principle, the triumph of the whigs in the nation in 1848 was assured. In Illinois they were not successful. So strongly cemented was the fabric of the democratic party, so great was the power of the democratic name that the destruction of the party supremacy there had to be the work of years. That supremacy was not to be ended by any defection to the old rival parties. The whig name and organization had first to disappear. Yet the forces in the democratic party that ultimately were to end the day of its power were, by 1847, plainly apparent to the student. In the study of the political as of the animal organism the first detection of a morbid condition is more significant than the following out of its development to the inevitable result.

[19] *Chicago Daily Journal,* April 8, 28, 29, May 8, 27, 29, September 16, 1847; *Alton Telegraph,* April 30, December 10, 31, 1847; *Belleville Advocate,* October 7, December 9, 1847, February 2, 1848.

XIX. THE MORMON WAR

O F ALL the settlements inspired by peculiar ideas or beliefs that grew up on the fertile soil of the Military Tract, the most ambitious, the most tragic, the one most abid: ing in its effects on the nation, if not on the state, was the community of Latter Day Saints or Mormons at Nauvoo. The religion revealed by Joseph Smith drew converts from the old and new world until almost in a night a city of perhaps fifteen thousand people grew up in Illinois as the capital of an even larger community, and after thus overtopping Alton, and for a time even Chicago, passed away as suddenly as it rose. Today only a village of scarce a thousand can recall to the student of the past the passions, the ambitions, and the tragedies of the holy city of the Mormons in Illinois.

Of the Mormon belief itself it is difficult to write with the balanced detachment of the historical student. The story of the miraculous golden plates, protected by the direct intervention of angels from improper approach in their hiding place on the hill at Palmyra, New York, which had seen the overthrow of the Nephites by the barbarian invaders,[1] is too much for this age of incredulity to accept; the evidence of the eleven witnesses who testified to the existence of the plates would hardly survive the cross-examination of a court of law. The *Book of Mormon,* which Smith claimed he had translated from the plates by direct divine assistance, is a book of tedious histories, each of which seems to the careless reader much like the rest. It contains blunders in grammar which, if we accept Joseph Smith's account of the translation, must be laid to the charge of the divine power that word by word gave him the English equivalents of the characters on the plates. The evidence that

[1] *Times and Seasons,* April 15, 1841.

the book is really an historical novel written by the Reverend Solomon Spaulding is unsatisfactory; in any case from a literary point of view the book is incapable of conferring honor on its author. Had Mormonism begun and ended with the book on the golden plates, it would have made little noise in the world.

Doctrinally Mormonism has little that is distinctive. Its theology is usually referred to Sidney Rigdon, a Campbellite preacher, who, as an early convert, may have devised its creed. Mormonism based itself on a literal interpretation of the word of God; it adopted from the Old Testament what is least spiritual in the stories of the patriarchs and neglected what is finest in the New. The problem of how God can be man that perplexed early christian theology and that was but partially solved by the doctrine of the two natures, Mormonism met in easier fashion—its God was a God with passions like men, with physical parts, the God who turned his hinder parts to Moses, a God who might delight in blood, a God from whom frail men might expect not mercy but sympathy. In place of the authority of an infallible church, speaking with the weight of eighteen christian centuries, or by the application to a holy book of reason sent from God, Mormonism substituted a religion of revelation to Joseph Smith by a God who could announce the names of the trustees of the Nauvoo House and prescribe that his servant Joseph Smith and his seed should forever receive free board there.

To the revelation Smith ever turned to keep his followers in order. There were revelations commanding that this man should tarry here and that man should go there, revelations admonishing, reproving, and praising his followers by name. By revelation God commanded the building of the Temple, and by revelation he ordained also the discipline of the Mormon faith. By revelation Smith held under control the followers who had swallowed greedily the marvel of the dead races of the past and of the golden plates. The church services were ceremonious; the sacraments were rites to preserve the faithful from the devil and to comfort their souls with the assurance of salvation for some specific performance. Mormonism, always prefacing its teaching with a reflection on the dissensions and differences of opinion on matters of faith of the christian denominations, proffered a certainty and counted its converts by ten thousands.

The influence of Smith's character on the development of Mormonism cannot be overestimated. Though educated only by his own efforts and not highly intellectual, he was possessed of a vigorous will in a powerful body; and he ruled his followers with absolute sway. He had efficient adjuncts in his brothers, notably Hyrum Smith, and in his father and mother. The family traced its descent from a long line of Puritan ancestors and pointed with pride to its record in Indian wars and the Revolution; although in its New York home its reputation had not been of special distinction, on the larger stage on which it was called to play it seconded with reasonably good support Joseph Smith's performance in the rôle of prophet.[1a]

But although he was able to gather to the standard of his religion a hundred thousand converts, at first chiefly New Englanders and New Yorkers already having strong religious traditions, Smith had certain limitations in his character that fatally hindered him from organizing them into an irresistible phalanx. He could dominate his humbler followers, but there his power stopped. He had not the imagination necessary to comprehend or to harmonize with the men outside his faith with whom he had to deal; neither was he a judge of the character and ability of the men that he gathered around him. Hence, perhaps because of the moral weaknesses of his religious dispensations — though Smith to the last retained his grasp on the church — the history of Mormonism is the history of the secession of one trusted leader after another; and Smith, not understanding or grasping the forces of the American frontier, led

[1a] Salisbury, "The Mormon War in Hancock County," Illinois State Historical Society, *Journal*, 8:281 ff.; Berry, "The Mormon Settlements in Illinois," Illinois State Historical Society, *Transactions*, 1906, 88 ff.

his followers repeatedly to failure and death in his effort to build up a theocracy in the American backwoods. In so doing he arrayed against himself and his followers all the strongest elements in every community where he sought to establish himself. The christian churches were outraged by his denunciation of them; the powerful proslavery party and its sympathizers were incensed at his antislavery teaching; and the democracy of the frontier was alarmed at his autocracy and at his insidious interference in local politics. The opposition was intensified by the provincialism of the frontier, impatient of anything different from itself and ready to enforce conformity even outside the law.

Joseph Smith was eighteen years old when in 1823 celestial visitants first announced his mission to him and showed him the plates, and twenty-two when the golden plates were finally given to him. On the sixth of April, 1830, the church was founded. Then followed a series of persecutions, the church seeking a home now at Kirtland, Ohio, now in Missouri. Whether the fault was theirs or their opponents', whether the causes of their unpopularity were their antislavery sympathies, their clannish proclivities, their denunciation of the churches, or their belief that the wealth of the gentiles belonged to the Saints, they finally in 1838 were driven out of Missouri, with the loss of their property and of many lives, and took refuge in Illinois.[2]

In Illinois they encountered a favorable reception. Their doctrines had previously awakened passing curiosity, and their earlier persecution at the hands of the people of Missouri had called forth occasional comments from the newspapers. The outburst of 1839 provoked indignant comment from the Illinois papers, especially those of whig political affiliations, possibly with a view to attracting to the whig standard a considerable body of voters.[3]

[2] *Times and Seasons*, March 1, April 1, 1842.
[3] *Chicago Democrat*, December 3, 17, 1833, June 18, 1834; *Chicago American*, July 23, October 3, 1839, June 11, 1842; *Peoria Register*, May 18, July 27, 1839; *Sangamo Journal*, January 19, 1839; *Illinois State Register*, November 9, 1838.

Mormonism at first throve in Illinois. On October 5, 1839, Commerce, the site of Nauvoo, was adopted as a "stake" of the church. The plat of the city, it was said later, was bought of a Connecticut firm for $53,500, on long time. A remarkable charter was secured from the legislature with little trouble, the member reporting it merely saying that the document had an extraordinary militia clause which he believed harmless. At Nauvoo a stringent temperance ordinance was passed, if not enforced, and a university was founded, which had sufficient vitality at least to bestow the honorary degree of Doctor of Laws on James Gordon Bennett, editor of the *New York Herald.* Missionaries were sent far and wide in the old as well as in the new world and communities of Saints grew up in other places than Nauvoo; though even as early as 1841, it is ominous to notice the appearance against them of charges of immorality, polygamy, and of harboring thieves.[4]

The beginning of the troubles of the Mormons in Illinois was their interference as a body in politics. Both parties had courted them, the whigs more openly than the democrats. In the presidential election of 1840, the Mormons voted for all the Harrison electors except Abraham Lincoln, substituting the name of one democratic elector for his, as they alleged out of complacency to the democrats. Lincoln was too good a politician, however, not to congratulate the Mormons warmly on the passage of their charters which apparently neither party opposed.[5]

Though the Mormons voted for Stuart in 1841, the democrats, for some reason, won the race for the favor of the prophet. On January 1, 1842, *Times and Seasons,* the official newspaper of the Mormons, published a proclamation declaring that the Mormons had voted for Harrison as a gallant

[4]*Times and Seasons,* December 30, 1839, November 15, 1840, March 1, April 1, November 1, December 15, 1841, January 1, 1842; *Chicago American,* July 29, 1842; *Warsaw Signal,* February 10, 1845. Bennett's paper was indicated as worthy of the patronage of the Saints, its attitude toward them being distinctly friendly.
[5]*Times and Seasons,* January 1, 1841; *Chicago American,* November 16, 26, December 26, 1840, June 8, 1842.

soldier but that he was now dead and there was no obligation on them to support his friends. "Douglass," Smith said, "is a Master Spirit, and his friends are our friends — we are willing to cast our banners on the air, and fight by his side in the cause of humanity, and equal rights — the cause of liberty and the law. Snyder, and Moore, are his friends — they are ours." The *Sangamo Journal* commented that if this pronunciamento did not set the citizens of the state to thinking it did not know what would. The democratic papers were taken a little back at this zealous missionary work for their candidate, the *Register* refraining from publishing the address in full.[6]

With Smith thus openly arrayed on the side of his opponent, Duncan in the campaign of 1842 for the governorship naturally took an anti-Mormon stand. He attacked the loose provisions of the Mormon charters, which, by allowing laws to be passed so long as they were not counter to the state or federal constitutions, permitted the city council a power of legislation almost concurrent with that of the state. He pointed out the evil legislation which had been passed under this arrangement, such as the ordinance providing heavy fine and imprisonment for any person speaking lightly of the established religion. He called attention to the violence of the Mormons in Missouri and to the charge that they were more or less openly engaged in plots against their old enemies there.[7] Suddenly a series of exposures by a man hitherto among the most prominent of the Mormon leaders threw the whole state into excitement and centered the climax of the campaign on the Mormon issue.

General John C. Bennett, after a more or less checkered career in the west, had joined the Mormons at about the time of their arrival in Illinois. Educated in medicine, he had become, for some reason, quartermaster-general of Illinois militia; and it soon became generally understood among the

[6] Ford, *History of Illinois*, 262; *Times and Seasons*, January 1, 1842; *Sangamo Journal*, January 21, February 11, 1842; *Illinois State Register*, January 14, 1842.
[7] *Sangamo Journal*, May 14, June 10, 1842; *Alton Telegraph*, May 14, 1842.

Mormons that he was a military genius of the first rank. He had had a large share in the political negotiations by which the Nauvoo charter was secured, and he was generally believed to have acted as a political go-between on other occasions. He commanded the "Nauvoo Legion" into which the militia of the city was organized and wrote communications to the *Times and Seasons* signed "Joab." For some reason he quarreled with Smith and was cast out of the church in 1842, the Mormons discovering that his character was scabrous in the extreme. The tone of his exposures indicates that there was nothing inherently improbable in the charge, though it is a little strange that his iniquity was not sooner found out.[8]

Undoubtedly Bennett was able to tell many things regarding the aims, methods, and morals of the Mormon leaders; but his exposures appear unreliable. It is possible that men like the Smiths, who were prone to use their spiritual authority for their pecuniary advantage, did not refrain from using it to win over women devotees who took their fancy; but it is difficult to believe that the elaborate societies and orders for debauchery which Bennett detailed existed outside his own evil imagination. It is doubtful if the doctrine of "spiritual wifery" existed at so early a date; indeed, the Mormons claimed that the doctrine was Bennett's own invention. Too much weight, however, should not be given to the denials of Bennett's charges as to the injuries inflicted or attempted to be inflicted on Orson Pratt, Sidney Rigdon, and Nancy Rigdon. Certainly in spite of the Mormon denials there was a Danite band with which Bennett had been threatened; but as a whole, except where Bennett's charges can be verified from other sources, they are to be discounted, if for no other reason because he claimed that he had originally joined the Mormons in order to expose them.[9]

<hr/>

[8] *Times and Seasons,* January 1, June 1, 1841, August 1, 1842, November 15, 1844; *Wasp,* October 1, 1842.
[9] *Times and Seasons,* April 15, August 1, September 15, 1842; *Wasp,* September 3, 1842; *Chicago American,* July 7, 1842; Bennett, *History of the Saints,* 5.

The charges of Bennett, especially the commentary on the danger to the state from the Mormon scheme supported by Mormon militia with state arms in their hands and the accusation of attempts on the life of Governor Boggs of Missouri by Mormons, rang through the whig papers in the last weeks of the campaign; but the Mormon vote was cast solidly for Ford; and he was elected by a safe majority. The *Telegraph* was inclined to believe that the charges because of apparent improbability might actually have injured the cause of the whigs.[10]

In his message of 1842 Ford stated that the people of the state desired that the Mormon charters be modified so as to allow the people of Nauvoo no greater privileges than were enjoyed by their fellow citizens; but the suggestion was not followed out by the legislature, since both parties hesitated to take a decided stand. The old doctrine of vested rights was invoked in behalf of the charters, and the friends of the Mormons were always ready with a suggestion to repeal all municipal charters in case that of Nauvoo were touched.[11] In the congressional campaign of 1843 the Mormon votes were apparently thrown for Hoge, the democrat, against Cyrus Walker, in spite of what the Mormons alleged were attempts on the part of the whigs to win them over. The democrats declared that in the fifth district the Mormons under the orders of the prophet voted for Orville H. Browning against Douglas.[12]

An important factor in the conduct of the Mormon leaders was their constant dread of extradition to Missouri. On September 15, 1840, Governor Boggs issued a requisition on Illinois for the surrender of Smith, Rigdon, and others as fugitives from justice. The warrants were not executed; but in

[10] *Alton Telegraph*, August 13, 1842.
[11] *Sangamo Journal*, December 15, 1842, January 19, 1843; *Alton Telegraph*, December 17, 24, 1842; *Illinois State Register*, March 31, 1843; *House Journal*, 1842-1843, 1 session, 50.
[12] *Chicago Democrat*, August 23, 1843; *Nauvoo Neighbor*, August 2, September 27, 1843; *Illinois State Register*, July 7, September 22, 1843; Ford, *History of Illinois*, 317.

the next June, Smith was arrested at Carlin's direction. Douglas in the Warren county court on June 10 decided the writ was not good. In August Smith and Rockwell, the latter Smith's alleged tool in his attempt on Governor Boggs, were again arrested, charged with the attempted murder; but they eluded arrest; and on the accession of Ford, Smith asked to have the validity of the writ tested. Justin Butterfield argued Smith's case before Judge Pope in the United States court and secured his discharge. Rockwell was finally taken to Missouri, but no evidence could be found against him sufficient to hold him, and he was released.[13]

Nauvoo meanwhile was growing rapidly. How prosperous the enterprise was so far as the rank and file are concerned cannot be known certainly. Taking the accounts of the Mormons themselves, and even of some travelers, one gets the impression that the city was marked by a prosperity in which all citizens alike shared. They commented on the industry of the inhabitants, the fine brick houses rising in considerable numbers, the stately public structures such as the Nauvoo House and the Temple. Yet as one studies the newspapers of the town, it is hard to find any evidences of business activity. There are few or no advertisements of commission houses, few advertisements of stores. On one or two occasions deliberate attempts were made to keep money at home and to preach abstinence from purchasing goods made outside the town. That was hardly the policy which a town aspiring to be the commercial metropolis of any important district would pursue; and the town of Nauvoo with a population twice as numerous as that of either Chicago or Alton had an agricultural hinterland depending on it less important than that of either of its rivals. From the point of view of the economist one wonders how such a population without extensive manufacturing could sustain itself.

Indications are not lacking that the leaders of the Saints

---

[13] Smith, *History of the Church of Jesus Christ of Latter Day Saints*, 524-525; *Nauvoo Neighbor*, January 10, 1844.

realized this difficulty and that they made repeated efforts to attract capital which might furnish employment to the floods of mechanics who, bringing little more than their strength and their skill, flocked in as a result of the preaching of the faith in the Old World and in the eastern cities of the United States. Skilled labor for varieties of industries was ready at hand; and Joseph Smith and his successors issued appeal after appeal to Latter Day Saints living elsewhere who possessed a few thousand dollars to come to Nauvoo and invest it in manufacturing that would supply an economic basis for the vast political and theocratic structure that Smith aspired to build up in Illinois. Repeated warnings against the immediate immigration of persons without capital had to be issued. One or two communications to the Mormon papers rebuking English immigrants for grumbling indicated that some of the newcomers did not find Nauvoo a land flowing with milk and honey and that they were inclined to denounce as oppressors the little group of well-to-do men in the community whose capital was so precious to Smith.

There was more than one possible solution to the problem. In spite of the fact that much of the work on the Temple and the other public structures was done by men donating their labor one day in every ten, there are indications that the work was used to feed and clothe the men employed on it. Farmers of the Mormon faith around Nauvoo were urged in payment of tithes to bring produce for the support of the men laboring on the Temple; and the sisters were urged to prepare articles of clothing for the persons engaged on it. On several occasions payment of the tithes was demanded in produce, money, or building material; and guns and old watches were pronounced unacceptable. Possibly in this way materials and subsistence for the workers on the Temple were obtained, and a certain amount of unemployment taken care of.

A precocious trade organization in the city that grew up may have been one result of this. The shoemakers planned at one time to have a common shop supplied by their work;

associations of carriage builders announced themselves ready to receive orders; at one time a trades council was held to consider the building of a factory on a mutual stock subscription. But many of the Mormon men who emigrated to the city of promise scattered to the nearby towns and to gentile farms to find work, while Mormon girls proved a blessing to overworked housewives of the Military Tract or in some instances met an evil fate in the little river towns. To this necessary scattering of their coreligionists some Mormons were inclined to lay the fact that the church was not strong enough to withstand the assaults of its foes. Had certain well-to-do men in the east, it was said, come to Nauvoo with their money as they had been adjured to do, there would have been sufficient numbers of the people in the town and the county to have defied all enemies and to have controlled the state politically.

It was not surprising that aside from any partisan motives for wishing ill to the Mormons the fact that this predominance in the state was the ideal of the Saints was enough to stir up against them a local opposition that deepened and became more bitter till the final expulsion of the Mormons. In part this antagonism may be ascribed to the jealousy of Warsaw at the development of its rival up the river; but the causes of it were more deep rooted; and by 1843 hostility to the Mormons in the state was open enough to have become a serious issue. On August 19, 1843, an anti-Mormon meeting held at Carthage adopted resolutions condemning in vigorous language the régime at Nauvoo, and denouncing the violence, the defiance of law, and the thievery that flourished there and pledged the convention to offer resistance. Furthermore, Missouri was assured that if another warrant was issued against Smith the people of Carthage would do all in their power to see it executed.[14]

Events moved rapidly. For some reason, instead of throwing his support to one presidential candidate or the other in

[14] *Alton Telegraph,* September 23, 1843.

1844, Smith decided to announce himself as a candidate. What he can possibly have hoped to gain from his candidacy is hard to see, unless it was to demonstrate that he held the balance of power in the nation as he already held it in the state. At all events he began newspaper agitation in support of his aspirations and sent out Mormon emissaries to electioneer for him.

Meanwhile another secession from the church was imminent. On June 7, 1844, there appeared at Nauvoo the first number of the *Expositor*, a paper supported by a group of men of whom the most prominent were William and Wilson Law, F. M. and C. L. Higbee, and Robert D. and Charles A. Foster. The Laws and Robert Foster had been cut off from the church in the preceding April.[15] The *Nauvoo Neighbor* promptly found a string of accusations to bring against the various members of the group; but in view of the fact that the Laws were well-to-do members of the community, the defection was, to say the least, a serious one.[16] The *Expositor* in the single number that was permitted to issue went straight to the mark. It accused the Smiths of embezzling church funds, of enticing immigrants too hastily in order to sell them property at exorbitant prices and of then leaving others to provide them with work to support themselves. It denounced the activity of the church in politics and the high-handed procedures in freeing by writs of habeas corpus, issuing from the municipal court, persons arrested by the United States marshal. More damaging still, it again accused the Smiths of the deliberate seduction of women and the secret practice of plural marriage. The authorities at Nauvoo to meet the attack had no other recourse than a council order to suppress the paper as a nuisance, and accordingly the press was totally destroyed.

The crisis was at hand. The anti-Mormons gathered at Warsaw and passed resolutions for the extermination of the Mormon leaders. They resolved that if the governor would not order out the militia to secure the execution of a warrant

[15] *Times and Seasons*, April 15, 1843.
[16] *Nauvoo Neighbor*, June 26, 1844.

they would rely on the rallying of the *posse comitatus* with assistance from other counties and from Missouri and Iowa. Throughout the county and in neighboring districts in Illinois, Iowa, and Missouri, men were gathering under arms. A bolder man than Joseph Smith might have lost his nerve in the emergency. For a time he appears to have thought of fleeing to the wilderness. From this resolution he was dissuaded; and with Hyrum, he surrendered to arrest at Carthage, June 24, on a charge of rioting. Next day a warrant charging them with treason was prepared and served.[17] Leaving the Smiths in the jail at Carthage, Governor Ford, who had arrived on the scene with state troops and taken command of the militia that had mustered, disbanded all the forces but three companies and, leaving two at Carthage, marched with the third to Nauvoo to urge a surrender of the state arms still there. Meanwhile, on June 27, the Smiths were set upon and murdered in the Carthage jail.[18] Ford, who returned from Nauvoo before the news of the murder reached that place, inclined to believe that it was a plot to procure his own assassination there, as a preliminary to a state war on the Mormons. Feeling he could trust neither Mormon nor anti-Mormon, he returned to Quincy to watch the excitement gradually quiet itself.

So perished Joseph Smith and his brother, Hyrum, at the hands of a mob, which was too panic-stricken at the Mormons' theocratic schemes to show mercy or allow fair fight. By this shedding of blood the anti-Mormons probably believed the freedom of Illinois and the dissolution of the dangerous power had been purchased. The *Alton Telegraph* commenting two years before on a keen analysis of Mormonism by that insatiable student of ideas, Jonathan Baldwin Turner, had pronounced the opinion that Smith's empire would not long survive him. But from among all the hands stretched out to grasp at a fraction of the sway enjoyed by Smith one man seized

[17] *Times and Seasons*, August 1, 1845; *Nauvoo Neighbor*, June 26, 1844.
[18] *Times and Seasons*, July 1, 1844.

the reins more firmly than Smith himself had ever held them, proving that while he lacked the qualities of imagination and boldness needed to found a new religion, he had the strength of will and ruthlessness of purpose to dominate it for his own uses.

At the time of his death Smith governed the church as a member of the first presidency, of which Hyrum and Sidney Rigdon were the other members. Rigdon at once hastened from Pittsburg to Nauvoo to endeavor to assert his constitutional right as surviving member of the first presidency to lead the church. But he was not the man to obtain power that Brigham Young had marked out for himself. Violent in speech, irresolute in action, continually grasping at an authority denied him by the stronger willed men who surrounded him, he stood helpless, while Young, controlling the people like a second Joseph, carried through a complete usurpation in the name of another part of the hierarchy — that of the "Twelve."

Secession movements from all sides had first to be checked. James J. Strang professed to have received from Smith a revelation June 18, commanding him to establish a "stake" at Voree; and he was promptly cut off from the church, a number of followers going with him. According to other accounts William Law attempted to establish a Mormon settlement at Rock Island.[19] The return of the "Twelve" and the personal influence of Young finally brought unity out of confusion.

On August 8 a meeting of the church was held. Young put the question to the people whether they wished a guardian, a prophet, a spokesman; but no one answered. Young then defined the position of the "Twelve," claiming for them the power to regulate the church. Amasa Lyman and Sidney Rigdon, he admitted, had been councilors in the first presidency, but if either wished to act as spokesman for Joseph, he must go behind the veil where Joseph was. Doubtless the double *entendre* was not lost on the men to whom it was addressed.

---

[19] *Chicago Democrat,* September 18, 1844; *Times and Seasons,* September 2, 1844.

Rigdon refused to have his name voted for as spokesman or guardian, and all voted to sustain the "Twelve." Notice of this decision was duly published with the remark that "the elders abroad will best exhibit their wisdom to all men by remaining silent on those things they are ignorant of." The presence of a firm hand had been apparent in the proclamation already issued by Young to the effect that the branches abroad must be tithed as soon as organized. A day of closer organization of the church was at hand.[20]

Rigdon could not refrain from one more snatch at the power passing from his grasp. It was said that Joseph Smith before his death had received a revelation designating Rigdon as a prophet, seer, and revelator. On the night of the second of September, according to his enemies, claiming to have the "keys" above the "Twelve," he ordained certain men to be prophets, priests, and kings. His enemies heard of his proceeding almost at once and acted promptly. First they apparently bullied him into surrender with threats of physical violence and on September 8 called a meeting to try him. Young adjured those who were for Joseph and Hyrum Smith, the *Book of Mormon,* the Temple, and the "Twelve" to stand forth; those who were for Rigdon or Lyman Wight or James Emmett might also stand forth, for they were known. William Marks bravely defended the right of Rigdon as a member of the first presidency to receive the oracles from Smith and to give them to the church. Rigdon was overwhelmed by his enemies with ridicule and invective, however, and he and his followers were cast out.[21]

Further opposition had to be met from the Smith family. For the time Young quieted Mother Smith's insistence on the rights of the young son of the prophet by promises that in due time his rights would be recognized, but that for the present she must remember that by pushing his claim she would expose him to danger. William Smith, the younger brother of the

[20] *Times and Seasons,* August 15, September 2, 1844.
[21] *Alton Telegraph,* September 21, 1844; *Times and Seasons,* September 15, 1844; *Nauvoo Neighbor,* October 2, December 15, 1844.

prophet, was persistent in his protest; and, after it became apparent that he could not be kept quiet, he was ridiculed in the Mormon papers and finally bullied into keeping silence while he was at Nauvoo. In the autumn of 1845 he was cut off from the church.[22] He openly charged that the "Twelve" were leading the church out into the wilderness to have the absolute sway of it, that they disregarded the claims of the Smiths and of the infant Joseph and even treated them with derision; he laid the spiritual wife doctrine to the charge of Young and the "Twelve," claiming that they had first taught it at Boston. A conference in Cincinnati in January of 1846 reiterated William Smith's attacks on the "Twelve," and pronounced in favor of the right of little Joseph. Thus the schism began among the Mormons that has continued to our own day.[23]

Meanwhile the necessity of removal from Illinois was doubtless becoming increasingly apparent to the leaders of the party at Nauvoo. The legislature of 1845 had repealed their charter, leaving them without any government adequate for the city. In these circumstances for the purpose of keeping strangers in order they had to take up certain uncouth practices of which the mildest was "whittling out of town." [24]

The fetish of the "Twelve" was the completion of the Temple at Nauvoo. Probably this policy was dictated partly by the fact that according to them, Sidney Rigdon had tried to draw the people away to Pittsburg and to scatter the church, prophesying that the Temple would never be completed. To save their faces the Nauvoo Mormons were compelled to wait until the Temple was completed so that the people could receive in it their promised endowments. On May 28, 1845, the *Nauvoo Neighbor* announced that the capstone was in place. In April of 1846 the Temple was dedicated, admission to the ceremony costing one dollar.

[22] *Times and Seasons*, November 1, 1845; *Nauvoo Neighbor*, June 11, 1845; *Warsaw Signal*, October 29, 1845; see also Lee, *The Mormon Menace*, 207.
[23] *Warsaw Signal*, October 29, 1845; broadside in Chicago Historical Society.
[24] Lee, *The Mormon Menace*, 213.

Since early in 1845 the leaders had been considering the idea of removal to some more remote site where the church could be governed without exciting the hostility of the gentiles. The pine region, Wisconsin, Texas, the country west of Missouri, and Oregon were mentioned as possible locations.[25] The delay of departure caused in a year and a half two armed conflicts between the Mormons and their opponents that have gone down in the history of the state as the "Mormon Wars."

Early in the spring of 1845 attacks on the Mormons and on the dangerous political tendency of their settlement at Nauvoo, controlled in its voting strength by the will of a few men, began to appear in such papers as the *Warsaw Signal*. The anti-Mormons denied apparently with some truth that their propaganda was a whig device to control the district by driving out the Mormon allies of the democrats; on the contrary, they alleged that the movement comprised the old settlers in Hancock of both parties. The old charges against the Mormons of harboring thieves, of counterfeiting, and of general lawlessness were reiterated.[26] But the *Nauvoo Neighbor* of January 22, 1845, declared that the thievery was that of a gang in Iowa, unconnected with the Mormons, who carried their stolen property through Nauvoo.

In the fall of 1845 the anti-Mormons initiated a regular campaign designed to drive the Mormons out of the county. Early in September a mob one or two hundred strong began burning the houses of Mormons in the country, requiring them to move their household goods to Nauvoo. Jacob B. Backenstos, the sheriff of the county, was a Mormon sympathizer, or what at the time was called a "jack-Mormon," a man put in office by Mormon votes. In the spring the feeling against him in the county had run high because of a speech he was alleged to have made in the legislature; and the Carthage Grays had ordered him out of the county, charging among

<hr/>

[25] *Times and Seasons,* September 15, 1844; *Hancock Eagle,* April 24, 1846; *Nauvoo Neighbor,* February 15, 26, 1845.
[26] *Warsaw Signal,* January 15, May 14, 1845; *Alton Telegraph,* June 21, 1845.

other things against him that he had engineered the deal to cast the Mormon vote for Hoge in the congressional election of 1843; indeed, it was said that Hoge's recent defeat for a renomination had been due to public dissatisfaction with the appointment of Backenstos, at his instance, as superintendent of the lead mines. Whatever his political affiliations were, there can be no doubt that Backenstos did his duty in the riots of the fall of 1845, even though the motive from which he did it may not have been disinterested.[27]

When apprised of the activity of the rioters, Backenstos on September 13 attempted to raise a posse at Warsaw for the purpose of stopping the disorder. Failing to get any assistance from the old settlers, he ordered the Mormons in Nauvoo to hold themselves in readiness; in a second proclamation of September 16 he stated that Colonel Levi Williams, the leader of the rioters, had called out the militia of Hancock, McDonough, and Schuyler counties, and he warned men against obeying the call. On the same day he called out a force of mounted men to rescue his own family and others from the territory terrorized by the mob. Proceeding against the mob, he encountered them at their work of burning houses and put them to rout with the loss of two of their number killed and others wounded. The Mormons in their turn fell to plundering, and a state force under Hardin had to be sent to disperse them.[28]

Meanwhile meetings held in nearby counties, notably at Quincy, at Mendon, and an important one held on October 1 at Carthage, at which eight or nine counties were represented, resolved that the only solution was the breaking up of the Mormon settlement in Hancock. The Nauvoo common council offered to remove in the spring in case the gentiles would assist them in selling or renting their property and would refrain from vexatious lawsuits. These terms were accepted by the

[27] *Illinois State Register*, April 24, 1845; *Sangamo Journal*, April 1, 17, 1845; *Nauvoo Neighbor*, April 23, September 24, 1845; *Warsaw Signal*, September 17, 1845.
[28] *Nauvoo Neighbor*, September 17, 1845; *Warsaw Signal*, September 17, 1845.

anti-Mormons on condition that an armed force should occupy Nauvoo during the winter to prevent continuance of the alleged depredations of the Mormons on the property of the old settlers.[29] The Mormons at the time were said to be almost in military control of the county and were accused of driving away the cattle and harvesting the crops of their opponents. It was the uncompromising attitude of the people of the neighboring counties that compelled them to give way.[30] The next session of the circuit court found several true bills against Mormons, but all except one against Backenstos for a murder connected with the reducing of the county to order were nol-prossed.   On this remaining bill Backenstos was acquitted.[31] Meanwhile attempts to serve warrants in Nauvoo as late as October 25 had been defeated by a show of force on the part of the Mormons.   The Mormon county commissioners, according to their opponents, attempted to have the expenses of Backenstos' posse charged to the county exchequer.[32]

The Mormons feared a renewal of disorder when the militia guard under Major Warren stationed in Nauvoo during the winter was withdrawn the first of May.   In answer to protests against its withdrawal Ford answered that the force was an expense to the state and was not large enough to prevent violence if either side were inclined to use it.   The Mormons, whose progress in removing was not so great as it should have been at the time, were warned that it was out of the power of the governor to protect them at Nauvoo, since the people of the state would not fight for them.   Although Ford disclaimed any responsibility on the part of himself or the state for the agreement made the preceding fall by which the Mormons had promised to emigrate, he told them plainly that there was nothing else for them to do.   The Mormons asserted that they were departing as fast as possible and that the only cause of

[29] *Quincy Whig,* October 1, 1845; *Sangamo Journal,* October 2, 1845; *Nauvoo Neighbor,* October 29, 1845.
[30] *Chicago Democrat,* October 4, 6, 1845.
[31] *Nauvoo Neighbor,* October 29, 1845; *Illinois State Register,* December 19, 1845.
[32] *Warsaw Signal,* October 29, 1845, January 8, 1846.

the uproar against them was the fear on the part of the whigs that they might cast a few votes. They asserted that at a meeting they had declared their intention not to vote again in Illinois. On May 15 the *Hancock Eagle,* ostensibly a "new citizen" paper, though Mormon in sympathy, declared that about fourteen hundred teams had crossed the river and that about twelve thousand souls had already left the state. Major Warren, who had received orders the day after his men disbanded to muster them in again, assured the anti-Mormons that the Mormons were leaving as fast as possible and that regulations were in force sufficient to guard against any disorder on their part.[33]

Within a few days, however, bands of anti-Mormons were again at work driving isolated Mormons in the county off their property. Early in June the anti-Mormons, alleging that the Mormons to the number of several hundred were planning to stay at Nauvoo, using it as a base from which to commit depredation on the old settlers, proposed to march a force to Nauvoo as a demonstration; to this end they applied for aid to the counties represented in the Carthage convention. The result, according to the new settlers in Nauvoo, was a desperate rush on the part of the few remaining Mormons to get over the river. The new citizens who were already moving in had held a public meeting on May 29 to determine the question of establishing a city government. The anti-Mormons, however, affected to believe that the Mormon leaders were still dominating the policy of the town. They affirmed that the committee of new citizens had been put down by Backenstos, who had raised a force of five hundred men. On June 9 the new citizens, according to the *Hancock Eagle,* passed conciliatory resolutions; but the advance of the hostile army next day led the opinion to be expressed that the prosperity of the town was what was really aimed at. By June 13 an anti-Mormon force of about four hundred was encamped before the town, and

[33] *Alton Telegraph,* May 2, 9, 1846; *Hancock Eagle,* April 10, 17, May 8, 15, 1846.

about three hundred new citizens were mustered to defend it. The anti-Mormons insisted that they be admitted to the town to force the remaining Mormons to leave, but the new citizens repulsed them, and forced them to retreat. By the middle of July the *Warsaw Signal* declared that an open state of war between Mormon and anti-Mormon forces existed in the county.[34]

In the summer the trouble broke forth with redoubled force. The anti-Mormons assembled in arms with the intention, as the *Hancock Eagle* professed to believe, of plundering Nauvoo and the new citizens and of murdering those who had been forward in the suppression of lawlessness. The Nauvoo party, whether directed by Mormons or new citizens, late in August summoned a posse to serve warrants against members of the opposite party accused of acts of violence. A few days earlier a similar posse was summoned to serve writs in Nauvoo. The anti-Mormons professed to believe that the Mormons were actually in control in Nauvoo directing the policy of its newspaper and that with three thousand Mormons in town and three thousand more within easy reach in Iowa they controlled and terrorized the new citizens, while they sent out parties to stir up confusion in the county by deeds of violence.[35]

The anti-Mormon army once more marched on Nauvoo to force the withdrawal of the Mormons. They were intolerant in the terms of departure that they insisted on; they rejected terms negotiated by James W. Singleton, one of their officers, who thereupon resigned his command. After several other attempts at negotiation, in which the anti-Mormons insisted on unconditional surrender, they undertook to force their way in. A battle occurred which resolved itself into an artillery engagement without decisive result, from which the anti-Mormons withdrew to await an additional supply of cannon balls, with

[34] *Hancock Eagle,* May 25, June 5, 19, July 13, 1846; *Warsaw Signal,* June 14, July 16, extra, 1846; broadside of the New Settlers' committee, June 15, 1846, in Chicago Historical Society.
[35] *Belleville Advocate,* August 27, 1846; *Hancock Eagle,* extra, August 21, 1846; broadside of August 29, 1846, in Chicago Historical Society.

seven men wounded and their supply of ammunition exhausted.[36]

Meanwhile the two parties entered into negotiations through the intervention of a committee of citizens from Quincy. The anti-Mormons tried to secure the surrender to civil authority of all who had resisted them, but finally were content with the withdrawal of the Mormons from the city and their agreement to surrender their arms to the Quincy committee, to be returned to them after they had crossed the river. Five of the Mormons were to be allowed to remain to dispose of the church property. On marching into Nauvoo on these terms, Thomas S. Brockman, the commander of the county forces, at once gave the Mormons five days to leave, requiring the "jack-Mormons," such as Backenstos and William Pickett, to leave at once. In addition Brockman forced a number of the new citizens, estimated by the *Warsaw Signal*, October 20, as not over thirty families, to leave Nauvoo. Unfriendly papers such as the *State Register* asserted that a reign of terror marked by plunder and violence was proceeding in Nauvoo.[37]

The opinion even of democrats in Illinois was turned against the anti-Mormons on account of their high-handed proceedings in Nauvoo, whig papers like the *Chicago Journal* and democratic papers like the *State Register* similarly condemning them. Ford once more marched with militia into the county, only to find that anti-Mormon opinion was strongly against him. The local papers treated with derision the marching and counter-marching of his forces; and the anti-Mormon women presented him with a petticoat, which his loyal troops decreed should be carried outside the camp and burned by three Negroes.[38]

[36] *Quincy Whig*, September 12, December 2, 1846; *Warsaw Signal*, extra, September 14, 1846; circular to the public by James W. Singleton, September, 1846, in Chicago Historical Society.

[37] *Warsaw Signal*, October 27, 1846; *Quincy Herald*, October 16, 1846; *Quincy Whig*, September 23, 1846.

[38] *Chicago Journal*, September 30, 1846; *Quincy Whig*, November 4, 1846; *Warsaw Signal*, November 14, 1846.

From first to last the party rivalries of whigs and democrats had complicated the problem of the Mormon disorders. Thus in 1844 despite Ford's denials the whigs insisted that his course toward the rioters was designed to curry favor with the Mormons and to secure their votes for the democratic candidates. In reply the democratic papers accused the whigs of trying to stir up a civil war in the state, although themselves welcoming the Mormon support.[39] In 1845 the *Sangamo Journal* affected to believe that the *State Register* was attempting to combine the Mormon vote with that of northern Illinois to outbalance the south.[40] Even in 1846 the democrats were charged with encouraging the retention of enough Mormon votes in the county to secure the triumph of the democratic candidates,[41] though the democrats denied that the Mormon vote had been necessary for the triumph of their candidate.

So after having for six years played a leading rôle in the life of Illinois, the Mormons disappeared from its history save as the state in future years had to bear its part in the solution of the problem of Mormonism in Utah.[42] After full allowance is made for the violence and perhaps the greed of the opponents of the Mormons in Illinois, it must be admitted that they saw clearly how terrible an excrescence on the political life of the state the Mormon community would be, once it had attained full growth. Because legal means would not protect them from the danger they used violence. The machinery of state government was then, it must be remembered, but a slight affair; and to enforce the will of public opinion, the resort to private war, though to be deplored, was inevitable.

[39] *Sangamo Journal*, August 22, 1844; *Alton Telegraph*, August 24, 1844; *Illinois State Register*, October 4, 11, November 8, 1844; *Chicago Democrat*, August 28, 1844.
[40] April 17, July 24, 1845.
[41] *Sangamo Journal*, January 1, March 12, 1846.
[42] A few members, many of them relatives of Joseph Smith, refused to follow Young and remained in Illinois where their descendants are still to be found in Hancock county. Here they continue to worship in the Reorganized Church of Jesus Christ of Latter Day Saints.

XX. THE SLAVERY QUESTION

THE slavery question in Illinois remained in a state of quiescence for at least a decade after the decision of the convention struggle. The black laws remained and even increased in severity; the shameful kidnapping of free blacks out of the state went on in defiance of legislation, aided in some sections by a proslavery public opinion which was prone to sooth itself with the excuse of the kidnappers that they recovered runaway slaves for their masters and therefore were merely vindicators of a just property right. On the other hand the underground railroad had its obscure beginnings as the escaping Negroes found sympathy and assistance at an increasing number of doors; there were always communities in the state where the slave was safe from his hunters. Little interest in the antislavery movement was publicly evidenced. In 1831 a Presbyterian layman of Bond county — that source of much propaganda in early Illinois — William M. Stewart by name, put forth a vigorous protest against the toleration of slavery by the churches. On January 9, 1831, an antislavery meeting at Shoal Creek, Bond county, made a vigorous protest against buying, selling, or holding slaves, declaring that the participation of its members in these things was a disgrace to the Presbyterian church. Along with the protest came the establishment of a local colonization society.[1]

During the next year or two the colonization movement attracted more notice, especially as it came to be contrasted favorably with abolition. The increased activity of the abolitionists and the gag rules began to bring the subject of slavery under wider discussion. The *Sangamo Journal, Alton Spectator, and Chicago American* were all strongly anti-aboli-

[1] *Illinois Intelligencer,* February 19, March 12, 19, May 7, 1831.

tion in their utterances. The *Alton Telegraph,* on the other hand, denounced the gag and interference with the right of petition in round terms.[2] It is rather hard to define the attitude of the Illinois representatives in the national house of representatives on the subject. They voted for the gag resolution designed to cut off abolition petitions in 1836; but on motions and petitions involved in Adams' diplomatic fencing with his adversaries, the delegation, Zadoc Casey particularly, occasionally voted with him. In Illinois the general assembly in the session of 1837 passed some violent anti-abolition resolutions. These passed the senate unanimously; but in the house, Abraham Lincoln, Andrew McCormick, Gideon Minor, John H. Murphy, Parven Paullin, and Dan Stone cast their votes in the negative. Before the end of the session, Abraham Lincoln and Dan Stone recorded on the *Journals* of the house their formal protest against the resolutions. Declaring their belief that abolition agitation tended to increase rather than diminish the evils of slavery, they pronounced the peculiar institution founded on injustice and bad policy; and they based their dissent to the abolition of slavery in the District of Columbia, not on the lack of power on the part of congress to do away with slavery there, but on the fact that congress should act only on the petition of the people of the district. In view of the increasing rage against abolitionism rising in the state and even more in the country at large, the men who signed this document took their political futures in their hands.[3]

In originating abolition propaganda in Illinois even the bold act of the man destined to be the freer of the slaves takes for the time second place to that of the martyr of abolitionism, Elijah Parish Lovejoy. At the time of his death, Lovejoy had just attained the age of thirty-five years. He was born in

[2] *Sangamo Journal,* November 3, 1832, May 11, September 21, 1833, August 6, 1836; *Illinois Advocate,* January 19, 1833; *Alton Spectator,* November 19, 1835, February 19, 1836; *Alton Telegraph,* February 17, 1836; *Chicago American,* September 5, 1835.

[3] *Congressional Debates,* 1834–1835, p. 1141; 1835–1836, p. 2535, 2608, 2660, 2662, 2779, 4051; *House Journal,* 1837, 1 session, 311; *Senate Journal,* 1837, 1 session, 297.

Maine, the son of a Presbyterian clergyman. He had graduated from Waterville College and at the age of twenty-five set
out to seek his fortune in the west, becoming first school teacher
and then newspaper editor in St. Louis. In 1832 he entered the
ministry and in 1833 graduated from Princeton Theological
Seminary and returned to St. Louis to edit a religious paper,
the *St. Louis Observer*. Lovejoy's fearlessness of speech in
an intolerant community soon led him into a series of difficulties. His paper manfully denounced the mob rule and disorder
that arose in St. Louis. When it struck straight from the
shoulder in denouncing the burning of a Negro by a St. Louis
mob in April, 1836, and expressed its indignation at the opinion of a judge, appropriately named Lawless, to the effect that
what was a crime when committed by one person was not such
when committed by a mob, the printing office was repeatedly
attacked and damaged. Lovejoy then moved his press to
Alton where the presence of a group of New England business
men, favorably known for piety and charity, seemed to offer it
a better field. It was destroyed presumably by a St. Louis mob
immediately after it was landed, but indignation in Alton found
expression in a public meeting which promised funds for a new
press. The meeting denounced abolition in vigorous terms;
and Lovejoy, while declaring his antislavery principles and his
determination to publish what he pleased in his paper, declared
he was not an abolitionist.

It is doubtful if Henrik Ibsen ever saw the newspaper
materials in which lie hidden the outlines of the story of the
tragedy staged at Alton, but the tragedy of Lovejoy is the
tragedy of Brand in real life almost to the letter. Lovejoy
mentally and spiritually was a Puritan of the Puritans. His
paper in every issue reveals the sharp, unflinching New England view of life. There are no sentimental and emotional
tales or religious appeals; Lovejoy was content with preaching
obedience to the law of God rather than ravishing his hearers
with the divine love. His temperance preaching was not the
usual sentimental appeal for the drunkard's wife and children

but hard common sense or biting contempt. There was much politics, much practical agriculture, clipped into the paper. In fact it might have been framed for entrance to a balanced, regulated, disciplined New England home.

Lovejoy's denunciations of vice were sharp and hard. He referred to a French dancer, then the rage in New York, as " Celeste, the obscene and lascivious danceress (danseuse she calls herself)." "This," he continued, "is no longer the country of the Pilgrims. Parisian courtesans are paid $26,000 per quarter for the indecent exposure of their persons in public." [4] The popularity of the dancer he believed but one more instance of the luxury and licentiousness, the apologizing for slavery, the sabbath breaking that had accompanied the speculative rage and money madness of the last few years. This attitude inevitably irritated the free and easy westerner, and to this irritation the character of the well-to-do New England merchants prominent among Lovejoy's supporters must have added. "Although," said the proceedings of an anti-abolition meeting of July, "the combination of wealth, interest, and moral power were assiduously brought to bear upon the community in order to deter them from such a course—yet like men born to live and die untrammeled by party,—by mercenary motives, they met as freemen." [5] Further, John Mason Peck, who was already editing the *Western Pioneer* at Alton, had for some time looked on Lovejoy and his methods with ill-concealed dislike.[6] Peck could not indorse Lovejoy's statement that the way to stop mobs was to hang a few mobbers; Peck, while a New Englander, was not a Puritan.

In this situation events were drawing Lovejoy's attention irresistibly to the subject of slavery. He believed that the old and new school split in the Presbyterian church was caused by slavery, and during the first half of the year 1837 he was drawing nearer and nearer to abolition. On June 8, he urged the

[4] *Alton Observer,* May 25, 1837.
[5] *Alton Telegraph,* July 19, 1837.
[6] *Western Pioneer,* July 29, 1836, March 29, October 27, 1837.

formation of an antislavery church in St. Louis; and, on July 6, he called for the organization of a state antislavery society. The charge began to spread that Lovejoy had violated a supposed pledge not to publish an antislavery newspaper. He was threatened with violence, and on the night of August 21 his press was destroyed. The *Telegraph* (August 23) termed the act an outrage. A second press was obtained and destroyed on September 21. Still a third press was ordered, and meanwhile Lovejoy was subjected to continual threat of mob violence. At St. Charles, Missouri, only the bravery of his wife saved him from a mob.[7]

In the hope of finding some way to restore order and peace at Alton public meetings were held in the first days of November. Lovejoy stood out for his right to be heard. He delivered an eloquent and impressive but uncompromising defense of his course. It might have had its effect had not Usher F. Linder's insane desire to exhibit oratory of a type more pleasing to western audiences caused him to take the floor after Lovejoy and destroy the effect of the latter's words. The *Pioneer* hoped that the meeting of the colonization society, the invariable counter-irritant to abolition, might set things on the right path even though "a very few restless spirits will be disappointed, vexed, mortified, and may struggle for a little time to enjoy notoriety" only to find that "the benevolent and real friends to humanity will co-operate to benefit the oppressed in a way consistent with the peace of our Union and the happiness and rights of all concerned."[8]

For a time Lovejoy may have hesitated. The story is well authenticated that he handed to the *Telegraph* editor a note resigning as editor of the *Observer*. A friend of Lovejoy's asked to borrow it, and it was never returned. Lovejoy had finally resolved, if indeed he had ever faltered, to force the issue then and there. A third press was landed at Alton and

[7] *Alton Observer*, June and July, December 28, 1837; *Western Pioneer*, July 29, 1836; *Alton Telegraph*, September 27, October 4, 1837; Harris, *History of Negro Slavery in Illinois*, 80 ff.; *Illinois State Register*, October 6, 1837.

[8] *Western Pioneer*, October 27, 1837.

stored in the warehouse of Godfrey, Gilman, and Company. A few men under the command of Enoch Long undertook to guard it there. On the night of November 7 a mob attacked the warehouse. In the first assault one of the attackers was mortally wounded. In a second, they attempted to fire the wooden roof of the warehouse. Lovejoy and a few more sallied out to prevent it. A first volley drove the attackers away from their ladder. A second sortie was made for the same purpose, and Lovejoy fell mortally wounded. The besieged gave up the fight and fled; the mob broke into the warehouse and threw the press into the river.

The murder of Lovejoy was a thing not done in a corner; it trumpeted the ill-fame of Alton to the ends of the United States and placed on the name of the city that aspired for commercial prominence a brand that has scarcely been removed even up to the present time. Probably to most of the people of the United States the word which associates itself intuitively with the name of Alton is Lovejoy. The papers of the north, and many in the south, some nearby like the *Peoria Register* spoke out manfully in condemnation of this assault on the freedom of the press and of speech even while they condemned abolition. In later days the abolitionists took pleasure in believing that the curse of God had fallen upon the city.[9]

Alton was not convinced. The defenders of the warehouse were indicted for "resisting an attack made by certain persons unknown to destroy a printing press" and "unlawfully defending a certain ware-house." In spite of the fact that Linder prosecuted, the defenders were acquitted, as were the assailants. The *Telegraph* was thoroughly cowed and protested it was best to say nothing which would stir up further ill-feeling. Peck's *Pioneer* at the time expressed its opinion that denunciation would do no good.[10] Six months after the Lovejoy affair

---

[9] *Peoria Register*, November 18, 1837; *Illinois State Register*, November 24, 1837; *Western Citizen*, May 18, 1843, April 20, 1847; *Alton Telegraph*, June 28, 1845.
[10] *Western Pioneer*, May 11, 1838; *Alton Telegraph*, November 15, 29, 1837, June 24, 1838.

was over, it undertook to justify its course in allaying excitement among an exasperated people. "But they (the editors of the *Pioneer*) believed in gospel expediency. They had not discarded the old fashioned virtue of prudence, and a due regard to consequences. And they have not the least occasion to regret their course. . . . An entire revolution has been produced. Moral influence, religion, temperance, order, respect for law, a better understanding of each other's rights, have all been gainers. A revival of religion in most of the congregations in that city, and the conversion of more than one hundred souls — the progress of the temperance cause, — of sound morality — of quiet and good order, of a spirit of kind feeling amongst all parties are the proofs."[11]

Doubtless long and tedious wars with "two seed Baptists" and similar opponents had blunted the edge of Peck's New England conscience to accord with the dictates of expediency and prudence that he so blandly preached over the corpse of the man he had disliked in life. Because Peck had learned the lesson of prudence he had twenty years more of a peaceful and useful career to round out. Because the high temper of Lovejoy's Puritanism would not let him repress an iota of what he conceived it his duty to say, because he would not spare a word or swerve an inch from his path, he died at thirty-five leaving a nerve-wrecked and destitute wife. Yet his career and death had not, as Peck easily supposed, merely caused an awakened revival of formal religion. The shadow of the Puritan had fallen across the page of Illinois history, not to recede.

For Illinois Lovejoy was the protomartyr of a movement already under way — the organization of the antislavery forces in Illinois. On July 4, 1836, an antislavery society in Putnam county held its second semiannual meeting. Early in 1837 an antislavery society was organized in Will county, and one was meeting in Bureau county, one in Jersey and one in Adams

[11] *Western Pioneer*, June 1, 1838.

(formed in 1836), and one in Macoupin. On July 6, Lovejoy had issued a call for the formation of a state antislavery society. Delegates met at Alton, October 27, but Linder with others got possession of the meeting and passed anti-abolition resolutions. Next evening, however, the antislavery men organized by themselves.[12] There was the usual attempt in various parts of the state to apply the counter-irritant of colonization to these ebullitions of abolitionism.

Though Lovejoy was gone there were men left to take up his work. On April 2, 1838, a meeting at Princeton resolved that an antislavery newspaper should again be established at Alton, but in September a meeting at Hennepin resolved to support Benjamin Lundy, who had grown old in the editing of abolition papers, with the *Genius of Universal Emancipation* at Hennepin, Illinois. The paper first appeared late in 1838, being actually printed at Lowell nearby, though dated at Hennepin. The issue of February 26 recorded the meeting of the Illinois antislavery society, and through its columns there began to pass the resolutions of the county societies denouncing slavery as contrary to the law of God and to natural right. Lundy showed a fine reasonableness, as for instance when he refused to attack an old antislavery warrior like John Quincy Adams because he was not an abolitionist. He was inclined to disapprove the uncompromising attitude of Garrison as tending to divide supporters of the cause by his vagaries. But Lundy's long warfare was at an end. On July 19, 1839, he apologized for missing a week's issue; a small wheat harvest had required the editor's care. If, he wrote gallantly, some country editors would farm a little they might write more independently. Next week he had to apologize for a lack of editorial matter because of a light fever which had yielded to treatment. On August 23, a paper with head line dated the sixteenth announced that he had died of a bilious fever on Au-

[12] *Chicago American*, August 6, 1836, April 1, 1837; Harris, *History of Negro Slavery in Illinois*, 82, 87, 125; *Alton Observer*, June 15, July 13, August 3, 17, 1837; *Alton Telegraph*, November 1, 1837; *Illinois State Register*, September 15, October 13, 1837.

gust 22.[13] The last number of the paper appeared on September 13, 1839.

A new paper, the Lowell *Genius of Liberty*, was begun December 19, 1840, by Zebina Eastman, a former associate of Lundy, and by Hooper Warren. Warren edited it with acid reminiscences of the old struggle of 1822–1824 in which he had participated. In 1842 the paper, transferred to Chicago under Eastman's editorship, became the *Western Citizen*. Its circulation, which soon entitled it to claim patronage as an advertising medium, was an indication that the movement was gaining fast.[14]

Meanwhile the work of agitation and organization in the state had advanced. In 1838, Reverend Chauncey Cook was chosen traveling agent of the state society, and he also labored with effect in enrolling members and forming new societies. For a time Cook and Reverend W. T. Allen, the traveling agents, had to support themselves by collections. In southern Illinois they encountered mobs and refusals of churches in which to hold meetings. In 1843–1844 they again invaded the south, but with not dissimilar results.[15]

The antislavery men in Illinois had launched their cause in politics; in 1840 they cast one hundred votes for James G. Birney for president. Next year at a state society meeting, despite opposition from many who opposed political action of any sort, partly on the ground of the iniquity of acting under a United States constitution which supported slavery, it was resolved that no antislavery man should vote for any proslavery candidates. A convention in the third district nominated Frederick Collins for congress, and he obtained 527 votes. In 1842, at the call of a state correspondence commit-

[13] *Peoria Register*, April 14, October 6, 1838; Harris, *History of Negro Slavery in Illinois*, 126; *Genius of Universal Emancipation*, March 8, 29, June 28, July 26, August 25, 1839.

[14] Harris, *History of Negro Slavery in Illinois*, 135; *Western Citizen*, September 7, 14, 1843, March 21, 1844, August 28, 1845, June 3, 1846.

[15] Harris, *History of Negro Slavery in Illinois*, 129, 131; *Genius of Universal Emancipation*, July 5, 1834, January 30, April 24, June 5, 1841; *Western Citizen*, August 3, November 9, 1843, April 5, June 20, July 23, 1844.

tee, a liberty convention was held at Chicago which nominated
a candidate for governor and urged in its resolutions nominations for all local offices. It defined its position as resistance
to the advance of the slave power rather than unconstitutional
opposition to it. It savagely arraigned the national losses and
misfortunes of the last few years as the work of the southern
slavocracy, and for the state it demanded the repeal of the
black laws. In 1844, the party put a presidential electoral
ticket in the field which received 3,469 votes. In 1846 it
adopted an elaborate plan of organization, reaching down even
to the school districts for the gubernatorial campaign.[16] It
declared alike against the annexation of Texas, the black laws,
and Garrisonism. Its vote for governor ran up to 5,147, and
in the fourth district Owen Lovejoy received 3,531 votes for
congress.

    Antislavery in Illinois in the forties was the center of a
whirlpool of new ideas in politics and in life that is the delight
of the student of human belief. When men are thinking intensely on one ideal, others group around it. Thus in 1839 a
peace society at Mission Institute near Quincy adopted resolutions declaring that wars promoted for the glory of rulers were
paid for by their subjects. Women participated on an equality
with men in antislavery societies, despite the sneers of whig
editors; and this participation led to discussion of woman's
rights. The new wine of Garrisonian abolition, however, was
a little too strong to be safely introduced into the bottles of
Illinois antislavery effort; a nonresistance and the alleged in-
fidelity of Garrison were usually eschewed as stumblingblocks
to antislavery men in southern Illinois.[17] There were, however, denunciations of holding communion with churches or
mission boards that tolerated slavery and declarations that

    [16] Harris, *History of Negro Slavery in Illinois*, 146, 147, 155; *Western
Citizen*, July 26, 1842, April 6, 1843, June 3, 10, 1846; *Genius of Universal
Emancipation*, February 6, 27, May 29, June 19, 1841; *Genius of Liberty*, Jan-
uary 1, 1842.
    [17] *Genius of Universal Emancipation*, August 30, 1839; *Western Citizen*,
November 2, 1843, May 2, June 20, September 7, 1844, September 22, October
13, 1846, February 23, 1847.

agnostics who were liberty men were better than christians who were not.

The theoretical antislavery argument is a magnificent thing to the student of ideas. On the one hand it begins with the statement that to justify slavery it is necessary to twist and alter the principles of the American Revolution and of the Declaration of Independence. On the other it built its foundation on the old Puritan concept, in which seventeenth century Englishmen had sought their guidance, of the law of God. The Puritan in Illinois in 1840 walked as genuinely as his English predecessor had done two centuries before in the faith that the law of God remained binding upon rulers and people and that any enactment or practice contrary to it was null and void. This to them was not an abrogation of human law but rather its fulfillment, for only where the divine law ruled could there be perfect liberty. To the antislavery men the law of nature and the common law of the land were alike in accord with the law of God in opposition to slavery. How could a slave father train up his child in the nurture and admonition of the Lord as the divine law bade him? Owen Lovejoy went back to Coke to find the law of nature in opposition to slavery.[18] And when James Wallace of Hill Prairie, Randolph county, sat down to write against slavery under the haughty caption of the old Puritan challenge: "The supremacy of God and the equality of man," Puritans reached over two centuries to guide his pen, so that one might almost swear his discourses were plagiarized from forgotten pamphlets written in the seventeenth century by such champions of freedom as Lilburne and Overton. The leaven of Puritanism remained unchanged.

On the political side, it was inevitable that antislavery propaganda should deal with economic conditions. The temptation to blame slavery for hard times was too great. Thus in 1843 Alvan Stewart attributed hard times to the fact that in the south but one person in five was a laborer, that therefore for

[18] *Western Citizen*, November 20, 1842, March 30, April 20, July 27, September 14, 1843, March 28, 1844, November 3, 1846, February 9, 23, June 22, 1847.

sustenance the south had borrowed three hundred millions of northern labor and then had failed. More significant by far was the idea advocated by William Goodell, which spread as far as Illinois, that the true course of the party was to stand for the right of the white as well as for the colored laborer and to advocate free trade and direct taxation. The repeal of the English corn laws seemed destined to let the product of the free laborer of the north into England as well as that of the slave laborers of the south. In 1847 Goodell, issuing a call for a national convention of the free-trade wing of the liberty party, based it on the highest and best ideals of democracy — the inalienable rights of men to trade freely and to use the earth freely — therefore, no tariffs, no laws permitting land monopoly, and no laws permitting slavery. An Illinois man, G. T. Gaston, wrote to the *Western Citizen* urging similar doctrine, on the ground that if the liberty party were to be a well-rounded party, it must have a complete policy.[19]

One wonders what might have chanced, had the liberty men in 1847, perhaps on a less radical platform, been able to unite with what was best in the democratic party and set forth on a crusade for the liberty of labor of whatever color the laborer might be. Wentworth for years had preached genuine democracy to the people of northern Illinois, except for the inevitable concession to the south in the matter of slavery. In 1847 the rejection of river and harbor improvement by southern votes had driven him and many another northern democratic politician to the point of revolt against slavery. It was one of these rare moments when the faces of men seemed turned directly toward the millennium.

It was not to be. The sins of the southern aristocracy were not yet full. The policy of "one-idealism" — of confining the party to the antislavery issue — triumphed in the liberty party. The *Western Citizen* preached it assiduously, perhaps from dread of Wentworth's skill in pilfering votes from abo-

[19] *Western Citizen*, April 27, 1843, July 7, September 1, 1846, January 19, May 25, October 12, 1847.

litionists.[20] Wentworth professed himself satisfied with the nomination of Cass and fell back into his party, though always a disturbing element in it because of his championship of justice and common sense. When a great antislavery party arose, it was to draw its principles except on slavery from the whigs rather than from the democrats; and fifty years of wandering in the wilderness have been necessary to make the American people realize as a nation that while rejecting slavery, they accepted the principles that their forefathers rejected when offered to them by Clay and Webster.

In the attitude of the Illinois churches on slavery one has a study of interest, fascinating because of its vagaries and inconsistencies. There was for instance the little Reformed Presbyterian group at Sparta and Eden who on occasion went so far as to pronounce the dissolution of a union tainted with slavery as not the worst misfortune that might befall. The church at Hill Prairie in 1843 sent to congress a strenuous antislavery petition. In northern Illinois the Presbyterian churches and synods gave repeated testimony against the sin of slaveholding and repeated declarations that they would have no fellowship with slaveholders. On the other hand, the Alton Presbytery discreetly smothered such a resolution in 1844. A northern Congregational church occasionally hedged on similar tests, but generally the churches of this communion were outspoken in favor of antislavery.[21]

Methodism hardly gave so many evidences of protest against the general proslavery attitude of the order as did Presbyterianism. The antislavery leaders came to expect opposition from the Methodists. One finds appeals to the Illinois conferences to take a decisive stand against the institution. In 1844 a "Wesleyan" circuit was formed on Fox river on the principle of "no fellowship with slavery." There were about

[20] July 7, September 8, 15, 1846, January 5, May 18, July 27, 1847.
[21] *Western Citizen*, July 26, 1842, January 25, May 2, July 4, 25, 1844; *Belleville Advocate*, October 25, November 1, 1845; Presbytery of Ottawa, *Minutes*, May 25, 1843; Synod of Peoria, *Minutes*, December 7, 1843, December 11, 1845; *Genius of Liberty*, September 18, 1841.

eleven churches on it and twenty appointments. There was a hot antislavery protest from Methodists at Florid as early as 1839. In 1845, however, in connection with the case of Bishop Andrews, antislavery pronouncements began to appear in the ranks of the Methodists proper. Still, next year the *Western Citizen* complained that the Rock River conference had done nothing but denounce abolitionists in its last meetings.[22] A year later the *Visitor* accused it of trying to cover up attacks on its members for holding and selling slaves.

The Baptists dealt more in accord with their inherent centrifugal qualities. In 1843 the *Citizen* complained that in Shurtleff College free speech on slavery was gagged. The Northwest Baptist Association, it was complained, defeated by trickery in 1844 a non-fellowship pronouncement. In the same year an antislavery mass meeting of all the Baptist churches in Illinois was called to meet at Warrenville. This meeting called for the establishment of an antislavery newspaper and accordingly on January 16, 1845, the Elgin *Western Christian* began publication under the direction of the Northwestern Baptist Antislavery Convention. In its first number it explained its appearance by the disappearance of the *Northwest Baptist*, as a result, it claimed, of an attempt to remain neutral on the slavery issue. It attacked in the course of the year the Quincy and Illinois river associations for not standing up to the issue. The paper was not abolitionist, but it was outspoken against slavery, and it maintained a war on the *Baptist Helmet* for printing advertisements of Negroes committed to jail. The Universalists were frankly antislavery, but the Episcopalian bishop, Philander Chase of Jubilee College, was repeatedly attacked for hedging.[23] With Chase the needs of his dear college swallowed up all other considerations.

[22] *Genius of Liberty*, March 29, 1839, July 10, November 27, 1841; *Western Citizen*, July 26, 1842, August 3, 1843, March 21, 1844, February 13, 1845, September 15, 1846; *Sangamo Journal*, June 5, 1845.

[23] *Western Citizen*, April 27, December 14, 1843, October 31, December 26, 1844, September 15, October 20, 1846; *Western Christian*, August 14, 22, 1845; *Baptist Helmet*, July 16, August 13, 1845; in 1844 the Quincy association voted down an antislavery resolution and Elgin did the same on September 19, 1844.

In considering the existence of slavery in Illinois, it is necessary to review a line of supreme court decisions which defined its nominal status, remembering always that, since the slave or Negro was less capable than his owner of defending his alleged rights, the probability is that much illegal servitude existed. Legally whatever servitude there was had to be based on the territorial act of September 17, 1807, as adopted by the Illinois legislature on December 13, 1812. This act allowed the bringing into Illinois of Negroes above fifteen years of age owing service or labor and the indenturing them for terms of years; Negroes so brought in under the age of fifteen could be held, the males till thirty-five years old and the females till thirty-two. Children born of them were to serve, the males until the age of thirty and the females until the age of twenty-eight. Further the act provided for the registration of Negroes brought into the territory, who might lawfully be held till thirty-five or thirty-two years old. Between these two classes of registered and indentured Negroes, as will be seen, the courts were later to distinguish. The state constitution prohibited the further introduction of slavery except for the indenturing of persons of age while at perfect freedom. It required, however, that all persons indentured without fraud or collusion should serve out the terms of their indentures and that registered Negroes should serve out their appointed times; and it provided that children born of them thereafter should become free, males at twenty-one, females at eighteen.

In the twenties the state supreme court decided that indentures to be valid must correspond with the form prescribed by the act of 1807 and that registered Negroes might be sold like other property.[24] But in Phoebe v. Jay in the December term of 1828, Justice Lockwood undertook an analysis of the whole legal support of existing slavery in Illinois. He pronounced the act of 1807 in contravention of the Ordinance of 1787 and therefore *per se* void. Whatever validity it had arose from

[24] Cornelius v. Cohen, *1 Illinois (Breese)*, 131; see also Choisser v. Hargrave, *2 Illinois (1 Scammon)*, 317 (318); Nance v. Howard, *1 Illinois (Breese)*, 242; Phoebe v. Jay, *1 Illinois (Breese)*, 268.

the constitutional confirmation of indentures and property rights arising from it. Indeed he pronounced that nothing less than the voice of the people in their sovereign capacity could have rendered such contracts of effect. A legislative reënforcement would have been of no avail. The Ordinance of 1787, he believed, had been so far abrogated by the implied assent of the people of the state and of congress in framing the constitution and in accepting it.

In 1836 the legal basis for existing slavery was sharply reduced by the decision in Boon v. Juliet. Speaking for the court, Judge T. W. Smith pronounced it illegal to hold to service the child of a servant registered under the act of 1807. He argued that the constitutional allowance of service from children of registered Negroes was based on a misapprehension of the intent of the act of 1807 and as designed to limit that act could not be interpreted to confer a right not granted by it. It had in no way affected the rights of the children of registered Negroes; and, anything in the constitution to the contrary therefore, they remained free. In 1840 and 1841 the court emphasized the fact that the freedom of a Negro must be assumed unless proof of his being legally held to servitude by indenture or otherwise was forthcoming.[25]

In 1843 Andrew Borders, a slaveholder of Randolph county, was involved in a suit designed to test once more the validity of the act of 1807 as it concerned indentured servants. For the slave, Trumbull and Koerner argued that the Ordinance of 1787 was still binding in every respect and would be until every state of the original thirteen consented to abrogate it,[26] and that as the territorial indenture laws were nullities no constitutional provision could be construed to give them effect. Judge Scates, however, went back to the old reasoning in his decision. The old law remained,[27] though in the case of Jarrot

[25] Kinney v. Cook, 4 Illinois (3 Scammon), 232; Bailey v. Cromwell et al., 4 Illinois (3 Scammon), 71.
[26] Borders v. Borders, 5 Illinois (4 Scammon), 341.
[27] Jarrot v. Jarrot, 7 Illinois (2 Gilman), 1. I can not see that this necessarily ended holding by indenture as is usually supposed.

Jarrot, the court decided that in view of the prohibition of 1787, slavery could not exist in the state even in the case of a Negro descended from the slave of a French *habitant* of the days before George Rogers Clark. To the end the best legal opinion of the state laid upon the state's own constituent assembly and the state's own conscience the sole responsibility for the continuance of slavery in its borders.

Several decisions were needed to define exactly the right of masters to bring their slaves into or through the state and as to the rights of free Negroes within it. In 1842 Judge Treat in the circuit court of Sangamon county had decided the law of 1829 allowing the taking up and selling of the blacks without freedom papers to be unconstitutional. In 1843 John D. Caton in a decision in the circuit court of Bureau county laid down the principle that a slave voluntarily brought to the state was thereby freed.[28] That same year, however, in Willard v. People, Scates laid down the principle that the slave of a master passing through the state was not therefore freed.

Fine legal distinctions and principles apart, slavery and antislavery men in Illinois contended as light and darkness. Kidnapping on a wholesale scale went on in the south; at Shawneetown an attempt was made to sell south sixty free blacks on the pretext of flaws in their papers of manumission. On the other side there was as much assiduity and as much provoking defiance in the attitude of those who sought to help runaways to escape. In 1844, Cross was in jail for seeking to help runaways to escape. The year before Owen Lovejoy was indicted in Bureau county for helping two Negro women — the occasion of Caton's decision. In 1843 too, Dr. Richard Eells of Quincy was, in the circuit court under Stephen A. Douglas, fined $400 for aiding a fugitive slave, a decision later sustained by Judge Shields of the Illinois supreme court. On the strength of the notoriety gained in this case Eells was elected president of the Illinois Antislavery Society in 1843 and nominated as the liberty party candidate for governor in 1846.

[28] Harris, *History of Negro Slavery in Illinois*, 109, 112.

Chicago was a dramatic center of activity. In 1846 a mob of some two thousand assisted in spiriting away two fugitive slaves under the very nose of a justice of the peace. At Chicago and in Kendall county, Negroes put up to sale were hired out for twenty-five cents and similar sums. Slaveholders were served notice by the *Western Citizen* that if their slaves ever reached northern Illinois their chance of recovering them was slim, and a Kane county convention in the same year resolved that Kane county was as safe for runaways as Canada. In its issue of July 13, 1844, the *Western Citizen* printed a cartoon of the underground railway that is perhaps Illinois' first political newspaper cartoon. Missouri slave hunters on the other hand threatened and perhaps did commit arson in revenge and offered rewards for the delivery across the river of prominent officials of the underground railway. In the Illinois legislature petitions began to appear against the black code, with whig as well as abolitionist support; and on the other side measures were passed penalizing the assisting of fugitive slaves.[29]

The slavery conflict too had its reflection more and more in national politics within the state. *The Chicago American* was disposed to praise John Quincy Adams' stand on the right of petition. In 1842–1843 all the Illinois representatives voted against abolition petitions. In 1843–1844 all the representatives but Hardin voted for the gag resolutions; but the next year the abolition vote had perhaps caused Wentworth to see the light, and he had voted with Hardin against the gag. In the election of 1844 the whigs had been inclined to play for abolition votes, and such papers as the *Citizen* endeavored to head them off by attacks on Clay. After the election they attempted to lay on the shoulders of the abolitionists the blame for the admission of Texas to the union by the proslavery

[29] *Sangamo Journal*, December 5, 1844, January 16, April 3, 1845; *Western Citizen*, November 18, 1842, January 13, March 23, 30, November 2, 1843, January 11, July 18, August 3, December 11, 1844, February 20, March 6, 1845, June 23, October 27, November 5, 17, 1846; *Chicago American*, April 25, 1842; *Illinois State Register*, January 24, 1845; *Belleville Advocate*, May 6, 1845; *Chicago Daily Journal*, January 9, 28, March 12, 1845.

democrats of the south. They affected to believe that at Chicago the *Democrat* and the *Citizen* were trying to break up the whig party and to divide it on the issues of abolitionism and nativism.[30] And they entreated the southern whigs not to be misled by such attempts.

It was the democratic party, however, that was destined to be broken by the slavery issue. Wentworth, in his opposition to the southern leaders of his party on rivers and harbors and the tea and coffee tax, moved toward antislavery in politics so far as the Wilmot proviso. This action the *Western Citizen* ascribed to the influence of Lewis Cass. Wentworth nevertheless was the only Illinois member who supported the Wilmot proviso in 1846, Douglas, Ficklin, Hoge, and McClernand voting to lay it on the table and Baker and Smith not voting. The whig papers in Illinois, while continuing to berate the abolitionists severely, especially for opposing the Mexican War, were inclined to be antislavery in their attitude. In the next session Wentworth's opposition to the south and to southern measures was as strongly marked as ever, but Hoge was the only other Illinois member he could draw with him on the vote for the proviso. In the coming election Wentworth affected to believe that it would be a northern democrat against a slaveholder such as Taylor; and he naturally denounced as mere pretense the whig antislavery attitude, in view of their prospective candidate. He was disposed to have the democrats stand against slavery and for free trade on necessities not provided by American labor.[31]

A little more than two decades since the decision of the state on the exclusion of slavery had seen the question develop

[30] *Chicago American*, March 16, 1842, December 11, 1844, March 31, 1845; *Congressional Globe*, 27 congress, 3 session, 31, 106, 28 congress, 1 session, 56, 133, 28 congress, 2 session, 7. *Western Citizen*, December 21, 1843, March 28, May 23, June 27, July 18, 1844; *Illinois State Register*, April 26, 1844; *Chicago Democrat*, April 28, 1844; *Chicago Daily Journal*, March 11, 15, 21, 1845; *Alton Telegraph*, March 22, 1845.

[31] *Chicago Democrat*, February 2, 23, March 2, June 30, 1846, February 9, March 2, 30, April 27, May 11, 25, 1847; *Western Citizen*, July 28, 1846; *Congressional Globe*, 29 congress, 1 session 1217, 29 congress, 2 session, 425; *Chicago Daily Journal*, March 17, June 13, August 26, 1846; *Sangamo Journal*, September 17, 1846.

in unexpected ways. A process of legal limitation on the toleration of slavery and indenture was to have been expected. But otherwise as against the lawless kidnapping of free blacks always prevalent, there had arisen on the antislavery side an elastic organization for the assistance of runaway slaves. Garrisonian abolitionism arose in the east and spread to Illinois, quickening the minds of intelligent men whether they approved or disapproved. Antislavery sentiment waxed till once more it could support newspapers and muster respectable votes for its candidates. Thirty years after the admission of Illinois to the union, the United States was once more riven on the question of slavery; and the two great political parties that had meanwhile developed on other issues were, as against the abolition and liberty parties, seeking their advantage in it.

XXI. ILLINOIS IN FERMENT

THE closing years of the period under review witnessed the eager efforts of Illinois to find itself economically. From 1830 to 1840 the population had grown from 157,000 to 476,000; and still growing, the state was trying to give expression to the pent-up energy within it. Experiments flourished; the inhabitants of Illinois, conscious of hidden riches, sought by means of a diversity of crops, a multiplication of towns, and sectional divisions to discover the key which would unlock the treasure and open the way to high reward.

Farmers began to grope somewhat uncertainly for better methods in securing the bounty of the rich prairie soil. In the late thirties and early forties the dwellers in the Illinois river counties led in the formation of county agricultural societies for the discussion of farm problems. In 1841 the Union Agricultural Society began publishing the *Union Agriculturist and Western Prairie Farmer*, which two years later became the *Prairie Farmer*, a newspaper that in time both directed and reflected the agricultural activities of the state.[1] Experiment followed experiment; flax, mustard seed, cotton, and tobacco, the cultivation of hemp, of the castor bean, and of the mulberry tree were in turn get-rich-quick crazes of the day. At one time a nursery in Peoria had 200,000 mulberries and 100,000 cuttings for sale; with every purchase of trees, silkworm eggs were furnished free. In 1841 agricultural societies were awarding prizes for the best cocoons.[2] The great staple crop still remained wheat; in 1833 the Illinois crop was esti-

[1] Scott, *Newspapers and Periodicals of Illinois*, 53.
[2] Bateman and Selby, *Historical Encyclopedia of Illinois*, 2:243-244; *History of Winnebago County*, 303-304.

mated at 1,500,000 bushels, and farmers were urged to plant more of it.[3]

There could be no great expansion in agricultural activities, however, without even greater improvements in implements. Throughout the thirties there was still in use the most primitive bar-share plows, which made no pretense of "scouring." In an effort to improve these, moldboards of cast-iron were first substituted, in turn to give way to those of polished steel. Necessity was, indeed, the mother of invention, and every blacksmith with a knack of "tinkering" was trying his hand at a plow. There was the early "Clark," then the "Diamond," the "Tobey and Anderson," the "Cary," the "Jewitt," with rivals not so well known in every county, all warranted to "scour."[4]

Efforts to improve or invent farm machinery were not confined to one form of labor-saving device. Cotton gins, headers, self-rakes, corn planters were tried out with varying success. An advertisement in the *Illinois Advocate* in 1835 declared that a machine had been invented that successfully performed the five operations of harrowing, opening the furrow, dropping and covering the seed corn, and finally, removing all clods not broken by the harrow. A letter to the *Alton Spectator* as early as 1833, while urging the farmers to clean their wheat better, suggested the use of the threshing machine; and this continued to be discussed until in 1846 and 1847 the reaping machines of Bachus and Fitch of Brochport and of Cyrus McCormick absorbed interest.[5] To the farmer on the treeless prairies of northern Illinois fencing was a problem — a very serious one. The earliest substitutes for rails were sod ditches or embankments; in 1839 thorn hedges began to be suggested; and by 1847 Jonathan Baldwin Turner had paused from his other interests to experiment with the possibilities

[3] *Illinois Advocate,* June 22, 1833.

[4] *Belleville Advocate,* March 10, 1842; Hicks, *History of Kendall County,* 400; Ballance, *History of Peoria,* 124-125; Rice, *Peoria,* 1:284.

[5] *Alton Spectator,* April 23, 1833; *Alton Telegraph,* August 21, 1841, August 9, 1845; *Chicago Daily Journal,* June 12, July 2, 24, 28, 1846.

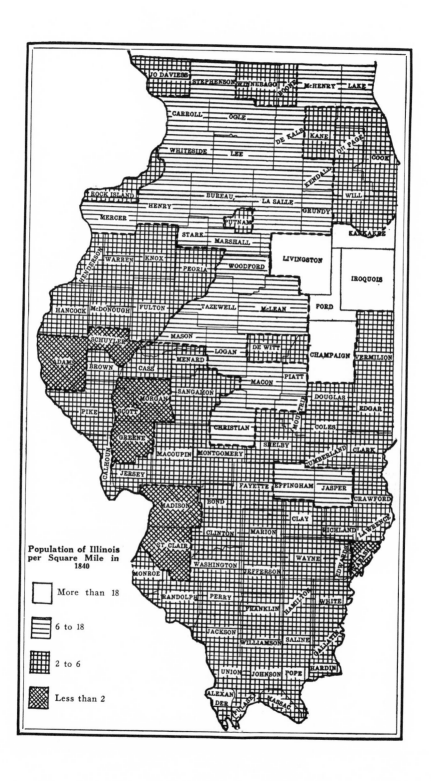

**Population of Illinois
per Square Mile in
1840**

More than 18

6 to 18

2 to 6

Less than 2

of the Osage orange which was to be popular until the advent of modern wire fencing.[6]

Throughout this period the handling of livestock in Illinois was, with a few rare exceptions, unscientific, inefficient, and haphazard. In the northern part of the state there was the very practical difficulty of housing and feeding during the severe winters. In 1836 Dr. J. W. S. Mitchell of Champaign county believed he had demonstrated that his herd of blooded shorthorn Durhams could be wintered as well as ordinary stock; a year later, however, he sold out.[7]

Aside from these practical considerations stock improvement met a curious and unintelligent opposition from the small farmers. Among the influential the necessity of developing better herds was so clear that "the legislature passed a law," writes Governor Ford, "for the improvement of the breed of cattle, by which small bulls were prohibited, under *severe* penalties, from running at large. On this last occasion no one dreamed that a hurricane of popular indignation was about to be raised, but so it was: the people took sides with the little bulls. The law was denounced as being aristocratic, and intended to favor the rich, who, by their money, had become possessed of large bulls, and were to make a profit by the destruction of the small ones."[8]

Leading stock growers of the day, notably Richard Flower, were as much interested in the raising of sheep as of cattle. Attempts were made to improve the breeds of sheep and to foster wool growing. Interest spread to such an extent that in 1842 wool in considerable quantities was brought to the Chicago market.[9]

Marketing of farm produce wove itself deeply into the business life of the state. Trade had many centers — every thriving village hoped to become an Alton. Belleville was

[6] *Sangamo Journal*, July 26, 1839, November 19, 1841; *Belleville Advocate,* October 7, 1847.

[7] *Western Citizen*, April 13, 1836.

[8] Ford, *History of Illinois*, 107-108.

[9] *Sangamo Journal*, December 17, 1841, October 23, 1842; *Chicago American,* June 27, 1842; *Alton Telegraph*, July 26, 1845.

boosted in season and out by a group of citizens headed by John Reynolds. The *Belleville Advocate* was eager that Belleville, closely allied to St. Louis in trade, should grow as its greater neighbor grew but pointed out the danger of being engulfed in the prosperity of that city. Farmers of the vicinity were urged to avail themselves of the advantages to be derived from marketing their goods at Belleville instead of at the larger place. It was pointed out that they avoided thereby the bad roads, inclement weather, the mishaps of the long trip, and the crossing of the Mississippi river, at times so dangerous, with the uncertainty of the market price at the end. In Belleville was a ready market for wheat and hogs at cash.[10]

Belleville papers were quick to resent the "cracking up" of the northern part of the state at the expense of the southern. They repudiated the idea that their section was made up of "swamps," and "low, flat, inundated prairies," that its population was "thriftless," or its seasons "sickly;" they stated that "notwithstanding the depression of all kinds of business, embarrassment from debt, and the number of emigrants that have left this part of the State within half-a-dozen years, the increase of the population in the counties south of a line drawn across the State from Alton by Vandalia to Palestine, from September, 1840, to September, 1845, by the State census, has been 48,574 in 32 counties . . . a gain of 31 per cent."[11] The *Belleville Advocate* for January 20, 1842, set forth how Illinois could be "disenthralled from her present prostrate condition. . . . The important object is to discover *the central river port* . . . whence the whole State might be recruited and resuscitated and which might be employed as the *commercial fulcrum,* moving either end of the State by its power of centrality — and where is this central point if not *opposite to St. Louis?* . . . If the State has now *small means,* the only rational plan is to select a spot where small

[10] *Belleville Advocate,* December 30, 1841, December 10,. 1846.
[11] *Ibid.,* July 2, 1846.

means will produce *the greatest amount of effect,* and where is this . . . but opposite St. Louis?"

In spite of jealous assertions that the population of Alton was declining and its population withdrawing, that city still held its commanding position as the market of the state. Its newspapers bitterly protested at the absurdity of irreverent legislators declaring that its market was glutted by one keg of butter and two dozen chickens. It pointed out its very real advantage over Chicago, where lake navigation was suspended by ice when Alton's port was still open. The *Telegraph* in 1847 declared that the older business houses had been swept away in the panic of 1837–1838, scarcely two or three out of forty or fifty surviving and that only a few of the former citizens remained. The ultimate consequences, however, were beneficial; business was on a better and more healthy basis; there was less selling to retailers on long credits, goods being sold for cash or produce. In the fall the *Telegraph* regularly celebrated the huge pork packing business done; it commented on the fact that more beef and pork packers were attracted to Alton year by year; and it assured the farmers that they could get the best prices there—better than at St. Louis or New Orleans, since Alton pork packers, in return for offal, paid ten cents for slaughtering. In 1843 farmers were bringing beeves to Alton to be slaughtered instead of selling them, as hitherto, to drovers to be driven to the eastern markets. The *Telegraph* was similarly loyal in its insistence that Alton was destined to be the grain market of the west.[12]

So strove the southern cities, while in the northern corner of the state, close to the lake it was rapidly controlling, Chicago waxed mighty. A shift in the avenue of trade assisted its growth. Ever since 1763 Philadelphia, and later Baltimore, had monopolized the trade in Illinois by way of the Ohio river. But clever advertising, offers of long credit, the building of the Erie canal had rapidly shifted this commerce from

[12] *Alton Telegraph,* January 4, March 21, 1840, June 23, November 13, 20, 1841, August 27, November 12, 1842, January 7, October 14, 21, 1843, October 19, 1844, October 11, 18, 1845.

Philadelphia and Baltimore to New York; and Chicago was the child of the new alliance.[13] In 1832 it had been a tiny market with two stores, and when incorporated the following year it had but little more than one hundred and fifty inhabitants. Then within the next few years there sprang up such an incredible mushroom growth as would seem to belie stability. In May of 1833 a newcomer saw a few houses huddled upon the shore of a great lake; by September he records "the extraordinary growth of Chicago which only a little while ago was nothing but a small village. Now there is a street a mile long, and soon there will be two others of the same length." When the town was a year old there were "two thousand inhabitants . . . and every day you see vessels and steam boats put in here from the lake crowded with families who come to settle in Chicago. Every day new houses may be seen going up on all sides." [14] Its wide streets were constantly filled with a bustling, busy throng; in August of 1835 immigration was so considerable, that with flour selling at $20 a barrel, there was fear of a famine. When the city was four years old it had a population of about 8,000; and one hundred and twenty stores, twenty of which were wholesale, were required to transact its business.[15] The immediate result of this immigration was to make Chicago a large importing center; in 1833 only two boats had visited her port; but, during the season of 1836, 456 entries were made, bringing in goods worth $325,203; the exports they carried away were

[13] Though Chicago papers did not ignore the packing industry, in 1847 "Long John" Wentworth described a Chicago packing house which had instituted marvelous economies by utilization of waste parts, had a daily capacity of one hundred and thirty head of cattle, and exported its products mainly to the English market. *Western Citizen*, December 23, 1842; *Chicago American*, December 29, 1840, December 14, 1842; *Chicago Democrat*, October 18, 1845, October 16, 1847.

[14] Father St. Cyr to Bishop Rosati, Chicago, September 16, 1833, and June 11, 1834, quoted by Garraghan, "Early Catholicity in Chicago, 1673-1843," in *Illinois Catholic Historical Journal*, volume 1, number 1; Quaife, *Chicago and the Old Northwest*, 349.

[15] For much of the material on the commercial growth in Chicago credit is due to Judson Fiske Lee, "Transportation. A Factor in the Development of Northern Illinois Previous to 1860," in Illinois State Historical Society, *Journal*, 10: 17-18.

valued at only a thousand dollars. Though Chicago used much of this incoming merchandise, a great deal was destined for inland towns that had discovered the cheaper northern route. But an economical route for imports would present similar gainful inducements to exports, and the fast settling north country began hauling its grain to Chicago, and within the next two years the prices this central market was able to offer brought wheat pouring into the city. Throughout the season of 1841 when places in southern, central, and northern Illinois offered but fifty cents for wheat, Chicago paid an average of eighty-seven cents; the day that the Peoria market bought wheat at forty cents, Chicago paid one dollar. Farmers, singly or in groups, and throngs of teamsters for inland merchant middlemen, hauled wheat to Chicago, sometimes from 250 miles away.[16] Lines of thirteen, twenty, or even eighty wagons loaded with wheat were to be seen en route for that city. Though 150 vessels a month docked at Chicago in the season of 1841, they were insufficient to carry away the grain. In 1842 there were 705 arrivals with a tonnage of 117,711, and 586,907 bushels of grain were sent from the port. In that year imports were valued at $664,347 and exports at $659,305, for Chicago had become the market for "about one-half the State of Illinois, a large portion of Indiana, and a very considerable part of Wisconsin."[17] Until 1848 the volume of wheat exported continued to increase and Chicago's strength to arise from its preëminence as a grain market.

A prevalent opinion among the farmers of the day was that dealers and commission men cheated them on the market price, an idea that Wentworth in his editorials was ready to foster. Year after year he claimed that dealers and whig papers — despite the angry denials from both — were in league to cheat the producer; and in the face of the great warehouses Chicago dealers were continually building, came Wentworth's

[16] At Ottawa one firm alone, in 1842, advertised for fifty teams to haul wheat to Chicago. *Ibid.*, 23.
[17] *Ibid.*, 24.

warning that the usage farmers received in Chicago would force them to seek Illinois river markets. In 1846 the remedy for poor prices advocated by the *Prairie Farmer* was the stacking of wheat until a larger return could be obtained, but the *Chicago Journal* believed that in the climate of Illinois it would not keep without injury. So keen a contemporary observer as Thomas Ford, however, regarded the practice of hoarding produce as one of the formidable difficulties of the day. "Let the price be what it might, many would hold up their commodity a whole year, expecting a rise in the market. . . . I have known whole stacks of wheat and whole fields of corn to rot, or to be dribbled out and wasted to no purpose; and whole droves of hogs to run wild in the woods so as never to be reclaimed, whilst the owner was saving them for a higher price. . . . By holding back for a higher price, he suffered loss by the natural waste of his property, by laying out of the use of his money, by losing the many good bargains he could have made with it in the meantime, and by being compelled to purchase dear on a credit, and pay a high interest on the debt if not paid when due. . . .

"This practice of holding up property from the market unless the owner can receive more than the market price, still [1847] prevails extensively in the southern and some of the eastern parts of the State, and fully accounts for much of the difference in the degree of prosperity which is found there, and in the middle and northern part of the State." [18]

Economic conditions were, of course, profoundly affected by a new factor that was just beginning in this period the important rôle it later played in Illinois life—the coming of the foreigner and his assumption of citizenship. Up to this time settlers had come from sister states and, like all Americans,

[18] Ford, *History of Illinois*, 99-100. The large barns characteristic of northern farming — it was said that in the north a farmer frequently spent $250 on his house and $1,000 on his barn — helped no doubt to enable them to take such advice without the losses pictured by Ford, though he asserted that "the New England population make it a rule to sell all their marketable property as soon as it becomes fit for market, and at the market price." *Ibid.*, 100.

were of many parentages — English, Irish, Scotch, and Scotch-Irish, with some Pennsylvania Dutch; but all had been in the new country long enough to have become essentially American. In the thirties, however, conditions in most of the northern countries of Europe were such as to make emigration imperative. Illinois, with vast fertile prairies, easy of access, drew more than its quota of the newcomers.

From Germany there came such numbers that the admixture of Teutonic blood in the people of Illinois was to furnish much of the bone and sinew of the state. At the close of the Napoleonic wars political, religious, and economic conditions in Germany were distinctly bad; crop failures, over-population and production with the resulting dire poverty, were evils from which thousands of peasants, laborers, tradesmen, students, and professional men were eager to escape by emigration.

At just this time was published Gottfried Duden's *Bericht über eine Reise nach den westlichen Staaten Nordamerika's.* In 1824 Duden, a graduate in law and medicine, had gone to the Mississippi valley and bought a fertile tract of land in Missouri. He was a man of means; and, while his land was being cleared, he occupied himself in writing a romantic account of his "Garden of Eden," as his plantation came to be known. Imagination colored his experiences; he exaggerated the freedom and blessings of the country and minimized its hardships.[19] To many Germans the book was like an answer to prayer; they read it daily, regarded it as an infallible guide, and under its sway thousands emigrated to Missouri. The only other influence directing settlement to the middle west which compared with this book in strength was that of the "Giessener Gesellschaft." This was an immigration company — the practical vehicle by which the dream of founding a German state within the United States was to be realized; in it the oppressed, the exploited, the idealistic, were to find a refuge and there rear a model society. The company finally

[19] Koerner, *Memoirs,* 1:325-326.

chose Missouri as the destination for the thousands who responded to the plan.

This wave of immigration was increased by the failure of the revolution of 1830 in Germany; many highly educated Germans, leaders in their own country, left the fatherland for America; and, since the stream of immigration had started toward the Mississippi valley, it was natural that large numbers of them turned their footsteps in the same direction. Preferring a free to a slave state, however, the leaders determined to settle within the regions of Illinois. St. Clair and Madison counties, having already a sprinkling of German settlers, were chosen with Belleville as the center of the first important German settlement of the state.[20]   Friends in university days, fellow members of the " Burschenschaften," the German student fraternities of a political cast, here began together a new life in a new country.   Conspicuous among them were Gustave Koerner, Theodor Hilgard, George Bunsen, and George Englemann.   It was this group who became known as the " Latin farmers" of Belleville, for they knew more of Latin than of land.   Most of them had no agricultural experience, and their wives were unaccustomed to doing their own housework.   On the prairies, however, were to be found neither workmen nor housemaids, so that these people, accustomed to the luxuries of Europe, were obliged to suffer the privations and hardships of frontier life.   Some succeeded and some failed.   But they brought to Illinois an element of culture and education that was in the long run to affect the life of the community.   From the first they made no effort to isolate themselves from that life; though they furnished themselves with new and better houses, flowers and fruit trees, books and music, they at the same time adapted themselves to the simpler social standards of the people about them and thereby gradually elevated the ideals of western life.   Their influence was

[20] In Madison county Highland became the home of an important German-Swiss colony, led by the families of Köpfli and Suppiger. Faust, *German Element in the United States*, 1: 460; Koerner, *Memoirs*, 1: 327.

felt in farming, in commerce, in journalism, science, art, and government.

They were all men of books, and it is therefore not surprising to find that in 1836 they formed a " Deutsche Bibliotheks-Gesellschaft," and started a library in Belleville, which was one of the first important libraries in the state; in it were found Latin books, Greek books, books on philosophy, books on subjects of which the pioneer community scarcely knew the name.[21] From the first they manifested their interest in education and gave their support to the public schools. During the first winter a schoolhouse was erected, and Koerner appointed schoolmaster. Their genuine love of music modified and cultivated the crude singing of the frontier, and the first music school of any moment owed its origin to their initiative.[22]

In 1850 there were thirty-eight thousand foreign born Germans in Illinois.[23] From Belleville they had pushed out over the whole state, but particularly into that region opened up by the Black Hawk War. By 1847 several German newspapers had been organized.[24] Gustave Koerner had become the accepted leader in politics and he soon established himself as

[21] The first public library was founded at Albion in 1818 and a year later Edwardsville had a subscription library. Buck, *Illinois in 1818*, p. 169-170.

[22] Beinlich, "Latin Immigration in Illinois," Illinois State Historical Society, *Transactions*, 1909, p. 213. Ferdinand Ernst had brought over a colony of Germans to Vandalia in 1820 and 1821. When he died in 1822 his personal property was listed for public sale in the *Illinois Intelligencer*, October 5, 1822; besides German carriages, fine broadcloth coats, and pantaloons, elegant table linen and glassware, looking-glasses, clocks and watches, thermometers, hydrometers, and spy glasses, there were: "one elegant wing piano forte; one small do, one elegant steel musical instrument; clarinetts, flutes; french horns, bassoons; contra bass; bass, tenor & Common fiddles &c. with a large and elegant assortment of music."

[23] It must be remembered that the census figures connote "foreign born" alone. They do not take into account the second generation, which, though native born were "German" to their neighbors, nor does it indicate German emigrants from other states. In the thirties a stock company of Cincinnati Germans formed a settlement at Teutopolis in Effingham county; Germans from St. Louis and Cincinnati had settlements at Havana and Bath, Mason county, Perry in Pike county, with other considerable colonies in Woodford and La Salle counties. Pooley, *Settlement of Illinois*, 495-496.

[24] *Der Freiheitsbote für Illinois*, 1840; *Adler des Westens*, 1844; *Stern des Westens*, 1845; *Chicago Volksfreund*, 1845; *Illinois Staats-Zeitung*, 1847; Koerner, *Das Deutsche Element*, 268, 276-278.

one of the powerful figures in Illinois through the influence which he exercised over his countrymen.[25]   The Germans, in no sense susceptible to the sway of a political "boss," could, however, be molded into agreeing with their public men by rational means.[26]   Koerner, a thoroughly trained and capable lawyer, early perceived that in this country law and politics went hand in hand. He acquainted himself with the language, customs, public policies, and opinions of his new home and used his knowledge to bridge the gap that its absence caused between Germans and natives. He wrote a legal treatise in German to inform the former of the laws of the state, and that they might learn of politics he published a paper and wrote its editorials to supplement his activities as a public speaker.

In spite of the fact that leading Germans had shown marked public spirit, and that the majority were for some years too much occupied with the economic struggle to avail themselves of political privileges, the Germans aroused the antagonism of the "native Americans." German solidarity, the idealistic project of the "Giessener Gesellschaft," and the violent criticism of American institutions and customs by a few of their number aroused a resentment and fear that about 1838 stimulated the formation of nativistic American societies. The Germans, affronted at this misunderstanding of them as a group, drew closer together; they vented their anger at the nativists' propaganda in most outspoken communications to the German newspapers. Koerner translated some of the strongest and most exhaustive of these articles and carried them to the democratic newspapers, which up to this time had been only lukewarm in their attitude toward the foreigners. Faced now by a definite issue, the press was afraid to alienate so numerous a body of voters who had shown a preference for democratic party principles. They took the leap, published Koerner's translations, and thus the democratic party became the official and powerful sponsor for the aliens. This action

[25] For the political phase of German life in this period I have drawn largely upon an unpublished monograph by Miss Jessie J. Kile.
[26] Koerner, *Memoirs*, 1:427.

was sufficient to cement the imminent alliance between democrats and Germans; at the same time nothing could have more impressed the state with the strength of the newcomers. It "made the American people and particularly American politicians aware that there was a large population among them who knew their rights and were willing to maintain them and that they had to be taken into account." [27] Still "native born citizens" continued throughout the forties to raise the cry against aliens, in spite of the spirit that the Germans often expressed.[28]

The feeling of the Germans toward their adopted state is illustrated by the following resolution of thanks to Koerner for his stand on the canal bill and stay law: "Resolved, That the German citizens of Chicago and Cook county feel pride and gratification that one of their countrymen was in a position to repay to some extent, by useful action as a public servant, the obligations we all feel to the State of Illinois for the liberality towards us in providing us a haven in a land of freedom and extending to us the privileges of native born citizens." [29]

German antagonism to those who persistently misunderstood them never abated, and they joined the nativist issue with vigor. It was the big plank in Koerner's campaign for the legislature in 1842;[30] and his election served, not only to please the Germans, but to allay in them all suspicion of nativism in democratic ranks. He was the first German legislator; and in fact his political prominence continued conspicuous, since, in spite of the respect that politicians paid the German vote, the aspirations of these new citizens were modest, and they seldom in this period held office. In 1846 a meeting of Chicago Germans recommended the appointment of one of their number as deputy sheriff, and the following year only one

[27] Koerner, *Memoirs*, 1:424.
[28] It was sometimes suspected that the democrats used the cry of "nativism" to keep the Germans from joining the whigs.
[29] *Chicago Democrat*, March 21, 1843.
[30] Koerner, *Memoirs*, 1:464-469.

German was elected as delegate to the constitutional convention.

Although the German element in Illinois was by far the most numerous and powerful of foreign groups, yet other nationalities were making significant contributions. Illinois had long felt the influence of the coming of individual Irishmen — such men as John Reynolds, Thomas Carlin, and James Shields. But in the thirties general conditions in Ireland, religious, political, and economic, with the terrible famines of 1845 and 1846 as a climax to misery, led all who could to flee from the country. Irish experience in agriculture was not conducive to a desire for further knowledge of it even in a new environment, and the Irish tended to remain in the large cities as day laborers or factory employees. In Illinois the great need of canal labor and the promise of good wages and steady employment drew thousands of this class to the state. They settled in large groups all along the line of the canal — at Joliet, Peru, La Salle, and over the adjacent counties.

For ten years the work on the canal dragged on, but the financial embarrassments of the state operated to change many Irish laborers into Irish farmers. Canal scrip could often be redeemed only in canal land. Moreover, when in the early forties work on the canal was abandoned altogether for a time, the laborers went into neighboring counties and took up sections of land. As a result the farming population along the line of the canal, and that from Peoria northward along the Illinois river was largely Irish. But whenever possible their gregariousness and their fondness for politics and excitement induced them to remain in the cities, or to return as soon as the outside demand for their labor declined; Chicago continued their favorite residence.[31]

In 1850 there were twenty-eight thousand Irish in Illinois; their Celtic adaptability, facility, and enthusiasm tended toward their rapid assimilation into the general population. At the same time a certain hot and aggressive loyalty to all things

[31] Pooley, *Settlement of Illinois*, 499-501.

Irish, together with the bristling qualities of their primitive Celtic temperaments, drew a sharp line of antagonism between them and their Anglo-Saxon neighbors.

English emigration to Illinois was led by Morris Birkbeck and the Flowers into Edwards county in the early days of statehood, and from that time many isolated English families continued to make their way to the Illinois prairies. In the thirties, however, agricultural and industrial conditions in England were similar to those throughout northern Europe; they fell with crushing weight on the small tenant farmers and were scarcely to be borne even by the more fortunate classes. Wages were low, tithes and taxes exorbitant. "Clergymen urged their parishioners to emigrate to America where wages were good. The London Roman Catholic Emigration Society hastened to complete preparations whereby various parties, each with its clergyman at its head might find new homes in America." [32] Farmers, trade-unionists, day laborers, and professional men left the country.[33] From 1845 to 1847 emigration to the United States doubled, and by 1850 there were 18,600 English settlers in Illinois. They were not the most happy and successful settlers. Adaptation to life on the prairies was difficult. "Their minds were hampered with prejudices in favor of the customs and habits of the mother country, which, combined with the lack of those qualities that make good pioneers, kept the English from being classed with the successful settlers of the new country." [34]

The Scotch, on the other hand, upon whom economic distress had also forced immigration, were markedly successful. About 1834 they began to form settlements in Illinois and by 1850 there were forty-six hundred settled chiefly in the northwestern part of the state. Their frugality, industry, and so-

[32] Pooley, *Settlement of Illinois*, 502.
[33] Mormon missionaries sent to England were there singularly successful in making converts. In 1840 the first band was brought over and by 1844 it was estimated that of the sixteen thousand Saints at Nauvoo ten thousand were English. *Ibid.*, 503.
[34] *Ibid.*

briety, together with their high rank as agriculturists, made them a valuable asset to the state.

It was a religious rather than an economic or political motive that first brought Norwegians to America; in 1825 a band of fifty persecuted Quakers, under the leadership of Kleng Peerson, came to New York, and ten years later, still under his guidance, most of them moved to the more promising Illinois country. They settled along the Fox river in La Salle county, and, after a preliminary year or so of hardship, prospered. Their glowing accounts were sent back to friends suffering from hard times, scarcity of money, and shortage of crops; to tell such people about " rich, rolling prairies stretching away miles upon miles, about land which was neither rocky, nor swampy, nor pure sand, nor set up at an angle of forty-five degrees, about land which could be had almost for the asking in fee simple and not by semi-manorial title," was to fire their imaginations with "America fever." [35]   Of this country many had never before heard the name, and now came these fabulous tales, first from letters, copied by hundreds and circulated from parish to parish, and then from Ansted Nattestad, who in the spring of 1838 came from the far land to visit relatives in Norway. Eager inquirers sometimes traveled one hundred and forty miles to see him and learn the facts concerning America and Illinois. Nattestad brought with him the manuscript of Ole Rynning's "True Account of America for the Instruction and Use of the Peasants and Common People," in which the author, a man of education and sympathy, answered the questions that he and many less informed than himself had asked about America. Hardly any Norwegian publication has been purchased and read with the avidity of the " American-book," which was packed with information and advice that reached many a circumscribed parish and sent adventuring spirits to the new land.[36]

[35] Babcock, *The Scandinavian Element,* 28, 81.
[36] Rynning was the leading spirit of the ill-starred Beaver creek colony — a party of fifty Norwegians who first intended to join the Fox river settlement. They chose their site in the late summer of 1837 when its grassy verdure gave no

ILLINOIS IN FERMENT 399

It was natural that these parties of emigrants should seek the Illinois settlements; the towns of Mission, Miller, Rutland, Norway, Leland, Lisbon, Morris, and Ottawa sprang up and grew rapidly at their coming. About 1840, however, the principal stream of Norwegian immigration was deflected into Wisconsin, just when Swedish settlers began pouring into Illinois. Swedish emigration, instigated at the outset almost entirely by economic motives, was early directed to this state through the influence of the brothers Hedström. Olaf Hedström, who was one of a handful of Swedes emigrating as early as 1825, had been converted to ardent Methodism, and in 1845 was put in charge of a New York mission where he accomplished a unique work among the incoming Swedes. His brother Jonas had settled in Knox county, and it was to this region as well as to Andover and Chicago that the fatherly missionary sent the multitudes dependent upon him for advice and direction.[37]

In 1846 the persecuted religious sect of Jansonists founded the first Swedish settlement of considerable size at Bishop Hill in Henry county. A year later the thriving communistic and religious colony numbered four hundred settlers, and five years after their coming they had grown to eleven hundred members or almost one-third the population of Henry county.[38]

By 1850 Scandinavian immigration had added to the state thirty-five hundred thrifty, industrious, and intensely Protestant citizens. Though chiefly agriculturists, concerned with winning a freehold for themselves and founding an honorable family competence, they held a high educational standard and were remarkable for their loyalty to the public school system.

hint of the swamps that in the spring made cultivation impossible nor of the unhealthfulness that during the summer caused the death of two-thirds of the company. Rynning, who in the winter had employed the leisure of illness by writing his *Account,* was one of the victims of the depopulating malaria the following summer. Babcock, *The Scandinavian Element,* 28-31; Blegen, "Ole Rynning's True Account of America," in *Minnesota History Bulletin,* 2:221-232

[37] Babcock, *The Scandinavian Element,* 54.
[38] *Ibid.,* 56-60.

So rapidly did this large body of recently foreign citizens take their place in the body politic, that when the national issue of the Mexican War arose, no cleavage in the state occurred. Such companies as that of Captain James F. Eagan, who organized the Ottawa Irish Volunteers with one hundred and forty-eight on the roll,[39] and that of Captain Julius C. Raith made up of young Germans from St. Clair and Monroe counties were among the first to volunteer.[40]

The war had come at a time to make it extremely popular throughout Illinois. The people were suffering from the most stringent "hard times:" money, except that of broken banks, was not to be had; repeated failure met any attempt at commercial or industrial enterprise; farmers, unable to market their abundant crops, used what they could and left the rest to waste in the field. Suddenly, to the pent-up energy of the state and to the spirit of adventure, came the call to arms. Causes and issues were hardly considered; party lines were swept aside in the response that, swift and enthusiastic, came from the people.[41]

A favorite employment of the young men of the state had been the organization of rifle companies which drilled and marched and displayed themselves in full regalia in Fourth of July parades and at patriotic meetings. Now these companies saw a chance for real service and at once offered themselves. The quota which Governor Ford had been asked to furnish from Illinois was three brigades of infantry. His call went out May 25, 1845; ten days later thirty-five companies or four thousand men reported to the governor. Eager captains of hurriedly mustered companies rode posthaste to the governor with letters certifying the worth of their men; he who first arrived was accepted, though a shift was sometimes

[39] *Alton Telegraph and Democratic Review,* July 18, 1846.
[40] Koerner, *Memoirs,* 1:495-496; Faust, *German Element,* 1:459.
[41] Enthusiasm, however, was keener in the southern and central parts of the state than farther north where the New England element was stronger. Koerner remarked on the lack of ardor in Stark and especially in the more northern counties as contrasted with that in St. Clair and Madison. Koerner, *Memoirs,* 1:501.

made when the credentials of another indicated that his men were more desirable. There was much jealousy and rivalry, and the four thousand who had not been in time to be accepted loudly complained.[42]

The colonels of the first three regiments, enlisted for twelve months, were John J. Hardin, William H. Bissell, and Ferris Forman. E. D. Baker, authorized to raise an additional regiment, had only to select the required number of companies from those already tendered. When a second call for troops was made in April, 1847, two additional regiments enlisted for the duration of the war and went out under Colonels W. B. Newby and James Collins. Besides these six regiments, four independent mounted companies were accepted; and one hundred and fifty Illinoisians enlisted in the regular army.

The troops composed chiefly of "the well taught youths of our farming communities, and our quiet, moral country towns,"[43] started south with an enthusiasm only equaled by that at home which sped them on their way.[44] Companies rivaled each other in the assiduity with which they drilled, marched, and perfected their organization. They furnished themselves with new uniforms; that of one company, for instance, consisted of a grey forage cap, a gray frock coat trimmed with black, and black pantaloons; and in addition to their rifles this company was armed with artillery swords, two feet long, two inches broad, and double edged — a formidable addition to their offensive at close quarters.[45]

The trip down the Mississippi, across the gulf to Texas, and the march into Mexico was an education to these provincial lads. Plantations, sugar cane, cypress trees, Spanish moss, levees, seasickness, drill, march, discipline, prickly pear, chaparral, tarantulas, and Texans were words that appeared in

[42] *Alton Telegraph and Democratic Review,* July 18, 1846.
[43] *Belleville Advocate,* August 12, 1847.
[44] Citizens voluntarily furnished provisions, blankets, provisional uniforms, and flags to the departing boys. Koerner, *Memoirs,* 1:495.
[45] Everett, "Narrative of Military Experience," Illinois State Historical Society, *Transactions,* 1905, p. 195, 196. Although percussion rifles had been invented some years before, the war with Mexico was fought with flint locks.

letters home and indicated a wealth of new experience. In spite of the hot, steamy climate, the dust, poor roads, and frequent sicknesses, the men made the most of this trip. As venison and wild grapes varied their diet of salt pork and beans, so did the sight of a new vegetation, architecture, and people vary and add interest to the monotony of long marches under trying conditions.

General John A. Wool, U. S. A., and other officers of the regular army had a merry time in impressing the men with the serious necessity of discipline, for an artless insubordination pervaded both volunteers and officers. Colonel Forman at one time threatened to walk his men home, and when Colonel Hardin landed he did not march his men directly to camp. "I will take away your commission, sir," said Wool. "By God, you can't do it, sir," Hardin hotly replied. Wool, admitted by the volunteers as a splendid soldier and first rate disciplinarian, was still thought to possess "too much *regular* contempt for volunteers."[46]

At home, the doings of the boys at the front were eagerly followed. The spirit of democratic papers throughout the state did not flag. The *State Register* praised the legislature for passing unanimously instructions to members of congress to do their utmost for the vigorous prosecution of the war and for its memorial asking bounty lands for those that serve.[47] A meeting of democrats in St. Clair county late in November, 1847, appointed a committee consisting of Gustave Koerner, John Reynolds, William H. Bissell, Lyman Trumbull, and William C. Kinney to express the sense of the meeting in a series of resolutions. They declared that the object of the war was to force Mexico to relinquish her claims, that the invasion of Mexico had not made it an offensive war, but that indemnity in land or money had become a legitimate object of the United States. They repudiated the idea that any portion of the people of the United States wished to conquer territory for slavery

[46] *Belleville Advocate,* September 3, 1846.
[47] *Illinois State Register,* February 5, 1847.

extension, but they asserted that the United States had a right to govern provisionally the conquered territory until the conclusion of peace; they claimed that no declaration of congress as to the cause of war should have any weight, but that all citizens should support the government in attaining indemnity in land or money. The *Register* was strongly in favor of the tea and coffee tax for it supplied the money necessary to prosecute the war, and the state submitted gladly to it for that reason.[48]

Although the outbreak of the war had been hailed with enthusiasm by the people of the state, the whig press at best had merely acquiesced in the war and became gradually more and more outspoken in its condemnation of the national aims. In September, 1847, the *State Register* charged the whigs with being traitors to the country and devoted three columns to quotations from party organs in which they were giving "aid and comfort" to the enemy. Whig opposition to territorial extension was in democratic eyes analogous to the opposition of federalists to the Louisiana purchase. At the same time the democrats declared it a political move to deprive their party of the glory of adding territory to the country, while forced to bear the responsibility for a heavy war expenditure.[49] Whig papers in turn charged that democratic members "think it a cardinal quality of national greatness that we are able to trounce and conquer a weaker one, and in justification of our course with Mexico," lay down "the supposition that because we have driven out the Indians from their ancient homes, and the deed being just and humane, the people of New Mexico and California, being in a more degraded condition, deserve the same treatment.[50] They pointed out the dangers, responsibilities, and resulting evils from annexation that the war-loving portion of the people seemed light-heartedly to desire. The *State Register* clung staunchly to its position that national

[48] *Illinois State Register*, January 29, December 10, 1847.
[49] *Ibid.*, September 24, October 1, November 5, 26, 1847.
[50] *Rockford Forum*, April 26, 1848.

prestige required the war to be carried to a successful close; readiness to avenge insult of national honor, it regarded as a protection; the whigs on the other hand cried for "peace, commerce and honest friendship with all nations," and a "speedy close of the bloody tragedy, too long enacted at our expense, on the soil of another Republic."[51]

Democratic condemnation of individuals who opposed the war was severe. In particular Abraham Lincoln, whig representative in congress, drew this fire. Lincoln in speech and by consistent vote had stigmatized the war as one of "rapine and murder," "robbery and dishonor." He felt that Illinois had sent her men to Mexico " to record their infamy and shame in the blood of poor, innocent unoffending people, whose only crime was weakness."[52] On December 22, 1847, he presented in the house the famous "spotty resolutions" in which he challenged the president's statement that Mexico had "involved the two countries in war, by invading the territory of the State of Texas, striking the first blow, and shedding the blood of our citizens on our own soil;" he pointed out that the particular spot on which the first blood was shed was Mexican soil, from which the citizens fled at the approach of the United States troops; and that it was the blood of our "armed officers and soldiers," whose blood was first shed.[53] To Lincoln, the facts admitted no other interpretation than that the war was "unnecessarily and unconstitutionally commenced by the President."

In a speech before the house, January 12, 1848, he declared that President Polk "is deeply conscious of being in the wrong; that he feels the blood of this war, like the blood of Abel, is crying to heaven against him; that originally having some strong motive . . . to involve the two countries in a war, and trusting to escape scrutiny by fixing the public gaze upon the exceeding brightness of military glory,— that attrac-

[51] *Rockford Forum,* March 22, 1848; *Illinois State Register,* November 5, 1847.
[52] *Belleville Advocate,* March 2, 1848.
[53] *Writings of Abraham Lincoln,* 2: 20-22.

tive rainbow that raises in showers of blood, that serpent's eye that charms to destroy,—he plunged into it, and was swept on and on till, disappointed in his calculation of the ease with which Mexico might be subdued, he now finds himself he knows not where. How like the half-insane mumbling of a fever dream is the whole war part of his late message!"[54]

Though Lincoln's charges may have borne some little fruit in enlightening public opinion and though such papers as the *Rockford Forum* gave Lincoln unqualified support, the great majority of the press and the people were uninterested in hearing whys and wherefores; to them this was an attack direct on their dearest enthusiam. Newspapers and public meetings, flaunting their own patriotism, declared Lincoln a second Benedict Arnold.[55] At a meeting without distinction of party held in Clark county, the following resolution was adopted:

"*Resolved,* That Abe Lincoln, the author of the 'spotty' resolutions in Congress, against his own country, may they long be remembered by his constituents, but may they cease to remember him, except to rebuke him—they have done much for him, but he has done nothing for them, save the stain he inflicted on their proud names of patriotism and glory, in the part they have taken in their country's cause."[56]

The fact that the conduct of the Illinois troops had been especially valorous made enthusiastic supporters more bitterly resent any criticism of the war. Illinoisians had markedly distinguished themselves at the battle of Buena Vista, February 23, 1847. General Zachary Taylor commended their services as follows: "The First and Second Illinois, and the Kentucky regiments . . . engaged the enemy in the morning, restored confidence to that part of the field, while the list of casualties will show how much these three regiments suffered in sustaining the heavy charge of the enemy in the afternoon. In this last conflict we had the misfortune to sustain a

[54] *Writings of Abraham Lincoln,* 2:38-39.
[55] *Illinois State Register,* March 10, May 26, 1848.
[56] *Belleville Advocate,* March 2, 1848.

very heavy loss.   Colonels Hardin, McKee, and Lieut.-Colonel Clay fell at this time, while gallantly leading their commands. . . .   Col. Bissell, the only surviving colonel of the three regiments, merits notice for his coolness and bravery on this occasion." [57]

When Colonel Hardin fell while recklessly leading his regiment in a desperate charge, Illinois lost a popular hero.   A man without much outward balance — crude, artless, almost stammering in speech — he had become the leading whig of the state, being a member of three general assemblies, and a representative in congress, 1843–1845.   Handsome, impulsive, ingenuous, his very handicaps attracted warm friends.

The Third and Fourth Regiments distinguished themselves in the campaign against the city of Mexico and in the battle of Cerro Gordo, April 18, 1847, while the Fifth and Sixth, though they lost severely through sickness and exposure, arrived too late for active service.

Illinois treated the returning volunteers as heroes, every one.   Not only were such men as William H. Bissell, John A. Logan, Richard J. Oglesby, James Shields, Benjamin M. Prentiss, and James D. Morgan rewarded with high places in the state, but in their home communities humbler men were recognized with county and township offices.   In Menard county, for instance, five returned volunteers were elected in August of 1847 to the county offices of judge of probate, clerk of the county commissioners' court, assessor, treasurer, and recorder.   Towns and counties gave public dinners, barbecues, and Fourth of July celebrations to welcome the returning volunteers.   Addresses, speeches, brass bands, fireworks, cannon salutes, and enormous crowds of enthusiastic people graced these occasions.   Five thousand people gathered in Springfield while an equal number sat at the public board in Belleville at the barbecue. [58]

Throughout this busy period Illinois had so grown and de-

[57] Moses, *Illinois*, 1:495-496.
[58] *Illinois State Register*, July 9, August 13, 1847.

veloped that the old constitution, designed for a frontier community, was felt as a hampering restraint. Never entirely satisfactory, twenty years' experience demanded a change. Popular opinion, newspapers, whigs, and democrats condemned the old constitution and urged drastic modification. The question of revision was narrowly defeated in 1842: four years later the answer came strongly in the affirmative. One hundred and sixty-two delegates were elected who met in Springfield in June, 1847, to begin what proved to be the work of drawing up a new constitution. Of this body, large and unwieldy, a majority were democrats though it was claimed the proceedings were carried forward in a strictly nonpartisan spirit. The convention was representative of western democracy in the fact that contrary to custom, there were only fifty-four lawyers to seventy-six farmers in the body. The debates which the newspapers anxiously watched were heated and long drawn out. After a three months' session the convention finished its work on August 31 and presented for the consideration of the people a new body of fundamental law.

A mongrel affair—the natural result of trying to meet the demands of all—the document throughout its detailed length made a valiant effort to render impossible to the future the unhappy experiences of the past. Stupendous debts, reckless banking, extravagant legislation, "life" offices—these were to be eliminated together with the particular aversions of each party; above all the will of the people was to be consulted and heeded in new places and to a much greater extent than formerly.[59] During the six months that intervened before the referendum the newspapers never allowed the issue to languish. The united support of the organs of each party, as a result of the compromises with which the new document bristled, was given with a sort of careful lack of enthusiasm; each, jealous of the victories gained by the other side, was accused of raising the cry of a "party constitution;" yet each was solicitous

[59] *Quincy Whig,* March 1, 1848; *Sangamo Journal,* April 1, 1847; *Illinois State Register,* February 26, 1847.

that party bickering should not alienate the final support of the people. It was said that only six papers within the state consistently opposed the constitution and were alone upheld in their opposition by the judges, their political appendages, and the small fry politicians.[60]   The German was the one other element of opposition to be really feared. The whigs had insisted upon the limitation of the franchise: could the Germans swallow so bitter a pill?   Although suffrage was to be guaranteed to all adult males residing in the state at the time of adoption of the constitution, would they suffer the substitution of naturalization and a year's residence for the six months' residence alone required before?   With Koerner combating ratification, it remained a question whether the gains in other reforms would lead the Germans to overlook the measure that had won unqualified whig support.[61]

For this victory of their opponents the disgruntled democrats found some compensation in the heads of the obnoxious supreme court judges, whose duties were now divorced from the circuit, and who, along with all other state and county officers, were made elective by the people.[62]

To meet the insistent demand for retrenchment and at the same time to clip the wings of the distrusted legislature, the number of representatives and state officers was reduced and all salaries were fixed at absurdly low sums; moreover, the session of the legislative body was practically limited to forty-two days, for any time in excess of that period was paid at just one-half the regular stipend of two dollars a day.[63]   With the keen remembrance of internal improvement bills still heavy, the state was forbidden to contract any debt exceeding fifty thousand dollars — and that was "to meet casual deficits or failures in revenue;" nor was the credit of the state "in any manner to be given to, nor in aid of, any individual associa-

[60] *Quincy Whig*, February 23, 1848; *Illinois State Register*, August 6, 1847.
[61] *Belleville Advocate*, February 10, 1848; Koerner, *Memoirs*, 1: 523.
[62] *Chicago Democrat*, January 14, 1848.
[63] *Illinois State Register*, January 22, 1847; *Belleville Advocate*, January 20, 1848; *Quincy Whig*, February 2, 1848.

tion or corporation." Neither the charter of the State Bank, or any bank hitherto existing was to be revived though new banks could be established by the sanction of a popular referendum.

The cry for economy did not, however, prevent the taking of an important stand on state indebtedness; the fund arising from a two mill tax was to be devoted exclusively to debts other than school and canal indebtedness; advocates of repudiation were thus rendered entirely powerless.

The council of revision with its unwholesome effect on legislation was lopped off, while the governor, his term and eligibility remaining unchanged, was invested with a veto which might, however, be overridden by the same majority that originally passed the bill.

An agitation for the granting of civil rights to Negroes met so prompt and spirited an opposition that it resulted in a fundamental strengthening of the black code. An article was introduced to "effectually prohibit free persons of color from immigrating to and settling in this State; and to effectually prevent the owners of slaves from bringing them into this State for the purpose of setting them free." [64]

The newspaper campaign of judicious enthusiasm continued throughout the winter. It was generally conceded that "the new Constitution is not perfect, for it is the work of fallible men. Critics and hypercritics, many good men, and some who might be suspected of sinister motives, may condemn it; but it is, on the whole, a good Constitution — a republican one — and an immense improvement upon the old instrument." [63] Such support won the day; in March, 1848, the people of the state ratified the new constitution with the large majority of 49,060 to 20,883, and on April 1, 1848, it went into effect.

[62] Constitution, 1848, article XIV.
[63] *Aurora Beacon*, February 10, 1848.

XXII. SOCIAL, EDUCATIONAL, AND RELIGIOUS ADVANCE, 1830–1848

COMPARED with the Illinois of 1818, the Illinois of 1848 was a community quickened into mental life and independence. On its accession to statehood, Illinois was intellectually provincial; its leaders came from older states, bringing with them tastes already established; and mental culture was the possession and badge of a social class. In 1848 this was in a measure still true; but Illinois colleges and schools had begun the work of democratizing education. Moreover, Illinois numbered among its citizens men like J. B. Turner and Thomas Ford whose thought, keen and original, was molded by the environment the state afforded them. Easterners came to quicken the life of the state, and their own intellectual life affected by the freedom of their new surroundings ceased to be purely eastern.

The cities growing up in the state were superimposing new and more complex social conditions on the older rural communities.[1] The old-time Fourth of July celebration continued in vogue though sometimes under temperance or Sunday school auspices. As early as 1845, however, newspapers were descanting on the number of accidents during such celebrations and were calling for a sane Fourth. Chicago had queens of the May on May day and kept the old-fashioned New Year's custom of calls and refreshments. There were donation parties and church fairs. There were traveling circuses to carry amusement to the village, though these were condemned by the fastidious as indecent. There was dancing. There were theatricals in Chicago and other cities, amateur and professional, the latter becoming from the critic's point

[1] *Chicago Daily Journal,* October 9, 1846.

of view, increasingly valid. Among sports there were horse races which at least in Chicago were sometimes scenes of disorder. Of course there was hunting, sometimes in the form of community wolf drives. At Chicago there was a boxing academy in 1845. In 1840 there was even a cricket match between Chicago and Auplaine.[2]

Chicago was growing up; by 1842 it recognized a need of shade trees, deprecated its ineffective system of checking the frequent fires, and dilated on the route northward it offered southern travelers. Moreover, it was acquiring, as had formerly Little Fort and even forgotten Salem, a reputation for bad morals; in 1842 women of evil fame scandalously accused pious men before grand juries. The advantages which Chicago offered as a market for products and the frequency with which the farmer availed himself of them, made it appropriate for the newspapers to offer advice concerning his conduct in town. He must beware of taverns that assign him to garret rooms and set before him shinbone steak. He must never go to a house merely because a runner recommends it. He must be sure on the register to bracket his name with that of the bedfellow he chooses and to bespeak a room when he first enters.[3]

Any attempt to reconstruct the cultural life of the state must leave out of account the great circles of ignorance and illiteracy; they have passed leaving no record. For the rest, the newspapers afford perhaps the best criterion, although, with the exception of such a sheet as J. B. Turner's *Illinois Statesman*, they fell below the plane of the best in the state. It was the papers which encouraged the lyceums that came

[2] *Chicago American*, May 2, July 8, September 21, 25, 1840, December 31, 1841, February 1, April 1, May 31, 1842; *Chicago Democrat*, January 3, 1844, July 9, October 28, 1845; *Belleville Advocate*, August 22, 1840, May 23, 1841, June 11, 18, July 16, 1846, April 8, 1847; *Alton Telegraph*, August 2, 1845; *Little Fort Porcupine*, September 19, 1845, June 23, 1846; *Chicago Daily Journal*, January 16, March 3, 1845.

[3] *Chicago American*, December 28, 1840, February 10, March 31, 1842, February 15, 1847; *Alton Telegraph*, October 19, 1844; *Illinois Journal*, November 11, 1847; *Chicago Democrat*, September 15, 1841, June 28, December 14, 1842, June 25, October 28, 1845; *Little Fort Porcupine*, April 30, May 28, 1845; *Sangamo Journal*, May 13, 1847.

intermittently to the towns to afford training in debate, to offer
lectures on science, literature, and phrenology, and to urge the
preservation of the history of the state; as early as 1831 a
state lyceum projected an elaborate writing up of the history
and curiosities of Illinois. The newspapers, moreover, forwarded this interest in history directly by publishing in their
pages numerous discussions of past events, often written by
men who had participated in them. More ambitious was the
scheme of a meeting at Vandalia in 1837, which deputed Peck
to write a complete history of the state. Two years later a
Peoria Scientific and Historical Society was organized, and in
1843 the Illinois Literary and Historical Society was at work.
The following year the latter issued an appeal for books and
manuscripts calculated to throw light on the history of the
state; and three years later it was still working with some
measure of success. Into these historical activities, it is to be
marked, contemporary politicians threw themselves with enthusiasm. Sidney Breese, William H. Brown, Thomas Ford,
and John Reynolds all have left their interpretation of the
state's past; to an amazing degree they have shaped the tradition of Illinois history.[4]

Book advertisements did not indicate the existence of a
more cultivated literary taste than that which the clippings in
newspapers satisfied. These clippings were marked by an
affected romanticism, though for some reason, the democratic
papers published less sentimental stuff than the whig; little
of the "literary" material, which filled such papers as the
Sangamo Journal and the *Alton Telegraph*, even approached
good melodrama or romance. It was a farrago of tales of the
American bourgeoisie: the marriages of merchants' daughters
to poor but virtuous clerks, the connubial felicities resulting,
and the final relenting of the hard-hearted father when, as was

---

[4] *Belleville Advocate,* March 25, 1841, November 3, 1842; *Chicago American,*
January 7, 1837, June 26, July 15, 1839, December 2, 23, 1841, February 15, 1842;
Sangamo Journal, April 29, 1837, November 15, 1839; *Peoria Register,* Feb-
ruary 9, July 6, 1839; *Alton Telegraph,* September 2, 1843, August 31, 1844,
September 3, 1847.

PECK-MESSENGER MAP, 1835

First sectional map of the state

[From original owned by Wisconsin Historical Society]

the usual *dénouement,* hard times had swept away his fortune. Or, in the time of the excitement stimulated by the Washingtonians, one gets tragic sentiment on the woes of drunkards' wives, of starved children fading under neglect, and similar tales, *ad nauseam.* In these, however, democratic papers also occasionally indulged. One is hardly surprised when the *Belleville Advocate* pronounces "To Lucasta on Going to the Wars" to be lacking in simplicity and fit only for corrupted tastes.[5]

There were, however, occasional indications of discrimination. Now and then there are reprints of such tales as that which is the basis of William Morris' "Written on the Image" or an imitation of Poe's "The Cask of Amontillado."[6] Poe's "Gold Bug" appeared in the *Alton Telegraph* of August 19, 1843, in the midst of a mass of sentimental and romantic trash. In the *Chicago Democrat* of 1845 N. P. Willis' "Letters from London" are a welcome relief. The one great exception to a deprecatory classification, however, is found in the enthusiastic cult of Dickens which existed before his strictures on America and especially on Illinois had turned popular feeling against him.[7] Wellerisms were common in the papers — even rivaling the Negro joke, which playing on the misuse of long words was the principal form of humor.

The attitude of the whig newspapers toward morals and manners is, to say the least, generally disappointing. The *Chicago American* within a few months managed to comment on the morals of Fanny Ellsler and of Dionysius Lardner, to remark on the relative beauties of the Venus of Canova and the Venus de Medici and withal to comment much on crimes of sex. Comparing favorably with this policy is the frank broadness of several of the democratic papers whose stories represented the naïveté of rural Illinois.[8]

[5] April 25, 1840.
[6] *Belleville Advocate,* April 17, 1841.
[7] *Chicago American,* November 23, 1841, January 19, 1842; *Belleville Advocate,* April 11, 21, November 29, December 22, 1842.
[8] *Chicago American,* December 2, 1841, June 4, 1842; *Belleville Advocate,* September 30, 1847.

The medical profession showed evidence of a growing social consciousness in the change from early individual efforts at medicine and hygiene to the organization in the thirties of medical societies and sodalities.[9]   In 1837 Rush Medical College was incorporated — at that time no such institution was to be found west of Cincinnati and Lexington.[10]   The trustees did not, however, effect an organization until 1843 when the first course of lectures was given by four instructors to twenty-two students; the following year the first college building was erected.   In 1846 a medical library of six hundred volumes and improved apparatus for study were added for students and a free dispensary and operating clinic opened to the public. By 1848 the school enrolled one hundred and forty students, and that year graduated thirty-three physicians.

The faculty of the institution not only contributed their services but kept up all expenses of maintenance and alteration of the college, the only donation either to its establishment or support being the lot upon which the college was originally erected.   To Dr. Daniel Brainard is due chief credit for the founding and directing in its early years of this first institution of science, which made Chicago a recognized center of medical instruction.[11]

The life of the people of the early state found its most typical expression in their churches.   They offered an immediate escape from the unending struggle with physical forces, a promise of future compensation for the privations that now pressed hard, and furnished a social center of varied and exciting interest.

For the religious denominations already strongly established in Illinois, the period from 1830 to 1848 was one of more or less steady growth.   The Methodists, who in 1830 numbered about six thousand communicants, were just entering on a decade of tremendous growth; in the next five years

[9] The first meeting of the Cook County Medical Society was on October 3, 1836.
[10] *Chicago American*, March 25, 1837.
[11] Andreas, *History of Chicago.* 464-466.

they increased to fifteen thousand, and that number was doubled by 1840. The growth of the next eight years, while not so remarkable, was still sufficient to insure this denomination with over forty thousand members first place in numerical strength.[12]

The Baptists had grown from thirty-six hundred to twelve thousand in the decade between 1830 and 1840; in the following ten years, increasing absolutely as much as the Methodists during the same time, they almost doubled their membership with twenty-two thousand communicants in 1850. Their annals throughout this period, however, had not been peaceful. The "anti-mission" Baptists, later confused with the "two seed" Baptists, strove against John Mason Peck and the supporters of the "religious institutions falsely so-called" which taught young men to preach and sent them forth under perpetual pay to displace the old Baptist preachers; their associations disfellowshipped those who had to do with missions.

In spite of opposition the main currents of opinion ran in the channels in which Peck would have had them, and the aid of the Baptist Home Mission Society in sustaining the ministry in the state was gratefully acknowledged by the Edwardsville association in 1836. That same year saw the formation of the Illinois Baptist Education Society designed to aid candidates for the ministry. Peck in defending the movement argued that the educated minister would not drive out the old illiterate preacher simply because of his illiteracy. If he was so narrow as to stand in the way of others, he deserved it; but a minister hearty in the cause would find no one inclined to take notice of slips in grammar.

The Illinois Baptist Convention, in connection with the Home Mission Society, had their traveling missionaries wholly or partly supported in the work of building up churches. Between April, 1836, and January, 1837, Moses Lemen traveled a distance of 2,100 miles, visited fourteen churches, and gave

[12] *Minutes of the Annual Conference of the Methodist Episcopal Church*, 2:46; 3:90, 99, 297, 399, 513; 4:79, 261, 281.

one hundred and five religious discourses. In a similar period of time his brother James had traveled 1,595 miles and preached ninety-six sermons. In 1837 the Illinois Baptist Convention agreed to assume one-third the expense of the Baptist missionaries. The indefatigable Peck was appointed general agent to visit the churches, to stir them to renewed activity, to seek out students, and to look after the interests of Shurtleff College and of the societies. Already for some years he had edited the *Western Pioneer*, a Baptist paper; and he was now urged to prepare sketches of religious history in the west. A Baptist leader such as Peck had to be a man of tact; not only was his attitude toward slavery under scrutiny but a sharp lookout had to be kept lest such matters as the informal shedding of a heavy coat in warm weather should offend the sensibilities of a visiting eastern brother.[13]

The slavery crisis of 1845, resulting from the refusal of the Baptist board to allow slaveholding missionaries, ended in the promotion of an independent Northwest Baptist Association including northern Illinois and finally in its dissolution and the promotion of an entirely new Baptist central body, the Baptist General Association of Illinois. The *Western Christian* was the supporter of the new body in contradistinction to the *Helmet* which was inclined in the slavery direction.[14]

The most significant event in the religious history of the period 1830–1840 is the rise of Presbyterianism and Congregationalism in Illinois. The two denominations working together in the west under the plan of union undertook, in the belief that Congregationalism of the Yankee type was exotic in the latitude of Illinois, to win the state to a modified Presbyterianism. Eventually, however, the compromise was denounced on the one hand by Presbyterians who claimed that Congregational influence was demoralizing the discipline of

[13] Hicks, *Outline of Baptist History*, 11; *Illinois Advocate*, December 9, 1831; *Western Pioneer*, June 30, September 2, November 25, December 16, 1836, March 29, April 14, May 5, September 22, October 27, 1837, February 9, 1838.
[14] *Western Christian*, June 14, 28, October 23, November 6, 13, 1845; *Baptist Helmet*, April 24, May 22, 1845.

the church, and on the other by Congregationalists who claimed that Congregational brains and money had been used by Presbyterians to establish themselves in the west. In the annals of the two denominations the same men and enterprises are described as Congregational or Presbyterian according to the writer's point of view, and it is difficult to find the real truth.

Illinois Presbyterianism which in 1830 had but four hundred and ninety-two members established in the one " Presbytery of the Centre of Illinois" had expanded to twenty-three hundred communicants in eight presbyteries by the end of the decade, and had with eleven presbyteries and two synods more than doubled their numerical strength by 1848.[15] Throughout this period, however, their chief energy was devoted to educational and mission society effort; the supporters of the movement had to be on the alert lest they arouse western pride by a too frank declaration of their belief that the west was a moral desert.[16] The Reverend John Milcot Ellis, when soliciting money for Illinois College, was embarrassed by the charge of having acquiesced in such malignant eastern statements. As a fitting retaliation to former aspersions, in 1833 the *Alton Spectator* called on the citizens to meet "in the splendid Cong. ch. soon to be built" to consider means of saving the east from its moral degradation.

Jealous opposition met the sedulous Presbyterian activities. In 1834 Peter Cartwright, on behalf of the Methodist preachers who had borne the heat of the pioneer day, testified against non-sectarian societies on the ground that they were controlled by "new school" presbyteries and that they paid money to agents who really worked for their own denominations and against the Methodists, breaking up Methodist Sunday schools and establishing their own. Had not an agent, lately sent east to procure some thousands for Illinois College, said: " give me this sum and the Mississippi Valley is ours?"

Illinois Presbyterianism felt the effects of the split of 1837

[15] *Minutes of the General Assembly of the Presbyterian Church*, 1830, p. 116-117; 1840, p. 58; 1849, p. 273.
[16] *Illinois Intelligencer*, January 23, 1830.

between the new and old school. In the national general assembly of 1837, the old school forces — gaining control, their opponents declared, by a bargain with the south on the subject of slavery — abrogated the plan of union of 1801; they cut off from the churches all synods believed to be tainted with lax discipline and new school, or " New Haven," theology which was regarded as not quite severe enough in its phrasing of the predestination doctrine; they denounced the activity of non-sectarian boards and established for their denomination its own particular missionary societies. Their act was interpreted rightly as the earnest of their determination to drive the new school element out of the church.

At this time it is possible to strike the balance with some fairness between the parties. Ostensibly at least the old school forces had certain grievances that may justify their course.[17] They were convinced that the union had brought into the church Congregationalists who were not only lax in doctrine but also disinclined to take seriously the exact and elaborate organization of their church. It has been well said that the essence of Presbyterianism is discipline; and the old school men, while the violence of their proceedings may be condemned, may be forgiven for thinking that without the full discipline Presbyterianism would not be Presbyterianism.

As might be inferred the split had a peculiar effect in Illinois, because there the new school forces had nourished Presbyterianism. Thus the synod of Illinois in 1836 had denounced ministers who bought or sold slaves or approved such actions. The synod by a small vote refused to condemn the abolitionist doctrine, that all slaveholding is sin; instead, it merely declared immediate emancipation inexpedient and prescribed a sermon on slavery at each annual meeting. This policy satisfied even Elijah P. Lovejoy, not yet an abolitionist. In April of 1837 the Alton presbytery appointed a committee to draft a memo-

17 For an account of the assembly from an Illinois new school source, see *Alton Observer*, June 8, 15, 22, 29, July 6, 20, 1837. Lovejoy believed that slavery was at the bottom of it, Princeton catering to the south, which formerly had been new school. *Ibid.*, June 29, 1837; *Peoria Register*, July 1, 1837.

rial to the synod against receiving into communion persons from the south who had sold their slaves instead of freeing them. In the convention of old school men which preceded the general assembly of 1837 there were many complaints of Illinois Presbyterianism. Ministers in the Schuyler presbytery denied with impunity the doctrine of imputation; the *Alton Observer* denied that all sinned and fell in Adam; three-fourths of the ministers were said to be New Haven men, brought in by the Home Missionary Society. Worst of all a Presbyterian minister, a professor of Illinois College, had said "What New Haven is in Connecticut I would make Jacksonville in Illinois." The general assembly of the church enjoined the Illinois synod to purge itself from errors in church order and doctrine. When the Illinois synod met in 1838 there seceded from it all the delegates from the Kaskaskia presbytery, three out of four ministers and one out of four elders from Sangamon; five ministers out of fifteen and seven elders out of fourteen from Schuyler, and one elder from Peoria. Those who remained condemned in a resolution the action of the general assembly and declared it the duty of ministers to preach against slavery as counter to the law of God. The year before there had been several appeals to the new school Presbyterians to organize before they were borne down by the old school power. A loose synodical organization was suggested in which they could continue to coöperate with New England associations and with the Congregationalists.[18]

Congregationalism in Illinois as an organization began in 1833. Up to that time the communion of Congregational churches through the arrangement with the Presbyterians contributed money, brains, labor, and members to the establishment of another denomination and had continued to do so even after it was realized that the arrangement was having such an unequal result. Presbyterian churches had been founded, sustained by Congregationalists in New England, and made

[18] *Alton Observer*, October 27, December 15, 1836, April 20, June 8, July 6, 13, 27, 1837, April 19, 1838; *Peoria Register*, October 27, 1838.

up in Illinois largely of emigrated New England Congregationalists.   In that year, however, the first three Congregational
churches were established, and by 1835 seven more had been
added.   In 1836 the first meeting of the Illinois Congregational Association was held, churches at Jacksonville, Quincy,
Fairfield, Pond Prairie, St. Mary, Griggsville, and Long
Grove being represented.[19]   A general association was founded
in 1844 with two local associations embracing sixty-four
churches, forty-eight ministers, and 2,432 members.

The pioneering Congregational missionaries were usually
men of thorough collegiate and theological training and were
of indomitable energy though they showed varied talents
and adaptation for pioneer work.   The Reverend Nathaniel
C. Clark, for example, founded the first Congregational church
in northern Illinois — that near Naperville — in 1833 and
afterwards organized thirty-seven churches in the Fox river
valley.

A great part of their energy, however, was given to the
planting and nourishing of educational institutions.   Here
again it was not only their own denominational schools that were
aided, but the heartiest coöperation was extended to others.
Illinois, Knox, and Beloit colleges, Whipple, Dover, Princeton, and other academies, Monticello, Jacksonville, Rockford,
and Galesburg female seminaries were all the fruit of their
inspiration, planning, or labor.   Nearly every one of the
founders, presidents, and early professors of Illinois colleges,
nominally Presbyterian, were Congregational ministers.

From the beginning Congregationalists were inflexibly
opposed to slavery.   The state association in 1844 made a
standing rule to which its members must assent: "No one
shall be admitted to membership in this body who does not
regard slaveholding as a sin condemned by God." For this

---

[19] In 1833 the first Presbyterian church of Chicago was founded, made up of
New England Congregationalists: "In fact, Philo Carpenter is said to have been
the only one . . . who had always been a Presbyterian." Moses and Kirkland, *History of Chicago*, 331, 375.   There was no Congregational church in
Chicago until 1851.   See also *Alton Observer*, January 26, 1837, March 22, 1838.

united and outspoken stand, and for the equally bold advocacy of temperance reform, Congregationalists for a long time aroused the abhorrence of conventional religionists.[20]

One of the most interesting religious developments of the period was that of the Christians or Disciples of Christ. They had a few scattered churches before 1830, but it was that decade which saw the organization of many churches, particularly in the southern and central parts of the state. Settlers from Kentucky, Ohio, and West Virginia, already imbued with the western spirit, found in this movement for the restoration of apostolic christianity a religion most suited to their needs. The freedom and simplicity of a church that refused to be limited by human creeds, that admitted to membership all who, after a scriptural confession of faith, were baptized by immersion was too inherently western not to make a strong appeal to the hardy, independent spirits of a developing frontier. The fact that they as a body incurred the most spirited and bitter antagonism from other established denominations[21] could not prevail over the warmth, good fellowship, and simplicity of their religion; by 1840 they had sixty churches, twenty-seven ministers, and four thousand members; the next ten years they more than doubled their strength having in 1850 one hundred and twenty-five churches, sixty ministers, and ten thousand communicants.[22]

In 1834 three Episcopal churches were organized in Illinois; and a year later the first annual convention of this body was held, seven ministers being present. By 1845 there were

[20] Savage, *Pioneer Congregational Ministers in Illinois, passim.*

[21] Sturtevant, *Autobiography,* 246, gives the following striking example of the attitude toward this body in their early history. He had been asked to preach to a congregation of Disciples and at its close he said: "I could say with Peter, 'I perceive that God is no respecter of persons.' God taught me that day to beware how I called any body of professed Christians 'common or unclean.'

"The report of my doings in that Sabbath startled the community, the story could not have been circulated with greater rapidity or repeated with more emphasis had I committed an infamous crime. A few defended my action, but most of my good neighbors were shocked."

[22] Thrapp, "Early Religious Beginnings in Illinois," in Illinois State Historical Society, *Journal,* 4:311; Moses, *Illinois,* 1077.

twenty-five clergymen in twenty-eight parishes, with over five hundred members; by 1848 the number of communicants had grown to over a thousand.[23] The interest in the denomination centers around the figure of the missionary bishop, Philander Chase, who came to Illinois in 1833. One knows more about Chase than about most men in Illinois of that day because he was continually breaking into print with pamphlets appealing for support for his pet, Jubilee College, or protesting against attacks on the college or on himself. His attempts to be discreet on the question of slavery brought him wordy wars with the abolitionists.

In the earlier years of statehood Illinois comprised a part of the Roman Catholic diocese of Bardstown, Kentucky, though it was administered by Bishop Joseph Rosati at St. Louis, who acted as vicar-general.[23a] During this time there were a few scattered congregations, mostly French, in southern Illinois; in 1826 there were, according to Bishop Rosati's report, twenty missions, whose needs were supplied by missionaries sent out from St. Louis. But beginning slowly in the thirties and increasing rapidly in the forties came that tide of Catholic immigrants, predominantly Irish and German, who, settling in great numbers in the northern section of the country, shifted ecclesiastical emphasis to the north and made Catholicism an important factor in state development.

When Chicago was incorporated in 1833 the Catholics there numbered 130, or ninety per cent of the population; they were largely French, or French and Indian — the latter including the half-breed Potawatomi chiefs, Billy Caldwell and Alexander Robinson.[23b] In April of 1833 these Catholics sent a

[23] *Alton Telegraph,* July 26, 1845; *Journal of Annual Conventions of Episcopalian Church of Illinois,* 1843-1857.

[23a] For the great part of the material here used on the Catholics of Illinois I am indebted to the proof of Gilbert J. Garraghan's article, "Early Catholicity in Chicago, 1673-1843," which is to appear in the *Illinois Catholic Historical Journal,* volume I, number I.

[23b] These were the chiefs so widely and favorably known as friends of the whites; it was their influence which saved the Kinzies and others from the fury of the Indians when the former arrived on the scene the day following the Fort Dearborn massacre; both were later instrumental in preventing the Potawatomi from participation in the Winnebago and Black Hawk wars.

petition for a resident pastor to Bishop Rosati, who, less than a month later, was able to comply with their request in the person of a zealous and intelligent young French priest, Irenæus Mary St. Cyr. He at once began his duties, saying mass in a laborer's cabin given him by the hotel keeper Mark Beaubien, until the first Catholic church of Chicago could be erected. This, a small, unplastered, unpainted chapel, on the south side of Lake street, was completed in October, 1833; and the following day the first mass was said in St. Mary's to a visiting band of three hundred Indians.

Father St. Cyr ministered to Indians, French, Canadians, Germans, Irish, and Americans, who, notwithstanding the priest's poor English, did "not fail to come in crowds to our church every Sunday." [23c] In the spring of 1835 there was a Catholic population of four hundred in Chicago, and Catholics were thickening throughout the state. Galena had a resident pastor, Father McMahon, in 1833, and at his death Father Charles Fitzmaurice, a native of Ireland, was sent out from St. Louis as his successor. Missions were established at Bourbonnais Grove, Joliet, in Lake and La Salle counties; in the central part of the state, Father Van Quickenborne was, in 1832, ministering to Springfield and other localities in Sangamon county; while Catholics near Peoria and Quincy were needing pastors. To meet these fast changing conditions Rome, when erecting the see of Vincennes in 1834, divided the state longitudinally; the western half, according to a suggestion of Bishop Rosati, was attached "not only *de facto* but *de jure*" to the see of St. Louis, while the eastern half, including Chicago,[23d] became a part of the see of Vincennes under Bishop

[23c] In 1836 Father Bernard Schaeffer, a native of Strassburg in Alsace, arrived in Chicago to care for the German speaking Catholics; at his death the following year he was succeeded by Father Francis Fischer. Father St. Cyr was removed to Quincy in the spring of 1837, and that summer Father Bernard O'Meara succeeded to the pastorate of St. Mary's. Father Maurice St. Palais, the future Bishop of Vincennes, came to Chicago in 1838 [?]; at the coming of Bishop Quarter in May, 1844, Fathers Fischer and St. Palais were the only priests in the city — as was the enlarged St. Mary's the only church, the new church of brick begun by Father St. Palais at the southwest corner of Wabash avenue and Madison street being then unfinished.

[23d] By special arrangement Chicago, in the pastorate of Father St. Cyr,

Simon Gabriel Bruté; such remained the status of Illinois during the next nine years of tremendous expansion and growth. A petition from Chicago Catholics in 1837 states that "we have in this town two thousand and perhaps more Catholics as there are a large number of Catholic families in the adjacent country particularly on the line of the Chicago and Illinois canal. . . ." The Catholic population continued to grow with the city, until on November 28, 1843, the diocese of Chicago, consolidating the entire state of Illinois, was canonically established by Pope Gregory XVI. The following spring the Right Reverend William Quarter, a native of Ireland, arrived in Chicago as its first bishop. During his service of four years, he founded the University of St. Mary's of the Lake, built thirty churches, ordained twenty-nine priests, and left forty clergymen and twenty ecclesiastical students in the diocese.

The influx of German and Scandinavian immigration in the forties brought many Lutherans into the state. In 1846 the first German Lutheran church was founded in Chicago; in 1847 the Norwegian Lutherans there organized themselves into a church. The first meeting of the Evangelical Lutheran synod of Illinois was called at Hillsboro, October, 1846, and reported seven ministers, fifteen congregations and six hundred and eighty-five communicants. The Illinois synod, German, was organized in 1848, and with the steady increase of German and Scandinavian immigration the Lutheran church grew with great rapidity.[24]

The work of Bible societies, Sunday school societies, and similar institutions in Illinois was actively continued. In 1836 the Illinois Bible Society employed a general agent who the following year reported that in forty-seven out of seventy-one counties one or more Bible societies had been established. He

---

remained for a year longer under Bishop Rosati at St. Louis. In the preceding year it would appear that Chicago was in the see of Detroit, the original southern line of that diocese, as erected in 1833, having run from the Maumee west to the Mississippi.

[24] Moses and Kirkland, *History of Chicago*, 356, 358; Moses, *Illinois*, 1075; Neve, *Brief History of the Lutheran Church in America*, 93.

estimated that two-thirds of the Bibles in the state were there as a result of the societies' operations. Like the Bible society the Sunday school union was an interdenominational affair with the support of at least the more liberal members of the various Protestant denominations. Such men as Kinney and Cartwright, believing that the movement was designed by the hated Yankees to civilize the valley, felt a natural jealousy that held them aloof from the enterprise. Indeed local utterances indorsing such a design were not wanting on the part of the American Sunday School Union, whose agents from this time were active in the state. The underlying purpose of the movement was variously defined; sometimes, in default of ordinary schools, to afford education that might train for intelligent citizenship; sometimes, to prepare the young for church membership. One of the reports for 1836 made by the three organizing agents of the Illinois Sunday School Union was rather diverting; among other things it was stated that there was no Sunday school in Johnson county, and it was not possible to establish any; in one place only two families wanted one, since the experience with a singing school which had broken up in a stabbing row had rendered the inhabitants fearful of any further educational projects. In general a slowly waning opposition to Sunday schools, especially on the part of the Baptists was reported, as was also the fact that no more day schools than Sunday schools existed. Multitudes of young men were growing up unable to read, and the state was slow in supplying the greatly needed schools.[25]

The general effect of religious propaganda in the state can be set down as nothing but good. It is true there were occasional complaints of lukewarmness or hypocrisy on the part of the church members, complaints that people went to church to show fine clothing or to indulge the newfangled habit of munching candy in church. Sabbath breaking persisted,

[25] *Alton Observer,* December 8, 1836, April 20, 1837; *Western Pioneer,* June 30, July 22, August 5, 1836, December 8, 1837; *Illinois Intelligencer,* July 3, August 21, September 18, 1830, February 26, April 2, 1831; *Galena Advertiser,* April 26, 1830.

the old habits of carrying produce to market and starting a
journey on Sunday continuing as before. This disregard of the
Sabbath was constantly noticed by visitors from the east. In
1847 a convention was held at Belleville to promote better
Sunday observance. There were the old complaints that the
people who in the east professed religion became irreligious
in the west. In 1838, however, the *Peoria Register* affirmed
that not a settler in the Military Tract but was within ten or
twelve miles of divine service on Sunday.[26]

In the cause of temperance during the early thirties there
were occasional bursts of activity throughout Illinois, notably
at Alton. In 1836 a state temperance agent was appointed,
and in the fall of that year the Illinois State Temperance Society celebrated its third anniversary at Alton. Timothy
Turner, its agent, reported the organization of fifteen societies
and the taking of twenty-five hundred pledges as a result of
one hundred and twenty addresses in thirty-three counties. By
the end of 1837 there were two hundred and fifty local societies
in the state.[27]

Prohibitory legislation followed in the wake of organization. In 1838 Alton prohibited the selling of spirituous liquors
producing thereby much excited language. At Peoria the
question was brought up coupled with the direction of attention
to the number of "doggeries" kept by aliens and with a suggested appeal to the state legislature to prohibit retailing of
spirituous liquor in Illinois. In January there were petitions
for and against the granting of liquor licenses in the town.
In Henry county it was said no license had ever been granted.
In 1837, owing to the refusal of the county commissioners to
license, there was not a grocery in the county of Wabash.

[26] *Illinois State Register*, July 9, 1841; *Chicago American*, September 26,
1839; *Alton Telegraph*, June 11, 1847; *Western Citizen*, April 18, 1844; *Baptist
Helmet*, April 24, 1835; *Belleville Advocate*, April 29, 1847; *Western Pioneer*,
April 7, 1837, February 18, 1845; *Peoria Register*, September 1, 1838.
[27] *Illinois Intelligencer*, October 29, 1831; *Alton Telegraph*, September 26,
1833, March 16, 1836; *Alton American*, January 3, 1834; *Alton Spectator*, January 4, 1834; *Alton Observer*, December 8, 1836; *Chicago Democrat*, February 4,
1834; *Western Pioneer*, December 8, 1837.

Monmouth was a dry town in 1839, and Peoria, Knoxville, and Oquawka all had temperance hotels.[28]

The difficulty in dealing with the problems was the all pervasive character of the traffic. It wound itself into almost every phase of life. The bargain or the store trade was not complete without the glass of whisky; it was a political expedient used on every hand. Drinking, and hard drinking, was everywhere prevalent. Men delighted to number and classify in routine the various potations of a day and to give each its own name — eye opener, phlegm cutter, stomach cleaner, fogmatic, anti-fogmatic and so on.[29] To wean men from so constant an attendant as John Barleycorn more was required than legislation or temperance organizations of the old type.

The Washingtonian movement took root in Illinois toward the end of 1841 and gave a completely different trend to the temperance propaganda in the state. It differed from the earlier temperance agitation in that the latter was closely guided by ministers and paid agents, suspected of fanaticism, and that it was designed to save the temperate man while leaving the drunkard to his fate. The Washingtonian movement on the other hand, frankly emotional, appealed to the drunkard through the mouth of the converted drunkard.[30] Here there was no chance of raising the cry of church and state. The signing of a pledge to abstinence set in motion a psychological force sure to have some effect. The excitement died down somewhat after the first burst of enthusiasm of 1842, but thereafter the Washingtonian interest can be traced from time to time.

The crimes of the day were more numerous than those of the earlier period though in both instances they arose from the contact of the wilderness with the property rights of civilization. Robberies, at times involving large sums, were not

[28] *Alton Telegraph*, May 23, September 12, 1838; *Peoria Register*, December 29, 1838, January 19, May 25, July 20, August 3, 1839; *Western Pioneer*, October 27, 1837.

[29] *Chicago American*, January 11, 27, 1842.

[30] *Sangamo Journal*, December 17, 31, 1841, January 21, March 26, 1842; *Chicago American*, January 13, 1842.

infrequent. There was an occasional murder not the work of a gang; one notes but few cases of crimes of sex. Counterfeiting and forgery, especially of land titles, were prevalent. Gangs frequently combined several activities, making and circulating counterfeits, horse stealing, and occasional murder. The large scale operation and organization of these gangs, especially such a one as the banditti of the prairies in northern Illinois, went far beyond the ability of the slight legal machinery of the county to compass.[31]

This being the case the citizens had occasional recourse to extraordinary means. Sometimes a mob would wreck a little hamlet, the resort of crime of all sorts, sometimes it would break up a gambling booth at a race course. Sometimes societies would be formed to put down horse stealing. Occasionally a man of doubtful life in a community who had excited the wrath of his neighbors might be visited with the extreme penalty of mob violence.[32]

In southern Illinois, Massac and Pope counties had for years been terrorized by a powerful gang of horse thieves, counterfeiters, and robbers until in 1846 the honest portion of the citizens formed themselves into a band of regulators to torture and harass the rascals into leaving the state. Suspected persons were taken to the Ohio and held under water until willing to confess; "others had ropes tied around their bodies over their arms, and a stick twisted into the ropes until their ribs and sides were crushed in by force of the pressure"[33] in order that information of their confederates might be gained. Such methods did not settle the matter, however, for the "Flatheads," as the outlaws were called, were too numer-

[31] *Alton Telegraph,* September 25, October 23, December 11, 1841, January 1, 1842, January 15, 1847; *Chicago Democrat,* June 25, July 6, 16, 23, August 9, 27, September 24, October 8, 15, 21, November 5, 11, 1845, July 21, 1846, September 28, 1847; *Belleville Advocate,* September 24, 1836, January 21, 1847; *Illinois State Register,* March 23, 1838, October 15, 1841; *Sangamo Journal,* September 14, 1833, January 18, 1834; *Chicago American,* February 18, 1837, July 15, 1839, September 5, 1840.

[32] *Belleville Advocate,* July 30, 1841, July 23, 1846, September 9, 1847; *Sangamo Journal,* October 11, 1834; *Alton Telegraph,* November 1, 1837; *Chicago American,* June 22, 1839.

[33] Ford, *History of Illinois,* 438.

ous and had been powerful for too long a period to be summarily disposed of. In Massac they gained the control of the county offices and in August made application to the governor for a militia force to sustain the authority of the law. "This disturbance," writes Governor Ford, "being at a distance of two hundred and fifty miles from the seat of government, and in a part of the country between which and the seat of government there was but very little communication, the facts concerning it were but imperfectly known to the governor."[34] In the interval of inquiry that ensued, disturbances broke out more violently than ever. Regulators from Pope county and from Kentucky joined their fellows in Massac, drove out the officers, and defied the judgments of the circuit court—forcibly liberating those of their number who were arrested; they became so sweepingly tyrannical that the counties were almost as terrorized as under the outlaws. The militia, however, refused to turn out to protect officials in league with horse thieves. Thus the regulators were left undisputed masters of the county; they whipped, tarred and feathered, and drove out of the country both rascals and honest opponents. Conditions became somewhat quieter that winter through state intervention; special legislation was passed creating a court to try offenders and at the same time vesting the governor with additional powers in that region. Notwithstanding all efforts, however, spasmodic outbursts continued for years.[35]

The struggle of the state to master its problem of education, despite its rich endowment, was marked with only a measured success. The main reliance for the education of the young was still on private schools. A report to the legislature of 1832 frankly admitted that the state policy must be one of grants in aid rather than one of forming by enact-

[34] Ford, *History of Illinois*, 439.

[35] In August, 1849, a civil war was anticipated. The "Flatheads," who had killed a regulator informer by tying him naked to a tree in a mosquito infested district, barricaded themselves with ammunition and two cannon taken from the regulators, who, determined to arrest the murderers, sent for cannon and aid from their friends in Kentucky. *Western Citizen*, August 14, 1849.

ment a complete system. In Illinois finance the school, college, and seminary funds went into the state treasury to pay state expenses, the state holding itself responsible for the payment of interest for school purposes to teachers presenting proper schedules of teaching.[36]

The absence of anything like uniformity or organization in the state's primary school system was keenly felt by those intimately connected with it. Teachers complained that parents afforded them no moral support in disciplining their children, that neighborhoods by preference employed the lowest bidders and therefore had the worst teachers. They complained of cold ill-ventilated schoolrooms, of the thousand and one different methods of teaching, use of books, and of other difficulties. The actual workings of the Illinois system under moderately favorable conditions may be gathered from the report of a school township secretary in Peoria county. His fund was $6,455.96 all loaned at ten to twelve per cent. Of the accrued interest, however, only $178.96 was collected; and this with $184.42 from the state school fund was paid to five teachers in amounts varying from $24.75 to $118.79. The schools, with two hundred and fifty pupils ran two, four, six, eight, and eleven and one-half months respectively. With this may be compared the account of a school teacher in Tazewell, in whose school one hundred and ten scholars were registered with a maximum attendance on any day of fifty-eight. In addition to the "common school branches" this man taught astronomy, philosophy, chemistry, surveying, algebra, and bookkeeping.[37]

Nevertheless in the thirties there was real and sometimes intelligent interest in educational problems. The demonstration of a new method of teaching English grammar by lectures would be the occasion of a newspaper invitation to the public to attend the meeting. In 1832–1833 the formation of an Illinois institute of education was undertaken to deal on the

[36] *Sangamo Journal*, March 2, 1833; *Laws of 1836*, p. 249.
[37] *Alton Telegraph*, June 11, 1837; *Sangamo Journal*, July 22, 1837; *Peoria Register*, January 26, September 21, 1839.

basis of educational statistics with the difficult problems of education in the state. In 1834 delegates to a state educational convention were chosen. That convention recommended the establishment of school districts by voluntary action but mainly devoted itself to recommendations regarding seminary and college funds. As early as 1837 one finds an appeal for the establishment of the office of superintendent of public instruction. Interest began to be directed in particular toward two different methods of school management and teaching — the New England system and the Prussian.[38]

With the forties, however, the state moved on toward a unified system. Attention was called to the fact that one hundred thousand children in Illinois were said to be out of school and that 28,780 adults were accounted illiterate. The act of 1841 provided for township administration of school lands in the familiar way with an added provision that congressional townships might on vote of the people be incorporated for school purposes. The *Belleville Advocate* urged a similar organization in St. Clair county. An attempt in 1843 to secure an act allowing the taxation for schools by local vote called out a flash of the same opposition to taxation for education that had defeated the school law of 1825. O. H. Browning pleaded for it referring to what Connecticut's school system had done for that state, to which Orlando B. Ficklin retorted that taxing one class for the benefit of another was unjust — witness the fact that Connecticut had inundated the west with clockpeddlers and men who lived by their wits. In 1845 an act was passed incorporating all congressional townships as school townships and allowing voters in school districts to levy a special tax for the support of the schools. More than this, the school system of the state for the first time was given unity by the designation of the secretary of state as state superintendent of public schools. An attempt was

[38] *Sangamo Journal*, November 10, 1831, March 2, 1833, November 15, 22, 29, 1834, January 24, 1835, September 3, 1837; *Alton Telegraph*, June 11, 1837; *Alton Observer*, January, March, 1838; *Chicago Tribune*, July, 1840; *Chicago American*, September 17, 1836.

made to secure state recognition of German schools, but in vain.[39]

The last years of the old constitution were marked on the part of educators by a renewed interest and hopefulness in their profession. A teachers' convention called at Jacksonville in 1845 set itself to discuss education for professional, agricultural, mechanical, and commercial pursuits, differentiation of education for the sexes, the possibility of an efficient school system without a complete township system, and possible state aid to colleges and seminaries in training teachers.[40] A teachers' convention at Belvidere that same year considered the possibility of a normal school that appears to have been near akin to the teachers' institute.

The broadening interest in education perceived the possibility, and consequent necessity of teaching the blind and deaf. The bill for the establishment of the deaf and dumb asylum was passed in 1839, but because of insufficient funds, the building contract was not let until 1843; three years later the school opened with thirteen pupils. In 1847 a blind man had undertaken, at the expense of private charity in Jacksonville, the instruction of six blind children. The success of the experiment was instrumental two years later in the passage of "an act to establish the Illinois Institution for the Education of the Blind." Through the influence of the "Jacksonville crowd," that city, after much bickering in the legislature, secured both schools.[41]

If Illinois lacked for a unified school system, it did not lack for much private effort in behalf of schools, seminaries, and colleges, a surprisingly large number of which struggled on. As early as 1830 one notes high schools and academies, sometimes free to subscribers' children, sometimes combined with a young ladies' school to teach the polite accomplishments

[39] *Alton Telegraph,* April 17, 1841, February 11, 25, 1843, March 22, 1845; *Chicago American,* November 10, 1841; *Belleville Advocate,* December 30, 1841; *Sangamo Journal,* February 2, 1843; *Laws of 1841,* p. 259; *Laws of 1845,* p. 51.

[40] *Sangamo Journal,* June 5, 1845.

[41] Through the same influence Jacksonville was named as the site of the Illinois State Hospital for the Insane, in an act passed in March, 1847.

of that day. In 1833 the Convent of the Ladies of Visitation was established in connection with Menard Academy at Kaskaskia which three years later opened a commodious building to pupils. By 1842 eighteen sisters had the care of seventy pupils, twelve of whom were orphans taught free of charge. Tuition for the curriculum of literature, music, and arithmetic was one hundred and twenty-five dollars a year for boarding pupils, and twenty-five dollars for day students. In 1844 the school building was practically destroyed by the Mississippi flood, and this academy was removed to St. Louis; but Catholic day schools were maintained at Cahokia, La Salle, and other places in this state.[42]

Every denomination was concerned with similar efforts to provide instruction for its children. Cartwright advertised a school at Pleasant Plains that began with the three R's and ended with natural and moral philosophy and Latin and Greek, with promise of other sciences and "female accomplishments" as soon as suitable teachers could be found. Meanwhile, common branches were taught at the rate of five dollars for a five months' session and one might board with Cartwright for one dollar a week if paid in advance, otherwise the rate was a dollar and a quarter.[43]

In 1835 the Jacksonville Female Academy was incorporated by the legislature, a majority voting to apply the stern republican principle of making trustees liable for debts contracted in their corporate capacity. The year 1836 saw a much larger crop of school corporations, a favorite type being the "manual labor" seminary in which the students were required to labor with their hands partly to lessen the cost of their education, partly for their health's sake. Session after session of the legislature added to the number of these schools, many of which had real life and energy. They offered studies similar to those in Cartwright's curriculum.[44]

[42] Salzbacher, *Meine Reise nach Nord-Amerika im Jahre 1842*, p. 227.
[43] *Illinois Intelligencer*, February 6, November 27, 1830; *Galenian*, May 16, 1832; *Alton Spectator*, August 28, 1832, April 2, 1833.
[44] *Laws of 1835*, p. 192; *Laws of 1836*, p. 154, 158, 160, 163, 167, 170, 182;

For children of well-to-do parents, however, outside schools held greater attractions. The Menard children went to Georgetown University or to Missouri schools. One school at Linden Wood, St. Louis, which asked two dollars and a half a week for plain tuition and board, prescribed a uniform that speaks a certain degree of luxury. Sabbath uniform dresses for summer were white dress, pink sash, handkerchief, straw bonnet trimmed with light blue ribbon, white cape, and black silk apron; for winter a crimson dress of English merino, white collar, black silk apron, and dark green cloak.[45]

The legislature had never evidenced any intention of using immediately the college and seminary funds for establishing the schools for which they had been set aside. Popular opinion did not greatly protest. In 1840 the *Chicago Weekly Tribune* believed the time not yet ripe for a state college or university, though it did insist that the state should have a competent system of high schools and a school of education.[46] In such a situation it was perhaps inevitable that, though deprecated by some, collegiate education would develop along sectarian lines. In 1835 an act incorporating four colleges, specified that no particular christian faith be held or taught in any, but the prohibition prevented only for the moment theological seminary training for it was soon evaded. In 1840 the state had twelve colleges, though Illinois College was the only one granting degrees.

The foundations of certain of these colleges had been laid before 1830. Shurtleff grew out of Peck's seminary at Rock Spring, which in 1831–1832 had been removed to Alton and opened there as Alton Seminary. It rejected in 1833 a charter which forbade the teaching of theology by any professor; but in 1835 a somewhat objectionable compromise was ac-

2 *Laws of 1837,* p. 43, 87; *Laws of 1841,* p. 1, 5; *Peoria Register,* June 22, 1838; *Alton Telegraph,* October 10, 1838; February 22, 1840; *Belleville Advocate,* August 20, 1841, June 5, 1843; *Chicago American,* April 6, 1841.
    [45] *Alton Observer,* May 25, 1837.
    [46] *Sangamo Journal,* December 8, 1834, August 22, 1835; *Senate Journal,* 1833, 1 session, 538; *Laws of 1835,* p. 177; *Chicago Weekly Tribune,* July 11, 1840.

cepted, a seminary being conducted side by side with the college until 1841, when the restriction was repealed. In 1836 the name of the college, in recognition of the donations of Dr. Benjamin Shurtleff, was changed to Shurtleff College.[47]

For a time men cherished great dreams of what might be done with it. In 1840 the trustees projected a school of dignified agriculture, designed to teach the farmer his profession scientifically. The project as it took shape in their minds seemed to be to give the farmer a better intellectual background; labor on the farm and in the workshop was to be combined with study. A few days later the *Telegraph* printed a letter purporting to come from a farmer, praising the scheme, and enlarging upon it. He denounced the Latin and Greek colleges that gave only a smattering to their students, leaving them ignorant of their mother tongue, and praised the plan for a professorship of English. For an agricultural department he suggested courses in horticulture, lower mathematics, natural philosophy, chemistry, mineralogy, botany, comparative anatomy, physiology, with the cause and cure of animal and vegetable diseases. More broadly he urged an education to obliterate the line between gentlemen and laborers. This idea was a full quarter century ahead of its time. The college continued to develop; in 1841 it had thirty-one preparatory and collegiate and four theological students. In 1841–1842 the opening of a medical school was announced. In the later years of the period the more radical Baptists attacked the college on account of its proslavery views, and the founder was denounced as "one of the greatest proslavery men in the state."[48]

McKendree College, a Methodist institution, developed from Lebanon Seminary founded in 1828. At first there was strong opposition in the board of trustees itself both to abolition and to the establishment of a school of theology. The institution emphasized the manual training principle and

[47] *Jubilee Memorial of Shurtleff College, passim.*
[48] *Western Christian,* June 28, 1848; see also *Alton Telegraph,* March 4, April 4, 1840, August 14, 1841, January 22, 1842.

boasted a female department. Students' board bills were payable two-thirds in produce, one-third in good bacon, pickled pork, beef, flour, or milch cows with young calves; tuition for a five months' term in the higher branches was eight dollars. The school was taken successively under the patronage of the Missouri and the Illinois conferences, and in gratitude for a donation from Bishop William McKendree it was renamed, first, McKendreean College, then, McKendree. It was incorporated with other colleges in 1835. The college had to suspend in 1845 but reopened in the next year with three professors and a principal for the preparatory department.[49]

In 1835–1836 Bishop Philander Chase collected funds in England for an Episcopal college in Illinois; the corner stone of Jubilee College was laid in 1839 at Robins Nest, Peoria county, but a charter was not secured until 1847.[50]

In 1837 the Presbyterians and Congregationalists laid the foundations for two small colleges. Through the Reverend Gideon Blackburn funds were obtained for a theological institution at Carlinville. He entered lands for eastern investors at two dollars an acre, keeping twenty-five cents of the surplus over government price for himself and appropriating the remainder to the purchase of lands for the college. In 1837 the future Blackburn University had in trust an endowment of seventeen thousand acres; the enterprise, however, lay dormant for twenty years, when in 1857 the college was formally incorporated.

The Reverend George W. Gale, a new school Presbyterian of New York, was responsible for the inception of the other educational venture. In order to combine study with wholesome physical labor for students he conceived the idea of buying at government prices a township of fertile western land, reserving a town site and large farm for the use of a college,

[49] Catalogue of McKendree College, 1916-1917, p. 90; Sangamo Journal, September 13, 1834; Western Pioneer, February 8, 1838; Alton Telegraph, December 6, 1845; Belleville Advocate, April 11, 1846.
[50] Sangamo Journal, February 13, 1836; Peoria Register, December 22, 1838, April 6, 1839; Illinois Advocate, December 16, 1835.

and selling the remainder which carried tuition rights in the college at five dollars an acre; the surplus would endow the college. The project met with favor; in 1835 a committee inspected and purchased land in Knox county, and forty-six colonists there undertook to carry out the plan. In 1837 Knox Manual Labor College was incorporated, and a year later forty students were enrolled at the formal opening of the academy. By 1842 there were one hundred and forty-seven preparatory students, and the collegiate department had been opened with ten freshmen.[51]

Illinois College, the greatest educational venture of the Presbyterians and Congregationalists in Illinois, was the fruit, but a partial fruit indeed, of the imperial dream of a group of young students, the famous "Yale band." In Yale Theological Seminary, Theron Baldwin, John F. Brooks, Mason Grosvenor, Elisha Jenner, William Kirby, J. M. Sturtevant, and Asa Turner, with the magnificent enthusiasm of youth planned to be workers in an enterprise, both educational and religious, to raise the west out of intellectual darkness. Some of them were to serve as settled ministers or missionaries, some of them to give their time to seminaries and to a college that was to crown the whole educational system.[52] At the time that this idea was taking form the Reverend J. M. Ellis, a Presbyterian missionary in Illinois since 1826, was busy with the scheme of a college in the state of Illinois at Jacksonville; and the little group, accepting it as the center of their enterprise — the seat of a new and greater Yale to be reared on the western prairies — enlisted the American Home Missionary Association in its support. Illinois College opened in January of 1830 with Julian Sturtevant as teacher in it; during the year the Reverend Edward Beecher came to be president; three years later, a brother of Asa Turner, Jonathan Baldwin Turner, arrived and began his connection with the state. In 1835–1836 there were

[51] *Alton Observer*, October 27, 1836, June 15, 1837; *Catalog of Knox College*, 1914-1915, p. 52.
[52] Sturtevant, *Sketch of Theron Baldwin, passim;* Sturtevant, *Autobiography, passim.*

four seniors, seven juniors, thirteen sophomores, sixteen freshmen, and forty preparatory students. In 1839 the preparatory
department was abandoned as tending to lower the tone of the
college.[53] Meanwhile in 1837, Baldwin, who had served as a
pastor and as editor of the *Common School Advocate,* became
principal of the Monticello Female Seminary. The college
had to meet the question of finance. Its founders were able to
supplement local resources with contributions from the treas-
uries of the society in the east. A subscription of seventy-five
thousand dollars was lost in the panic of 1837. Finally in
1843 the Society for Promoting Collegiate and Theological
Education at the West, with Theron Baldwin as its secretary
and financial agent, took Illinois College over together with
Western Reserve, Wabash, Marietta, and Lane colleges. In
1846 Sturtevant urged that the property of the college be sold
for Illinois bonds than at a heavy discount, but the scheme was
too visionary for the trustees, and they preferred to sell for
cash.[54]

From a larger point of view the college never met the ideal
of its founders, but by no fault of theirs. To begin with the
scheme excited jealousy both from rival denominations and
from those who believed New England was plotting to federal-
ize the west. Hardly had Sturtevant arrived when Peter Cartwright delivered himself of a sermon, anathematizing and
caricaturing Presbyterian doctrine and ridiculing learned ministers; and Sturtevant, at the time just painfully learning to
preach without reading his sermon, was at a disadvantage.
Further the jealousy between old school and new school, and
new school and Congregational was to do its work. The
"Yale band" had imbibed at their alma mater the theology of
N. W. Taylor which was anathema to the strict Presbyterian.[55]
In 1833 Edward Beecher, Julian Sturtevant, and William
Kirby were accused of heresy in the presbytery at Jacksonville;
but subsequently they were acquitted. In 1839, despite previ-

[53] *Alton Spectator,* February 12, 1836; *Peoria Register,* October 6, 1839.
[54] Sturtevant, *Autobiography,* 268.
[55] *Ibid.,* 125-132, 161; *Galena Advertiser,* November 30, 1839.

ous attempts on the part of Beecher and Sturtevant to prevent it, a Congregational church was organized at Jacksonville. Sturtevant later gave some countenance to it; and as the tide of New Englanders sweeping into the north disregarded the plan of union and organized churches of their own, distrust and suspicion deepened. The antislavery views of men like Beecher and Sturtevant were an added difficulty. Finally, in 1844, Beecher resigned, possibly from necessity. Turner followed him a few years later; but Sturtevant remained to round out a long career at Jacksonville.

The story of Illinois College leads naturally to the consideration of one of the most remarkable men intellectually in the state of that day — Jonathan Baldwin Turner. The fact that of what he offered her, his country, and especially his adopted state, cared to take only the Osage orange hedge and the agricultural college, should not blind the student to the fact that Turner's intellectual interests were far broader than either scientific agriculture or highly technical education. In 1843–1844 for example, he edited at Jacksonville the *Illinois Statesman;* and that paper to the student of ideas is a land flowing with milk and honey in a desert otherwise relieved only by half-arid oases. From other papers one can learn only by indirection of the intellectual life of Illinois of that day; from Turner one gets the comment on it of a powerful and keenly interested mind.

It was not to be expected that Turner would compromise with the public tastes of his day. Sensational news had so little interest to him that he would not vex himself to give it to his readers. Under the head of "Crimes and Casualties" he printed: "Our paper is small, and if our readers will for the present just have the goodness to imagine a certain due proportion of fires, tornadoes, murders, thefts, robberies and bully fights, from week to week, it will do just as well, for we can assure them they actually take place." [56] The man who, when the thunders of denominational denunciation were rolling forth

[56] Scott, *Newspapers and Periodicals of Illinois,* lxxiv.

against Mormonism, was moved to analyze the sect as a fascinating study in comparative religion was not likely to blind his eyes to the violence of the deeds and plans of the anti-Mormons. He urged the people of the Military Tract to abide by the law and to have pity on the helpless at Nauvoo. What would Europe think of the state, if one year she granted Smith lawmaking powers and the next made open war on him?[57]

Because of Turner's keen, trenchant comment on politics the *Illinoisan* made fierce war on the "crack-brained, gaping, half-witted theorist Yankee," who cheerfully replied in abusive rhetoric that Milton himself might have envied. Turner's paper reflected a popular disgust with political partisanship and party manipulation on either side, declaring that the politicians on both sides were usually men who could not be trusted with any of the ordinary concerns of life. Turner was disgusted with Van Buren as a political manipulator and hoped for a time that Calhoun might lead the party to a higher plane of statesmanship, until he saw the latter's slavery drift. At the same time he regarded the possible defeat of Clay, the duelist and gambler, as a moral triumph. Further he tore to pieces mercilessly the whigs' argument for protection and other of their pet doctrines. He was keen enough to see that the democrats really stood in theory at least for certain fundamental truths as well as for certain very important measures. To the whigs he was willing to ascribe the conservative function, that of promoting steadiness and stability of progress, remarking that they necessarily had to show greater statesmanship than their opponents for this very reason.[58]

In his consideration of the slavery question Turner steered as original a course as he did elsewhere. He was not an out and out abolitionist, and he occasionally deprecated the violence of referring to all slaveholders as kidnappers and man-stealers. As to runaways he was disposed to think the proper course somewhere midway between turning all the people of

[57] *Illinois Statesman*, September 18, 25, 1843.
[58] *Illinoisan*, November 17, 1843; *Illinois Statesman*, July 17, August 14, 28, October 2, 16, November 27, December 4, 1843, February 19, March 11, 27, 1844.

Illinois into slavecatchers and enticing slaves away. As a result he had one or two tifts with the *Western Citizen*. He denounced slavery bitterly enough in his own way, as an institution in monstrous contrast with the nation's principles of political liberty, or an imposition on a majorty of the whites for the benefit of an aristocratic ruling-class minority. He professed, however, that he could not support the liberty party on the ground that he could not vote for a man like James G. Birney who was not a tried statesman.[59] On the exclusion from church membership of slaveholders he remarked with a full vision of the essential barrenness of "one idealism" that "no one conformity or non-conformity can make a man good or bad."[60] His final comment, however, on the intellectual ferment that followed on the train of abolitionism in the east was, "there is always some good in all protestantism."

Religiously that was Turner's ideal. His creed was simply christianity, including belief in the atonement and in the Sermon on the Mount as containing all the doctrine necessary to man's salvation. It had, however, no place in it for heresy hunting and little for denominational organization. Baptism to him was a rite which any minister without regard to church bounds was entitled to perform for all believers. His notion of church membership ended with the association of men into voluntary societies having no control of baptism or of the Lord's Supper. He was Congregational in his belief solely from a pragmatic view of the essential flexibility of that system.[61] There was to him no halfway house between the entire independency of the local church and the centralization of government under the vatican at Rome.

Turner emphatically was the critic rather than the exponent of the Illinois of his day. Yet he introduced into the intellectual life of the state a freshness of view, a cosmopolitanism that by the very fact that it jars no more sharply upon its

---

[59] *Illinois Statesman*, November 27, 1843, February 19, 23, 26, March 4, May 27, 1844.
[60] *Ibid.*, February 26, 1844.
[61] *Ibid.*, April 29, 1844.

surroundings shows how Illinois had traveled since the early days of statehood. Society in the state, conventionalized and stiff, posing in every intellectual attitude, original in nothing, had had a change worked in it. Men had come to think broadly in terms of general political principles; they had come to think more independently on the set forms of law, of slavery, and, as Turner exemplified, of the set dogmas and forms of church doctrine and discipline. The Illinois of 1818 like the nation it existed in was dreaming dreams and interpreting the future in terms of the past; in the Illinois of 1848, there were many men of vigorous mind who had visions of the future.

BIBLIOGRAPHY

I

MANUSCRIPTS

Eddy manuscripts, Shawneetown, Illinois. Transcripts in Illinois Historical Survey, University of Illinois, Urbana.

Edwards papers in Chicago Historical Society manuscripts.

Kane manuscripts in Chicago Historical Society manuscripts.

II

NEWSPAPERS

Newspapers form a source of inestimable value in writing Illinois history of this period. Indeed, for any approximately full or continuous record, it is only through them that the pioneer state may be pieced together; economically, socially, and in especial politically, they preserve, for the critical student, a reflection of early Illinois.

For a complete bibliography of Illinois newspapers, as well as for additional data on those here listed, see: Scott, Franklin W., *Newspapers and Periodicals of Illinois, 1814-1879* (Springfield, 1910) [*Collections of the Illinois State Historical Library*, volume 6]. Files in the Chicago Historical, Springfield State, and University of Illinois libraries have been utilized where possible, but files of papers at Belleville have supplemented these.

Alton American, 1833-1834, Alton, Illinois.

Alton Observer, 1836-1837, Alton, Illinois.

Alton Spectator, 1832-1839, Alton, Illinois.

Alton Telegraph, 1836-1848, Alton, Illinois.

Aurora Beacon, 1847-1849, Aurora, Illinois.

Baptist Helmet, 1844-1845, Vandalia, Illinois.

Belleville Advocate, 1839-1848, Belleville, Illinois.

Chicago American, 1835-1839, Chicago, Illinois [continued as *Daily American*].

Chicago Daily Journal, 1844-1848, Chicago, Illinois.

Chicago Democrat, 1833-1848, Chicago, Illinois.

Chicago (Weekly) Tribune, 1840-1841, Chicago, Illinois.

Congressional Globe, see in the division of federal and state documents.

Edwardsville Spectator, 1819-1826, Edwardsville, Illinois.

Farmers and Mechanics Repository, 1842-1843, Belleville, Illinois.

Galena Advertiser, 1829-1830, Galena, Illinois.

Galenian, 1832-1836, Galena, Illinois.

Genius of Liberty, 1840-1842, Lowell, Illinois [continued as *Western Citizen*].

Genius of Universal Emancipation, 1838-1839, Hennepin, Illinois.

Hancock Eagle, +1845-1846+, Nauvoo, Illinois.

Illinois Advocate, 1831-1832, Edwardsville, Illinois, and 1832-1833, Vandalia, Illinois. Its title was changed to *Illinois Advocate and State Register,* 1833-1835, then to *Illinois Advocate,* 1835-1836, then to *Illinois State Register and Illinois Advocate,* 1836, and to *Illinois State Register and People's Advocate,* 1836-1839.

Illinois Emigrant, 1818-1819, Shawneetown, Illinois [continued as the *Illinois Gazette,* 1819-1830].

Illinois Gazette, 1819-1830, Shawneetown, Illinois.

Illinois Intelligencer, 1818-1820, Kaskaskia, Illinois, and 1820-1832, Vandalia, Illinois [then combined with *Illinois Whig*].

Illinois Journal, 1847-1848, Springfield, Illinois.

Illinois State Register and People's Advocate, 1836-1839, Springfield, Illinois [became *Illinois State Register* in 1839].

Illinois Statesman, 1843-1844, Jacksonville, Illinois.

Illinoisan, 1837-1844, Jacksonville, Illinois.

Kaskaskia Republican, 1824-1825, Kaskaskia, Illinois.

Little Fort Porcupine and Democratic Banner, 1845-1847, Little Fort and Waukegan, Illinois.

Miner's Journal, 1826-1832, Galena, Illinois.

Nauvoo Neighbor, 1843-1845, Nauvoo, Illinois [continued as *Hancock Eagle*].

Peoria Register and Northwestern Gazetteer, 1837-1842, Peoria, Illinois.

Peoria Register, 1842-1845, Peoria, Illinois [had been *Peoria Register and Northwestern Gazetteer,* 1837-1842, Peoria, Illinois].

Quincy Whig, 1838-1848, Quincy, Illinois.

Rockford Forum, 1844-1848, Rockford, Illinois.

Sangamo Journal, 1831-1847, Springfield, Illinois. It was called the *Sangamon Journal* until 1832; in 1847 the name was changed to *Illinois Journal.*

Times and Seasons, 1839-1846, Nauvoo, Illinois.

Vandalia Free Press, 1836-1837, Vandalia, Illinois [continued as *Free Press and Illinois Whig,* 1837-1841; continued as *Vandalia Free Press,* 1843-1844].

Vandalia Whig and Illinois Intelligencer, 1832-1834, Vandalia, Illinois.

Warsaw Signal, 1841-1843, Warsaw, Illinois.

Wasp, 1842-1843, Nauvoo, Illinois [continued as *Nauvoo Neighbor*].

Western Christian, 1845-1848, Elgin, Illinois.
Western Citizen, 1842-1848+, Chicago, Illinois.
Western Monthly Magazine, a continuation of the *Illinois Monthly Magazine*, Cincinnati, 1833-1835.
Western Pioneer and Baptist Standard Bearer, 1836-1837, Alton, Illinois [continued as *Western Pioneer*, 1837-1838].

III

FEDERAL AND STATE DOCUMENTS

ILLINOIS

Bluebook. Compiled by the secretary of state (printed by authority of the state of Illinois).
Journal of the House of Representatives of the State of Illinois, 1818-1847 (published at the state capitols, 1819-1847).
Journal of the Senate of the State of Illinois, 1818-1847 (published at the state capitols, 1819-1848).
[*Law*] *Reports. Reports of Cases at Common Law and in Chancery, argued and determined in the Supreme Court of the State of Illinois, from its first Organization in 1819, to the end of December term, 1831.* Volume 1 by Sidney Breese (Chicago, 1877), volume 2, 3, 4, 5 by J. Young Scammon (Chicago, 1886, 1887, 1880, 1886), volume 7, by Charles Gilman (Chicago, 1888).
Laws, 1819-1847 (published at the state capitols, 1819-1847).
Reports made to the Senate and House of Representatives of the State of Illinois, volumes 1839-1845, 1863, volume 1 (Springfield, 1840-1846, 1863) [Cited as *Reports General Assembly*].

UNITED STATES

American State Papers, 38 volumes (Washington, 1832-1861).
Annals of Congress, 42 volumes (Washington, 1834-1856).
Congressional Globe . . . containing sketches of the debates and proceedings of . . . congress, 17 volumes (Washington, 1835-1848).
Executive Documents of the House of Representatives (Washington, 1831-1846).
Journal of the Convention, assembled at Springfield, June 7, 1847, . . . for the purpose of altering, amending, or revising the Constitution of the State of Illinois (Springfield, 1847).
Journal of the House of Representatives of the United States (Washington, 1818-1848).

Journal of the Senate of the United States of America (Washington, 1818-1849).

Kappler, Charles J., (ed.) *Indian Affairs, Laws, and Treaties.* Compiled to December 1, 1902 (Washington, 1903) [*Senate Documents,* volume 34, 57 congress, 1 session, number 452].

Register of Debates in Congress, . . . important State Papers and Public Documents, and the Laws, of a public nature, enacted during the session, 18 volumes (Washington, 1824-1837) [Cited as *Congressional Debates*].

Senate Documents (Washington, 1818-1847).

Sixth Census or Enumeration of the Inhabitants of the United States, as corrected at the Department of State in 1840 (Washington, 1841).

IV

CONTEMPORARY ACCOUNTS

Bennett, John C., *The History of the Saints; or, an exposé of Joe Smith and Mormonism* (Boston, 1842).

Birkbeck, Morris, *Letters from Illinois* (London, 1818).

Birkbeck, Morris, *Notes on a journey in America, from the coast of Virginia to the territory of Illinois* (London, 1818).

Blair, Emma H., (ed.) *The Indian Tribes of the Upper Mississippi Valley and Region of the Great Lakes, as described by Nicolas Perrot, French commandant in the Northwest; Bacqueville de la Potherie, French Royal Commissioner to Canada; Morrel Marston, American army officer; and Thomas Forsyth, United States agent at Fort Armstrong* (Cleveland, 1912).

Blane, William Newnham, *An excursion through the United States and Canada during the years 1822-1823 by an English gentleman* (London, 1824).

Broadsides in Chicago Historical Society.

Caswall, Henry, *The Prophet of the Nineteenth Century: or the rise, progress, and present state of the Mormons, or latter day Saints: to which is appended, an analysis of the book of Mormon* (London, 1843).

Circular to the public by James W. Singleton, September, 1846, in Chicago Historical Society.

Cobbett, William, *A Year's residence in the United States of America. Treating of the face of the country, the climate, the soil, the products, the mode of cultivating the land, the prices of land, of labor, of food, of rainment; of the expenses of house-keeping, and of the usual manner of living; of the manners and customs of the people; and of the institutions of the country, civil, political, and religious.* In three parts (London, 1822).

Coles, Edward, to Joseph Duncan, April 28, 1835, in *House Journal, 1835-1836,* 2 session (Vandalia, 1835).

Delafield, John, to Edward Coles, April 20, 1835, in *House Journal, 1835-1836,* 2 session (Vandalia, 1835).

Duden, Gottfried, *Bericht über eine Reise nach den westlichen Staaten Nordamerika's und einem mehrjährigen Aufenthalt am Missouri* . . . (Elberfeld, 1829).

Edwards, Ninian, *The Edwards Papers; Being a portion of the Collection of the Letters, Papers, and Manuscripts of Ninian Edwards* . . . edited by E. B. Washburne (Chicago, 1884) [Chicago Historical Society's *Collection,* volume 3].

Expedition against the Sauk and Fox Indians, 1832. Narrative of the Expedition against the Sauk and Fox Indians, furnished to the Military and Naval Magazine, by an Officer who served in General Atkinson's Brigade (New York, 1914) [Reprinted from the *Military and Naval Magazine of the United States* of August, 1833].

Faux, William, *Memorable Days in America: being a Journal of a tour to the United States* . . . (London, 1823) [Reprinted in Thwaites, Reuben G., *Early Western Travels,* volume 11, Cleveland, 1905].

Fearon, Henry B., *Sketches of America. A Narrative of a Journey of Five Thousand Miles through the Eastern and Western States of America:* . . . with remarks on Mr. Birkbeck's "Notes" and "Letters" (London, 1819).

Flower, George, *History of the English Settlement in Edwards County, Illinois, founded in 1817 and 1818 by Morris Birkbeck and George Flower.* Edited by E. B. Washburne (Chicago, 1882) [Chicago Historical Society's *Collection,* volume 1].

Flower, Richard, *Letters from Lexington and the Illinois, containing a brief Account of the English Settlement in the latter Territory and a Refutation of the Misrepresentations of Mr. Cobbett* (London, 1819) [Reprinted in Thwaites, Reuben G., *Early Western Travels,* volume 10, Cleveland, 1904).

Flower, Richard, *Letters from the Illinois, 1820, 1821; containing an Account of the English Settlement at Albion and its vicinity, and a Refutation of the various Misrepresentations, those more particularly of Mr. Cobbett* (London, 1822) [Reprinted in Thwaites, *Early Western Travels,* volume 10, Cleveland, 1904].

Ford, Thomas, *A History of Illinois from its commencement as a state in 1818 to 1847* (Chicago, 1854).

Fordham, Elias Pym, *Personal Narrative of Travels in Virginia, Maryland, Pennsylvania, Ohio, Indiana, Kentucky; and of a Residence in the Illinois Territory: 1817-1818.* Edited by Frederic A. Ogg (Cleveland, 1906).

Forsyth, Thomas, "Manuscript account of the causes of the Black Hawk War written in 1832" printed as appendix to *Wau-Bun—the early Day in the Northwest.* By Mrs. John Kinzie (Philadelphia, 1873).

Gale, George W., *History of Knox College and Galesburgh, Illinois* (Cincinnati, 1845).

Greene, Evarts B., and Clarence W. Alvord (ed.), *Governors' Letter Books, 1818-1834* (Springfield, 1909) [*Collections of the Illinois State Historical Library,* volume 4].

Harris, William T., *Remarks made during a Tour through the United States of America in the years 1817, 1818, and 1819* (London, 1821).

Hulme, Thomas, *Journal of a Tour in the Western Countries of America, September 30, 1818–August 8, 1819* (New York, 1818) [Reprinted in Thwaites, Reuben G., *Early Western Travels,* volume 10, Cleveland, 1904].

Journal of the Annual Convention of the Protestant Episcopal Church in the Diocese of Illinois, 1843-1857 (Peoria, 1843, 1845, Alton, 1846, Jubilee College, 1847-1853, Chicago, 1856, 1857).

Lee, John D., *The Mormon Menace. Being the confession of John Doyle Lee, Danite, an official assassin of the Mormon Church under the late Brigham Young.* Introduction by Alfred Henry Lewis (New York, 1905).

Lincoln, Abraham, *The Writings of Abraham Lincoln,* federal edition. Edited by Arthur B. Lapsley, volume 2, 1843-1858 (New York, 1905).

Minutes of the Annual Conference of the Methodist Episcopal Church, volumes 2, 3, 4 (New York, 1829-1837).

Minutes of the General Assembly of the Presbyterian Church, in the United States of America (Philadelphia, 1826-1831, 1840-1851).

Parker, Amos A., *Trip to the West and Texas. Comprising a Journey of eight thousand Miles through New York, Michigan, Illinois, Missouri, Louisiana, and Texas, in the autumn and winter of 1834-1835* (Concord, N. H., 1835).

Peck, John M., *A gazetteer of Illinois, in three parts: containing a general view of the state, a general view of each county, and a particular description of each town, settlement, stream, prairie, bottom, bluff, etc.,* alphabetically arranged (Jacksonville, 1834).

Presbytery of Ottawa, *Minutes of the Presbytery of Ottawa* (Ottawa, 1843).

Salzbacher, Joseph, *Meine Reise nach Nord-Amerika im Jahre 1842* (Vienna, Austria, 1845).

Sparks, Edwin E., (ed.) *The English Settlement in the Illinois.* Reprints of three rare tracts on the Illinois country. With maps and a view of a British colony house at Albion (London and Cedar Rapids, Iowa, 1907).

Synod of Peoria, *Minutes of the . . . Annual Session of the Synod of Peoria of the Presbyterian Church in the United States of America* (Peoria, 1844, 1846).

Wakefield, John A., *History of the Black Hawk War* (Jacksonville, 1834) [Reprinted by Frank E. Stevens, Chicago, 1908].

Whittlesey, Charles, "Recollections of a Tour through Wisconsin in 1832," *Collections of the State Historical Society of Wisconsin,* volume 1 (Madison, Wisconsin, 1855).

Woods, John, *Two Years' Residence in the Settlement on the English Prairie, in the Illinois Country, United States, with an account of its Animal and Vegetable Production, Agriculture, &c., &c., A description of the Principal towns, villages, &c., &c., with the habits and customs of the back-woodsman* (London, 1822) [Reprinted in Thwaites, Reuben G., *Early Western Travels,* volume 10, Cleveland, 1904].

V

BIOGRAPHY AND REMINISCENCE

Adams, John Quincy, *Memoirs of John Quincy Adams, comprising portions of his diary from 1795 to 1848.* Edited by Charles Francis Adams, 12 volumes (Philadelphia, 1874-1877).

Black Hawk, *Autobiography: life of Ma-ka-tai-me-she-kia-kick, or Black Hawk.* With an account of the Cause and general History of the late War, his Surrender and Confinement at Jefferson Barracks, and Travels through the United States. Dictated by himself. Edited by J. B. Patterson (Boston, 1834).

Cartwright, Peter, *Autobiography of Peter Cartwright, the backwoods preacher.* Edited by W. P. Strickland (Cincinnati, 1856).

Clark, John, *"Father Clark," or the Pioneer Preacher. Sketches and Incidents of Rev. John Clark.* By an old pioneer (New York, 1855).

Clark, Satterlee, "Early Times at Fort Winnebago, and Black Hawk War Reminiscences," *Report and Collections of the State Historical Society of Wisconsin, 1877, 1878, and 1879,* volume 8 (Madison, Wisconsin, 1879).

Drake, Benjamin, *The Life and Adventures of Black Hawk. With sketches of Keokuck, the Sac and Fox Indians, and the late Black Hawk War* (Cincinnati, 1838).

Edwards, Ninian, *History of Illinois from 1778 to 1833; and life and times of Ninian Edwards* (Springfield, 1870).

Hubbard, Gurdon S., *Incidents and Events in the life of Gurdon Saltonstall Hubbard.* Collected from personal narrations and other sources and arranged by his nephew, Henry E. Hamilton (Chicago, 1888).

Johnson, Allen, *Stephen A. Douglas. A Study in American Politics* (New York, 1908).

Koerner, Gustave, *Memoirs of Gustave Koerner, 1809-1896.* Life sketches written at the suggestion of his children. Edited by Thomas J. McCormack, volume 1 (Cedar Rapids, Iowa, 1909).

Nicolay, John G., and John Hay, *Abraham Lincoln, a history,* volume 1 (New York, 1890).

Peck, John M., *Memoir of John Mason Peck. [Forty Years of Pioneer Life.]* Edited from his journals and correspondence by Rufus Babcock (Philadelphia, 1864).

Reynolds, John, *My own Times, embracing also the History of my Life* (Belleville, 1855).

Snyder, John F., *Adam W. Snyder and his Period in Illinois History, 1817-1842* (Virginia, Illinois, 1906).

Sturtevant, Julian M., *Julian M. Sturtevant: An Autobiography.* Edited by J. M. Sturtevant, Jr. (New York, 1896).

Sturtevant, Julian M., *Sketch of Theron Baldwin* (Boston, 1875) [Reprinted from *Congregational Quarterly,* April and July, 1875].

Tillson, Christiana H., *Reminiscences of early life in Illinois by our mother* (Amherst, Mass. [?], 1873).

Washburne, Elihu B., *Sketch of Edward Coles, second governor of Illinois and of the slavery struggle of 1823-1824* (Chicago, 1882).

VI

MONOGRAPHS AND SPECIAL WORKS

Abel, Annie H., "The History of Events resulting in Indian Consolidation West of the Mississippi," *Annual Report of the American Historical Association,* 1906, volume 1 (Washington, 1908).

Andreas, A. T., *History of Chicago from the earliest Period to the present Time,* 3 volumes (Chicago, 1884-1886).

Babcock, Kendric C., *The Scandinavian Element in the United States* (Urbana, 1914) [*University of Illinois Studies in the Social Sciences,* volume 3].

Bancroft, Hubert H., *History of Utah* (San Francisco, 1889) [*Works of Hubert Howe Bancroft,* volume 26].

Beinlich, B. A., "The Latin Immigration in Illinois," Illinois State Historical Society, *Transactions,* 1909.

Berry, Orville F., "The Mormon Settlements in Illinois," Illinois State Historical Society, *Transactions,* 1906.

Ballance, Charles, *The History of Peoria, Illinois* (Peoria, 1870).

Bateman, Newton, and Paul Selby, (ed.) *Historical Encyclopedia of Illinois,* volume 2, *History of Peoria County.* Edited by David Mc-Culloch, 2 volumes (Chicago and Peoria, 1902).

Blegen, Theodore C., "Ole Rynning's True Account of America," *Minnesota History Bulletin,* volume 2, November, 1917 (Saint Paul, 1917).

Boggess, Arthur C., *The Settlement of Illinois, 1778-1830* (Chicago, 1908) [Chicago Historical Society's *Collection,* volume 5].

Breese, Sidney, *The Early history of Illinois from its discovery by the French, in 1673, until its cession to Great Britain in 1763 . . .* Edited by Thomas Hoyne (Chicago, 1884).

Brown, William H., *An Historical Sketch of the early Movement in Illinois for the legalization of slavery* (Chicago, 1876).

Buck, Solon J., *Illinois in 1818* (Springfield, 1917) [*Illinois Centennial Publications,* introductory volume].

Buck, Solon J., "The New England Element in Illinois Politics before 1833," Mississippi Valley Historical Association, *Proceedings,* volume 6 (Cedar Rapids, Iowa, 1913).

Catalog of Knox College, 1914-1915 (Galesburg, Illinois, 1915).

Catalogue of McKendree College (Lebanon, Illinois, 1912).

County histories have in general been found useful for local information. For complete bibliography of Illinois counties see: Buck, Solon J., *Travel and Description 1765-1865 together with a List of County Histories, Atlases, and Biographical Collections and a List of territorial and state Laws* (Springfield, 1914) [*Collections of the Illinois State Historical Library,* volume 9].

Dowrie, George W., *The Development of Banking in Illinois, 1817-1863* (Urbana, 1913) [*University of Illinois Studies in the Social Sciences,* volume 2].

Elliot, Isaac H., (ed.) *Record of the services of Illinois Soldiers in the Black Hawk War. 1831-1832, and in the Mexican War, 1846-1848.* Prepared and published by authority of the thirty-second General Assembly (Springfield, 1902).

Everett, Edward, "Narrative of Military Experience in Several Capacities," Illinois State Historical Society, *Transactions,* 1905 (Springfield, 1906).

Fairlie, John A., *County and Town Government in Illinois* [Reprinted from the *Annals of the American Academy of Political and Social Science,* Philadelphia, May, 1913].

Faust, Albert B., *The German Element in the United States, with special Reference to its political, moral, social, and educational Influence* (Boston, 1909).

Garraghan, Gilbert J., "Early Catholicity in Chicago, 1673-1843," *Illinois Catholic Historical Journal,* volume 1, number 1 (Chicago, 1918).

Harris, Norman D., *History of Negro Slavery in Illinois and of the Slavery Agitation in that State* (Chicago, 1906).

Hicks, E. W., *Outline of Illinois Baptist History* (Toulon, Illinois).

Hicks, E. W., *History of Kendall County, Illinois, from the earliest discoveries to the present time* (Aurora, Illinois, 1877).

History of Winnebago County, Illinois, its Past and Present (Chicago, 1877).

Jubilee Memorial of Shurtleff College, Upper Alton, Illinois (Alton, 1877).

Koerner, Gustave P., *Das deutsche element in den Vereinigten Staaten von Nordamerika, 1818-1848* (Cincinnati, 1880).

Kofoid, Carrie P., "Puritan Influences in the Formative Years of Illinois History," Illinois State Historical Society, *Transactions,* 1905.

Leaton, James, *History of Methodism in Illinois, from 1793 to 1832* (Cincinnati, 1883).

Lee, Judson Fiske, "Transportation. A Factor in the Development of Northern Illinois previous to 1860," Illinois State Historical Society, *Journal,* volume 10.

Lockwood, James H., "Early Times and Events in Wisconsin," *Second Annual Report and Collections of the State Historical Society of Wisconsin,* 1855, volume 2 (Madison, 1856).

Moses, John, *Illinois, Historical and Statistical, comprising the Essential Facts of its Planting and Growth as a Province, County, Territory and State,* 2 volumes (Chicago, 1889).

Moses, John, and Joseph Kirkland, *History of Chicago, Illinois* (Chicago, 1895).

Neve, J. L., *A Brief History of the Lutheran Church in America* (Burlington, Iowa, 1916).

Pease, Theodore C., *The County Archives of the State of Illinois* (Springfield, 1915) [*Collections of the Illinois State Historical Library,* volume 12].

Pooley, William V., *Settlement of Illinois, 1830-1850* (Madison, 1908) [Reprinted from *Bulletin of University of Wisconsin,* history series, volume 1].

Putnam, James W., *Illinois and Michigan Canal. A study in economic history* (Chicago, 1917) [Chicago Historical Society's *Collection,* volume 10].

Quaife, Milo M., *Chicago and the Old Northwest, 1673-1835. A study of the evolution of the northwestern frontier, together with a history of Fort Dearborn* (Chicago, 1913).

Rice, James M., *Peoria, City and County, Illinois; a Record of Settlement, Organization, Progress and Achievement* (Chicago, 1912).

Royce, Charles C., (ed.) *Indian Land Cessions in the United States* (Washington, 1899) [Bureau of American Ethnology, *Eighteenth Annual Report,* 1896-1897, part 2. In *House Documents,* volume 118, 56 congress, 1 session, document 736].

Salisbury, Herbert S., "The Mormon War in Hancock County," Illinois State Historical Society, *Journal,* volume 8.

Savage, G. S. F., *Pioneer Congregational Ministers in Illinois* (Chicago).

Smith, Joseph and Herman C., *History of the Church of Jesus Christ of Latter Day Saints,* 1836-1844, 1844-1872, volumes 2 and 3 (Laomi, Iowa, 1908).

Stevens, Frank E., *The Black Hawk War, including a Review of Black Hawk's Life* (Chicago, 1903).

Stevens, Wayne E., "The Shaw-Hanson Election Contest," Illinois State Historical Society, *Journal,* volume 7.

Thompson, Charles M., *The Illinois Whigs before 1846* (Urbana, 1915) [*University of Illinois Studies in the Social Sciences,* volume 4].

Thrapp, Russel F., "Early Religious Beginnings in Illinois," Illinois State Historical Society, *Journal,* volume 4.

Thwaites, Reuben G., *The Story of the Black Hawk War* (Madison, 1892) [*Collections of the State Historical Society of Wisconsin,* volume 12].

Treat, Payson J., *The National Land System, 1785-1820* (New York. 1910).

Wisconsin Historical Collections, volumes 1-12 (Madison, 1855-1892).

INDEX

A. B. plot, 98, 99, 101, 102, 103
Adams, James, 149; gubernatorial candidate, 145, 206n
Adams, Captain John G., 163n
Adams, John Quincy, 92, 240, 268, 289, 328, 364, 370, 380; charges against in campaign 1828, 116, 117, 118, 120, 121, 122; Cook supported, 96, 107, 108, 111-112; Edwards lost favor with, 98-99; elected president, 115; influence of, in local politics, 123, 124, 127, 128, 129, 131, 132, 133, 139, 141, 145; one founder of whig party, 236; presidential chances of, 106
Adams county, 174, 203, 206n, 325, 369
Africa, 85, 87
Agriculture, 122; abundant crops, 400; among Mormons, 348, 349; Birkbeck's influence on, and founding of society, 15-17; Bond encouraged, 105; crops, 383; estimated output of farms, 207; extent, 6-7, 15; German influence on, 393; improvements in, 383-385; Irish undertake, 396; methods of, and kind of land for, 179-181; products shipped to New Orleans, 52; Scandinavian interest in, 399; Scotch influence on, 398; slave labor and, 88-89; Turner's contribution to, 439
Alabama, 174-175
Albany, 190, 237, 254, 275
Albion, 82; Flower founded, 15; library at, 393n
Alexander county, 89, 112
Alexander, General Milton K., 287; in Black Hawk War, 165, 167
Alexander, William M., 61
Allen, W. T., organized antislavery societies, 371
Allen, William, 247; editor of *Madisonian*, 245; proposed for president, 329
Alsace, 423
Alton, 9, 84, 192, 198, 206, 209, 210, 340, 348, 375, 385, 386; all-Oregon meeting at, 328; anti-abolition resolutions passed at, 370; branch bank at, 305; commercial importance of, 189, 212, 221, 309-310, 387; Lovejoy killed in,

365-368; Peck edited paper in, 366; prohibition at, 426; proposed capital site at, 202, 203; school at, 22; Sunday school established at, 29
Alton and Mt. Carmel railroad, *see* transportation
Alton and Shawneetown railroad, *see* transportation
Alton and Shelbyville railroad, *see* transportation
Alton and Springfield railroad, *see* transportation
Alton Seminary, *see* education
Alton, Wabash, and Erie railroad, *see* transportation
Ambrister, Robert C., 114
American Bottom, 5, 42
American Fur Company, 3
Amusements, 150, 410-413
Anderson, Richard C., 70
Anderson, Stinson H., 284
Andover, 399
Andrews, Eliza Julia, 14
Andrews, Bishop James Osgood, 376
Anti-Edwards faction, *see* politics
Apple river, 165
Arbuthnot, Alexander, 114
Archer, William B., 116n, 142n
Arkansas, 331
Armstrong, Fort, 3, 160, 161
Arnold, Benedict, 405
Arnold, Isaac N., 298, 301
Atkinson, General Henry, commanded forces against Black Hawk, 160, 161, 163, 165, 166, 167, 170-171
Atlantic Bank, *see* banking
Atlantic ocean, 120, 219
Auplaine, 411
Axley, James, 25-26

Bachus and Fitch, 384
Backenstos, Jacob B., attempted to stop anti-Mormon riots, 356-357, 358, 359, 361
Bad Axe, battle at, 169-171
Bailhache, John, 338, 339
Baker, David J., 138
Baker, Edward D., 281, 286, 293, 296, 381, 401
Baldwin, Theron, 437, 438

455